ICSA Study Text

Company Compliance and Administration

ICSA Study Text

Company Compliance and Administration

Douglas Armour

The Governance
Institute

First published 2019
Published by ICSA Publishing Ltd
Saffron House
6–10 Kirby Street
London EC1N 8TS

Typeset by Paul Barrett Book Production, Cambridge

British Cataloguing in Publication Data
A catalogue record for this book is available from the British Library.

ISBN 9781860727450

Contents

How to use this study text   xi

About the author   xiii

Acronyms and abbreviations   xiv

Part one
The role of the company secretary, the board and other stakeholders 1

1   The role of the company secretary   4

1.   Introduction   4

2.   Role, functions and duties of the company secretary   6

3.   Appointment and vacation of the office of company secretary   10

4.   Relationship with the chair and directors   13

5.   Company secretary as adviser to the chair and directors   14

6.   Dissemination of information and decisions   15

7.   Communication with shareholders and other stakeholders   19

2   The directors   23

1.   Introduction   23

2.   Types of directors   23

3.   Recruitment, appointment, re-appointment and rotation   27

4.   Roles, duties, responsibilities and mandates   34

5.   Retirement, removal and disqualification   40

6.   Succession planning   45

7.   Directors' and officers' indemnification and liability insurance 46

8.   Co-option   47

3   Effective board practices — **49**

1.   Introduction — 49
2.   Board evaluation — 49
3.   Director education and guidance — 55
4.   Best practices, policies and procedures — 59

4   The members — **68**

1.   Introduction — 68
2.   What is a member? — 69
3.   Restrictions on membership — 72
4.   Shareholders — 76
5.   Guarantors — 77
6.   Other types of member — 78
7.   Member activism — 78
8.   Articles of association — 80
9.   Unfair prejudice — 85
10.   Derivative action claims — 87
11.   Membership — 90

Part two
Regulatory requirements for companies — **93**

5   Company compliance — **97**

1.   Introduction — 97
2.   Company formation — 97
3.   Filing of company returns — 104
4.   Offences under the relevant corporations or associations legislation — 106
5.   Corporate governance overview — 109
6.   Mergers, divisions, arrangements and reconstructions — 114
7.   Takeovers and acquisitions — 116
8.   Culture and corporate behaviours — 121
9.   Company insolvency, dissolution and restoration — 123
10.   Dormant companies — 127

6   Annual or integrated report   **129**
1.   Introduction   129
2.   Role and duties of the company secretary in the annual report cycle   129
3.   Statutory, regulatory and listing requirements   130
4.   Narrative reporting   145
5.   Disclosure of financial statements   160
6.   Legislative and other developments   161

7   External audit   **164**
1.   Introduction   164
2.   Roles and responsibilities of the company secretary in the external audit process   165
3.   Independence of external auditors   166
4.   Appointment of auditors   170
5.   Rotation of auditors   176
6.   Termination of auditor's appointment   177
7.   Role of external auditors   182

8   Securities exchange listing regime   **187**
1.   Introduction   187
2.   Listing requirements   188
3.   Ongoing reporting, filings and compliance   202
4.   UK corporate governance code   213
5.   UK stewardship code   214
6.   Insider dealing   215
7.   Dematerialisation   217

9   Maintenance of records   **219**
1.   Introduction   219
2.   Statutory registers   219
3.   Location of records and registers   227
4.   Access to records and registers   231
5.   Minute books   233
6.   Meeting materials/board papers   237
7.   Financial records   239
8.   Corporate records   241
9.   Retention periods for documents and registers   243

10   Company secretarial software   **247**

1.   Introduction   247

2.   Evaluation of needs for company secretarial software   248

3.   Implementation of appropriate software   252

4.   Security issues   253

5.   Potential uses and benefits of company secretarial software   254

6.   Ongoing maintenance and updates   255

11   Minutes and minute books   **257**

1.   Introduction   257

2.   Required information in minutes   257

3.   The six 'C's   260

4.   Proof of existence of an organisation and its historical development   262

5.   Record of decisions made and actions taken   263

6.   Demonstration of due diligence on part of decision-makers   263

7.   Legal evidence in support of actions taken   264

8.   Records retention   266

9.   Risk management – protecting the organisation   268

12   Oversight by regulators   **271**

1.   Introduction   271

2.   Governance practices – processes and procedures   272

3.   Assessment of performance in carrying out governance responsibilities   274

4.   Protection of stakeholders   279

5.   Investigation powers of regulators   283

13   Regulation and disclosure   **295**

1.   Introduction   295

2.   Disclosure requirements for listed companies   296

3.   Link between disclosure, accountability, transparency and trust   312

4.   Data protection   318

5.   Public access to corporate information   324

Part three
Meetings   **329**

14   Meetings of shareholders and members   **332**
1.   Introduction   332
2.   Member meeting or written resolution   333
3.   General meetings   335
4.   Regulations governing general meetings   337
5.   Role of the company secretary before, during and after the annual general
      meeting   338
6.   Notice of meetings   342
7.   Quorum, agenda, meeting materials   346
8.   Resolutions   347
9.   Role of the chair   348
10.   Rules of order, standing orders   349
11.   Proxies   350
12.   Polls   353
13.   Attendance   355
14.   Voting   357
15.   Meeting technology   358
16.   Share registrar and role of scrutineer   359
17.   Communication with members and other stakeholders   361

15   Meetings of the board and its committees   **362**
1.   Introduction   362
2.   Board meetings   362
3.   Role of the company secretary before, during and after board meetings   367
4.   Delegation of authority and responsibility   369
5.   Reliance on management and advisers   372
6.   Committees – types, purpose and composition   373
7.   Matters reserved for the board   375
8.   Executive discretion   381
9.   Motions and written/circular resolutions   382
10.   Conflicts of interest   383

**Part four
Shares**   **389**

16   Shares, share capital, share register and debt capital   **391**

1.   Introduction   391
2.   Regulation of the securities industry   392
3.   Types of share and debt capital   395
4.   Share capital   398
5.   Company share registrar function   412
6.   Register of members   413
7.   Share transfers   413
8.   Transmission of shares   415
9.   Registration of documents affecting title   415
10.   Share certificates   417
11.   Distributions   418
12.   Rights and warrants, debentures and bonds   421
13.   Capital events and role of share registrar   422
14.   Key features and establishment of employee share schemes and their ongoing
      administration   425

Test yourself answers   429
Directory of Resources   451
Glossary   456
Index   464

How to use this study text

This study text has been developed to support the Company Compliance and Administration module of the ICSA's qualifying programme and includes a range of navigational, self-testing and illustrative features to help you get the most out of the support materials.

The text is divided into three main sections:

- introductory material
- the text itself
- reference material.

The sections below show you how to find your way around the text and make the most of its features.

Introductory material

The introductory section includes a full contents list and the aims and learning outcomes of the qualification, as well as a list of acronyms and abbreviations.

The text itself

Each part opens with a list of the chapters to follow, an overview of what will be covered and learning outcomes for the part.

Every chapter opens with a list of the topics covered and an introduction specific to that chapter.

Chapters are structured to allow students to break the content down into manageable sections for study. Each chapter ends with a summary of key content to reinforce understanding.

Features

The text is enhanced by a range of illustrative and self-testing features to assist understanding and to help you prepare for the examination. You will find answers to the 'Test yourself' questions towards the end of this text. Each feature is presented in a standard format, so that you will become familiar with how to use them in your study.

These features are identified by a series of icons.

The text also includes tables, figures and other illustrations as relevant.

Reference material

The text contains a range of additional guidance and reference material, including a glossary of key terms and a comprehensive index.

Stop and think

Test yourself

Case law

Case study

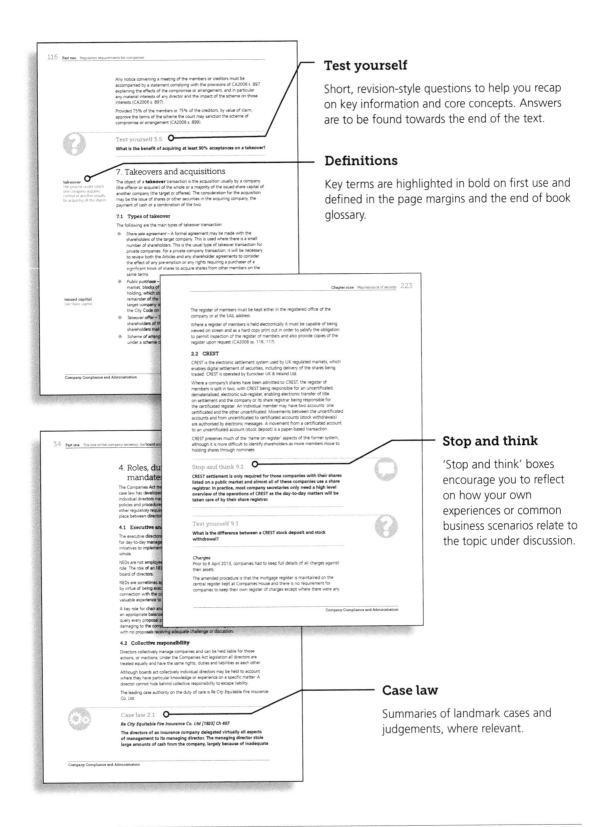

Test yourself

Short, revision-style questions to help you recap on key information and core concepts. Answers are to be found towards the end of the text.

Definitions

Key terms are highlighted in bold on first use and defined in the page margins and the end of book glossary.

Stop and think

'Stop and think' boxes encourage you to reflect on how your own experiences or common business scenarios relate to the topic under discussion.

Case law

Summaries of landmark cases and judgements, where relevant.

About the author

Douglas Armour FCIS is Senior Governance Manager at Intertrust Group, a global leader in providing expert administrative services to clients operating and investing in the international business environment. He also founded Doug Armour & Company, a governance and compliance consultancy service, offering tailored advice to a range of clients.

He has over 30 years' experience in providing company secretarial services to client companies and has written and contributed to a number of company law reference books. He has a wealth of experience of all aspects of company secretarial and corporate governance procedures and has and continues to act as company secretary for a wide range of public and private companies.

Acronyms and abbreviations

2008 Regulations	The Large and Medium-sized Companies and Groups (Accounts and Reports) (Amendment) Regulations 2008
ABI	Association of British Insurers
ACCA	Association of Chartered Certified Accountants
Act	Companies Act 2006
AGM	Annual general meeting
AIM	Alternative Investment Market
APB	Auditing Practices Board
Articles	Articles of association
BEIS	Department for Business, Energy and Industrial Strategy
C(MR)R2018	Companies (Miscellaneous Reporting) Regulations 2018 (SI 2018/860)
CA1998	Competition Act 1998
CA2006	Companies Act 2006
CDDA1986	Company Directors Disqualification Act 1986
CEO	Chief executive officer
CFO	Chief finance officer
CIC	Community Interest Company
CIMA	Chartered Institute of Management Accountants
CIPFA	Chartered Institute of Public Finance and Accountancy
City Code	City Code on Takeovers and Mergers
CJA1993	The Criminal Justice Act 1993
CMA	Competition and Markets Authority
CSDR	Central Securities Depositaries Regulations
DPA1998	Data Protection Act 1998
DPA2018	Data Protection Act 2018
DTR	Disclosure and Transparency Rules
DVD	Digital versatile disc
EA2002	Enterprise Act 2002
EA2010	Equality Act 2010
EU	European Union
FCA	Financial Conduct Authority
FOIA2000	Freedom of Information Act 2000
FRC	Financial Reporting Council
FSMA2000	Financial Services and Markets Act 2000
FTSE	Financial Times Stock Exchange Index
GDPR	General Data Protection Regulations

GM	General meeting
Governance Code	UK Corporate Governance Code 2018
Governance Code Guidance	Guidance On Board Effectiveness (2018)
HMRC	HM Revenue & Customs
HSWA1974	Health and Safety at Work Act 1974
IA	Investment Association
IA1986	Insolvency Act 1986
IAS	International Accounting Standards
ICAEW	Institute of Chartered Accountants in England and Wales
ICAI	Institute of Chartered Accountants in Ireland
ICAS	Institute of Chartered Accountants of Scotland
ICSA	Institute of Chartered Secretaries and Administrators
IFRS	International Financial Reporting Standards
IOD	Institute of Directors
ISS	Institutional Shareholder Services
JSA1856	Joint Stock Act 1856
LLP	Limited liability partnership
LR	Listing Rules
LSE	London Stock Exchange
M&A	Mergers and acquisitions
MAR	Market Abuse Regulations 596/2014/EU
MiFID	Markets in Financial Instruments Directive 2004/39/EC
MLRO	Money laundering reporting officer
Model Articles [Plc], [Ltd] or [Guar]	Companies (Model Articles) Regulations 2008 (SI 2008/3229) [Sch. 1], [Sch. 2] or [Sch. 3]
NAPF	National Association of Pension Funds
NED	Non-executive director
NIC	National Insurance Contributions
OECD	Organisation for Economic Co-operation and Development
PAYE	Pay as you Earn
PCA	Person closely associated
PDMR	Person discharging management responsibility
PECR	Privacy and Electronic Communications Regulations
PIE	Public Interest Entity
PIRC	Pensions & investment research consultants
POCA2002	Proceeds of Crime Act 2002
PR	Prospectus Rules
PRA	Prudential Regulation Authority
PROOF	PROtected Online Filing
PSC	People with significant control
Registrar	Registrar of Companies
RIS	Regulatory information service
RLE	Relevant legal entity
SAIL	Single alternative inspection location
SATCAR2016	Statutory Auditors and Third Country Auditors Regulations 2016 (SI 2016/649)

SBEE2015	Small Business, Enterprise and Employment Act 2015
SMS	Short message service
SRO	Self-regulatory organisation
STA1963	Stock Transfer Act 1963
Table A	Companies (Tables A to F) Regulations 1985
The Panel	Panel on Takeovers and Mergers
TUPE	Transfer of Undertakings (Protection of Employment) Regulations 2006
UCITS	Undertakings for Collective Investment in Transferable Securities Directive 2009/65/EC
UKLA	UK Listing Authority

Part one

Chapter one
The role of the
company secretary

Chapter two
The directors

Chapter three
Effective board
practices

Chapter four
The members

The role of the company secretary, the board and other stakeholders

Overview

This part introduces and examines the key roles in the creation, management and ownership of a company being the company secretary, directors, the board and the members. This part looks at the legislative and best practice framework that governs the authority, interaction and obligations each has to the others. There is a review of the protections afforded to the members who entrust the management of the company to the directors.

Chapter 1 explores the historical context of the role of the company secretary and the evolving nature of that role up to the present day. It reviews the qualifications, duties and responsibilities of the company secretary, the appointment process as well as the circumstances in which a company secretary might resign or be removed. Finally, there is a review of the company secretary's relationship with the chair of the board and the other directors and their role in facilitating the flow of information from the board to those within the company as well as externally to members.

Chapter 2 is an in-depth review of company directors, the types of director, the appointment process from recruitment, formal appointment, induction through to Companies House requirements and protection from disputed or defective appointments. There is an examination of the rights, duties and obligations of directors to the company, members and other stakeholders under the Companies Act, common law and other regulations. The chapter concludes with a review of the processes to follow when a director's appointment terminates whether by resignation, removal or disqualification, the importance of succession planning and the financial protection available for directors.

Chapter 3 examines the importance of effective board practices, and in particular the benefits to be derived from regular board evaluation, the need for continuing education and access to guidance for directors. The chapter then looks at the need for relevant board practices, policies and procedures to ensure that individual directors and the board collectively have the necessary tools to effectively, efficiently and transparently manage the company.

The final chapter in this part, chapter 4 looks at the company members including the restrictions on becoming a member and the different types of member. There is a review of the contractual basis of the relationship between the company and its members contained in the articles of association and the protection afforded to members from acts of the directors and other members. The chapter ends with an explanation of the difference between registered and beneficial interests in membership.

Learning outcomes

At the end of this part you will be able to:

◆   understand the role of the company secretary and the differing responsibilities of the company secretary, the board, management, shareholders and other stakeholders;

- discuss the historical evolution of the role of the company secretary;

- explain the processes for the appointment and termination of appointment of a company secretary together with an understanding of the qualification requirement and general duties of a company secretary;

- explain the relationship between the company secretary and the chairman, CEO and other directors and executives;

- understand the distinction between different types of director qualifications and prohibitions of appointment as a director;

- know that directors act collectively as a board and not as individuals and that the directors can exercise all the powers of the company subject to any powers reserved to the members by statute or the Articles;

- explain that if directors abuse the exercise of the company's power or their position as directors, they can be held to account and even be disqualified from acting as a company director or otherwise involved in company management;

- know the seven general statutory duties of directors;

- discuss and explain the different types of member and who can or cannot be a member of a company;

- explain the purpose behind member activism and the offences against members and remedies; and

- understand the relationship between members and the articles of association.

Chapter one
The role of the company secretary

CONTENTS

1. Introduction
2. Role, functions and duties of the company secretary
3. Appointment and vacation of the office of company secretary
4. Relationship with the chair and directors
5. Company secretary as adviser to the chair and directors
6. Dissemination of information and decisions
7. Communication with shareholders and other stakeholders

company
An association of persons which, on incorporation, becomes a legal entity entirely separate from the individuals comprising its membership. In the Companies Act 2006, 'company' is restricted to companies registered under that Act or previous Companies Acts.

company secretary
An officer of the company with a number of statutory duties, such as to sign the confirmation statement and accompanying documents, and usually charged with a range of duties relating to the company's statutory books and records, filing requirements, etc. Under the Companies Act 2006, private companies are no longer required to appoint a company secretary.

1. Introduction

All public **companies** must appoint a **company secretary**, **private companies** may choose not to appoint a company secretary (sections 270 and 271, Companies Act 2006 (the Act or CA2006)). The option for private companies not to appoint a company secretary was one of a series of de-regulating measures brought into force by the Act with effect from 6 April 2008.

Where appointed, in addition to their traditional compliance role, the company secretary usually occupies a position of considerable influence at the heart of governance within an organisation.

Compliance encompasses the systems put in place to record and maintain records relating to the company's structure and that of any other companies in the same group, systems to document reporting and decision-making processes as well as the exercise of those processes, and to detect and prevent breaches of legislation by the **agents**, employees, **officers** and **directors** of the company. The extent of the legislation falling within the remit of the company secretary will vary considerably from company to company with larger companies having specialist roles or departments responsible for compliance with matters such as health and safety, insurance, intellectual property, finance, risk management or commercial **contracts** etc.

Although the role of the company secretary in a small private company is very much an administrative one for large private companies, **public companies** and especially listed companies, the role is increasing in importance as the regulatory environment continues to evolve placing more and more emphasis on governance structures and disclosure obligations.

Governance is the processes and procedures by which an organisation is directed and controlled and in particular the way that senior management and the board of directors are structured, exercise their authority, have transparent and accountable processes and interact with investors, employees and other stakeholders.

The **UK Corporate Governance Code** (Governance Code) is a collection of best practice for the processes and oversight to drive the highest standards of leadership, accountability and behaviour in **listed companies**. As will be discussed in later chapters good governance helps boards and organisations to achieve their goals by acting appropriately and providing the framework and mechanisms to be transparent in their dealings with **members** and investors, employees, customers and suppliers.

Until very recently large private companies had escaped much of the additional governance obligations of public companies. However, in part spurred on by the collapse of BHS the government launched a consultation into large private company governance and the Wates committee published its six core principles of governance for private companies in December 2018. This is examined in more detail in chapter 5.

private company
A company that is not a public company.

agent
Someone who is authorised to carry out business transactions on behalf of another (the principal), who is thereby bound by such actions.

officer
Includes a director, manager or (where appointed) the secretary of a company. Not everyone with the title of manager is sufficiently senior to be regarded as an officer, who must have a level of supervisory control which reflects the general policy of the company. Also includes the company's auditor.

Stop and think 1.1

In recent years a popular phrase used to describe the role of the company secretary is that of the 'conscience of the board/company'. This is perhaps an unfortunate phrase which might be seen to imply ethical or moral virtues on the part of the company secretary that are less developed or missing entirely in the case of directors. It is more likely a reflection that company secretaries rarely have front line revenue budgets and consequently are able view issues from an impartial neutral position without the potential to be compromised by the commercial drivers and personal targets that might distort the decision-making of executives.

An essential role in advising boards of directors and senior executives on any proposed course of action is to consider whether it should be undertaken, an ethical decision. The legality of any proposed course of action should have been determined before it reaches the board for consideration. It is this fundamental difference that differentiates the role of the company secretary from that of the general counsel. These two roles do not always make happy bedfellows when combined into one role, although, in practice, they are often combined.

director
An officer of the company responsible for determining policy, supervising the management of the company's business and exercising the powers of the company. Directors must generally carry out these functions collectively as a board.

contract
An agreement between two or more legal persons creating a legally enforceable obligation between them.

Company Compliance and Administration

public company (plc)
A company that meets specified requirements as to its minimum share capital and which is registered as a public company. Only public companies can offer shares and debentures to the public.

UK Corporate Governance Code
The code on corporate governance that applies to UK listed companies. It is a voluntary code rather than a legal requirement.

listed company
A company whose shares are listed by the Financial Services Authority on the Official List of the UK and admitted for trading on the London Stock Exchange or NEX Listed markets.

member
A subscriber to the memorandum of association and any other person who agrees to be a member and whose name is entered in the register of members.

2. Role, functions and duties of the company secretary

2.1 Background

The office of the company secretary can trace its roots back to the Joint Stock Act 1856 (JSA1856). The JSA1856 laid the foundations of modern company law and many of the principals first established by JSA1856 remained in force and are largely unchanged to this day. Unlike the modern company secretary, the nineteenth-century incumbent had a purely administrative function with no responsibilities or duties in the legislation at all.

Indeed, in a court case in 1887 (*Barnett, Hoares & Co v South London Tramways Co (1887)*), the Master of the Rolls, Lord Esher, stated that 'A [company] secretary is a mere servant; his position is that he is to do what he is told, and no person can assume that he has any authority to represent anything at all'.

Over the years that followed, recognition of the role gradually gained momentum with the first major step forward set out in the Companies Act 1948 being the recognition of the company secretary as 'an officer of the company' together with a requirement for all companies to appoint a company secretary (s. 177 Companies Act 1948). There were no specific duties; however, the company secretary was authorised to sign prescribed forms on behalf of the company and make statutory declarations as to matters of fact concerning the company. Consequently, a company secretary may incur personal responsibility for not complying with requirements of the Act affecting the company.

The position gained further recognition as a responsible officer under a succession of Acts including the Trade Descriptions Act 1968, the Taxes Management Act 1970 and the Unsolicited Goods Act 1971.

The next big advance in the status of the company secretary came in a court case heard in the Court of Appeal in 1971 (*Panorama Developments (Guildford) Ltd v Fidelis Furnishing Fabrics Ltd [1971]*). In his judgement, Salmon LJ stated that that the position of the company secretary was formally noted as being the 'chief administrative officer'.

This was expanded upon in the same hearing by the then Master of the Rolls, Lord Denning, who stated:

> A company secretary is a much more important person nowadays than he was in 1887. He is an officer of the company with extensive duties and responsibilities. This appears not only in the modern Companies Acts, but also by the role which he plays in the day-to-day business of companies. He is no longer a mere clerk. He regularly makes representations on behalf of the company and enters into contracts on its behalf which come within the day-to-day running of the company's business. So much so that he may be regarded as held out as having authority to do such things on behalf of the company. He is certainly entitled to sign contracts connected with the administrative side of a company's affairs, such as employing staff,

and ordering cars, and so forth. All such matters now come within the ostensible authority of a company's secretary.

The importance of the role of the company secretary and the need to ensure the role was filled by a suitably qualified person was acknowledged in the Companies Act 1980 which introduced a requirement for company secretaries of public companies to be a member of one of the specified professional bodies or qualified by relevant experience. This requirement remains in force today (CA2006 s. 273), and is considered below.

In 1992, the key role of company secretaries in good corporate governance was recognised in a report issued by a committee chaired by Adrian Cadbury, titled 'Financial Aspects of Corporate Governance', but universally referred to as the Cadbury Report. This report has evolved over the years, is regularly updated and is now the Governance Code which sets out recommended good practice covering issues such as board composition and effectiveness, the role of board committees, risk management, remuneration and relations with **shareholders**. The Governance Code is considered in chapter 5.

shareholder
A member holding shares of a company with a share capital. The most common form of company member.

In 2008, the role of the company secretary took a backward step. As part of the programme to deregulate private companies in the general review of Company Law, the Companies Act 2006 saw the position of the company secretary become optional for private companies.

The office of the company secretary does not in itself carry any management responsibility under the legislation. Many company secretaries do occupy senior executive functions and their authority derives from their employment contract and not, like directors, through any authority under the Companies Act and associated legislation.

A corporate body may, subject to certain restrictions, be appointed company secretary. Use of a corporate company secretary is very common in groups of companies or where the role is outsourced to a corporate service provider. Use of a corporate company secretary facilitates the use of multiple signatories, where unlike the position of a natural person being their own sole signatory, a corporate body can appoint any number of authorised signatories to sign documents on its behalf.

A **partnership** may be appointed company secretary in the name of the firm. In England and Wales, this has the same effect as an appointment of all the partners as joint secretaries. In Scotland, where partnerships have corporate status, the firm may be appointed company secretary in its own right.

partnership
A business run by two or more persons where the owners share ownership (partners) and have unlimited liability for the business' debts.

A corporate body may, subject to certain restrictions, be appointed company secretary.

A partnership may be appointed company secretary in the name of the firm. In England and Wales, this has effect as an appointment of all the partners as joint secretaries. In Scotland, where partnerships have corporate status, the firm may be appointed company secretary in its own right.

limited liability partnership (LLP)
A corporate body where the partners have limited liability but undertake the management themselves rather than appointing directors to manage the company on their behalf.

A **limited liability partnership (LLP)**, as a corporate body, whether registered in England and Wales or in Scotland, can be appointed as company secretary.

It is also possible to appoint deputy or assistant company secretaries, who may act in the office of company secretary if that office is vacant or there is no company secretary capable of acting (CA2006 s. 274).

2.2 Duties

The duties of the company secretary are not specified in detail in the Companies Acts. However, in various sections of the Companies Acts, the company secretary is named as one of the people who may sign prescribed forms on behalf of the company, make statutory declarations and sign the confirmation statement. As noted above the company secretary is recognised as a responsible officer in other legislation including the Taxes Management Act 1970, the Trade Descriptions Act 1968 and the Unsolicited Goods and Services Act 1971.

model articles of association
The specimen articles of association for a company limited by shares incorporated under the Companies Act 2006. Unless specifically modified or excluded, the version of the Model Articles in force at the time of a company's incorporation automatically applies to the company.

Table A
The specimen articles of association for a company limited by shares incorporated under former Companies Acts. Unless specifically modified or excluded, the version of Table A in force at the time of a company's incorporation automatically applies to the company.

All companies have articles of association (Articles) which supplement the CA2006 and may be amended to suit the particular requirements of the company. Usefully the Act sets out **model articles of association** for public, private and guarantee companies (Model Articles Plc, Ltd and Guar) which are set out in Appendix 1. In addition to these Model Articles it is important to also be aware of the previous model articles set out in Companies (Tables A to F) Regulations 1985 (**Table A**) and which remain in force for many companies incorporated under that Act. As well as the statutory requirements, a company's Articles frequently contain provisions with regard to the appointment of the company secretary, as in Table A reg. 99. For those companies incorporated on or after 1 October 2009 that adopted the Model Articles, there are no provisions in relation to the appointment of the company secretary. However, those companies may include specific provisions in relation to the appointment of a company secretary in their Articles if they wish to do so.

In addition to these limited legislative duties in practice the role of the company secretary can encompass all areas of a company's activities, depending on the size and nature of the company, and the qualifications and experience of the individual. These activities can be divided into three broad principal categories.

The board
The company secretary should ensure that proper board procedures are in place and are adhered to, and that all relevant papers are circulated to board members in advance of meetings. They should also provide practical support and guidance, particularly to non-executive directors, and monitor and guide the company's corporate governance policies.

The company
The company secretary should ensure the company's compliance with relevant legislation and codes of conduct specific to the company's business activities. The company secretary will often provide a central source of information to the board and senior executives.

The shareholders

The company secretary is often the primary point of contact for shareholders and institutions, particularly in matters related to corporate and environmental governance.

2.3 Qualifications

The company secretary of a private company need have no professional or other qualification nor have any previous experience.

In the case of a public company CA2006 s. 273 provides that the directors must take all reasonable steps to ensure that the company secretary is a person who appears to have the knowledge and experience necessary to discharge the functions of company secretary, and who also meets the qualification requirements laid down in that section.

CA2006 s. 273 lists four categories of persons who are automatically deemed to have the relevant qualifications to be appointed as company secretary of a public company. These categories are:

◆ a barrister, advocate or solicitor, called or admitted in any part of the UK;

◆ a member of the following specified professional bodies: The Institute of Chartered Secretaries and Administrators (ICSA), Institute of Chartered Accountants in England and Wales (ICAEW), the Institute of Chartered Accountants of Scotland (ICAS), the Association of Chartered Certified Accountants (ACCA), the Institute of Chartered Accountants in Ireland (ICAI), the Chartered Institute of Management Accountants (CIMA) or the Chartered Institute of Public Finance and Accountancy (CIPFA);

◆ a person who by being a member of any other body or having held any position appears to the directors to be capable of discharging the functions of the company secretary; and

◆ a person who, for at least three of the five years immediately preceding their appointment as company secretary, held the office of company secretary of another public company.

2.4 Prohibited appointees

The auditor of a company and any employee of the auditor may not be appointed as company secretary (CA2006 s. 1214).

The sole director of a company is no longer prohibited from being appointed as its company secretary. However, there is little to be gained in practice from doing so, as any documents requiring signature by a sole director and the company secretary cannot be signed by the same person acting in both capacities (CA2006 s. 280).

Accordingly, while it is now possible for a private company to have one person as sole director and shareholder, it may occasionally be necessary to seek assistance from a second person when signing certain documents for these to be countersigned by an authorised signatory, which can be anyone authorised by the director(s), or for the signature of the sole director to be formally witnessed (CA2006 s. 44).

Stop and think 1.2

When considering the appointment of a company secretary the directors must consider the role required and whether it will be focused on corporate compliance and governance or if there will be a wider role encompassing areas such as insurance, risk management, and health & safety.

Private company directors will also need to consider if the role requires the formal appointment of a company secretary or not. Things to bear in mind include the additional signing capacity an appointed company secretary brings for official documents and contracts.

3. Appointment and vacation of the office of company secretary

3.1 Appointment

The appointment process is the same for private and public companies and will take one of two forms.

The company secretary may be appointed with effect from the date of incorporation by virtue of being the person named as company secretary on form IN01 (not obligatory for a private company), and is deemed to have been appointed as the first company secretary of the company (CA2006 ss. 12 and 16). For more information on the incorporation process, see chapter 5.

In all other cases and whether the appointment is as company secretary to a public or private company the appointment is made by the directors in accordance with the provisions of the Articles and CA2006 ss. 275–8.

The checklist below shows the common appointment process for a company secretary.

Checklist to appoint company secretary

1. **Ensure that for a public company appointment that the proposed appointee meets the qualification criteria set out in CA2006 s. 273.**

resolution
A decision at a meeting reached by a majority of members voting.

2. **At a meeting of the directors or by written resolution, the directors must resolve to appoint a new company secretary. Where the new appointment is to replace an incumbent company secretary rather than to fill a vacancy, the resolution will also include the replacement of the previous company secretary, be it by way of resignation, retirement, removal or another cause.**

3. The appointee should formally consent to their being appointed as the company secretary and the presenter is required to confirm on form AP03 or AP04 that the appointee has consented.

4. The particulars relating to the new company secretary must be entered in the company's register of secretaries and notified to the **Registrar of Companies** (Registrar) using Form AP03 or Form AP04, for personal or corporate appointments respectively, within 14 days of the appointment (CA2006 s. 276). The form can be filed either in paper form or electronically. Where the company has elected to hold its register of company secretaries on the central register the obligation under CA2006 s. 276 to give notice of the appointment is replaced with a matching obligation under CA2006 s. 279D.

Registrar of Companies
The official responsible for maintaining the company records filed under the requirements of the Companies Act.

5. If the company secretary is to be an authorised signatory of the company's bank account, notification of the change of company secretary and a specimen signature should be sent to the bank, together with any additional verification of identity documents required by the bank.

6. If thought appropriate, announcement of the new appointment should be made to the company's staff, suppliers and customers. This would normally only be appropriate for company secretaries also having a senior executive role.

service contract
A director's contract of employment.

share
A unit of ownership of the company, representing a fraction of the share capital and usually conferring rights to participate in distributions. There may be several kinds of shares each carrying different rights. Shares are issued at a fixed nominal value, although the company may actually receive a larger amount, the excess representing share premium. Members may not be required to subscribe the full amount immediately, in which case the shares are partly paid. The members then await calls, which require them to pay further amounts until the shares are fully paid.

7. A formal **service contract** should be drawn up for signature by the company and by the company secretary. This will often contain details of the employee's executive responsibilities and not necessarily state that they are employed as company secretary. As a result, being removed as company secretary would not necessarily also terminate their employment contract.

8. If the company has an insurance policy covering officers of the company against the liabilities that they may incur in carrying out their duties, the insurance company should be notified, usually at renewal, of the appointment of the new company secretary.

9. In the case of a company with publicly traded **shares**, the company secretary should be supplied with the company's rules governing transactions in its securities, if any, which should comply with the terms of the Market Abuse Regulations (MAR), Disclosure & Transparency Rules (DTR), Listing Rules (LR), if listed, and the rules of the relevant exchange.

Test yourself 1.1

1. Which of these cannot be appointed as company secretary of a public company: company secretarial manager of the company's auditor, a chartered secretary or an unqualified compliance officer?

2. Which of these cannot be appointed as company secretary of a private company: company secretarial manager of the company's auditor, a chartered secretary or an unqualified compliance officer?

3. What is the basis of a company secretary's executive authority?

3.2 Resignation or removal

Subject to any service contract in force, a company secretary may resign by notice in writing to the board. The board may remove the company secretary and replace that person by simple majority. Any termination will be subject to the terms of any service contract, and removal of an individual from the office of company secretary need not necessarily also require termination of employment.

Whether the company secretary has resigned or been removed from office, the following procedures should be followed:

◆ In the case of a removal, the directors must approve a resolution to remove the company secretary, either at a meeting or by written resolution.

◆ The fact of the resignation or removal of the company secretary must be entered in the company's register of directors and secretaries and notified to the Registrar using Form TM02 within 14 days of the resignation or removal (CA2006 ss. 276 and 277). The form can be filed either in paper form or electronically. If an election to hold the register of secretaries on the central register maintained by the Registrar is in force, there is no obligation to update the company's own register and the obligation to notify the Registrar of the resignation under CA2006 s. 276 is replaced by a matching obligation under CA2006 s. 279D.

◆ If the company secretary is an authorised signatory on the company's bank account, notification of the change in company secretary should be given to the bank.

A new company secretary must be appointed to a public company as soon as practical and the procedure on appointment outlined above should be followed. As the position is optional for a private company, there is no such urgency if a replacement company secretary is to be appointed.

Stop and think 1.3

Many groups, especially those with a lot of subsidiary companies will appoint a corporate company secretary to its subsidiaries, which can also be a subsidiary. In addition to facilitating the use of multiple signatories

for documents required to be signed on behalf of the company secretary this also means that changes of staff within the company secretariat will not also require registration of changes in the named company secretary with the Registrar.

subsidiary
A company controlled by another, which usually holds a majority of the issued shares.

Although such subsidiaries are typically private companies, many groups continue to appoint a company secretary as the benefits of retaining the ability to have documents signed or authenticated by the company secretary outweigh any advantages, usually cost, of leaving the position vacant.

Test yourself 1.2

1. **Why are there two appointment forms for a company secretary, Forms AP03 and AP04?**

2. **Are there any benefits for a sole director appointing a third party as company secretary rather than themselves?**

3. **Does the removal of a company secretary also terminate their employment contract?**

4. Relationship with the chair and directors

The obligations and responsibilities of the company secretary outlined in the Act and built upon by governance guidance and best practice, such as that contained in the Governance Code, require the company secretary to fulfil a leading role in the good governance of their company by supporting the chair and helping the board and its committees to function efficiently.

The Governance Code recommends that the company secretary should report to the chair on all board governance matters (Governance Code Guidance para. 80). This does not preclude the company secretary also reporting to the CEO or another line manager such as the general counsel in relation to their executive responsibilities. The appointment and removal of the company secretary should be a matter for the board as a whole to consider, and the remuneration of the company secretary might be determined by the remuneration committee to ensure independence of the role from undue influence.

Among the key responsibilities of the company secretary included in the Governance Code and associated guidance are:

◆   advising the board on all governance matters;
◆   supporting the board to establish the necessary policies, processes, information, time and resources to function effectively and efficiently;

◆   ensuring that board procedures are complied with;

◆   ensuring good information flows within the board, its committees, between senior management and non-executive directors;

◆   facilitating induction, board training and board professional development;

◆   ensuring that the directors and in particular the non-executive directors have access to independent professional advice at the company's expense where they judge it necessary in the performance of their duties; and

◆   together with the chair, periodically reviewing corporate, board and committee governance and considering any improvements or initiatives that could strengthen these governance processes.

An extremely important skill which will enhance the company secretary's effectiveness is their ability to build and maintain relationships of trust and confidence with the three director groupings on the board being the chair, non-executive directors and the executive directors. A failure to maintain a positive relationship with some or all non-executive directors is unfortunate but often workable. However, losing the trust or confidence of the chair or CEO is often unsustainable.

5. Company secretary as adviser to the chair and directors

The company secretary is an adviser to the chair and the board on a company's values and governance framework achieved through assisting and guiding the directors in their pursuit of the company's aims. The company secretary must always act with integrity and independence to protect the sometimes-competing interests of the company, its members, its employees and other stakeholders.

Success necessitates that the company secretary takes a proactive and central role in the governance of the company. It involves strategic thinking around why and how the company is doing business and the governance procedures needed to ensure an appropriate corporate culture so that it operates in accordance with its values.

annual accounts, annual report and accounts
The accounts which are prepared to fulfil the directors' duty to present audited accounts to members in respect of each financial year. Annual accounts of limited companies must be filed with the Registrar of Companies.

In addition to this governance role, the company secretary's compliance duties will usually include maintaining the company's statutory registers, ensuring filings are made promptly and on time with Companies House, taking and drafting minutes of board and committee meetings, co-ordinating and often drafting the non-financial parts of the **annual report and accounts** such as the strategic report, directors' report, remuneration report as well as convening and managing meetings of the members.

Many company secretaries, especially in smaller companies, are also involved with HR, pensions, risk management, insurance and health & safety.

Stop and think 1.4

The company secretary occupies a unique position at the heart of a company's decision-making process, access to highly confidential information, and privy to opposing views which may or may not be discussed in the boardroom as well as either overseeing or actually running the evaluation process for their own line manager.

Test yourself 1.3

The Governance Code recommends that the company secretary report to two people. Who are they and for which aspects of the company secretary's role would each have oversight?

6. Dissemination of information and decisions

Although the directors have authority to convene board meetings this is usually delegated to the company secretary (Model Articles Plc reg. 9, Ltd reg. 8) who also plays a central role in the preparation for, convening and management of board meetings and is responsible for any administration tasks following the meeting.

Until relatively recently, board papers would be collated, hard copies printed and these packs distributed by hand, post or courier to each director. With the increasing use of secure email and remote access to corporate IT networks some companies will now also distribute their board packs using email or by making the pack available on a corporate network.

Additionally, a number of third-party vendors have developed board meeting management applications which among other features facilitate the distribution of board packs directly to a director's laptop or tablet. For the company secretary there are obvious advantages for the electronic collation and distribution of board packs and the consequent savings in time, cost and significantly enhanced levels of security. Another advantage is the ability to issue updated reports directly to directors' laptops or tablet devices. Some of these applications form part of an entity management application, which allows for all entity documentation to be retained securely in one database. Such applications are considered in more detail in chapter 10.

6.1   Before the board meeting

In circumstances where board meetings are held on a regular basis there are likely to be standing items on the agenda for topics that are discussed or reports received at every meeting such as finance update, business development, risk management, health & safety etc. In addition to these standing items the company secretary should make enquiries of the directors and senior executives as to whether there are any matters they wish to be discussed or brought to the attention of the board and from this list of topics a final agenda should be settled on after discussion with the chair and/or CEO. For listed companies the agenda will most often be agreed in consultation with the chair and in other companies it is often the CEO that leads the board meeting process.

Having agreed the agenda, the company secretary should request that any documents or reports be made available in good time prior to the deadline for issuing the board pack to allow time for the reports to be reviewed, amended and the board pack itself compiled. The time required to compile the board pack will vary considerably depending on how the board packs are distributed.

The lead time to distribute board packs in advance of the meeting will vary from company to company and will be driven by the length of the board pack, the frequency of the meetings and preference of the chair.

If any of the company's managers are to attend the whole or part of the meeting, e.g. the company's financial controller, internal auditor or risk manager, they should also be advised of the meeting and sent a copy of the agenda and supporting papers. If they are to attend only part of the meeting, it might be appropriate for them be sent the papers for those relevant items only.

It is a sensible precaution for the company secretary to ensure that spare copies of the agenda and supporting papers are available at the meeting itself. This will be the case even where the papers are distributed for viewing on an electronic tablet or laptop as these devices can fail during the meeting.

The company secretary must be familiar with the quorum requirements and process for declaration and handling any conflicts of interest with any item of business considered by the meeting.

6.2   During the board meeting

The company secretary should keep a note of those persons present at the commencement of the meeting, any apologies for absence and details of anyone joining or leaving the meeting. In this way the minutes will reflect those present at any particular point during the meeting.

The company secretary should ensure that a quorum is present at the commencement of business and whenever any decisions are reached. If any item in which a director has an interest is to be considered, they should ensure that there will still be an independent, disinterested quorum to deal with it.

The company secretary should take notes during the course of the meeting on any action decided on by the board and of its decisions reached, together with appropriate justification, if necessary. The minutes should not be a verbatim record of what is said but should provide the reader with an accurate summary of the matters being discussed, any challenges raised and all decisions reached. Although the exact style and detail of the minutes is for each board to decide for itself there will be external requirements to consider as well. Particularly for companies with external regulators it is likely that the minutes will provide more detail on reasons for any particular decision and where a director has raised concerns, objections or challenge to a proposal and the actions taken or discussions to satisfy that concern, objection or challenge.

Voting at directors' meetings is often informal and decisions usually reached by unanimous consent as directors have collective responsibility for their decisions and actions (Model Articles Plc & Ltd reg. 7). In rare cases, where, after discussion, a director remains opposed to any particular course of action a formal vote may be appropriate and a note of the views of the dissenting director should always be recorded in the minutes.

The chair may ask the company secretary to advise on any point of procedure regarding the conduct of the business of the meeting, although it would also be appropriate for the company secretary to intervene in the meeting (a company secretary who is also a director is, of course, free to speak at any time during a meeting) if the board were proposing to do something that was unlawful, contrary to the company's **articles of association** (Articles) or any other regulations the company is subject to such as the Governance Code or LR.

If a manager or external adviser is to be present for a specific agenda item, the Company Secretary should ensure that they are ready to be called when that item is reached on the agenda.

If any confidential papers are left behind on the board table by the directors, or any flip chart pages used, these should be collected by the company secretary before staff come in to clear the room.

6.3   After the board meeting

(*Companies with publicly traded securities only*) If the board has made a decision with regard to a notifiable event such as the payment of a dividend on the company's shares, yearly or half-yearly accounts have been approved, a decision for the appointment or resignation of a director, an issue of shares or **debentures**, or the postponement of the payment of a preference dividend or of interest, then an announcement via a **regulatory information service (RIS)** must be made as soon as possible. In practice the company secretary will be aware in advance of the meeting that such an announcement is likely to be required and a draft of the announcement should be available for approval by the board for immediate release following the meeting.

The company's managers should be notified of any action which the board requires them to take.

A note should be made of any item that has been deferred for future consideration to ensure that it is not overlooked.

If the directors have asked for a report on a specific subject to be prepared for their next meeting, the Company Secretary should ensure that the manager responsible for preparing it is notified.

The company secretary should prepare the minutes of the meeting according to the company's usual style and format. These should include details of any items

articles of association
The constitutional document setting out the internal regulations of the company. Unless modified or excluded, the specimen Articles in the relevant version of Table A/Model Articles in force on the date of incorporation have effect.

debenture
A written acknowledgement of a debt owed by a company, often – but not necessarily – secured. It is common practice for a debenture to be created by a trust deed by which company property is mortgaged to trustees for the debenture holders, as security for the payment of interest and capital.

regulatory information service (RIS)
An information provider approved by the FSA to disseminate information to the market.

carried forward for discussion at a future meeting. In addition, many boards prefer a schedule of action points to be circulated, often in advance of the minutes being available.

The procedure to be followed after preparation of the minutes will vary from company to company. However, it is usual to send a copy of the draft minutes to the chair or sometimes the CEO for comments and once a settled version of the minutes is agreed a copy will be forwarded to every director present with a request that they return any comments by a given date. The final form of the minutes will be agreed following which the minutes can be prepared for distribution to all directors.

If a director makes a comment about the wording of a particular minute, the alteration should be considered and if agreed the minutes updated accordingly. Other than obvious mistakes, alterations should be confined to what was said rather than what any particular director meant to say or, on reflection, would have preferred not to say.

Stop and think 1.5

Although board meeting management applications can be relatively expensive as a standalone cost the cost savings and increased level of security can often see this investment recouped even in the first year. In order to provide a degree of security many companies would courier their board packs to their directors and depending on the frequency of meetings and the length of the board packs the savings in courier and print costs alone can be considerable plus the associated staff time required to co-ordinate the production of the board packs.

Board packs will often contain confidential personal information and the increased level of protection required following the coming into force of the General Data Protection Regulations (GDPR) in May 2018 means that company secretaries must review their processes for the secure distribution of board papers.

Test yourself 1.4

1. **Who is authorised to convene meetings of the directors?**

2. **How might minutes of directors' meetings differ between a regulated and unregulated company?**

3. **Is it good practice to permit directors to amend meeting minutes to reflect what they meant to say?**

7. Communication with shareholders and other stakeholders

The Act sets out in detail communication provisions to be used by companies when communicating with their members and vice versa (CA2006 ss. 1143–8 and Sch. 4 & 5). In addition, members of a traded company may nominate a third party to receive copies of company communications (CA2006 ss. 146–51).

Traded companies will also be subject to one or more of the DTR and LR and any trading venues which also stipulate additional provisions in respect of communications with members and the wider (share) trading market.

Companies may only send communications to members by electronic means if the member has opted in or has been deemed to opt in following a specific request from the company to ascertain their preferred method of receiving communications from the company. The provisions dealing with communications by a company are set out in schedule 5 of the Act and apply not only to company communications to its members but also to any other company such as a **corporate director**, supplier or a company it itself is a member of.

Members, other than corporate members, may send documents by electronic means to the company if it has agreed, generally or specifically, or can be deemed to have agreed as set out in any provision of the Act (e.g. CA2006 ss. 333 or 333A).

The default method of communicating is in hard copy other than for communications being forwarded to a third party where the default method is via a website. A member reviewing a communication by electronic means has the right to request a hard copy version free of charge (CA2006 s. 1145).

The provisions in the Act take precedence over any contrary provision in a company's Articles except where the Act specifically allows for contrary provision to be made (e.g. CA2006 s. 1146(4)).

CA2006 s. 1146 sets out default authentication requirements for communications issued to the company, subject to any alternative provisions in the company's Articles. In the case of hard copy communications these should be signed by or on behalf of the sender and in the case of electronic communications must identify the sender in such manner specified by the company and in the absence of any specification in such a way as to identify the sender.

CA2006 s. 1147 sets out details of when documents or information required by the Act to be sent by a company are, subject to any alternative provisions in its Articles, deemed to have been received, as follows:

◆   documents and information sent by post are deemed to have been delivered 48 hours after posting provided the company can prove that the envelope was properly addressed, postage paid and was actually posted;

corporate director
A corporate entity that is appointed as a director of another company. Quite common within groups of companies.

◆ documents and information sent in electronic form are deemed to have been received 48 hours after they were sent provided the company can prove they were properly addressed; and

◆ documents and information made available on a website are deemed to have been received when published on the website or, if later, when the recipient received, or is deemed to have received, notification that the documents or information were available on the website.

When calculating the period of deemed delivery non-working days, or any part of them, are not taken into account.

Hard copy means any document on paper or similar form and capable of being read. Electronic form means by email, SMS message or fax or being delivered while in electronic form such as sending a DVD or memory stick by hand or post. A document sent in electronic form must enable the recipient to be able to read it and retain a copy of it. A document is deemed to be readable if it can be read with the naked eye (CA2006 s. 1168).

7.1 Delivery of documents and information to a company

CA2006 sch. 4 sets out detailed provisions for the sending of documents and other information to a company but does not apply to communications from another company, even one that is a member. Company to company communication is subject to CA2006 sch. 5.

Hard copy documents may be sent to a company by hand or post to:

◆ an address specified by the company for that purpose;

◆ its registered office; or

◆ an alternative address authorised by any provision in the Act.

(CA2006 sch. 4 paras 2–4)

Documents in electronic form may be sent to a company:

◆ if the company has agreed, generally or specifically, to permit delivery of that document in electronic form (e.g. CA2006 s. 333A); or

◆ in circumstances where the company can be deemed to have agreed by virtue of a provision in the Act (e.g. CA2006 s. 333).

proxy
A person authorised by a member to vote on his behalf at a general meeting. A proxy need not also be a member of the company.

The document must be delivered to an address specified for that purpose by the company or is deemed to have supplied that address. Where the electronic document is contained on a physical device such as a DVD or memory stick, delivery to the company is only permitted if it is to an address complying with the requirements for delivery of hard copy documents (CA2006 sch. 4 paras 5–7).

Documents and information may also be delivered to a company if delivered in a form that has been agreed by the company. This provision enables the use of online submission of information such as appointment of a **proxy** where the instructions are in a format that cannot be read or using pre-paid cards which do not meet the criteria for delivery by post as an envelope is not used (CA2006 sch. 4 para. 8).

7.2   Delivery of documents and information by a company

CA2006 sch. 5 sets out the detailed provisions for a company to issue communications.

Hard copy documents may be handed to the recipient or sent by a company by hand or post to:

◆   an address specified by the recipient for that purpose;

◆   a company at its registered office;

◆   a member of the company, in their capacity as a member, at the address in its register of members for that member;

◆   a director of the company, in their capacity as a director, at the address in its register of directors; or

◆   an alternative address authorised by any provision in the Act.

(CA2006 sch. 5 paras 2–4).

Documents in electronic form may only be sent by a company:

◆   if the recipient has agreed, generally or specifically, to permit delivery of that document in electronic form and supplied an address for that purpose; or

◆   if the recipient is a company, agreement may be deemed to have been given and the address may be deemed to have been provided.

The document must be delivered to an address specified for that purpose by the company or is deemed to have supplied that address. Where the electronic document is contained on a physical device such as a DVD or memory stick the company is only permitted to hand it to the recipient or deliver it to an address complying with the requirements for delivery of hard copy documents (CA2006 sch. 5 paras 5–7).

A company may also deliver documents or information by making it available on a website and notifying the recipient that it has done so. Communications via a website are only permitted where the company has a reasonable expectation that the recipient will be able to read it, with the naked eye, and retain a copy.

Website communication is only permitted where the recipient has given general or specific consent or is deemed to have done so by failing to respond to consultation conducted in accordance with CA2006 sch. 5. Member consent is required for a company to take advantage of the deemed consent provisions. Any consultation can only be conducted once in any 12-month period (CA2006 sch. 5 paras 8–14).

Documents and information may also be delivered by a company if delivered in a form that has been agreed by the recipient (CA2006 sch. 5 para. 15).

Stop and think 1.6

Companies even with only a few thousand members can make significant costs savings through reduced print run and the associated postage costs of distributing their annual report and accounts. In order to take advantage of these provisions a consultation must be conducted allowing members to elect to receive hard copy documents, those documents electronically and to provide a suitable address. If the member fails to respond, the company is entitled to deem that the member has consented to the documents or information being made available via a website.

In order to ensure that the necessary consents are available at the time of mailing the AGM documentation a company will need to either undertake a standalone mailing or enclose the consultation with their interim accounts or dividend mailing.

Test yourself 1.5

1. Can companies print documents in very small 'fine print'?

2. Can companies unilaterally decide to issue their report and accounts by email only to their members?

3. A company has developed its own secure encrypted web technology which requires anyone using the service to pay an annual subscription. Can the company use this platform to make its annual report and accounts available to its members?

Chapter summary

◆ Historical growth in the importance of the company secretary
◆ Appointment process
◆ Qualifications
◆ General duties
◆ Relationship with the chair, CEO and other directors and executives
◆ Communications to and by companies

Chapter two
The directors

CONTENTS

1. Introduction
2. Types of directors
3. Recruitment, appointment, re-appointment and rotation
4. Roles, duties, responsibilities and mandates
5. Removal, retirement and disqualification
6. Succession planning
7. Directors' and officers' indemnification and liability insurance
8. Co-option

1. Introduction

Directors manage the affairs of a company on behalf of its members. The majority of private company directors will also own a significant proportion of the company whereas in public companies their ownership will usually be quite modest.

This chapter looks at the processes for the appointment and termination of appointment of directors, the authority of directors to exercise the company's powers and the duties, responsibilities and liabilities of directors.

2. Types of directors

CA2006 s. 250 defines a director as any 'person occupying the position of director, by whatever named called'. A director of a company who has the title chief executive officer is a company director while the head of business development might be given the title of 'business development director' but is not a company director.

The Act makes no distinction between different types of company directors, and the rights, duties and liabilities set out in the Act apply equally to all persons occupying the position of director.

The definition in CA2006 s. 250 refers to any person rather than any individual and thus will include corporate bodies, which have a 'legal persona'. In this way, it is possible for one company to be appointed a director of another company.

2.1 Executive

Day-to-day management of the company's affairs is in the hands of the senior company executives. Where any or all of those senior management executives are also board directors, they will be executive directors.

In smaller private companies, typically all the executives will also be company directors. In a listed company it might only be the CEO and chief finance officer (CFO) who are also company directors.

The appointment of directors as executive directors is governed by provisions contained in the company's Articles, giving the directors power to appoint such directors, to determine the terms of their appointment and remuneration, and to delegate to them such powers of the board as may be desired (Model Articles Plc reg. 23, Ltd reg. 19).

Directors who also hold salaried executive positions with the company should have a contract of employment, usually called a service contract, specifying whether the remuneration stated in the contract is exclusive or inclusive of directors' fees. The agreement should also contain any provisions relating to confidentiality and some control over the director's activity, in the event of their leaving the service of the company.

For a smaller company, the terms of appointment could be set out in the minutes of the board meeting appointing the director and a letter sent to the director containing a copy of the minutes and asking them to confirm acceptance of the proposed appointment in writing.

2.2 Non-executive

A non-executive director (NED) is a director without executive responsibilities in the company. The role of NEDs is to contribute skills and experience to board decision-making that might not otherwise be available, and to provide balance and challenge to proposals brought forward by the executive team.

NEDs are not employees of the company, and accordingly will not have a service contract. Instead, the terms of their appointment will be set out in a letter of appointment.

The role of NEDs is seen as increasingly important for larger, listed companies, and the issue of the balance between executive and NEDs on boards has become a key tenet of good corporate governance practice.

In order to provide a firm foundation to challenge the executive management team NEDs should ideally be independent of the company and its management. Under the Governance Code it is recommended that half of the directors be independent NEDs, excluding the chair.

There are a number of situations and circumstances that might compromise the independence of an NED. Helpfully the Governance Code, provision 10 sets out a summary of these as shown in checklist 2.1.

Checklist 2.1 NED independence

Circumstances which are likely to impair, or could appear to impair, a non-executive director's independence include, but are not limited to, whether a director:

◆ **is or has been an employee of the company or group within the last five years;**

◆ **has, or has had within the last three years, a material business relationship with the company, either directly or as a partner, shareholder, director or senior employee of a body that has such a relationship with the company;**

◆ **has received or receives additional remuneration from the company apart from a director's fee, participates in the company's share option or a performance-related pay scheme, or is a member of the company's pension scheme;**

◆ **has close family ties with any of the company's advisers, directors or senior employees;**

◆ **holds cross-directorships or has significant links with other directors through involvement in other companies or bodies;**

◆ **represents a significant shareholder; or**

◆ **has served on the board for more than nine years from the date of their first appointment.**

2.3 Shadow

A **shadow director** is any person who has not been formally appointed as a company director, does not openly participate in managing the company but on whose instructions the appointed directors and employees usually act upon. This situation can occur where a majority or significant shareholder is not also a director. A shadow director of the company is deemed to be a director of the company for all purposes (CA2006 s. 251).

shadow director
A person, not appointed as a director, managing or directing the affairs of a company or who directs the actions of the directors.

This is of particular relevance to the individual if the company they are a shadow director of becomes insolvent, as their actions as well as those of the formally appointed directors will be reviewed by the liquidator/receiver to assess if any wrongdoing was committed and if any individual(s) should be held to account for any action or inaction.

Professional advisers are often invited to attend meetings of the directors, sometimes on a regular basis. Such advisers must take care to restrict their advice to their area of expertise such as accountancy or property transactions.

Otherwise, if they provide wide-ranging advice which the directors regularly take or act upon they are likely to become shadow directors.

Unlike a de facto director, a shadow director tries to conceal their involvement with the company.

2.4   De facto

A de facto director is a person who has not been formally appointed as a company director but holds themselves out to be a director and carries out the acts and duties of a company director. A de facto director of the company is deemed to be a director of the company for all purposes (CA2006 s. 250).

Unlike a shadow director a de facto director actively holds themselves out to be a director although not formally appointed.

2.5   Alternate

alternate director
A person appointed by a director to represent them, usually at board meetings, and who assumes the responsibilities and duties of their appointor when acting in their place.

An **alternate director** is a person appointed by an existing director to act on their behalf in their absence. There is no authority in the Act to appoint an alternate director, so alternates may be appointed only if the Articles specifically permit this.

Model Articles – Plc reg. 25 make provision for a director to appoint another director to be their alternate, or they may appoint any other person as their alternate subject to that person being approved by the board. The Model Articles for private companies and companies limited by guarantee do not provide for the appointment of alternate directors.

Alternate directors are included in the definition of 'director' in CA2006 s. 250 and accordingly, if they are not already a director, their particulars should be entered in the register of directors and details of their appointment notified to the Registrar using Form AP01. This form does not differentiate between the appointment of a person as a director or as an alternate director; however, it is possible to enter 'alternate director' in the occupation field if preferred.

Alternates are subject to the same rules as directors with regard to disclosure of interests in shares of traded companies and related party transactions with the company. Their names must also be shown on letterheads if it is company practice to show the names of directors on such stationery.

An alternate director may act only in the absence of the appointing director; it is not a complete assignment of office by the director.

In practice, alternate directors are most often appointed for specific board meetings in circumstances where their appointor is unable to attend but wishes their views or vote to be recorded.

Stop and think 2.1

In most cases it is obvious who the directors are, and they are formally appointed as such. If a company has a significant shareholder and a representative routinely attends board meetings consider what advice

should be provided to ensure that, if they are not to be appointed as a director, they do not become a shadow director. How would the advice differ if the person was a professional adviser to the board?

Test yourself 2.1

1. **What are the key differences between an executive director and an NED?**

2. **Must directors have the word 'director' in their job title?**

3. **What criteria prevent an individual from being independent?**

3. Recruitment, appointment, re-appointment and rotation

The nature of the relationships between companies and their directors, companies and their shareholders and shareholders and directors results in a patchwork of requirements governing the appointment process and any on-going requirement for re-appointment and/or re-election. These requirements are set out in the Act, the company's Articles, Governance Code, directors' service contracts, company policies and shareholder/investor agreements. The company secretary must ensure they familiarise themselves with all relevant requirements for their company.

3.1 Qualification

There are only two eligibility criteria in the Act to satisfy when appointing directors:

◆ There must be at least one **natural director** appointed at all times (CA2006 s. 155).

◆ On appointment, the person being appointed must be at least 16 years old (CA2006 s. 157).

The company's Articles may, however, contain additional eligibility criteria such as a requirement to hold a minimum number of shares or a particular professional qualification. It is very common for the directors of a residents' management company to be required to be property owners or tenants of the particular development.

Provided the two Companies Act eligibility criteria, together with any additional company or industry specific criteria, are met, anyone may be appointed to the office of director, provided they are not specifically prohibited. Prohibited persons are as follows:

natural directors
Companies are required to have at least one natural director by which is meant a human being rather than a corporate entity.

- A bankrupt person. If a director becomes bankrupt after appointment, they must immediately resign, unless leave to continue is given by the courts (Company Directors Disqualification Act 1986 (CDDA1986), s. 11).
- A person who has had a disqualification order made against them may not act as a company director, unless leave has been given by the courts (CDDA1986 ss. 2 and 5).
- The auditor of a company cannot also be a director of that company (CA2006 s. 1214).
- The director of an insolvent company cannot, without the leave of the court, be appointed as a director of a company with a 'prohibited' name (Insolvency Act 1986 (IA1986), s. 216).

The company's Articles may impose additional restrictions, including:

creditor
A person or company owed money.

- If a receiving order has been made against the director or proposed director, or if they compound with their **creditors** generally (Model Articles Ltd reg. 18(c)).
- If the maximum number of directors permitted by the Articles has been reached (not in the Model Articles).

3.2 Recruitment

Where an additional director is required either to fill a vacancy or as an additional director the board or the nominations committee will draw up a job specification and candidate profile. In drawing up the specification, care must be taken to ensure that these meet the requirements of the Equality Act 2010 (EA2010). Although boards are able to encourage or enable applications from a particular sector to address any board diversity imbalance, selection of the successful applicant(s) must be judged on individual merit and positive discrimination is not permitted.

audit
The independent examination of, and expression of opinion on, the company's accounts. All persons or firms offering audit services must be registered auditors and belong to one of the recognised accountancy bodies.

3.3 Regulatory approval

In some regulated industries appointment of directors is subject to regulatory approval or conditions including but not limited to:

- financial services companies;
- NHS Foundation Trusts;
- regulated **audit** firms; and
- solicitors firms.

Stop and think 2.2

In addition to the Companies Act requirements for the appointment of directors the company secretary must make themselves aware of any industry specific or regulatory requirements relating to the appointment of directors.

What additional approval or pre-vetting of new directors is required for appointments to an investment company or an audit company?

3.4   Procedure for appointment

The first directors of a company are those whose names are entered on Form IN01 and submitted to the Registrar for the purpose of incorporating the company. Subsequent appointments as directors are governed by the provisions of the company's Articles. These usually provide that the board itself may or the members in **general meeting** (GM) may fill any casual vacancies or appoint additional directors up to the maximum number, if any, specified in the Articles. A casual vacancy is one arising from the death or resignation of a director.

Before the meeting to consider the shortlist of candidates, the company secretary should circulate to the directors:

general meeting
Any general meeting of the company's members that is not an annual general meeting.

◆ all relevant information about the director;

◆ a summary of the proposed remuneration arrangements including any bonus and share incentive arrangements if an executive position;

◆ a summary of the company's remuneration policy to ensure compliance;

◆ a draft of the service contract; and

◆ copies of any regulatory notices or press releases that will be issued upon the director's appointment.

Once a suitable candidate has been identified and any qualification or regulatory criteria satisfied, the process shown in checklist 2.2 should be followed.

Members can either circulate their own resolution in writing or submit a requisition for a general meeting to be held to appoint a new, specified director. Members of public companies and traded companies can put forward resolutions to be considered at the AGM provided it is received at least six weeks prior to the meeting and is given by the requisite number of members or members holding the requisite percentage of voting rights (see chapter 14).

Checklist 2.2 Appointment of directors

◆ **Obtain written confirmation from the appointee that they consent to be appointed as a director. This is particularly important as Forms AP01/AP02 are no longer required to be signed by the appointee consenting to act. Without this consent, it may be difficult to prove that the person has consented to be appointed and if there is a dispute application can be made to the Registrar for the appointment to be struck out (see page 33).**

◆ **The board resolves to appoint the new director either at a meeting of the directors or by written resolution.**

The company secretary should confirm to the newly appointed director their appointment by the board and deal with the following:

◆ Request personal particulars, including full name, residential address, full date of birth, nationality and occupation which are required to complete Form AP01 or AP02 (there are different forms to be completed by natural persons and corporate entities) and to make the necessary entry in the register of directors (CA2006 s. 162). The date of birth is required for all directors (CA2006 s. 163 (1)(f)). Although the full date of birth must be provided to the Registrar on Form AP01 only the month and year of birth are placed on the public record. Two addresses may be supplied for each director. A service address, where documents may be served on the director, and their residential address. Use of a service address will also assist in prevention of identity fraud.

◆ On receipt of the relevant information from the director, make the necessary entries in the register of directors and the register of directors' residential addresses. The completed Form AP01 or AP02, whether on paper or electronic, must be sent to the Registrar within 14 days of the date of appointment.

◆ If the director will be signing cheques on the company's behalf, an amended bank mandate and a specimen signature should be sent to the company's bank.

◆ Providing details to the director of any share or other qualifications that must be acquired under the Articles and the time allowed in which to do this.

◆ Requesting the director to give a general or specific notice of any interests such as in contracts between the company and any customers or suppliers (CA2006 ss. 182 and 185).

◆ Inviting the director to give notice of their interests in shares in the company. Although there is no longer a requirement to keep a register of directors' interests in shares, any interests do need to be disclosed in the accounts and for listed companies interests and changes to those interests need to be disclosed.

◆ Providing dates of forthcoming board meetings.

◆ Enquiring how the director wishes their remuneration to be paid, e.g. sent to their home address or paid direct into their bank account, including information regarding their Pay as you Earn (PAYE) tax coding and National Insurance contributions (if they are already paying the maximum contributions in connection with another employment, they should obtain and submit to the company a certificate of exemption from contributions).

◆ Providing general information about the business of the company if the newly appointed director is not already involved in the company. Copies of the articles, reports and accounts for recent years and interim reports and circulars should be made available, if required.

◆   (*Traded companies only*) **Providing a copy of the company's rules for securities transactions, if any, and asking the director to acknowledge receipt.**

◆   (*Traded companies only*) **A regulatory information service (RIS) should be notified of the appointment by the end of the business day following the decision to appoint the director (LR 9.6.11). Details of the director's other business activities must be disclosed to a regulatory information service within 14 days. Details of any interests in shares of the company must also be disclosed within five days of their appointment.**

◆   **If appropriate, a press announcement should be sent to newspapers or through the company's press agents.**

◆   **Where a director is not required to have a share qualification, it is usual for the Articles to provide that the director may receive notice of, and attend and speak at, general meetings of the company. As a non-shareholder, they would not otherwise have such power except if acting as chair of the meeting.**

◆   **If the company has an insurance policy covering directors and officers of the company against liabilities incurred in carrying out their duties, the insurance company should be notified of the appointment of the new director, either at the time of appointment or at renewal, depending upon the wording of the policy.**

◆   **All newly appointed directors, even experienced directors should receive some form of director induction tailored to their specific requirements.**

3.5   Induction

In order for directors to contribute in discussions, it is important that all newly appointed directors receive induction and briefings. Individual induction arrangements and briefing materials should be prepared as appropriate covering three broad topics: internal policies and procedures, external legislation and codes of practice and industry specific information. Although particularly important for those who might not have been a director previously or to an external appointee not familiar with the company, induction and briefings are important for experienced directors as although many policies will have the same overall aim, the detail will vary from company to company.

For listed companies reference should be made to the Governance Code and related guidance which set out recommendations concerning director induction (Governance Code Guidance paras 81 and 82).

The company secretary should ensure that all prospective appointees are fully aware of the responsibilities, duties and potential liabilities of being a director. Additionally, there are several institutions (for example, ICSA, ICAEW or IOD) that provide training courses and written guidance material for new directors and specific courses for members of board committees.

It is often the duty of the company secretary, under direction from the chair, to arrange induction materials and site visits for new directors. This means that the company secretary needs to have a good understanding of how the business operates and who will be the most appropriate employees to meet the new director.

Tailored induction must be provided to all new appointees and it should not be assumed that a newly appointed director is already familiar with their duties and responsibilities simply due to their being a director of another company, whether listed or not.

3.6   Rotation and re-appointment

For public companies, and any private company that chooses to hold an AGM, their Articles typically provide that where a new director has been appointed by the other directors they must put themselves forward for re-election at the next AGM and that all directors must put themselves forward for re-election at the AGM at least every three years (Model Articles – Plc reg. 21(1)).

The Governance Code recommends that all directors offer themselves for re-election at every AGM.

At the company's first AGM, all the directors retire from office and have to be re-elected by the members at the meeting.

3.7   Directors' addresses

Directors are required to give details of a service address for the receipt of official notices. The service address can be their usual residential address, but if it is not, details of their usual residential address must be provided on Form AP01, on appointment, or any subsequent change in their usual residential address on Form CH01. Companies House routinely verify the address details supplied against the Post Office database and will reject any that appear to be an office address. Accommodation addresses and PO Box numbers cannot be used, as clearly these are not residential addresses. The Registrar does not place the residential address information on the public file unless it has reason to believe that mail addressed to the service address is being returned, not being actioned or not being forwarded to the individual concerned.

3.8   Number of directors

A public company must have at least two directors and a private company must have at least one director (CA2006 s. 154). All companies must have at least one director who is a natural person (CA2006 s. 155).

The Articles may stipulate a higher minimum number of directors. If the number of directors falls below this number, the remaining directors have the power to fill a casual vacancy or to convene a GM only for the purpose of allowing the members to appoint additional director(s).

If, for any reason, it is not realised that the number of directors has fallen below the minimum number, once the number has been restored it is recommended that the board ratify the decisions made while there were insufficient directors.

3.9   Defective appointment of directors

If the appointment of a director is found to be defective in any way, CA2006 s. 161 provides that, for the protection of third parties, any earlier acts made by the person acting as a director remain valid. CA2006 s. 239 provides that the members of the company may ratify prior acts of directors either individually or collectively for acts of negligence, default or breaches of duty or trust.

3.10   Disputed appointments

Under a new process introduced in 2016 CA2006 s. 1095(4A) enables a director to dispute their appointment or amend details filed in respect of their appointment and make application to the Registrar for the appointment to be struck out.

Application to the Registrar is made using form RP06. The Registrar will enquire of the company to ascertain whether consent was given or not and where consent cannot be proved the appointee's details will be removed from the record.

Consequently, it is recommended that specific written consent to act as a director be obtained for all proposed directors prior to their formal appointment.

3.11   Contracts of employment

A director's employment or service contract that cannot be terminated other than for breach of contract on less than two years' notice must be approved by the members in general meeting (CA2006 s. 188).

Members' approval may be given by an **ordinary resolution** passed at a general meeting, provided that a written memorandum setting out the terms of the proposed agreement or a copy of the service contract is available for inspection by members of the company at the registered office for a period of not less than 15 days prior to the date of the meeting. Companies are required at all times to keep copies of directors' service contracts available for inspection by members (CA2006 s. 228).

ordinary resolution
A resolution at a general meeting carried by a simple majority of votes cast.

Listed companies are encouraged to have service agreements with their directors with a notice period of not more than one year (Governance Code provision 39).

Test yourself 2.2

1.   What form should be used to notify the Registrar of the appointment of an individual as a director?

2.   Which statutory registers should be updated on the appointment of a director?

3.   What information should be obtained from the new director?

4.   Who cannot be appointed as a director?

4. Roles, duties, responsibilities and mandates

The Companies Act treats all directors equally in all respects. Over the years, case law has developed and there are now certain mitigating factors that individual directors may be able to rely on. Through the operation of board policies and procedures, services contracts, their Articles and where relevant other regulatory requirements different levels of authority and liability will be in place between directors and in particular between executive and NED roles.

4.1 Executive and non-executive roles

The executive directors are employees of the company and are responsible for day-to-day management of the business and for formulating policies and initiatives to implement the strategy agreed upon by the board of directors as a whole.

NEDs are not employees of the company and have no hands-on management role. The role of an NED is to bring expertise, experience and balance to the board of directors.

NEDs are sometimes appointed who are not independent of the company either by virtue of being executive directors or senior managers or some other previous connection with the company. These non-independent NEDs can also bring valuable experience to board discussions.

A key role for chair and nomination committees is to achieve and maintain an appropriate balance. A board where the NEDs constantly challenge and query every proposal put forward by the executive team is as dysfunctional and damaging to the company long-term as a board where 'group think' is the norm with no proposals receiving adequate challenge or discussion.

4.2 Collective responsibility

Directors collectively manage companies and can be held liable for those actions, or inactions. Under the Companies Act legislation all directors are treated equally and have the same rights, duties and liabilities as each other.

Although boards act collectively individual directors may be held to account where they have particular knowledge or experience on a specific matter. A director cannot hide behind collective responsibility to escape liability.

The leading case authority on the duty of care is *Re City Equitable Fire Insurance Co. Ltd.*

Case law 2.1

Re City Equitable Fire Insurance Co. Ltd [1925] Ch 407

The directors of an insurance company delegated virtually all aspects of management to its managing director. The managing director stole large amounts of cash from the company, largely because of inadequate

supervision by the other directors. It was held that the directors had been in breach of their duty of skill and care. In his judgement, Romer J laid down the directors' duties of skill and care:

◆ The director must exhibit the skill that would be reasonably expected of a person of their knowledge and experience.

◆ The director is not bound to give continuous attention to the company affairs.

◆ A director may delegate their duties to some other official in the company and trust them to perform them properly.

Stop and think 2.3

Although board decisions are taken collectively, they may not be agreed unanimously, and individual directors may have strong contrary views. In these circumstances, what options and actions are available to a dissenting director to protect their position?

4.3 Duties

The Companies Act 2006 codified directors' duties for the first time and introduced seven duties of directors drawn from the existing case law, with some amendments.

A director's prime duty, which they hold together with their fellow directors, is to manage the company for the benefit of its members. The directors may delegate some or all of their powers, usually to committees of the board or other senior officers in the company, but they cannot delegate their duties.

These codified duties are as follows.

To act within their powers (CA2006 s. 171)

Directors must act in accordance with the company's constitution and only exercise powers for the purposes for which they are conferred. Although the company's Articles are likely to be the primary source document the statutory definition of constitution also includes resolutions and other agreements and decisions (CA2006 ss. 17 and 257).

The company secretary must ensure that the Articles together with any other relevant authorities are up to date, that copies are available and circulated to the board members on induction and when any changes are made.

To promote the success of the company (CA2006 s. 172)

A director must 'act in the way he considers, in good faith, would be most likely to promote the success of the company for the benefit of its members as a whole, and in doing so have regard (among other matters) to':

- the likely consequences of any decision in the long-term;
- the interests of the company's employees;
- the need to foster the company's business relationships with suppliers, customers and others;
- the impact of the company's operations on the community and the environment;
- the desirability of the company maintaining a reputation for high standards of business conduct; and
- the need to act fairly as between members of the company.

To exercise independent judgement (CA2006 s. 173)

The duty to exercise independent judgement is not infringed in circumstances where an agreement, validly entered into, restricts the future use of discretion by the directors or where the directors' actions are authorised by the company's constitution.

To exercise reasonable care, skill and diligence (CA2006 s. 174)

The duties imposed by CA2006 ss. 173 and 174 require that a director owes a duty to exercise the same standard of care, skill and diligence that would be exercised by a reasonably diligent person with the general knowledge, skill and experience that may reasonably be expected of the person carrying out the same functions as a director in relation to that company (an objective test); and the general knowledge, skill and experience that the director actually has (a subjective test).

For example, a finance director would be expected to have a greater knowledge of finance issues than, say, the HR director (the objective test); but if the HR director is also a qualified accountant, then they would be expected to have a greater knowledge than would normally be expected of an HR director, although not necessarily the same knowledge as the finance director (the subjective test).

To avoid conflicts of interest (CA2006 s. 175)

Directors must avoid situations in which they have or might have a direct or indirect interest that conflicts or might conflict with the interests of the company. Of particular importance are conflicts relating to assets, information or opportunity, regardless of whether the company could take advantage of such opportunities (CA2006 s. 175(2)).

The duty does not apply to conflicts arising out of transactions or arrangements between the company and the director.

This duty is not infringed in circumstances where the remaining directors authorise the transaction provided:

- where the company is a private company and subject to any restrictions in the Articles, authorisation may be given by resolution of the directors; and
- where the company is a public company and subject to specific authority in the Articles, authorisation may be given by resolution of the directors.

mode.

Such authorisation, whether for a private or public company, is only valid if the necessary quorum for a meeting of the directors is present excluding the director with the conflict of interest and without that director voting (CA2006 s. 175(6)).

Not to accept benefits from third parties (CA2006 s. 176)

Directors must not accept a benefit from a third party being given by virtue of their being a director or due to any action or inaction by the director.

Benefits received by a director from a person by whom their services are provided are not to be regarded as paid by a third party.

The duty is not infringed if the acceptance of the benefit cannot reasonably be regarded as likely to give rise to a conflict of interest.

To declare interests in any proposed transaction or arrangement (CA2006 s. 177)

A director must declare the full nature and extent of any direct or indirect interest in any proposed transaction or arrangement before that transaction or arrangement is entered into. The declaration may be given at a meeting of the directors or by notice in accordance with CA2006 ss. 184 or 185.

Where a previous notification or interest becomes inaccurate or incomplete, additional notification(s) must be made.

Notification is not required where the director is not aware of the interest or is not aware of the transaction or arrangement.

Notification is not required where the nature of the interest is such that it cannot reasonably be regarded as likely to give rise to a conflict of interest, to the extent that the other directors are already aware of the interest without requiring specific notification, or where the transaction relates to the director's service contract.

Stop and think 2.4

While it is each director's responsibility to disclose any conflicts of interest or changes in any conflict it will often fall to the company secretary to remind directors of their responsibility. As company secretary, what actions and processes can be put in place to ensure directors meet their obligations to disclose conflicts of interest?

4.4 Other statutory duties

There are also a number of circumstances under which a director may be personally liable to the company or third parties from a breach of duty or statutory offence, including:

◆ acting as a director while disqualified, CDDA 1986 s. 15;
◆ a director of an insolvent company carrying on a business with a company with a prohibited name s. 217 Insolvency Act 1986 (IA1986);

- payment of a dividend or other distribution in contravention of the Act (breach of duty under CA2016 s. 171);
- employing illegal immigrants, s. 8 Asylum and Immigration Act 1996;
- evasion of VAT, ss. 13 and 14, Finance Act 1986;
- fraudulent preference (IA1986 ss. 238–40);
- fraudulent trading (CA2006 s. 993);
- public company trading prior to issue of trading certificate (CA2006 s. 767);
- trading with intent to defraud (IA1986 s. 213);
- wrongful trading (IA1986 s. 214); and
- health and safety offences s. 37 Health and Safety at Work Act 1974 (HSWA1974).

4.5   Common law

common law
The body of law based on custom and usage and decisions reached in previous cases. The principles and rules of common law derive from judgments and judicial opinions and not legislation introduced by parliament.

The codified general duties of directors are based on certain **common law** rules and equitable principles and have effect in place of those rules and principles. These common law rules and principles have evolved over the years as a result of judges interpreting, confirming and building upon previous judgments. The codified general duties are to be interpreted and applied in the same way as common law rules and equitable principles.

Directors' actions remain subject to the remaining, uncodified common law rules and equitable principles such as breach of trust or minority oppression.

4.6   Contractual

Directors may have obligations to take specific actions under the terms of commercial contracts entered into between the company and its customers and suppliers.

A breach of those terms in general might expose the company to legal action from the affected party. Deliberate or wilful action or inaction on the part of one or more directors may expose them to personal action in addition to any action against the company.

4.7   Regulatory

In addition to the general statutory duties noted above, directors of companies whose shares are publicly traded also have additional statutory and regulatory duties and responsibilities. These are considered in Chapters 8, 12 and 13.

4.8   Authority to exercise company's power

The directors are generally responsible for the management of the business of the company, but the extent of their authority depends on the provisions of the Articles and any overriding provisions in the Companies Act. Model Articles Plc reg. 3 provides that 'subject to the articles, the directors are responsible for management of the company's business, for which purpose they may exercise all the powers of the company'.

Directors act as agents of the company, and are therefore bound by all the provisions of agency law (i.e. actual and ostensible authority). In order to safeguard their position, directors should ensure that the company secretary makes full board minutes showing the directors' reasons, the factors they considered and the arguments against or for any proposed course of action (see chapter 11).

4.9   Liability for actions or inaction

Directors properly exercising the powers of the company and acting as agents for the company will not incur personal liability in the event of a breach of contract. However, directors may incur personal liability if they have given personal guarantees or if they have not made it clear that they are acting as agent of the company and not in a personal capacity.

Personal liability arises from a breach of duty or statutory offences including:

◆ acting as a director while disqualified;

◆ evading the payment of VAT;

◆ failing to show the company name on correspondence, cheques, etc.;

◆ fraudulent trading;

◆ wrongful trading; and

◆ employing workers without valid work permits.

In light of the significant potential liabilities to which directors and other officers are subject, it is becoming increasingly common, especially for companies with external investors, for companies to take out directors' and officers' indemnity insurance.

See section 7 in respect of the indemnification of directors and officers under CA2006.

Test yourself 2.3

1.   **What are the seven codified duties of directors?**

2.   **Do directors have unfettered authority to exercise the company's powers?**

3.   **Can directors delegate any of their powers and duties?**

4.   **How many directors may be appointed?**

5. Retirement, removal and disqualification

Regardless of the terms of a director's service contract or any provisions in the company's Articles shareholders always have the right to remove directors by ordinary resolution approved at a GM. In addition, there are other circumstances, explored below, under which directors may be required to vacate office including resignation, retirement, illness or disqualification.

5.1 Vacation of office

The office of director is vacated on the death of the office holder, under **statute** or under a provision in the Articles of the company. A relevant provision in the Articles might be that the directors are appointed for a fixed term and, on expiry of that term, their appointment automatically ceases.

Vacation of office may also arise under statute, as follows:

statute law
The body of law represented by legislation, and thus occurring in authoritative written form. Statute law contrasts with common law, over which it takes precedence.

- If the director becomes bankrupt, unless the court permits the appointment to continue (CDDA1986 s. 11).
- If the director is disqualified from being a director by court order (CDDA1986, ss. 1–6, as amended). A register of such disqualification orders is maintained by the Secretary of State and is available for inspection by the public at Companies House (CDDA1986 s. 18).

Under the Articles, further criteria for vacating office may be specified, including the following:

- Where the Articles stipulate any qualifying criteria such as a minimum shareholding or professional qualification and that criteria has not been met, the office of director would be vacated automatically at the conclusion of the qualifying period.

annual general meeting (AGM)
A general meeting of the company's members, which must be held in each calendar year within 15 months of the previous AGM. Under Companies Act 2006, private companies are (generally) no longer required to hold AGMs, although the requirement remains for public companies.

- In the case of a company where the director reaches a specified age set out in its Articles, the office of director would be vacated at the conclusion of the next **annual general meeting (AGM)**. Although such a general provision was included in Table A these provisions are now likely to be in contravention of age discrimination legislation under the Equality Act 2010 (EA2010).
- *Resignation.* This will usually take effect from the date on which the letter of resignation is received by the company, unless this states some subsequent date on which the resignation is to become effective. To be effective, the resignation does not need to be accepted by the board, unless the Articles provide otherwise.
- *Absence.* If the director is absent from board meetings for some specified period (often six months) without leave of absence. In order to monitor the operation of any such article, therefore, the secretary should arrange for the board to grant leave of absence where it is known that a director is likely to be absent for a period exceeding six months, e.g. because of overseas travel on the company's business or because of long-term illness.

◆ If a receiving order is made against a director or the director compounds with their creditors generally.

◆ If an order is made by the court on grounds of mental disorder. As with age-related provisions although previously found in Table A such a general provision is likely to in contravention of the EA2010.

◆ If the director is removed from office, e.g. by a notice signed by all remaining directors or by any **holding company**.

◆ Non-reappointment under **retirement by rotation**.

5.2   Retirement by rotation

The Model Articles for public companies provide for the retirement of one-third of the total number of directors by rotation every year (Model Articles – Plc reg. 21). There is no general requirement in the Act for directors to retire by rotation at annual general meetings.

It is usual for the Articles to provide that a person appointed as a director by the board to fill a casual vacancy, or as an additional director, must be re-elected at the next following AGM of the company. Such retirements and elections are not considered in determining the directors who are to retire by rotation at that meeting (Model Articles – Plc reg. 21(b)).

For a listed company, the Governance Code recommends that all directors should offer themselves for re-election every year (see chapter 8).

The procedure to be followed for the retirement of directors by rotation depends on the wording of the Articles, but typically will be as set out in checklist 2.3.

holding company
A company which has subsidiaries.

retirement by rotation
The annual standing down of directors (usually one third) for re-election by members at an annual general meeting.

Checklist 2.3 Rotation of directors

◆ **At the first AGM of the company, all directors must retire and offer themselves for re-election by the members.**

◆ **At subsequent AGMs, one-third of the directors or, where the number is not an exact multiple of three, the number nearest to one-third retire from office. Directors who are retiring because they have been appointed since the last AGM and directors who are excluded from the retirement by rotation provision (e.g. managing directors) are not taken into account for this purpose. Some companies' Articles differ from the Plc Model Articles by providing that the number of directors to retire by rotation shall be one-third of the directors or, if their number is not a multiple of three, then the number nearest to but not exceeding one-third shall retire.**

◆ **The directors to retire at any AGM are those who have been in office longest since their last election. If two or more persons became directors on the same day, those to retire (unless they otherwise agree among themselves) shall be determined by lot.**

◆ **Directors retiring by rotation are eligible for re-election, but the company in GM may elect some other person to take that director's place.**

◆ **In public companies, the resolutions at a GM for the appointment or reappointment of directors must be voted on individually unless those at the meeting first agree unanimously that the appointments or reappointments may be made by a single resolution (CA2006 s. 160).**

5.3 Removal of directors

The members may remove a director at any time by ordinary resolution. This provision cannot be overruled by any provision in the company's Articles, contract of employment, service agreement or any other agreement (CA2006 s. 168).

Removal does not stop the director from being able to exercise any rights they may have to compensation or damages payable in respect of the termination of their appointment as a director before the expiry of any fixed term or without due notice.

Special notice must be given to the company of the intention to propose such a resolution (see chapter 14). A copy of the notice must be sent to the director concerned, to give them the opportunity to make representations in writing to the company and to request that these be circulated to the members.

Where such special notice is received by the company, care must be taken to ensure that the requirements of CA2006 s. 169 are strictly complied with. It may be advisable to obtain legal advice as to the precise procedure.

In the case of a public company, a resolution could be proposed at the next annual general meeting. In all other cases, the removal will be dealt with at a GM. In either case the special notice must be given to the company not less than 28 days prior to the meeting, as specified in CA2006 s. 168(2).

The Articles may not exclude the provisions of CA2006 ss. 168 or 169, but may make additional provisions for removal of directors, such as by unanimous resolution of the other directors or by written notice of a holding company, if any.

A private company may not use the written resolution procedure to remove a director, which must be by way of a resolution approved at a GM (CA2006 s. 288).

Stop and think 2.5

Removal of a director is a serious step to take and the company secretary would be wise to seek external professional advice to ensure all the necessary procedural steps are taken. A removed director may still initiate legal action against the company. Consider what risks the company faces in these circumstances and what action can be taken to mitigate those risks.

5.4   Disqualification

Directors may be disqualified under the CDDA1986 either automatically, as a result of a specific event, or where application has been made to the court that a person is unfit to be a director.

A person who has been disqualified may not, during the period of disqualification, be a director, liquidator, **administrator**, receiver or manager of a company, whether directly or indirectly, without the consent of the court.

Contravention of a disqualification order is a criminal offence punishable by up to two years' imprisonment or an unlimited fine.

Application for disqualification is made under the appropriate provision of the CDDA1986 and disqualification may be automatic or discretionary.

Disqualification for unfitness
The court is obliged to disqualify a person who was or is a director of an insolvent company where their conduct makes them unfit to be involved in the management of a company.

A director can be found unfit to be a director as a result of either their actions or inaction.

Disqualification on conviction
The courts may make a disqualification order if a person has been convicted of an indictable offence in connection with the management, promotion, **formation** or **liquidation** of a company.

Disqualification for breach of statutory obligations
A disqualification order may be made for persistent failure to file accounts or **confirmation statements** or other documents required to be filed with Companies House or failing to keep statutory records.

In addition to disqualification under the provisions of CDDA1986 disqualification may also be sought in the following circumstances:

Disqualification for fraudulent or wrongful trading
A disqualification order may be made against a person if, during the course of a winding up, it appears that they are guilty of an offence under CA2006 s. 993 for fraudulent trading or have committed some other offence or breach of duty, or where the director is required to contribute to the company's assets for insolvent trading.

Disqualification in the public interest
The Secretary of State has power to apply to the courts for a disqualification order on the grounds of public interest. This would usually follow from an enquiry by the **Department for Business, Energy and Industrial Strategy (BEIS)** inspectors.

---

administrator
A person appointed by the court to manage a company in financial difficulties in order to protect creditors and, if possible, avoid liquidation. The administrator has the power to remove and appoint directors. Also a person who administers the estate of a deceased person in the absence of any executors.

formation
See registration.

liquidation
The process under which a company ceases to trade and realises its assets for distribution to creditors and then shareholders. The term 'winding up' is synonymous.

confirmation statement
A form filed each year with the Registrar of Companies, confirming that specified information about the company's directors, secretary, registered office, shareholders, share capital, notified to Companies House is correct or that any changes to the information are being notified at the same time as the confirmation statement. Replaced the annual return from 1 July 2016.

Department for Business, Energy and Industrial Strategy (BEIS)
The government department responsible for the administration of company law. The Companies Act confers certain powers on the Secretary of State. Formerly called the Department for Business, Innovation and Skills (BIS).

Disqualification undertaking

The Secretary of State may, where an individual would otherwise be subject to disqualification proceedings under CDDA1986 ss. 7 and 8, accept a disqualification undertaking from that person.

Competition disqualification order

The court must make a disqualification order (maximum 15 years) against a person if a company of which that person is a director commits a breach of competition law and the court considers the conduct of that person makes them unfit to be concerned in the management of a company (CDDA1986 s. 9A).

Competition undertaking

The Competition and Markets Authority (CMA) or the specified regulator may accept a disqualification undertaking from a person in circumstances where the CMA or the regulator believes a company of which that person is a director has committed a breach of competition law and that person's conduct makes them unfit to manage a company (CDDA1986 s. 9B).

Checklist 2.4 Vacation of office by a director

◆ Where the vacation of office is voluntary obtain a letter of resignation from the director to include any subsidiary companies where appropriate. If not covered by a separate compromise agreement the resignation letter should also confirm that there are no fees owing to the director, or if there are, relevant details.

◆ Listed companies should notify the UKLA and make a market announcement without delay.

◆ Although vacation of office does not require board approval, it is customary to note the vacation of office at the next board meeting.

◆ Note the date of ceasing to be a director in the register of directors.

◆ Notify the Registrar using form TM01 or TM02 within 14 days of the date of cessation.

◆ Any fees or expenses due to the period up to cessation should be paid and PAYE form P45 completed as necessary.

◆ If the director held any share options or bonus arrangements these may have been triggered by the vacation of office. If this is the case notify the director, or their personal representative if the vacation is due to their death or incapacity, of the steps required to be taken.

◆ If it is the company's practice to include the names of directors on headed stationery make arrangements for the stationery to be amended and old stocks destroyed.

◆ Amend any bank mandate(s) if required.

◆ Regulated companies should notify their regulator(s) as required.

◆ **The director should be requested to return all company documentation, or confirm its destruction, any company property held, office keys and make arrangement for the return of any bulky items held such as computers, printers, company car etc.**

Test yourself 2.4

1. **Under what circumstances can a director be disqualified?**

2. **Do the remaining directors need to approve the resignation of a director?**

3. **How soon must notification of the vacation of office by a director be notified to Companies House?**

4. **How many directors should retire at the first AGM of a public company?**

6. Succession planning

Key to the long-term effectiveness of a company board is proper succession planning for the key roles at board and senior management level. The Governance Code (Principle J) recommends that listed companies ensure that they have plans to ensure an orderly succession in director and senior roles so as to maintain an appropriate level of skills and experience and a planned refreshing of board membership.

In drawing up their succession plans, boards and nomination committees must ensure that their plans deliver appropriate skills, expertise, diversity, independence and balance while also being aligned to deliver the company's strategy both currently and in the future.

6.1 Diversity

Poor gender balance on company boards has been the focus of attention for many years, particularly during the five years of the Davies Review. During this period an increase in female board appointments in both FTSE100 and FTSE350 companies was seen. The work of the Davis Committee has now been taken on under the Hampton Alexander review which published its first review and recommendations in November 2016.

The review report advises companies on how to improve gender imbalance and to focus on development, accessibility and diversity in the senior management pipeline of talent.

The review recommends that FTSE350 companies should aim to reach a minimum of female representation on boards of 33% by 2020.

6.2 Independence

In drawing up succession plans the board and nominations committee need to ensure that there remain sufficient independent NEDs to maintain a proper balance of the board.

Under the UK Corporate Governance Code, excluding the chair, independent NEDs should hold at least 50% of board appointments.

6.3 Balance

The board should be balanced in terms of skills, experience, length of service and diversity.

Test yourself 2.5

1. **Why is succession planning important?**

2. **If a listed board has two executive directors, a chair and a non-independent NED, how many independent NEDs must be appointed?**

3. **Is positive discrimination permitted to address board diversity imbalance?**

7. Directors' and officers' indemnification and liability insurance

Directors are responsible for the general management of the company and it follows that they are liable to some extent for their actions and those of the company. CA2006 confirms that directors and officers may be indemnified against civil proceedings (both defence costs and damages) brought by third parties and criminal proceedings. It also permits companies to reimburse directors in respect of costs incurred prior to the outcome of those proceedings. Indemnities may only provide to reimburse costs incurred in a successful defence of any proceedings brought against them.

Subject to certain exceptions, the statutory position set out in CA2006 s. 232(1) is that companies cannot exempt a director from liability in respect of his negligence, default, breach of duty or trust.

Even in circumstances where it is the company bringing an action against one of its own directors, the director's defence costs may be paid by the company as they are incurred. Such defence costs are usually repayable by the director if he unsuccessfully defends the company's claim. The director is personally liable to pay any damages awarded to the company or any fines imposed on them.

Any qualifying indemnity provisions must be disclosed in the company's **directors' report** to the accounts (CA2006 s. 236).

directors' report
A statement attached to the annual accounts containing certain information laid down in the Act.

A copy of any qualifying indemnity provisions, or a memorandum of its terms if the original is not in writing, must be kept available for inspection by members or copies made available during its period of cover and for a further year after it has expired (CA2006 ss. 237 and 238).

Companies intending to indemnify their directors must check their Articles. Model Articles Plc reg. 85, Ltd reg. 52 provides that the company may indemnify every director or officer against any civil or criminal proceedings.

Test yourself 2.6

1.   **Can any company take out directors' indemnity insurance?**

2.   **Can a director be indemnified against personal liability to pay fines and damages?**

3.   **Can the details of any indemnity insurance be kept secret?**

Stop and think 2.6

You are the company secretary of Query plc, a listed company, and the board are to consider the appointment of a new NED.

The chair has requested that you prepare a briefing for the directors on the following matters:

1.   **Can the board appoint the new director?**

2.   **Is any external approval required?**

3.   **This will be the new director's first appointment as a director. What are the key details of directors' duties they should be informed about?**

4.   **How can the board assess the independence of the new director?**

8. Co-option

Co-option to be a director is not a term used in the Companies Act and, in any event, appointing a person to the position of a director without their consent is not possible and a person appointed without their consent can apply to the Registrar to have the appointment struck out.

However, co-option is sometimes used to refer to situations where a director is appointed in between AGMs. This is usually possible provided the directors have authority to fill casual vacancies, the person concerned consents and the maximum number of directors set out in the Articles has not been exceeded.

Test yourself 2.7

Can a person be co-opted to a board without their consent?

Chapter summary

- ◆ Distinctions between different types of director.
- ◆ Statutory qualifications required to become a director.
- ◆ Statutory obligations of people without 'director' in their title.
- ◆ Appointment of directors.
- ◆ Retiring by rotation, and re-election by members.
- ◆ Director's powers.
- ◆ Disqualification of directors.

Chapter three
Effective board practices

CONTENTS

1. Introduction
2. Board evaluation
3. Director education and guidance
4. Best practices, policies and procedures

1. Introduction

As companies grow the role of the directors evolves away from being the technical guru and source of all information pertaining to the company's business and moves into a management role setting and implementing strategy. The directors of large companies almost always have a much smaller percentage of ownership of the companies they manage.

For these large organisations, an effective board is key to the long-term success of the organisation and in order to maximise the board's effectiveness, as with any business process, it should be regularly reviewed, skills and knowledge must be developed and appropriate working practices adopted, reviewed and improved.

This chapter looks at the processes for the evaluation, training and establishment of appropriate working practices that combine to create the right conditions to create an effective board of directors.

2. Board evaluation

Board evaluation is not a statutory requirement but generally accepted good practice. Most managers and directors would not argue that employee appraisals are an effective tool that helps to ensure employees understand and are motivated and aligned to the corporate objectives and that any issues or grievances, on either side, are resolved at an early stage.

The same is true of boards of directors, although among some boards, and in particular those new to the process, there continues to be a degree of reticence to allowing the inner workings of the board to be reviewed, especially by outsiders.

However, like employees directors need to know how well they are performing both individually and collectively if they are to improve their own performance. Board evaluation may be a voluntary exercise or an obligation, willingly undertaken, under the Governance Code.

The Governance Code recommends that all listed company boards should undertake an annual, formal and rigorous evaluation of its performance and that of its committees and individual directors (Governance Code provision 21).

The Governance Code further recommends that for the boards of FTSE350 companies this review should be conducted by an external facilitator at least once every three years. Details of how the evaluation was undertaken should be included in the next annual report together with an overview of any issues found and steps taken to address them (Governance Code provision 23).

Although an obligation for listed companies many other organisations including charities, professional bodies, mutual bodies, regulatory bodies and pension trustee boards also voluntarily undertake board evaluation reviews.

The board evaluation process will examine one or more of the three major roles performed by the board being direction through setting strategy, control through monitoring the executives' progress in delivering the strategy and support though its advisory role. The overall effectiveness of the board depends on a wide variety of factors, some of which may be company or industry specific, and which cover four broad areas:

2.1 Board structure

As part of the board evaluation process, the structure, composition and processes of the board should be reviewed, though most likely not annually, to ensure they remain appropriate for the size and structure of the organisation and the tasks required to be completed by the board.

There is no one-size-fits-all template to establishing either the number or individual responsibilities of the board of directors and it is for each board to determine the most appropriate composition and constitution of its board. Among the factors to be considered are competencies, experience, diversity, independence and any applicable obligations such as the Governance Code for listed companies.

The governance code, while not prescribing the composition of the board, does make a number of recommendations for listed companies including:

- board to compromise both executive and NEDs (Governance Code principle G);
- at least half the boards in the FTSE350 should be independent NEDs, excluding the chair (Governance Code provision 11). Companies outside the FTSE350 should have at least two NEDs; and
- a majority of board committee members should be independent NEDs (Governance Code provision 17).

As with the composition of the board it is for each board to decide the frequency of its regular scheduled meetings. The cycle of issuing board packs sufficiently ahead of the meeting to allow time for the directors to read the reports, holding the meeting, drafting minutes and then call for papers for inclusion in the next board pack means that holding regular meetings more frequently than monthly is not practical. Meeting less often than quarterly is unlikely to provide sufficient oversight of the company's operations.

Many private companies with only one or two directors often do not hold regular board meetings managing the business on a day-to-day basis as required. Often the only formal meeting is the annual meeting to approve the financial statements formally. Similarly, for subsidiaries it can often be the case that the companies' trading activities are undertaken by managers with the directors, often directors of the group holding company, not involved in the day-to-day decision-making process.

Where meetings are held on a regular basis the board should establish board processes, often by the chair in conjunction with the company secretary. This should include:

◆   standing agenda items;

◆   the structure and format of board papers;

◆   the process for calling for board papers;

◆   circulation of the board pack;

◆   the process for non-standard items to be added to the agenda; and

◆   drafting and commenting on draft minutes.

2.2   Board and company governance

One of the key roles of a board is to set corporate strategy and establish relevant and appropriate systems and policies of governance to be able to adequately monitor the performance of those policies and systems and provide a framework to provide support and advice to the executive management team.

The strategy and monitoring process require regular review to both ensure that they are appropriate and functioning correctly and also the strategy and policies will need to evolve over time to meet the changing environment within which the organisation operates.

2.3   Board monitoring

All boards should have appropriate and relevant systems to monitor financial performance, internal control and risk management, processes to manage related party or controlling shareholders and whistle-blowing processes.

Any evaluation process of the board needs to consider these monitoring activities so that there can be assurance that they remain fit for purpose and that the scale and complexity of the business has not outgrown the monitoring processes originally developed.

2.4 Board processes and interactions

The evaluation cycle should include an in-depth review of the board processes including meeting calendar, agenda, availability of information, board packs, relationship between CEO and senior management and quality of discussion at board meetings.

As business information and accounting systems improve and are able to provide more and more granular detail this has led to the increase in size of many board packs. This availability of information has also led to a decrease in the need to accurately summarise the information which has resulted in many board packs lacking succinct overviews of the issue at hand and at the same time provide far too much ancillary background information. Managers sometimes take the view that by providing all the information they are doing the right thing. However, if it takes a director 18 hours to read the board pack the chances are that the pack will not be read in full in which case providing all that information has the opposite effect than that intended.

Another key area, sometimes grouped within board processes and interactions, and hugely important to a successful and effective board is the capability and effectiveness of the chair of the board.

For the majority of companies that undertake board evaluation, this is an annual exercise. There is no universally accepted methodology for undertaking board evaluation. The evaluation process is most often overseen by the chair and will be tailored to the board/company's requirements, any external obligations such as the Governance Code, the board and corporate structure, board culture and existing board processes.

The outcomes of a board evaluation process will be dictated to a large extent by the scope and remit of the evaluation methodology and will range from relatively minor changes to board processes, recommendations to add or change directors, additional board committees or changes to their terms of reference all the way to significant wholesale change to the board and governance structure, composition and processes.

In the early years of board evaluations, in particular where these were undertaken as a result of an obligation rather than through voluntary choice, the results of any board evaluation were often not circulated beyond the board itself and sometimes quietly ignored. As a consequence of this lack of transparency, the Governance Code was amended and boards of listed companies must now report the findings and recommendations of their board evaluations, provide details of how the recommendations will be implemented and in following years an evaluation of those changes (Governance Code provision 23).

After the initial few evaluations, the process becomes the 'norm' with evaluations naturally following the previous one and building on the recommendations and actions from the previous evaluations. The evaluation cycle also becomes embedded in the board's own processes and annual cycle of events.

The evaluation, however undertaken, should include elements of both self-assessment and peer review by the individual directors.

The NEDs led by the senior independent director, should carry out an evaluation of the chair considering the views of the executive directors.

With the exception of their own performance, the evaluation of the board, committees and individual directors is the responsibility of the chair although the mechanics are often delegated to the company secretary.

A key question is whether the evaluation is to be facilitated internally or externally. There are advantages and disadvantages of each approach and the decision is likely to depend on the scope and remit of the evaluation. In addition, the evaluation should include both qualitative and quantitative measures. Qualitative measure by their nature are subjective and open to different interpretations. Quantitative measures lack this subjectivity and can provide good data for subsequent analysis while missing the richness of information available from qualitative measures.

2.5 Internal

Listed below are some of the more common advantages and disadvantages cited by those arguing in favour or against the use of an internally facilitated board evaluation.

Advantages of internal board evaluation include the following:

◆ Those undertaking the evaluation will be familiar with the company, its culture and objectives.

◆ Those participating in the discussions may be more willing to speak to someone they know.

◆ Less financial cost.

Among the disadvantages are the following:

◆ Those undertaking the evaluation are likely to be in junior roles and may be influenced by or have a vested interest in the outcome.

◆ Internal facilitators are less likely to be skilled evaluators.

◆ A well-run evaluation is a time-consuming process and an internal evaluator may not be able to commit the appropriate time to the task.

◆ Those participating in the discussions may be unwilling to speak to people more junior in the organisations about their own faults or those of fellow directors.

◆ Especially if the outcomes are all or mainly positive the review process might lack credibility with external stakeholders.

An internal evaluation can take many forms including combinations of:

◆ questionnaires created in-house;

◆ questionnaires created from third party question banks;

◆ one-to-one interviews; and

◆ group discussions.

2.6 External

For a listed company where the evaluation is undertaken by an external facilitator they should be identified in the annual report and any other connections to the company disclosed (Governance Code provision 23).

Advantages of externally facilitated board evaluation include the following:

◆   Those undertaking the evaluation are likely to be more objective and freer from internal pressures.

◆   Those participating in the discussions may be more willing to speak to someone they view as independent.

◆   The evaluators will have suitable skills and experience.

◆   The evaluator will have appropriate time to commit to the review process.

◆   An externally facilitated evaluation is likely to have more credibility with external stakeholders.

Among the disadvantages are the following:

◆   Those undertaking the evaluation will be less familiar with the company, its culture and objectives.

◆   Internal facilitators are less likely to be skilled evaluators.

◆   Those participating in the discussions may be unwilling to speak to people they do not know about their own faults or those of fellow directors.

◆   Externally facilitated evaluations have a financial cost.

An external evaluation can take many forms including combinations of:

◆   bespoke questionnaires;

◆   questionnaires created from question banks;

◆   one-to-one interviews;

◆   group discussions;

◆   observation of board/committee meetings; and

◆   review of board pack/meeting material.

Test yourself 3.1

1.   **Which companies are required to undertake board evaluation?**

2.   **Which companies must carry out external facilitated board evaluation and how often?**

3.   **Who should evaluate the performance of the company chair?**

3. Director education and guidance

A director's very first appointment, certainly for a normal trading company, will be made on merit based upon technical or entrepreneurial prowess. For directors of standalone private companies this could very well be their only directorship. For small groups the directors of the holding company are likely to be also appointed to each of the subsidiary companies.

Some directors are asked or actively seek out non-executive appointments with other companies. Many large listed groups, as part of their succession planning processes, actively encourage their senior managers or divisional directors to become non-executive directors of smaller listed or AIM companies in order to gain experience of being a director of a listed company which they can then use for the benefit of their main employing company.

Whether appointed to their first directorship or as an additional inter group or external directorships directors should undergo an induction process on each appointment and receive regular updates, sometimes referred to as continuous professional development (CPD) during the course of their appointment. The form of the induction will vary greatly depending on the experience of the appointee, the size and operation of the company, the regulatory framework within which the company operates and if the company's shares are traded on any public market.

3.1 Induction

On appointment, all directors should undergo an induction exercise tailored to their individual experience and knowledge of the company and industry in which it operates.

For directors of listed companies this induction must also provide details of the additional responsibilities of a listed company director and the disclosure and transparency rules.

Newly appointed directors will wish to contribute at an early stage and a properly constructed and delivered induction programme will facilitate this goal.

It is important that any induction is tailored to the needs and experience of the individual on the receiving end of the induction. In addition to any company- or industry-specific information, the newly appointed directors should be asked if there are any areas in which they would like training. It is an understandable mistake to assume that because your new director has been a director before they are already fully aware of their rights, duties and responsibilities. They may, but equally they may not be.

The following checklist sets out a suggested induction programme that would need to be tailored to the needs of the individual as well as the company and the environment in which it operates.

Checklists: for director induction – listed company

1.   **The role of a director**

◆   An introduction to the role of a director and rights and duties of a director

◆   Details of the company's share dealing policy, requirement for notification of transactions to the UKLA and the need to inform the director's family members and other connected parties

◆   Support roles of the company secretary, general counsel, company secretariat and availability of external professional advice

◆   Policies relevant to the director as an individual (independent professional advice, expenses, data protection reporting of gifts and hospitality etc.)

◆   Directors' and officers' liability insurance, deeds of indemnity

◆   Personal development process

◆   Protocol, procedures and dress code (if applicable) for board meetings, general meetings, formal dinners, staff social events, site visits, etc.

◆   Any related roles and responsibilities (e.g. involvement in relevant trade bodies)

◆   Any restrictions on outside interests (e.g. restrictions on taking up other directorships)

2.   **Rules, regulation and guidance**

◆   Concept of the unitary board

◆   Up-to-date copy of the company's articles of association and any unusual features

◆   Overview of the UKLA's Listing, Prospectus and Disclosure and Transparency Rules and any other jurisdictions' securities and listing rules requirements, as applicable

◆   Overview of the UK Corporate Governance Code and associated FRC guidance and concepts of comply or explain and best practice

◆   Details of any investors' corporate governance guidelines which the company seeks to follow

3.   **Operation of the board**

Composition

◆   Board and committee structure, matters reserved for the board, delegated authorities, terms of reference of committee, items requiring approval outside of board meetings

- Board composition, succession plans for executive and non-executive directors and policy on directors' re-election by shareholders
- Board committee membership
- Biographical and contact details of all directors of the company, the company secretary and other key executives

Meetings

- Provide copies of the minutes of board meetings from the last 12 months and dates for future board and board committee meetings and dinners, financial reporting dates and close periods etc.
- Pro forma agendas of regular items
- Overview of board procedures covering details such as when papers are sent out, the method of delivery, the normal location of meetings and how long they last
- Training in the use of any board portal or online board paper/reading room facility
- Explanation of the chair's expectations of the board in terms of its output and behaviours
- Summary of the corporate culture and values, codes of conduct and ethics, etc.

Procedures

- Board, committee and individual director evaluation processes
- Board training and development programme
- Special procedures (accounts sign-off, company disclosures)
- Treatment and disclosure of inside information
- Bid and/or defence handbook

4. Business background

- Introduction to the company's history, the company's structure, any subsidiaries or joint ventures
- Major events over the last few years
- Company business model, products and services and mission
- Major elements of the company's business: key customers and markets, contracts, suppliers etc.
- Market analysis, market shares, trading backdrop, recent operational and financial performance, current challenges
- Previous annual report and accounts (and any interim reports)
- Any supporting material (e.g. marketing brochures)

5. **Running the business**

   ◆ Key individuals (other than the board): senior executives, their roles and contact details; any other key individuals

   ◆ Professional advisers and how they work with the board

   ◆ Key policies and procedures: e.g. health and safety; environmental management

   ◆ The company's risk profile and tolerance, risk management and internal control procedures and relevant disaster recovery plans

   ◆ Any other significant reports (e.g. if the company has conducted an environmental audit or a review of corporate social responsibility)

   ◆ Current performance of the business: financial position, budgets and management accounts, key performance indicators

   ◆ Financial and treasury issues: accounts and/or interim management statements, audit, management accounts, budgets, funding sources, dividend policy, credit-rating metrics

   ◆ Insurances in place, including any directors' and officers' liability insurance

   ◆ Any significant litigation the company is involved in or may become involved in

6. **Third party relationships**

   ◆ Investor relations policy and responsibilities

   ◆ Major shareholders, facilitate engagement and/or meetings as per the UK Stewardship Code

   ◆ The company's advisers (lawyers, bankers, auditors, registrars, brokers etc.) and the key internal contacts for any external advisers

   ◆ Other company advisers (e.g. PR, remuneration, or other relevant consultants)

   ◆ Key customers and suppliers

   ◆ Key stakeholders (regulators, unions, etc.)

7. **Practical issues**

   ◆ Premises layout and facilities (e.g. toilets, parking)

   ◆ Useful people and contact details

   ◆ Any support services (e.g. secretarial)

   ◆ Issue of any company phone number, email address

   ◆ What expenses can be reclaimed and the procedure

8. **Executive role**

    ◆ **Any additional information required if the director will also be taking up a new executive role (e.g. key duties, personnel, etc.)**

3.2 CPD

The induction process should be the start of a continuing programme of education and updates.

These updates will inevitably be delivered in a number of different formats from written or verbal board briefings, formal briefing notes and internally and externally delivered board presentations.

For directors, CPD helps them keep their knowledge and skills up-to-date as well as filling gaps in knowledge particularly where new legislation, regulatory requirements or technology are introduced.

Compliance and governance briefings will usually be the responsibility of the company secretary with company and industry briefings being provided by the appropriate executive director or senior managers.

A staggered approach to board education is best as otherwise there is a danger of information overload if these briefings are all delivered in only one or two concentrated sessions each year.

3.3 Availability of internal and external support

In addition to internal briefings directors should be encouraged to attend relevant seminars in particular the committee chairs so that they can keep abreast of legislative and regulatory developments and reporting preferences of investors to their particular committee.

Test yourself 3.2

1. **When should directors receive induction training?**

2. **Is it necessary for experienced directors to receive induction training?**

3. **Is it better for directors to receive training all in one session or spread out during the year?**

4. Best practices, policies and procedures

The Governance Code recommends that boards formally adopt written policies covering key governance matters. These policies are intended to ensure a clear division of responsibilities exists between the role of the board as a whole and the executive team, between the CEO and chair and the responsibilities delegated to board committees.

These policies should be formally adopted by the board and periodically reviewed. They will include some or all of the following.

4.1 Matters reserved to the board

Other than for small closely held companies, although the board controls the business, everyday decisions are delegated to the executive management. For this system to work there must be clear lines of demarcation between matters that the executive can approve and those requiring board approval.

To avoid these potential conflicts, it is recommended that the board set out, in as clear terms as possible, those matters which are reserved specifically for the decision of the board or a duly authorised committee thereof.

For listed companies and those other companies following its principles and provisions the Governance Code states: 'The responsibilities of the chair, chief executive, senior independent director, board and committees should be clear, set out in writing, agreed by the board and made publicly available' (Governance Code provision 14). The guidance goes on to note that 'Ensuring there is a formal schedule of matters reserved for its decision will assist the board's planning and provide clarity to all over where responsibility for decision-making lies' (Guidance note 28).

It is for each board to decide for itself the scope of matters to be reserved and the content will be driven largely by the size of the company and the nature of its operations. Large listed companies generally have an executive committee to which general authority will be delegated to manage the company day-to-day. Where such a committee is not present many of those authorities will most likely be retained by the board.

In drawing up a schedule of matters reserved for the board the schedule should identify those types of documents that must always be approved by the board, for example any documents requiring to be entered into as deeds or where the appointment can only be made by the directors i.e. auditor's appointment, those documents that require board approval due to the value of the contract exceeding pre-determined amounts and those where the nature of the matter is one which should be approved by the board.

Certain decisions should, in compliance with the Governance Code, only be made based on a recommendation by the audit, nomination or remuneration committee. The decision itself however remains the responsibility of the full board.

When drawing up a schedule of matters reserved for the board it is important to consider the frequency with which certain matters might occur as this may be relevant to deciding who should have authority to agree such matters.

As noted above, it is for each board to decide for themselves which matters should be reserved for the board. In general, however, any such schedule will be divided into the following subject areas.

Authority limits

Directors have a fiduciary duty to the shareholders. All directors should take great care that they are able to fulfil this duty, for their own personal protection as well as for the shareholders and other stakeholders.

Every organisation should have a robust system of financial controls in the business and for the directors and managers at all levels this should include appropriate authority limits. Like the schedule of matters reserved to the board the authority limits will depend on the size and nature of the company's operations and are likely to be a combination of monetary limits, length of contract and type of contract.

Code of conduct

A code of conduct sets out the standards of personal behaviour and conduct required of directors and senior executives. A code of conduct for directors will include some or all of the following aspects:

- qualification for office;
- commitment to corporate values and culture;
- carrying out the directors' responsibilities;
- standards of behaviour;
- confidentiality;
- conflicts of interest;
- taking independent advice;
- induction and ongoing professional development;
- hospitality and gifts;
- serving on the board of another organisation; and
- breach of this code.

Some companies may have a number of codes of conduct applicable to different levels or grades of employees, managers and directors with the company although these will share may common aspects and must reflect the overall corporate values and culture.

Tenure policy for NEDs

From a legislative perspective, there is no maximum period of appointment for a director whether they are executive or non-executive appointments. Similarly, the Governance Code does not refer to a maximum period of tenure for non-executive directors. It does however provide that any non-executive director serving more than nine years will be deemed to be no longer independent for the purposes of the Governance Code.

Some of the investor representative bodies have suggested that in order to be fully consistent with Governance Code principle K, which states that 'Consideration should be given to the length of service of the board as a whole and membership regularly refreshed', a shorter period is required to achieve that aim. A shorter overall appointment period would better reflect the rapid changes in technology experienced by many companies, the shorter duration of many CEO and CFO directors' years of service and the need for refreshed boards.

The desire and need to refresh boards with younger directors possibly more in tune with the latest trends and technologies does however need to be balanced with the need for continuity on boards and the experience gained through years of service.

Expense policy

An expenses policy will not apply just to the directors but should apply company wide. The policy will typically set out the types of expense for which an expenses claim can be made and also those costs which it is not, in the normal course of events, appropriate for directors or employees to pay for personally and then reclaim.

The policy should provide details of the evidence required and the payment cycle for expenses, together with the details of the process to claim expenses and the authorisation required.

Independence standards for independent NEDs

To provide appropriate challenge and counterbalance to the executive directors it is important for those non-executive directors identified as being independent to retain their independence. While a director may continue to query and question the executives' proposals, they will lose credibility for other stakeholders if they lose their independence, especially if this is due to other business connections or direct remuneration.

Although there are no statutory criteria of what constitutes independence the Governance Code provision 10 sets out the following examples of circumstances that could or might appear to impair independence of an NED:

- is or has been an employee of the company or group within the last five years;
- has, or has had within the last three years, a material business relationship with the company, either directly or as a partner, shareholder, director or senior employee of a body that has such a relationship with the company;
- has received or receives additional remuneration from the company apart from a director's fee, participates in the company's share option or a performance-related pay scheme, or is a member of the company's pension scheme;
- has close family ties with any of the company's advisers, directors or senior employees;
- holds cross-directorships or has significant links with other directors through involvement in other companies or bodies;
- represents a significant shareholder; or

- has served on the board for more than nine years from the date of their first appointment.

Any formal policy setting standards of independence for NEDs of a listed company will follow this guidance adapted for the particular circumstances of the company. Although these standards can be made more onerous on the NED if they are relaxed there will need to be an explanation in the annual report giving the rationale for the departure from the provisions of the Governance Code.

Committee terms of reference

Where a board creates any board committee there should be clear written terms of reference setting out the composition of the committee, the duties of the committee, any delegated responsibility, budgetary constraints and reporting requirements. The board will be generally authorised to constitute such committees as it deems fit in accordance with its Articles (Model Articles Plc & Ltd regs. 5 & 6, Governance Code provision 14).

Listed companies are recommended to constitute four standing committees:

- audit
- remuneration
- nomination
- disclosure.

Other committees might include specialist areas such as risk committee, health & safety committee or investment committee. Whether any additional committees are constituted will depend upon the size and nature of the company's operations.

Although the specific duties and remit of the committees will be worded individually for each committee overall the general content of a committee terms of reference will have the following elements:

- membership
- secretary
- quorum
- frequency of meetings
- notice of meetings
- minutes of meetings
- annual general meeting
- duties
- reporting responsibilities
- authority.

Listed companies generally will make their committee terms of reference available on their website.

Share dealing policy

Following the implementation of the Market Abuse Regulation (MAR) on 3 July 2016, Annex 1 of Listing Rule 9, known as the 'Model Code' was withdrawn as it was not compatible with MAR. Under MAR there is no obligation on listed companies to have a share dealing code as the responsibilities fall largely on the Persons Discharging Managerial Responsibilities (PDMRs).

A number of market participants agreed that it would be of great benefit for listed and quoted companies for there to be a single, industry-led dealing code rather than each company drafting their own code broadly similar but with subtle differences. Co-ordinated by the ICSA a model code was drawn up for use by all market participants.

Individual companies remain responsible for their own compliance with MAR obligations and establishing the necessary systems and procedures.

The specimen dealing code is split into two sections the first dealing with a company's internal processes to review requests from employees for clearance to deal in the company's own shares. The second part provides guidance to the company's PDMRs covering both clearance to deal with processes that will in certain circumstances be more restrictive than the general clearance processes for employees, as well as guidance on the need to formally notify both the company and the FCA on details of the trade. Although the notification obligations are obligations of the PDMRs themselves, these are often delegated to the company secretary although it cannot be a complete delegation as the PDMR does need to provide the company secretary with the necessary information.

Whistle-blowing policy

'Whistle-blowing' is the reporting by employees of suspected misconduct, illegal acts or failure to act within their company. The aim is to encourage employees who have serious concerns about any aspect of a company's operations to come forward and voice those concerns.

For listed companies the Governance Code provision 6 states that:

> There should be a means for the workforce to raise concerns in confidence and – if they wish – anonymously. The board should routinely review this and the reports arising from its operation. It should ensure that arrangements are in place for the proportionate and independent investigation of such matters and for follow-up action.

For companies in the financial services industry and regulated by the FCA, the Senior Managers and Certification Regime (SMCR) requires companies to take the following steps, which would usually be contained in a whistle-blowing policy:

◆ Appoint a Senior Manager as whistle-blowers' champion.
◆ Establish internal whistle-blowing arrangements able to handle all types of disclosure from all types of person.

- Ensure settlement agreements include an explanation that workers have a legal right to blow the whistle.
- Tell UK-based employees about the FCA and PRA whistle-blowing services.
- Present a report on whistle-blowing to the board at least annually.
- Inform the FCA if it loses an Employment Tribunal whistle-blowing case.
- Require its appointed representatives and tied agents to tell their UK-based employees about the FCA whistle-blowing service.

A whistle-blowing policy will obviously be tailored to the specific circumstances of the company but should cover the following areas:

- that the company takes malpractice seriously providing example types of concerns to be raised and how to distinguish them from a normal grievance;
- that employees have the option to raise concerns outside of line management;
- that employees are able to access confidential advice from an independent body;
- that the organisation will respect the confidentiality of a member of staff raising a concern;
- that concerns can be raised anonymously, although that might hamper any investigation or feedback to the complainant;
- that complaints may be made to a prescribed body or person rather than to the company; and
- that whistle-blowers are protected under legislation and may not suffer any harm as a result of making a complaint.

Whistle-blowing policies ought to be tailored to the particular employer's business and sector. For example, regulated businesses ought to address how breach of regulations should be dealt with and in what circumstances, if any, the employee should report to the regulator.

Some companies, in order to provide as much confidentiality as possible, use the services of an external party administrator to facilitate and log whistle-blowing utilising telephone hotlines, dedicated email and online submissions.

Companies that meet the disclosure obligations under the Modern Slavery Act should ensure that any whistle-blowing policy and process also enables disclosure of anti-slavery and human trafficking within the supply chain.

Stop and think 3.1

In 2018, the FCA and PRA jointly fined the chief executive of Barclays £642,430 over his handling of a whistle-blower.

The regulators announced that Barclays chief James Staley was fined for his failure to act with due skill, care and diligence in the way he acted in response to an anonymous letter received by Barclays in June 2016.

The whistle-blower case at Barclays revolved around concerns raised about the appointment of a friend of Staley who then tried to find out who raised the concerns.

Risk management policy

A risk management policy is an important tool to support the company's corporate strategy. The identification, classification and mitigation of both strategic and systematic risks should be a central part of every company's management processes. Listed companies are required to detail in their annual reports the principal risks and uncertainties facing the company and the steps taken to mitigate those risks.

An enterprise-wide approach to risk management enables an organisation to consider the potential impact of all types of risks on all processes, activities, stakeholders, products and services. Implementing a comprehensive approach will result in an organisation unlocking the benefits of well-understood and managed risks.

The risk management policy documents the risk management cycle as shown in Figure 3.1.

Figure 3.1 The risk management cycle

A risk management policy should contain the following elements:

◆   Risk identification
  –   Internal
  –   External
  –   Systemic
  –   Strategic

◆ Assess the impact of the risk event occurring
  – Avoid risks that are too great by not doing that activity
  – Rate risks by impact x probability
◆ Develop risk mitigation strategies
  – By understanding the risk develop strategies to reduce either the impact or probability of the risk – or both
◆ Implement risk mitigation
  – Implement the risk reduction mitigation
  – Shift the risk through insurance, joint ventures, ring fencing
◆ Review effect of mitigation
  – The resulting risks are acceptable (for now)
  – The end review is also the start of the next cycle of identifying risks and running through the cycle again

Test yourself 3.3

1. **Why should board committees have written terms of reference?**
2. **Who is responsible for notifying the FCA where a PDMR deals in the company's shares?**
3. **Can an employer legally sack a whistle-blower for blowing the whistle?**

Chapter summary

◆ Review of the benefits of board evaluation
◆ Consideration of the elements contributing to the full board evaluation cycle
◆ Discussion of the advantages and disadvantages of internal v externally facilitated board evaluation
◆ Overview of the need for board education and regular updating
◆ Checklist for a director induction programme
◆ Review of board best practice procedures and policies

Chapter four
The members

CONTENTS

1. Introduction
2. What is a member?
3. Restrictions on membership
4. Shareholders
5. Guarantors
6. Other types of member
7. Member activism
8. Articles of association
9. Unfair prejudice
10. Derivative action claims
11. Membership

subscriber
A person who subscribes to the memorandum of association and agrees to take up shares in the company on incorporation.

memorandum of association
A constitutional document setting out details of the subscribers on incorporation.

registration
Process by which companies are created by filing (or registering) several specified documents at Companies House.

capital
The money or money's worth used by a company to finance its business.

1. Introduction

The Act defines members as:

◆ The **subscribers** of the company's **memorandum of association** are deemed to have agreed to become members of it and on **registration** of the company become members and must be entered as such in its register of members.

◆ Every other person who agrees to become a member of the company and whose name is entered in its register of members, is a member of the company (CA2006 s. 112).

All companies are owned and controlled by their members who have the right to appoint and remove directors and make changes to the company's constitution – its Articles.

A company with a share **capital** is owned by its members. The nature of that ownership is dependent on the type of company, type of membership and the provisions contained in the company's Articles. The proportion of a company that any individual member owns is determined in proportion to the number of shares held.

Companies limited by **guarantee** have not been permitted to be formed or become a company limited by guarantee with a **share capital** in Great Britain since 22 December 1980 or in Northern Ireland since 1 July 1983. Any provision in the Articles of a company limited by guarantee which has effect as dividing the company's undertaking into shares or interests is deemed to be a provision for share capital and not permitted (CA2006 s. 5).

The members' liability is different depending on the type of company they are a member of, as follows:

◆ A company is a **limited company** if the liability of its members is limited by its constitution. It may be limited by shares or by guarantee.

– If the members' liability is limited to the amount, if any, unpaid on the shares held by them the company is limited by shares. A company limited by shares must issue a minimum of one share and there is no maximum number of shares that can be issued, subject to any provision in the company's Articles.

– If the liability of the members is limited to an amount the members have agreed to contribute to the assets of the company in the event of it being wound up the company is limited by guarantee. The amount of the guarantee is often a nominal amount such as £5 or £10. As a guarantee company has no shares a distribution of profit by way of **dividend** is not possible.

◆ If there is no limit on the liability of its members, the company is an unlimited company. An unlimited company may be constituted with or without shares (CA2006 s. 4).

An unlimited company without a share capital will have some other method, set out in its Articles, to determine the rights of its members.

2. What is a member?

All companies are owned and controlled by their members.

Subject to restrictions contained in the Act (see page 72), any natural person or corporate entity may be a member of a company.

Companies are owned and controlled by their members although managed on a day-to-day basis by their directors.

The overwhelming majority of companies are private companies, limited by shares with the shares being held by the company's members. As a consequence, the terms member and shareholder are often used interchangeably when referring to the owners of a company. This is not, however, correct as while all companies have members not every company has shareholders. Companies limited by guarantee or unlimited companies without a share capital do not have shareholders.

For companies with a share capital, there is a formal, transparent structure. Ownership and control are divided between the members according to the proportion of shares they hold.

guarantee
A formal agreement under which a guarantor undertakes to meet the contractual obligations of one person to another in the event of default. A company limited by guarantee is one in which the liability of the members is limited to a specified amount in a winding up.

share capital
The capital of a company contributed or to be contributed by members. Nominal capital represents the nominal value of the shares issued and excludes any premium paid.

limited company
The commonest form of company, in which the liability of members for the debts of the company is limited – either to the amount of share capital for which they have applied (a company limited by shares) or to a specific amount guaranteed in the event of a winding up (a company limited by guarantee).

dividends
The distribution of a portion of the company's assets (usually cash) to its members.

Guarantee companies also have a formal structure of ownership and control although in a lot of cases not as transparent. Guarantee companies are a popular choice for membership organisations where the Articles are supplemented by internal by-laws regulating how the organisation is run in general and specifically how directors are elected.

As noted in the preamble to this chapter, two elements are generally required to become a member:

◆ The person must agree to become a member.

◆ Their details must be entered in the company's register of members (CA2006 s. 112).

The exception to this general rule is that the subscribers to the memorandum agree to become members by virtue of signing the subscription clause and become the first members on registration of the company (CA2006 s. 112(1)).

2.1 Agreement to become a member

Agreement can be either explicit or implicit.

In cases where the company is issuing new shares, or a person wishes to become a guarantor of the company limited by guarantee they should complete an application form.

For an issue of shares this will incorporate both consent to become a member, agreement to pay the amounts due on the shares either in full or in part on application and a commitment to pay the balance, if any, due either on fixed date(s) or when called upon to do so by the company and finally consenting to be bound by the terms of the company's Articles.

For a guarantor the application form, in addition to consent to become a member, will incorporate a guarantee to contribute a fixed amount to the assets of the company in the event of it being placed into an insolvent winding up, and agreement to be bound by the terms of the company's Articles.

transfer
Process where ownership of shares passes from one person to another usually by way of a sale.

A person may, rather than acquiring a share allotted directly from the company, acquire an existing issued share by way of share **transfer** from an existing member. In such cases there is an implicit agreement to become a member by virtue of their agreeing to purchase shares in the company from a third party.

2.2 Entry in the register of members

allotment
Shares are taken as allotted when a person acquires the unconditional right to be included in the company's register of members which is generally accepted to be once the contract of allotment is completed and acceptance of the application notified to the applicant.

The subscribers to the memorandum are the first members immediately on the registration of the company and their details must be entered in the register of members as such (CA2006 s. 112(1)).

A person applying for new shares will have those shares allotted to them by the directors and once their details have been entered in the register of members, they become members and the shares become issued. A company must enter the details of any shares allotted as soon as practical and in any event within two months of the date of **allotment** (CA2006 s. 554(1)). This timescale applies regardless of whether the company maintains, directly or indirectly, its own register of members or it has opted to keep its register of members on the central register under CA2006 s. 128B.

The distinction between the allotment and the issue of shares can be critical for an investor. For example under a number of HMRC share investment schemes tax relief is only available from the date of issue. The allotment date is when the person acquires an unconditional right to be entered in the register of members and is usually taken to be the date of the directors' meeting to approve the share allotment. The date of issue however is the date when the person, the **allottee**, acquires legal title to the shares when their details are entered in the register of members. While this can be the same date as the date of allotment it can be some time later.

In instances where the person has acquired the shares by way of share transfer the company must either register the transfer by entering the details in its register of members or refuse to do so within two months of the date of receipt of a duly completed **stock transfer form** (CA2006 s. 771(1)).

2.3   How many members are required?

All companies, subject to any contrary provisions in their Articles, must have a minimum of one member (CA2006 s. 7(1)).

A private company limited by shares need only issue one share, and there is no minimum nominal or **paid-up capital** requirement.

Public companies limited by shares are required to issue at least £50,000 or the prescribed Euro equivalent, in nominal value of shares, with each share at least 25% paid up as to its nominal value and 100% of any premium (CA2006 ss. 761 and 763) before commencing to trade, and to maintain this minimum capital at all times. A public company could issue only one share and in order to meet the minimum capital requirement, it would need to have a nominal value of not less than £50,000 or the prescribed Euro equivalent.

allottee
A person or company to whom shares have been allotted.

stock transfer form
Document used to transfer ownership of shares from one person (transferor) to another (transferee).

paid-up capital
Refers to the amounts paid up on any issued shares.

Stop and think 4.1

It might appear a subtle difference between allotment of shares by the directors and the shares being issued, but this is hugely important and not remedied simply by the issue of a share certificate. It also clearly demonstrates the need to ensure that proper attention to detail and completing all the necessary steps to allot and issue shares are completed and especially the task of writing up the statutory registers.

Failure to write up the register of members, even if a share certificate has been issued means that the shares have not been issued and the investor is not a member and does not have full title to the shares. This in turn will mean that any member resolutions that would not have been approved or defeated without the votes relating to those shares are not valid, as the shares were not properly issued they do not exist in law and have no voting rights.

There can be financial consequences too, as a number of HMRC tax reliefs for investors depend on the date of issue of the shares. If the register of members has not been written up, either promptly or at all, this can prejudice the investors' ability to claim the tax relief they believe is available to them and without which they may not have invested at all. Failure to meet the tax relief criteria might lead to legal action to recover their loss.

This distinction was at the heart of a case in 1994 in which the meaning of the 'issue' of shares was critical to the availability of tax relief. The original case found in favour of the bank; however, the Inland Revenue won on appeal to the Court of Appeal and the case was then referred to the House of Lords. There it was held that allotment of shares provides the applicant with a choice in action, the right to have the shares issued to them, but the issue only comes when they (or if appropriate, a successor in title by one or more renunciations) are entered in the register as the holder of the shares; 'issue' is distinct from allotment and requires something to complete or perfect the title of an allotment of shares, which can be nothing short of registration or the issue of a certificate *(National Westminster Bank plc and another v Inland Revenue Commissioners: HL [1994])*.

Test yourself 4.1

1.   **What two criteria must be met in order to be a member of a company?**

2.   **Other than as a shareholder what other forms can company membership take?**

3.   **Is there a minimum or maximum number of members that a company must have?**

3. Restrictions on membership

3.1   Who can be a member?

As long as there is no provision to the contrary in the Articles, and the exceptions noted below, any legal person may hold shares in a company.

3.2   Restrictions on membership

The Act sets out a limited number of exceptions to the general position that any legal person may become a member of a company:

1.   CA2006 s. 126 prohibits companies from recognising trusts, whether express, constructive or implied, over their shares. Accordingly, holdings of shares cannot be registered in the name of a trust or settlement but must be held in the name(s) of the trustees. The exception to this being

companies whose name includes the words such as trust, trustee, nominee etc. In such instances, the company views the corporate entity as the legal owner of the shares and is not concerned with any underlying trust or nominee relationship.

2. Unless a subsidiary company is acting only as personal representative or trustee without having any beneficial interest in the shares or acting as an authorised dealer in securities, a subsidiary company is not permitted to be a member of its holding company (CA2006 s. 136). CA2006 s. 139 makes provisions to enable a company's subsidiary company to act as trustee for a group employee share scheme or pension scheme. There is, however, no prohibition on the holding of shares by a subsidiary in its holding company if it held shares in that company before it became its holding company. However, in this case, the subsidiary is not permitted to vote at meetings of the holding company (CA2006 s. 137(4)). It would not be lawful for any further shares in the holding company to be allotted to such a subsidiary company, a situation that could arise if the holding company undertook a rights issue. The allotment and issue of fully paid shares by way of a capitalisation of reserves is, however, permitted.

3.3   What is a legal person?

Only legal persons may become a member of a company. A legal person is any natural person or an incorporated entity with legal capacity.

Examples of entities and bodies without legal capacity include English partnerships (but not Scottish partnerships), sole traders, unincorporated clubs and associations. None of these should be entered in the register of members as a member of the company. If such an entity is entered in the register, a court order to rectify the register will be required. This is due to the inability of the entity to voluntarily transfer the shares into the correct name as the entity, having no legal capacity, has no power or authority to give the necessary instructions. If these bodies wish to acquire any shares they should be registered in the name(s) of one or more of the partners, business owners or managers on behalf of that body.

Similarly, the holder of an office should not be accepted as a member in that capacity unless it is an office created by statute, such as the Treasury Solicitor or the Accountant General. Some public officers are legally deemed to be a corporation, e.g. the Public Trustee, and as such may be registered as members of companies.

3.4   Restrictions in the Articles

◆ The Articles of some companies exclude certain categories of person from membership, e.g. persons who are not able to give a declaration of British or EU nationality may be prohibited from being registered as a member of an airline as these usually require a minimum level of ownership by nationals of a particular country or trading block such as the EU.

◆ Although historically many professionals traded through partnerships over recent years there has been an increasing move to moving away from partnerships to LLPs and limited companies. Where a limited company is used, the Articles may well require all or a minimum percentage of the members to hold a particular professional qualification.

◆ Shares in a company may be held by a number of persons in a joint account. However, some Articles limit the number of persons who may be so registered. In the case of a listed company, the maximum number of joint holders is not permitted to be fewer than four.

3.5 Minors as members of a company

Since becoming a member of a company may involve the assumption of liabilities in respect of the shares held, it is not considered good practice to accept minors as members of a company in their own name, as their responsibilities would be voidable during their minority (i.e. under the age of 18 in England, Wales and Northern Ireland; see below for details of the position in Scotland). This is especially important where the shares are partly paid, as this imposes an obligation to pay any **calls** that may be made by the directors. As the obligation to pay is voidable by a minor payment and any sanctions for non-payment are unenforceable against them.

The Articles may give express power to reject allotments and transfers in the name of a minor, but if not, a right of rejection is conferred by general law. Accordingly, the company may repudiate the contract for the allotment of new shares, and in the case of a transfer, the **transferor** may be reinstated as the holder of the shares. It may come to light at some later stage that a minor is a member of the company and until any repudiation or rejection of their membership, any minors can enjoy the full rights of membership. Rejection of a minor can take place only during that person's period of minority. LR 2.2.4 requires that the Articles of companies contain no restrictions on the transfer of fully paid shares, although the right of rejection is maintained under the general rule of law. From a practical point, especially for publicly traded companies, minors may well become members of the company without the company's knowledge.

Any member transferring shares to a minor, even in ignorance, is liable for any future calls on those shares while the minor is still the registered holder and a minor. Any person who arranges the purchase of shares and their registration in the name of a minor makes themselves liable to indemnify any transferor in respect of any future calls. In practice, this is most likely to occur in circumstances where parents purchase shares for their children and register the shares in the child's name.

In Scotland, persons are pupils until the age of 12 (girls) or 14 (boys), after which they become minors until the age of 18. Pupils have no capacity to contract, although their guardian (tutor) may contract on their behalf. Minors who live independently and hold themselves out as having reached the age of 18 have the capacity to contract. If a minor has a guardian (curator), contracts will normally be made only with that person's approval.

call
A formal notice issued by a company requiring shareholders to pay all or part of the amounts unpaid on partly paid issued shares.

transferor
A person disposing of shares by way of transfer.

A pupil or minor who validly acquires shares is able to reduce (cancel) the contract not only while still a pupil or minor, but until the age of 22 (this additional age limit does not apply to business contracts). In order to reduce the contract, the pupil or minor only has to show that the contract was unreasonable.

Where shares have been incorrectly registered in the name of a minor and a sale or transfer of the shares is required a parent or guardian will need to obtain a court order. This is typically a vesting order or general form of judgment to enable a sale or transfer to proceed. The court order is required to ensure the sale is being done in the best interests of the shareholder, the 'minor', as they cannot deal with the transaction for themselves and is undertaken under the authority of the court.

Stop and think 4.2

For major public share offers and privatisation share issues, such as the flotation of the Royal Mail, the rules of the share offer usually prohibit the making of multiple applications. This is in order that in circumstances where the applications are scaled back all applicants may be treated equally.

However, some applicants will attempt to circumvent this provision by making applications in the name of their children and in the absence of any information to the contrary these applications are accepted on face value and shares issued in the name of the child.

Subsequently, the parent will wish to sell those shares and will request the funds be paid to their bank account which is different from the name of the registered shareholder. On investigation, not only will the presence of a minor on the share register be discovered but the parent will need to obtain a court order in order to be granted the necessary authority to transfer the assets of their child. The costs of this may well wipe out any increase in value of the underlying investment.

It is quite common for small groups of individuals to join together as a share club or investment club to pool cash and make small investments in quoted companies. Most often these share clubs are unincorporated clubs. It is very common for these clubs to apply to acquire shares to be held in the name of the club and this is not permitted as the club does not have legal capacity and is therefore not a legal person. In such circumstances the shares should be registered in the name of one or more of the members or a corporate nominee used. Where the shares are registered in one or more of the members' names it is recommended that both a declaration of trust and a stock transfer form are signed to ensure that firstly there is no confusion as to ownership and that in the event of a dispute or death of one of the registered holders the shares may be readily transferred or sold as required.

Test yourself 4.2

1. **What are the main disadvantages of registering shares for a long-term investment in children's names?**

2. **Can anyone become a member of a company?**

3. **A professional partnership wishes to acquire some shares. How should they be registered?**

4. Shareholders

As noted in the opening paragraphs of this chapter the overwhelming majority of companies are limited by shares and accordingly their members will hold shares in the company. Consequently, for a company limited by shares the terms member and shareholder are used interchangeably.

Shareholders provide the working capital, often supplemented by bank loans or other forms of finance, to allow the company to operate.

Shareholders as owners of the company will benefit from any capital growth in the value of the company in proportion to the number of shares held. They also have the risk that the value of their shares may fall and potentially lose all of their investment. Their liability is, however, limited to the amounts paid or due and payable and once their shares are fully paid they have no further or additional liability for any losses incurred by the company.

Where shares in a company have different rights, they constitute a different share class. The majority of companies limited by shares have only one class of shares.

All companies limited by shares must have at least one share in issue at all times and as a consequence at least one shareholder.

4.1 Shareholder specific provisions

In contrast to the position for directors, the Act and the company's Articles contain many provisions governing the relationship between the company and its shareholders and as between shareholders including:

- allotment of shares – chapter 16;
- transfer of shares – chapter 16;
- buy back of shares – chapter 16;
- class meetings – chapter 14;
- payments to shareholders – chapter 16;
- disclosing ownership – chapter 13;
- protection from oppression – chapters 4 and 12; and
- shareholder activism – chapter 4.

Test yourself 4.3

1. **In order to establish the rights of a shareholder which documents should be referred to?**

2. **Are members always shareholders?**

5. Guarantors

For companies limited by guarantee, the members guarantee the company's **debts**, usually limited to a nominal amount. In general, although guarantors are the members, they are not true owners of the business, but should be viewed as trustees holding ownership temporarily until this is passed on to the next trustee.

Guarantors are usually not entitled to participate in profits or **distribution** of surplus assets, and in the event of a guarantee company ceasing to trade or being wound up, any assets remaining must be passed to another guarantee or charitable company with similar objects. However, this need not be the case and it is necessary to examine the Articles if a distribution of income (dividend) or capital is proposed, to ensure that this is permitted under the company's constitution.

debt
An amount of money owed by one person, the debtor, to another, being the creditor.

distribution
The transfer of some or all of a company's assets (usually cash) to its members, generally by way of dividend or on a winding up.

5.1 Transferring membership

It is not possible for a person to transfer their guarantee to another person. Instead they must resign as guarantor and a replacement must apply in their place. It should be noted however that the personal guarantee does not cease immediately but continues for a period of one year after resigning as a member (CA2006 s. 11(3)).

5.2 Guarantor specific provisions

Other than the provisions on incorporation or application to become a guarantor or resignation as a guarantor set out in CA2006 s. 11 there are no other provisions applicable only to guarantee companies in the Act.

Provisions relating to the convening and holding of members meetings, methods of communicating with members etc. apply equally to companies limited by guarantee or by shares.

Stop and think 4.3

At the end of 2017, there were 3,896,757 companies incorporated under the Companies Acts on the register maintained by Companies House. Of these 95.9% were private companies limited by shares, 3.8% were private companies limited by guarantee, 0.2% were public companies and 0.1% were private unlimited companies.

As a result, it is not surprising that many people use the terms member and shareholder interchangeably.

Source: Companies House – Companies register activities 2016/17.

Test yourself 4.4

1.   How can a guarantor transfer their membership to someone else?

2.   Does the guarantee cease immediately on the guarantor resigning?

3.   Which type of organisation is best suited to use a guarantee company structure?

6. Other types of member

Unlimited companies without a share capital will have some other method of determining ownership which will typically be a members' agreement similar in content to a partnership agreement setting out the members' rights to vote, share in profit, shares in assets and contribution to assets in the event that the company is unable to settle its debts in a winding up.

Other than on incorporation the Act has no specific provisions applicable to the members of an unlimited company.

7. Member activism

Member activism more often referred to as shareholder activism covers a number of differing methods employed by members to achieve hugely varying aims. Unlike directors, who have a duty to manage the company for the benefit of its members as a whole while also considering the interests of other stakeholders, shareholders need only take account of their own interests and aims.

Traditional corporate governance is focused on what has been referred to as vertical corporate governance and aligning the interests of senior managers and shareholders. This however is an impossible aim to fulfil as shareholders have differing reasons to become and remain as shareholders. Some will have invested due to real or perceived short-term opportunity for the share price to increase, others invest for the long-term based upon dividend yield and there will also be shareholders who have no particular interest in the company at all but invest on the basis of the composition of a particular share index. As a result, management will often rely on discussions with their largest shareholders to form a view of what is in the interests of the wider shareholder base.

In the UK institutional investors will usually invest in companies whose strategy they agree with and are not looking to change, in most instances are supportive of management and while not actively looking for change are prepared to listen to the ideas of activists.

7.1   Investor activism

Shareholder activists are typically investment funds and although making a significant investment in the target company would rarely be the largest shareholder. They invest in companies where they think change is needed to realise increase in shareholder value and actively seek to disrupt the status quo and current corporate strategy. They engage publicly and privately often aggressively with the management and use the full range of shareholder rights to promote their agenda for change. Such shareholder rights include campaigns to vote directors off the board, putting forward contrary resolutions at AGMs and calling for informal shareholder votes/meetings.

There is a broad area of potential interest for activist investors which can be summarised in the following wide categories:

- Corporate governance
    - Corporate governance changes
    - Board change
    - Directors' remuneration
- Balance sheet
    - Share buyback/dividends
    - Divestment of non-core assets
    - Adding value to existing underperforming assets
- Strategic transactions
    - M&A – promote, complicate, frustrate
    - Strategic direction
    - Corporate governance change

For companies and their company secretaries, investor engagement is key to managing their investors, be they the traditional 'hands off' investor or an activist 'hands on' investor.

As with most areas of the company secretary's work preparation is an essential tool. It is important to know the company's advisory team, be familiar with corporate processes, review and identify any vulnerabilities in the corporate strategy and the company's record at keeping to that strategy. The investor relations messages must be in sync with the corporate strategy and actual progress along that path. Monitoring the shareholder base and engaging at an early stage with new investors is a key role for the company secretary and keeping the board updated with changes in investors and their agenda.

As discussed in greater detail in chapter 13, member and investor trust can be greatly enhanced by making proper, meaningful disclosure, being transparent and clear with communications and providing accurate information in those communications. These disclosures and communications must also be aligned to the corporate strategy and accountability mechanisms of the directors.

7.2 Pressure group activism

Although rarely an issue for private companies, traded public companies often have another type of activist shareholder in the form of pressure groups who often purchase only nominal numbers of shares in order to attend and disrupt shareholder meetings with the intention of gaining publicity.

The motivation for these pressure groups is to attempt to force a company to change its behaviour or strategy in relation to a particular topic and to draw attention to their campaign. Over the years, there have been many such protests on topics such as animal welfare, fossil fuel usage, climate change, environmental issues, gender diversity and equal pay.

There are a number of practical steps that can be taken firstly to prevent or minimise any disruption at the meeting and either the meeting can be adjourned or the disrupting members can be ejected if there is persistent disruption during the meeting. These are considered in detail in chapter 14.

Test yourself 4.5

1. **Why is aligning the interests of directors and shareholders difficult to achieve in practice?**

2. **What are the main differences between activist and pressure group shareholders?**

8. Articles of association

Although the Act sets out the fundamental processes for the issue and transfer of membership, protection from their membership being diluted and protection from directors unfairly prejudicing their rights the Act provides little detail on the rights that membership enjoys. These rights are set out in each company's Articles.

8.1 Members' rights

Where all members are to have equal rights, the company need only have one class of shares (CA2006 s. 629). It is only where members or groups of members are to have different rights that the company's membership will need to be divided into different classes. Although possible in practice companies limited by guarantee usually only have one class of member. Where the company limited by guarantee is a membership organisation such as a sports club it is quite possible that by-laws will have been adopted whereby the underlying members, who are not guarantors, have rights to elect the directors which may differ according to the type of membership they hold.

In this section, we will only look at the rights relating to shares and contained in a company's Articles.

8.2 Classes of shares

The Articles will set out the division of shares into different classes, with the respective rights of each of the classes being stated. There is no statutory naming convention for share classes and while many share classes provide a clue to their rights or restricted rights, e.g. non-voting shares or fixed dividend shares, other classes may simply be distinguished as 'A' **ordinary shares** and 'B' ordinary shares. The exception to this is that CA2006 s. 560 defines ordinary shares as 'shares other than shares that as respects dividend and capital carry a right to participate only up to a specified amount in a distribution'.

The most common classes into which shares of a company may be divided are as follows.

1. Ordinary shares. As noted above, CA2006 s. 560 requires that ordinary shares must have rights to participate in distributions with no upper limit on that participation. As a consequence, where a company's share capital is divided into two or more classes the basic/default share class with full rights will most often be called the ordinary share class with the rights of the other class(es) being enhanced, fettered or removed when compared to the corresponding rights of the ordinary shares.

    Although the ordinary shares carry full rights to participate in dividends this does mean that they will rank behind other classes that have a preferred or fixed dividend entitlement as otherwise it would be necessary to limit the distribution applicable to the ordinary shares to allow for the dividend on the fixed income shares which is contrary to CA2006 s. 560.

    These shares constitute the company's 'risk capital' – i.e. each year, the directors declare a dividend to be paid on the ordinary shares out of the profits of the company. If the company does well, the dividends will be good and increase year by year; but if the company does badly, the dividends may be reduced or even (in a very bad year) omitted entirely. The word 'ordinary' is commonly omitted from the description of the shares in the Articles where a company only has one class of shares in issue. In some companies, the risk capital is called 'deferred shares' or 'deferred stock'.

2. Ordinary non-voting shares. Such shares are usually distinguished from the voting shares by calling them 'non-voting' or 'A' shares. Some companies have classes of ordinary shares which have restricted voting rights. In both cases, however, the shares otherwise have similar rights to those of the other ordinary shares as in point 1 above.

3. **Preference shares**. These are shares which carry a preferential right to a fixed rate of dividend and, on a winding up, to **return of capital** with or without a premium, together with arrears of dividend. They constitute part of the company's share capital, and repayment of capital on preference shares would rank ahead of repayment of capital on the ordinary shares (or the deferred shares or deferred stock) in a liquidation. The fixed rate of dividend is usually expressed as a percentage of the nominal value of the shares and not the issue price. Holders of preference shares get the same rate of dividend year in and year out, unless in any year the profits

ordinary shares
The most common form of share in a company, giving holders the right to share in the company's profits in proportion to their holdings and the right to vote at general meetings (although non-voting ordinary shares are occasionally encountered).

preference shares
Shares carrying the right to payment of a fixed dividend out of profits before the payment of an ordinary dividend or the preferential return of capital or both.

return of capital
An amount paid back to members being a repayment of the principal originally invested. A return of capital will occur if shares are redeemed or otherwise purchased by the issuing company.

of the company are insufficient to pay the preference dividends, which, of course, take priority over payment of dividends on the ordinary shares. Alternatively, the preference dividend might be expressed as a fixed percentage of the distributable profit in any **financial year**.

financial year
The period in respect of which the company's profit and loss account is drawn up; it need not coincide with the fiscal or calendar year and need not be a period of twelve months.

4. Deferred shares. As the name implies these shares have one or more deferred rights. These might have no right to dividends either at all or not until a specified level of profit is reached. Alternatively, in situations where a company has made significant losses and new investors have been identified the majority of the existing ordinary shares might be converted to deferred shares in order to provide greater ownership for the new investors without the costs and complexity of undertaking a reduction of capital.

5. Cumulative preference shares. This type of share is very similar to preference shares but has an additional right that if in any year the profits of the company are insufficient to pay the preference dividend in full or at all, any part of the dividend not paid will be carried forward to be paid when the company's fortunes improve. The payment of such arrears would rank ahead of payment of dividends on the ordinary shares.

redeemable shares
Shares which are issued as redeemable may be bought back by the company at a future date at the option of the company or members depending on the terms of issue.

6. **Redeemable shares** (preference shares) or cumulative redeemable (preference) shares. These are shares that will be redeemed by the company at a future date or on the achievement of a particular event. The redemption terms will be either set out in the Articles or determined by the directors at the time of allotment (CA2006 s. 685). The amount might be a fixed amount or may be determined according to a formula.

7. Debentures and loan stocks. Although sharing many of the features of shares these are not shares but loans to the company carrying a fixed rate of interest. Generally, debentures are secured loans on the assets of the company, whereas loan stocks are normally unsecured.

Payment of the interest on debentures and loan stocks ranks ahead of the payment of preference dividends and ordinary dividends. They would also rank ahead of preference and ordinary shares in repayment of capital in a liquidation. It should be noted, however, that debentures and loan stocks do not form part of the company's capital, although quite often they are colloquially referred to as 'loan capital'. The company's capital is confined to its share capital.

8.3 Rights attaching to a class of shares

As noted above, the rights attaching to shares will be stated in the Articles or in the case of redemption rights may be determined at the time the shares are allotted (Model Articles Plc reg. 43, Ltd reg. 22). The rights attaching to shares generally fall into three categories: rights to vote, rights to income and rights to capital.

The most common rights differentiating one class from another are as follows.

1. Right to vote. The right to attend and vote at meetings may be restricted or enhanced or the shares might be non-voting except in certain circumstances.

2. Right to receive dividend. The right to dividends can be excluded completely, or a class may be granted a preferential right to a dividend up to a specified amount with no further participation. As noted above CA2006 s. 560 requires that ordinary shares have an unrestricted right to dividends. Dividend right may be cumulative and in the absence of any express provision dividends are non-cumulative.

3. Right to capital. This right refers to the rights to participate in a distribution of surplus capital on a winding up or on a return of capital. Such rights are to a preferential right to return of capital. Share classes with enhanced dividend rights may have preferential rights to return of capital though this is frequently restricted to the amounts paid for the shares. Where external investors contributed significant amounts of capital to grow the business, they may well have enhanced rights to return of capital in excess of the amounts originally contributed and these are sometimes on a ratchet so that the greater the sale price or company valuation the greater the return although at a decreasing over-all percentage of the valuation. This provides an incentive for the existing management who typically retain the ordinary shares as they will achieve a greater return the higher the valuation: a win/win situation for both investors and managers. Deferred shares will often have no right to a return of capital unless a significant, and unrealistic, return has been paid on other share classes first.

4. **Pre-emption rights** on transfer. Pre-emption rights on transfer will ensure existing shareholders have the ability to purchase shares from selling shares in priority to any third party purchaser but can affect the shareholders' ability to realise their investment if the pre-emption rights contain a price mechanism or a cap on the number of shares that can be offered in a year.

pre-emption rights
Preferential right of existing members to purchase new shares to be issued or existing shares being offered for sale by way of transfer by an existing member.

5. Right of pre-emption on allotment. Pre-emption rights on allotment give protection from dilution in the event of an issue of shares of the same class by requiring that all new shares to be allotted are offered to the existing shareholders pro rata to their existing holding. Any untaken shares can then be offered to external investors.

6. Right of redemption. Normally given to shares carrying enhanced dividend rights but no right to capital, redemption rights allow investors to realise their investment at a predetermined date, upon the achievement of a pre-determined event or following a stipulated formula.

7. Right to conversion. Conversion rights are often used in conjunction with enhanced dividend rights to provide greater incentive for investors to invest in a company. The conversion rights will allow the conversion of shares normally into ordinary shares. The conversion rights will include not only the exchange rate for their conversion into the new class but also the trigger criteria. The trigger might be the passage of a set period, a particular company valuation or an event such as the listing or sale of the company. The exchange rate might be 1:1 but can also be on a multiple and can, like redemption criteria, be on a ratchet providing greater return in the event of a higher valuation hurdle being attained.

A company can create classes of shares with as many or few rights as it wishes. The rights will often depend on the investor where new capital is being invested to enable an existing business to expand. Although the majority of rights attaching to shares can be altered whether the shares have been issued or not, it is not possible to convert issued shares that were not redeemable into redeemable shares.

Companies must always have at least one share in issue that is not redeemable (CA2006 s. 684(4)).

8.4   Variation of rights

The Act provides that the rights attached to a class of shares or members can only be varied in accordance with the provisions of the company's Articles, or, if the Articles do not make provision for the variation of **class rights**, in accordance with the provisions of CA2006 ss. 629 – 640. This allows a company to specify less demanding procedures for varying class rights in its Articles.

class rights
Where a company has more than one class of shares, the rights attached to those different classes of shares.

special resolution
A resolution required either by the Companies Act or a company's Articles which must be carried by at least 75% of the members voting at a general meeting. Such resolutions tend to be required where the proposal would change the nature of the relationship between a company and its members, such as an amendment to the Articles.

CA2006 s. 630 provides that class rights may only be varied by the written consent of the holders of at least three-quarters in nominal value of the issued shares of the relevant class, or if a **special resolution** passed by the holders of that class sanctions the variation. Where the company's Articles impose a higher threshold for consent to the variation of class rights, the company must comply with the more onerous regime. It should be noted that provisions restricting the right to vote of a particular class only apply to general meetings of shareholders and not to class meetings of that class.

CA2006 s. 631 provides that for companies without a share capital, consent in writing from at least three-quarters of the members of that class and a special resolution passed at a separate class meeting of the members of that class sanctioning the variation will be required to vary class rights.

Holders of not less than the aggregate of 15% of the issued shares of a class (or 15% of the members of a class in the case of a company without a share capital) who did not consent to, or vote in favour of, the variation may apply to the court for it to be cancelled within 21 days of the resolution consenting to the variation being passed. In this case, the variation will not take effect until it is confirmed by the court. The application may be made by one or more of these shareholders (or members) on behalf of those entitled to make the application. The court will disallow the variation if it is satisfied that the variation would unfairly prejudice the holders (or members) concerned; otherwise, the court will confirm the alteration (CA2006 ss. 633 and 634). A copy of the court order must be filed with the Registrar within 15 days of it being made.

It should be noted that a variation of class rights will usually also require an amendment to the company's Articles and accordingly a special resolution of the members entitled to attend and vote at general meetings will also be required in addition to the class consent.

Companies creating new classes of shares or members, or varying the rights of existing classes of shares or members, are required to notify the Registrar of the particulars of the rights created or affected within one month of the date of variation (CA2006 ss. 636–40).

Stop and think 4.4

Given the number of variable attributes that shares have it is extremely important to check the Articles whenever any action affecting the members is contemplated. Failure to observe voting rights properly or consequential changes to rights for a particular class can create the possibility of a decision being challenged and possibly reversed or damages being payable where the effect of a decision cannot be reversed.

Test yourself 4.6

1. Rights attaching to shares can be divided into three broad categories, what are they?

2. What protection is given to members holding non-voting class shares if the members holding voting shares resolve to amend the articles in general meeting to increase their dividend rights?

3. Can a company with two classes of shares, ordinary shares and redeemable shares, purchase back all of the ordinary shares?

9. Unfair prejudice

9.1 Protection from unfair prejudice

Directors have a **fiduciary** duty under common law and under CA2006 s. 172(1) to act in the interests of the members as a whole and can be held liable in the event that they act for the benefit of a subgroup of members or for their own benefit rather than the members as a whole or even at all.

9.2 What is unfair prejudice?

CA2006 s. 994 provides that 'A member of a company may apply to the Court by petition for an order ... on the ground (a) that the company's affairs are being or have been conducted in a manner that is unfairly prejudicial to the interests of members generally or of some part of its members (including at least himself), or (b) that an actual or proposed act or omission of the company (including an act or omission on its behalf) is or would be so prejudicial'.

In order to bring a successful claim for unfair prejudice the aggrieved member must be able to demonstrate that the conduct complained of meets two tests:

◆ the conduct must be unfair; and

◆ the conduct must have caused or is causing prejudice or harm to the interest or rights of the members or some part of the members of the company.

fiduciary
Having a position of trust, such that the power and authority conferred by the position must be exercised solely in the interest of the person with whom the fiduciary relationship exists. Trustees are in a fiduciary position, as are solicitors in relation to their clients. Directors have a fiduciary duty to the company, obliging them to act always in good faith and not to derive a personal profit from their position.

9.3   What is unfair conduct?

Conduct may be unfair even in circumstances where there has been no bad faith or the intention to be unfair or prejudicial. The test is objective and there is no need to show that anybody acted in bad faith or with the intention of causing prejudice. The courts will regard the conduct as unfair if a hypothetical reasonable bystander (the so-called man on the Clapham omnibus) would believe it to be unfair.

9.4   Members' rights must be prejudiced

The conduct must be unfairly prejudicial to the complainant's interests in their capacity as a member of the company. The court does however take a broad view of what constitutes members' rights.

The court will consider wider equitable considerations that are not necessarily included in the Articles or are not strictly legal rights as a member. Accordingly, a member may have a legitimate expectation due to the way the company was set up, any agreements on how the company would be managed and profits shared. Such interests are routinely present in 'quasi partnerships' in which the members have an expectation to be included in the company's management and being excluded might be prejudicial to their interests.

In other cases, the complainant must be able to demonstrate abuse of their powers by the directors or an infringement of the members' rights under the Act or the Articles.

Stop and think 4.5

Unfair prejudice is a flexible concept, and common examples of what may constitute unfairly prejudicial conduct are:

◆   **exclusion from management in breach of express or implied agreement of participation;**

◆   **majority shareholder being granted excessive financial benefits;**

◆   **the diversion of business to another company in which the majority shareholder/director(s) are interested;**

◆   **failure to observe properly, or at all, rights of pre-emption on the allotment of shares thus denying an existing member from participating in a share issue thus their holding being diluted; and**

◆   **abuses of power and breaches of the Articles. For example, the passing of a special resolution to alter the company's Articles may be unfairly prejudicial conduct or failure to circulate accounts and depriving the members of their right to know the state of the company's affairs.**

9.5   Remedies available

If the courts find in favour of a complainant and agree that unfair prejudice has occurred the Act sets out several remedies available to the court (CA2006 s. 996(2)) in addition to a general provision to make any order it deems appropriate (CA2006 s. 996(1)):

◆   regulate the conduct of the company's affairs in the future;

◆   require the company to refrain from doing or continuing an act complained of, or to do an act which it has omitted to do;

◆   authorise civil proceedings to be brought in the name and on behalf of the company by such person(s) and on such terms as the court may direct;

◆   require the company not to make any, or any specified, alterations in its Articles without the leave of the court; and

◆   provide for the purchase of the shares of any members of the company by other members or by the company itself and, in the case of the purchase by the company itself, the reduction of the company's capital accordingly.

The power to authorise civil proceedings subject to terms directed by the court can be a particularly useful remedy for the complainant as it not only enables an action to be pursued by the Company, but also means the costs of the action will be borne by the company.

The most common remedy is to order that the shares held by the members whose interests have been prejudiced be purchased by those who caused the unfair prejudice.

Ordering that shares be purchased can cause considerable problems, as there are many conflicting methods of valuation. Although the court will not necessarily stipulate the valuation method to be used, they will often oblige the valuer to value the company at the date the prejudice initially took place and on the basis that the prejudicial conduct had not taken place.

Test yourself 4.7

What two tests must be satisfied in order to bring a claim for unfair prejudice?

10. Derivative action claims

The Act introduced a derivative action procedure, making it easier for members to sue directors or others for a broader range of acts or omissions than was previously possible under common law (CA2006 ss. 260–269). Due to the different legal systems in England, Wales, Northern Ireland and Scotland, the legislation is split, with CA2006 ss. 260–264 applicable to proceedings brought in England, Wales or Northern Ireland, and CA2006 ss. 265–269 applicable to proceedings brought in Scotland. The provisions themselves are intended to have the same effect in all territories.

A derivative action is an action made by a member, on behalf of and in the name of the company and for the benefit of the company. Any member may, on behalf of the company, bring a derivative action claim against a director or third party for an actual or proposed act or omission involving negligence, breach of duty or breach of trust (CA2006 ss. 260–69).

10.1 Grounds for bringing a derivative action

A derivative action claim may only be brought under the provisions of the Act or under a court order and may be brought in respect of an actual or proposed act or omission involving negligence, default, breach of duty or breach of trust. The claim may be brought by a member whether the cause of action arose before or after they first became a member (CA2006 ss. 260 and 265).

10.2 Application for permission to continue derivative claim

prima facie
On the face of it, at first sight.

A member who has brought proceedings must apply to the court for permission to bring the claim before the claim can continue, by establishing a ***prima facie*** case.

The court must dismiss the claim if the evidence filed by the member does not disclose a *prima facie* case for giving permission. In dismissing a claim, the court may make any consequential order it considers appropriate, including a costs order.

If the evidence does disclose a *prima facie* case, then the court may give directions as to the evidence to be provided by the company and may adjourn the proceedings to allow that evidence to be obtained (CA2006 ss. 261, 262, 266 and 267).

This step is designed to filter out frivolous and vexatious claims.

If a company has brought a claim and that claim could be continued as a derivative action claim, a member may apply to the court to continue the claim as a derivative action claim on the grounds that:

- the manner in which the company brought or is continuing the claim is an abuse of a process of the court; or
- the company has failed to prosecute the claim diligently; or
- it is appropriate for the member to continue the claim.

10.3 Application to continue action brought by another member

Where a member has commenced a derivative action against the director's claim, another member may apply to the court to continue the claim on the grounds that:

- the manner in which the first member brought or is continuing the claim is an abuse of a process of the court; or
- the first member has failed to prosecute the claim diligently; or
- it is appropriate for the second member to continue the claim.

The court must dismiss the claim if the evidence filed by the member does not disclose a *prima facie* case for giving permission. In dismissing a claim, the court may make any consequential order it considers appropriate, including a costs order.

If the evidence does disclose a *prima facie* case, then the court may give directions as to the evidence to be provided by the company and may adjourn the proceedings to allow that evidence to be obtained (CA2006 ss. 264 and 269).

10.4   Grounds for permission to continue

On hearing the permission application, the court must refuse permission to continue the claim if a person seeking to promote the success of the company for the benefit of its members would not continue the claim or if the conduct complained of has been authorised or ratified by the company (i.e. the members).

On any resolution to ratify a director's negligence, default, breach of duty or breach of trust, the votes of those members personally interested in the ratification must be disregarded.

In exercising its discretion to allow an action to be continued, the court must consider:

◆ the views of other 'independent' shareholders;

◆ whether the member is acting in good faith;

◆ the importance a director promoting the success of the company would attach to continuing the claim;

◆ whether the conduct would be likely to be authorised or ratified by the company;

◆ whether the company has decided not to pursue the claim; and

◆ whether the applicant should pursue a remedy in their own right instead of on the company's behalf.

The court must have particular regard to the evidence of independent members in deciding whether to grant permission (CA2006 ss. 263 and 268).

10.5   Alternative remedy

There is an additional shareholder remedy that may be more suited to a member's circumstances than an unfair prejudice petition, or a derivative action and that is a petition for 'just and equitable winding-up' under IA1986 s. 122(1)(g).

A just and equitable winding up is a bespoke petition to wind up a company under IA1986 s. 122. This type of winding up is used in circumstances where a shareholder dispute has caused a breakdown in mutual trust and confidence and is impeding the management of the company. The petition to wind up a company on a just and equitable basis may be made by the company, the directors, a majority of creditors, members or other persons liable to contribute to the assets of the company on a winding up. This type of action might be used in situations of 50:50 deadlock between members, mismanagement by one party or exclusion from management of a party.

Test yourself 4.8

Can anyone bring a derivative action claim against a company?

initial public offering (IPO)
An initial public offering is the first sale of shares issued by a company to the public and is usually associated with its stock market launch. Prior to an IPO a company will typically have a relatively small number of shareholders made up of the founders, early stage investors such as venture capitalists or angel investors, family and friends of the founders and employees. The IPO usually involves the raising of additional funds by the issue of shares to the public which will include both institutional and retail investors. An IPO might only add a few shareholders if the shares are all taken by institutions or many hundreds of thousands of retail investors if the IPO is more widely available such as the Royal Mail Group IPO in 2013.

11. Membership

11.1 Registered members

As noted above, to become a member requires consent and entry in the company's register of members. Such members are the legal or registered members. Companies are prohibited from entering details of trusts in their register of members, and must always treat the registered member as the member.

11.2 Beneficial ownership

Although companies are not permitted to note trusts over their issued shares in the register of members, shares are very often held by nominees on behalf of the true or beneficial owner of the shares (CA2006 s. 126).

The beneficial owner must always act in respect of the shares through their nominee, the registered holder.

In order to protect their position beneficial owners should obtain and hold a transfer form signed by the nominee in order that they can effect a transfer of their shares either to themselves or another nominee in the event of any dispute between the nominee and the beneficial owner.

Stop and think 4.6

Ensuring that only natural people or corporate entities are registered on a share register may not always be as simple as it sounds.

Small private companies routinely have investment from the directors' or members' pension fund and all too often these are registered in the name of 'J Smith Personal Pension' which is not permitted.

In October 2018, Aston Martin Group undertook an Initial Public Offering (IPO) and the company through its share registrars will have been at pains to ensure that shares were not subscribed for in the name of any of the unincorporated Aston Martin Owners Clubs or car enthusiast clubs who fancied owning a (small) slice of the famous car marque.

Test yourself 4.9

What is the difference between beneficial and legal ownership of shares?

Chapter summary

◆ Who can be a member of a company

◆ Restrictions on membership

◆ Types of member – shareholders and guarantors

◆ Member activism

◆ Members and the articles of association

◆ Offences against members and remedies

Chapter five
Company
compliance

Chapter six
Annual or
integrated report

Chapter seven
External audit

Chapter eight
Securities
exchange listing
regime

Chapter nine
Maintenance of
records

Chapter ten
Company
secretarial software

Chapter eleven
Minutes and
minute books

Chapter twelve
Oversight by
regulators

Chapter thirteen
Regulation and
disclosure

Part two

Regulatory requirements for companies

Overview

This part examines the obligations on companies and directors to maintain records relating to the constitution of the company, its offers and owners and the format of those records. Additionally this part reviews the obligation on companies to publish their accounts and other information about changes to a company's constitution and registered details. It also considers the additional obligations placed on listed companies, their directors and major shareholders.

Chapter 5 explores the incorporation process for companies and the restrictions around the choice of company name. There is an overview of the obligation to publish information on the company and changes to the information filed at the time of a company's incorporation such as changes of directors, issue of shares and accounting disclosures. The chapter examines the various offences for breaches of a company's constitution or for breaches of the Companies Act and other legislation. The chapter considers the consequences of companies being unable to pay their debts and the alternatives available to manage companies that are insolvent as well as those that whilst solvent have run their course and are no longer required.

Chapter 6 looks at the requirements to keep accounting records and publish annual financial statements. There is an in-depth examination of the numerous exemptions from full disclosure available to companies of different sizes and type as well as the additional disclosures required of listed companies. There is also a discussion on the future developments already signposted in corporate reporting and governance, especially for listed and large non-listed companies.

Chapter 7 examines the need for and purpose of external auditors and the importance of the independence of the auditor. The chapter explores the process for the appointment of auditors and the obligation for the rotation of audit partners and the compulsory audit firm rotation in listed company audit appointments. There is an overview of the processes to follow on termination of an audit appointment.

Chapter 8 provides an overview of the listing regime, the listing process and role played by the London Stock Exchange. There is an examination of the additional disclosure obligations on listed companies of accounting, financial and inside information as well as disclosure of significant shareholders' and senior company managers' dealing in company shares. The chapter provides an overview of the UK corporate governance regime. Finally, there is an overview of the legislative regime that prohibits insider dealing and the potential penalties for breaching those provisions.

Chapter 9 provides a detailed analysis of the requirements on companies to keep and maintain various registers, corporate records and copies of documents and contracts. It looks in detail at the statutory registers that must be kept, the format of the registers and where they may be kept. There is a review of who has the right of access to the registers and the fees that a company can charge for that access. Lastly the chapter explores the need to retain and the period of retention for a number of corporate documents.

Chapter 10 reviews the process to evaluate and implement the adoption of a software application for corporate statutory records administration and maintenance. The chapter explores some of the pitfalls and notes that, as with all databases, these applications are only as good as the data contained within them.

Chapter 11 examines the art of good minute taking and a discussion of what minutes should and should not contain. It considers the 'six Cs' to good minute writing, that minutes can have evidential status in legal actions as well as the requirement for the security of the minute books.

Chapter 12 explores the oversight of companies by regulators and the interaction between regulators, the directors and the company secretary and how the general day-to-day observance, or lack of it, can affect the nature of regulatory investigations. The chapter reviews the statutory powers of certain regulatory authorities to require the production of documents and/or undertake searches for those documents.

Chapter 13 provides an overview of the reporting and disclosure requirements of listed companies and examines the link and relationship between disclosure, accountability, transparency and trust. The chapter considers the requirement for disclosure together with the overriding obligation to keep personal data secure under the GDPR regime as well as an individual's right to require disclosure of details of their personal data being held and processed by companies and public bodies.

Learning outcomes

At the end of this part you will be able to:

◆ understand the nature and principles of the company's regulatory requirements and interpret and practise in the sector to ensure compliance;

◆ explain the options available for the incorporation of a company and the obligation to inform the Registrar of Companies of any changes to the constitution, officers and share capital;

◆   provide an overview of the various offences under the Act and the penalties on conviction;

◆   discuss the background to the UK corporate governance regime and its purpose;

◆   give an overview on liquidations and winding up;

◆   explain the different types of accounts available depending on the size of the company and the additional accounting disclosures for listed companies;

◆   understand the narratives, reporting requirements and publication requirements of financial statements;

◆   discuss the future developments in reporting, insolvency and corporate governance;

◆   understand the importance of audit independence, the role of the auditor and the process for appointment, resignation or removal of the auditor;

◆   provide an overview of the process for listing and admission to trading, the continuing obligations of listed companies and the corporate governance and stewardship responsibilities of listed companies and institutional investors;

◆   explain the criminal liability for abusing inside information relating to a company;

◆   discuss the proposed removal of paper share certificates for listed companies;

◆   explain the requirement to make and keep minutes of meetings;

◆   understand which corporate records are required, where and for how long they should be kept and who has the right of access;

◆   discuss the benefits of entity management platforms and have an understanding of the process of evaluating new platforms for upgrades or first-time deployment;

◆   explain the benefits to be gained from board and director effectiveness appraisals;

◆   give an overview of the investigation powers of the various government agencies charged with oversight of companies; and

◆   understand the data protection regime brought in by GDPR.

Chapter five
Company compliance

CONTENTS

1. Introduction
2. Company formation
3. Filing of company returns
4. Offences under the relevant corporations or associations legislation
5. Corporate governance overview
6. Mergers, divisions, arrangements and reconstructions
7. Takeovers and acquisitions
8. Culture and corporate behaviours
9. Company insolvency, dissolution and restoration
10. Dormant companies

1. Introduction

Companies are required to ensure that changes to the company's corporate structure and changes to its officers are notified to the Registrar for placing on public record at Companies House.

As a minimum, companies must file a confirmation statement each year (s. 853A) and file its **financial statements** in respect of each financial year.

This chapter looks at the processes for the formation of companies, compliance requirements during their life and the processes relating to the winding down of a company either through insolvency or through it having fulfilled its purpose and being wound up voluntarily.

2. Company formation

The process by which a company is created is described as incorporation, registration or formation. All three words refer to the same process but derive from different sections of the Act.

financial statements
The term adopted by the joint accountancy bodies to signify 'balance sheet, profit and loss accounts, statements of source and application of funds, notes and other statements' which collectively are intended to give a true and fair view of financial position and profit or loss.

◆ s. 1(1) … 'company' means a company **formed** and **registered** under this Act…

◆ s. 9(2) The application for **registration** must state…

◆ s. 14 If the registrar is satisfied that the requirements of this Act as to **registration** are complied with, he shall **register** the documents delivered to him.

◆ s. 15(1) On the **registration** of a company, the registrar of companies shall give a certificate that the company is **incorporated**.

Each particular word has a specific meaning with the effect that Companies Act companies are formed under the Act, incorporated in the United Kingdom and registered in England & Wales, Scotland or Northern Ireland.

A company, that is to say an incorporated entity, is formed under an Act of Parliament. While most will be formed under the Act, an incorporated entity may also be formed under other Acts including the Limited Liability Partnerships Act 2000, the Charities Act 2011 or the Risk Transformation Regulations 2017 under FSMA2000.

In most cases, company incorporation (registration or formation) is a relatively straightforward process and can be undertaken without any legal training, although the majority of companies are formed either by specialist registration agents (also referred to as formation or incorporation agents) or increasingly directly with Companies House, using their web incorporation service.

2.1   Matters to consider when incorporating a company

Table 5.1 summarises the four types of companies available to be incorporated under the Act and the range of factors to consider when deciding which type to incorporate.

Factors to consider	Plc	Ltd	Unltd	Guarantee
Profit	✓	✓	✓	
Not for profit				✓
Liability of members limited	✓	✓		✓
Liability of members unlimited			✓	
Financial information confidential			✓	
Financial information public	✓	✓		✓
Profits to be assessed for tax on trading vehicle	✓	✓	✓	✓
Shares to be offered to the public >100 persons	✓			
Shares to be offered to a defined restricted membership		✓	✓	✓

Table 5.1 Types of company

Other common forms of trading entity, but not formed or registered under the Act, are sole traders, partnerships and limited liability partnerships.

2.2 Types of companies

There are four types of companies that may be incorporated:

◆ public company limited by shares;

◆ private company limited by shares;

◆ private company limited by guarantee; and

◆ private unlimited company.

In addition to these four basic company types there are the following specialised variants:

◆ Charitable companies can be incorporated as guarantee companies and also registered under the Charities Act 2011. It should also be noted that it is now possible to incorporate a charity directly under the Charities Act without also requiring a guarantee company vehicle as an association or foundation of a Charitable Incorporated Organisation (CIO).

◆ Community Interest Companies (CICs) are private companies limited by shares or by guarantee that have lodged a community interest statement, either at the time of incorporation or subsequently, and are also required to have an asset lock provision in their Articles.

◆ Right to Manage Companies (RTMs) were introduced under the Commonhold and Leasehold Reform Act 2002. These are private companies limited by guarantee which must adopt articles of association prescribed by the RTM Companies (Model Articles) (England) Regulations 2009 (SI 2009/2767).

2.3 How to form a company

Registration

Registration is the process by which a company is incorporated and becomes a legal entity separate from its owner(s) (i.e. the members). This principle is stated in CA2006 s. 7(1): 'A company is formed under this Act by one or more persons – subscribing their names to a memorandum of association … and complying with the requirements of this Act as to registration.'

Registration is effected by delivering the relevant documentation to the Registrar. Guidance on incorporating a company is available from the Registrar by post or online at www.companieshouse.gov.uk.

Registration can be undertaken in three ways:

1. Electronic software filing using an approved software product. The filing fee is £10 for the standard service or £30 for the guaranteed same-day service. Standard incorporations are usually processed within 24 hours.

2. Paper filing. The filing fee is £40 for the standard service or £100 for the guaranteed same-day service. Standard incorporations are usually processed within five working days.

3.   Web Incorporation Service. The filing fee is £12 and there is no guaranteed same-day service. This service is only applicable for private companies limited by shares, adopting the Model Articles without amendment and those not adopting a company name that requires approval.

2.4   Registration of companies

The first step is to find a suitable name. An index of company names is maintained by the Registrar of Companies and must be checked to make sure that the proposed name will not be the same as or too similar to the name of any existing company.

Certain words and phrases require the consent of the Secretary of State and are referred to as sensitive words. Sensitive words and expressions are those that:

◆   imply pre-eminence or a particular status or function;

◆   imply a connection to government or any part of it, any local authority or public body in any part of the UK;

◆   represent regulated activities; and

◆   whose use could be an offence.

When a name has been selected, the documents listed below, having been completed and executed, must be sent to Companies House. The name of a public company must end with the words 'public limited company' or 'plc' or the Welsh equivalents 'cwmni cyfyngedig cyhoeddus' or 'ccc' (CA2006 s. 58). The name of a private company must end with either 'limited' or 'ltd' or the Welsh equivalents 'cyfyngedig' or 'cyf' (CA2006 s. 59). Qualifying charities, non-profit making organisations and CICs can apply for exemption from the requirement to include the word 'limited' or its alternatives (CA2006 ss. 60–2).

The following must be lodged with the Registrar to incorporate a company:

1.   *Memorandum of association*. There must be at least one subscriber to the memorandum, who must agree to take at least one share or agree to be a member if the company is not to have a share capital. The number of shares which each subscriber has agreed to take, if relevant, is shown against their name in the memorandum. One witness must sign against the name of each subscriber.

2.   *Articles of association*. All companies must register Articles, there are three options available:
(a) to adopt the relevant set of model articles in their entirety;
(b) to adopt the relevant set of model articles with modification; or
(c) to adopt an entirely bespoke set of Articles.

3.   *Form IN01*. Details of the proposed company must be submitted on Form IN01. Details to be provided include the proposed name, situation of the registered office, details of the proposed secretary (if any) and directors, together with their service address.

4.   *Name approval*. Formal approval of the name of the company (if required).

5.   *Registration fee.* Payment of the applicable registration fee either by cheque for paper filings or by account if using the software filing or WebFiling facilities.

If all is in order, the Registrar will issue a **certificate of incorporation** bearing the date of incorporation, the company's registered number and stating the company type.

A private company may commence business as soon as it is incorporated.

2.5   Additional requirements for the registration of a public company

A public company must have at least two directors (CA2006 s. 154) and a company secretary.

Unlike a private company, a public company cannot immediately commence business on the issue of the certificate of incorporation or exercise any of its borrowing powers. Before this can happen, the company must deliver an application for a borrowing certificate using Form SH50 following which the Registrar will issue the trading certificate, confirming that the company complies with CA2006 s. 761.

This application includes confirmation that the authorised minimum share capital has been subscribed. The authorised minimum requires that each share issued by a public company must be paid up as to a minimum of 25% of its nominal value and 100% of any premium (CA2006 s. 761).

If the company commences its business and exercises any of its borrowing powers before the issue of the trading certificate, the company and any officer in default may be liable to criminal penalties and are jointly and severally liable to indemnify any affected third party for any loss or damage suffered as a result of the failure to comply with s. 761. The transactions themselves are not affected by the failure to comply with CA2006 s. 761.

2.6   Additional requirements for the registration of a Community Interest Company

A Community Interest Company (CIC) may be registered under the Companies (Audit, Investigations and Community Enterprises) Act 2004 (C(AICE) 2004) and the Community Interest Company Regulations 2005, SI 2005/1788.

The Memorandum and Articles must comply with the provisions of the Community Interest Company Regulations 2005, which set out details of the asset lock and other features of a CIC.

The name of the CIC must, if it is not a public company, end with the words 'Community Interest Company' or 'CIC'. If the registered office is situated in Wales, the Welsh equivalent may be used instead: 'Cwmni Buddiant Cymunedol' or 'CBC'. If the CIC is a public company, the name must end with 'Community Interest Public Limited Company' or 'Community Interest plc', or their Welsh equivalent.

certificate of incorporation
A certificate issued by the Registrar of Companies on receipt of specified constitutional and other documents of the company. The company assumes its identity as a legal person on the date of incorporation shown on the certificate.

A CIC must clearly demonstrate how it will meet the community interest test. One way it can do this is to define closely its objects, rather than using the general commercial objects clause.

The proposed CIS must confirm using Form CIC36 that the company will benefit the community. The form sets out the intended activities of the CIC and demonstrates how these will benefit the community.

The final document is the Excluded Company Declaration (ECD), in the form approved by the Regulator of Community Interest Companies (Regulator), to confirm that the company is not excluded from being eligible from being a CIC.

The incorporation documents are all filed at Companies House. The filing fee for incorporating a CIC is £35. As the Regulator must confirm that the proposed company meets the eligibility criteria, same-day CIC incorporations are not possible.

2.7 Additional requirements for the registration of a Right to Manage Company

There are no registration requirements however in order to be an RTM company the company must:

- be a private company limited by guarantee;
- ensure its Articles comply with the provisions for RTM Companies;
- hold a freehold or leasehold interest in a qualifying premises;
- not be a commonhold association; and
- have as its members the tenants of flats in the premises or landlords under leases of those premises.

An RTM company ceases to be an RTM company if it no longer continues to fulfil any of these conditions.

2.8 Same-day registrations

The registration of private or public companies is usually completed within five days of receipt of the registration documents by post, or within 24 hours where one of the online services is used. Registration can also be effected on the date of the documents' receipt if they are sent to Companies House (Cardiff) or the London Information Centre, addressed to the 'New Incorporation Section – same day incorporations', or if the online service is used by selecting the same-day option.

2.9 Companies' registered numbers

On incorporation, every company is allocated a registered number; this consists of one or more sequences of figures or letters. The Registrar has the power to change a company's registered number but, for a period of three years the company may use either the old number or the new one on business letters and order forms (CA2006 s. 1066).

2.10   Re-registration – changing the status of a company

Provided certain conditions are met, most companies can change their company type by following a process known as re-registration.

The following changes of status are permitted:

◆ Private to public (unless previously re-registered as unlimited) (CA2006 s. 90).

◆ Public to private limited (CA2006 s. 97).

◆ Private limited to unlimited (unless previously re-registered as limited) (CA2006 s. 102).

◆ Unlimited to limited (unless previously re-registered as unlimited) (CA2006 s. 105).

◆ Public to unlimited (unless previously re-registered as limited or unlimited) (CA2006 s. 109).

It is not possible to change a company's type:

◆ to or from that of a company limited by guarantee; or

◆ from being a CIC company.

Stop and think 5.1

A company may not be incorporated for a purpose that is illegal, such as fraud, with the intention of the true perpetrators of the fraud attempting to evade justice by hiding behind the veil of incorporation.

Test yourself 5.1

1. **Certain words and expressions require consent before they may be used as part of a company name. Which of the following require consent?**

   ◆ **Britain**

   ◆ **French**

   ◆ **Accountant**

   ◆ **Insurance**

   ◆ **Royal**

2. **What are the different types of company that can be incorporated under the Companies Act 2006?**

3. **Why must a public company apply for a certificate under CA2006 s. 761 before it starts trading?**

3. Filing of company returns

All companies are required to give notice to the Registrar of changes to their constitution, officers, members, people with significant control (PSC), accounting information and **charges** over their assets. Notice is given by submitting the relevant statutory form, copy resolution, financial statements or other documents as required by the Act to the Registrar for registration and placing on the company's public file. Under CA2006 s. 1191 those submitting information to the Registrar are under an obligation to ensure that the information provided is accurate and true.

Stop and think 5.2

This was amply demonstrated in a case in March 2018 where a businessman was prosecuted and admitted a number of offences of providing false information to the Registrar. In this case, the director had incorporated two companies and falsely appointed two government ministers as directors and shareholders, without their knowledge.

charge
A means by which a company offers its assets as security for a debt. A charge is a general term that includes, but is not limited to, a mortgage. A fixed charge relates to a specific asset or assets. A floating charge relates to whatever assets of a specified class are in the company's possession at the time the charge crystallises (if it does so).

Paper versions of all statutory forms are available free of charge from Companies House.

Almost all forms are also available for completion and submission online from the Companies House website using the WebFiling service.

For certain filings such as incorporations, changes of name, re-registrations and confirmation statements, there is a fee payable and the fee is reduced where the forms or documents are submitted electronically.

Although all forms must be authenticated or signed it is not necessary for hard copy documents to bear an original 'wet' signature. There is a presumption that the use of an automated signature will be subject to internal controls. This relaxation does not extend to allowing submission of documents by fax, due to issues relating to document quality.

The Registrar has the power to reject documents if they are incorrectly completed, not signed, received late or are illegible. Illegible in this case means not only documents that cannot easily be read, but also documents that are not capable of being captured electronically or where capture is possible but would result in an unacceptably large file (CA2006 ss. 1068 and 1072). Accordingly documents may be rejected if they contain shading, colour text or images or are printed on glossy paper.

3.1 Online filing

Many companies will find it more convenient to file their statutory forms online. The WebFiling or software filing services have several advantages over paper-based filing including:

- quicker;
- cheaper (online filing fees are usually lower than the paper-based equivalent filing);
- rejection rates are lower due to inbuilt checks, pre-population of data;
- automatic confirmation of filing; and
- provides an environmentally friendly alternative.

Users of the online filing services can opt in to receive email reminders for submission of annual accounts and confirmation statement and can also opt in to the PROtected Online Filing service (PROOF). PROOF combats corporate identity theft by making changes of registered office or director only notifiable using either WebFiling or software filing.

3.2 WebFiling

Registering to use the WebFiling service is very simple requiring the online registration of a username and password and then requesting an authentication code for the company. The authentication code is posted to the company's registered office address. The authentication code acts as the signature on the forms.

3.3 Software filing

The software filing service allows companies to file most Companies House forms, some forms of accounts as well as incorporation documents using an approved third party software package or by developing their own bespoke solution in-house.

Use of the services requires registration with Companies House and the setting up of an account for the payment of any fees which are invoiced monthly.

The service works by the use of electronic transmission of documents to Companies House via an HTTPS link using Extensible Markup Language (XML). These documents must comply with the structure approved by the Registrar for electronic submission.

Stop and think 5.3

Prosecutions for failure to file statutory returns are rare and typically only in respect of no filing or late filing of confirmation statements or annual accounts. The fines are usually quite modest, however the implications are much broader as a successful prosecution will result in a criminal record and this is then accompanied by difficulties in obtaining bank loans and mortgages and can lead the person to be denied entry to some foreign countries.

Even where a prosecution is not brought a director's track record for filing or failing to file documents on time or at all is taken into account where other breaches of regulations are being assessed or a director's

behaviour is being assessed either in insolvency or disqualification proceedings.

Test yourself 5.2

1. **Hard copy, paper filing is available for all statutory forms and documents. What other methods of filing these documents are there?**

2. **Does it matter to which Companies House office documents are delivered?**

4. Offences under the relevant corporations or associations legislation

The Act sets out numerous instances where the company or its officers may be held criminally liable for an offence committed by the company under the Act. CA2006 ss. 1121–3 stipulate the circumstances under which the company is held liable and those where the officers are held liable and which officers this relates to.

Most of the offences are intended to hold companies and their directors to account for misconduct but some address the behaviour of members or third parties. Although many of the offences are for significant failings, others might seem to be trivial administrative details. Criminal offences under the Act include:

◆   failing to file accounts on time (CA2006 s. 451);

◆   failing to enter a director's details in the register of directors or failing to update those details within the prescribed timescale (CA2006 s. 162);

◆   failing to file an amended copy of the Articles following an amendment (CA2006 s. 26);

◆   failing to respond to a request for confirmation that the details on the central register are up to date (CA2006 s. 128F); and

◆   failing to show registered office and registered number on emails (reg. 25 Company, LLP and Business Names (Trading Disclosures) Regulations 2015).

The general principle is that where the only victims of the breach(es) of the Act are the company itself or its members the company should not be liable, but the officers are. In other instances where the victims are persons other than the company or its members liability rests with the company.

CA2006 s. 1121 sets out which persons are meant by 'every officer who is in default' which is widely used throughout the Act. An officer is defined as including any director, manager or company secretary and any person who is to be treated as an officer for the purposes of the particular provision giving rise to the default.

CA2006 s. 1122 sets out the position where a company is an officer of another company.

CA2006 s. 1126 sets out details of a number of instances where consent from the Secretary of State, or the Director of Publication Prosecutions (DPP), as appropriate, is required before proceedings can be brought in England and Wales or their counterpart for proceedings being brought in Northern Ireland.

The penalties on conviction for a breach of the Companies Act range from fines, stipulated by the relevant section, to imprisonment.

Summary proceedings for offences under the Act must be brought within the period of three years commencing on the date of the offence and within 12 months of the date on which evidence sufficient in the opinion of the Secretary of State or the DPP to justify prosecution comes to their knowledge (CA2006 s. 1128).

Although there are a great number of instances where a director or company might be liable for criminal prosecution these are extremely rare and are considerably outnumbered by the number of civil penalties imposed to late filing for accounts. During the 12 months ended 31 March 2017, 377 directors were disqualified for breaches of the Insolvency Act or Companies Act plus an additional 989 voluntary undertakings. During the same period there were 190,496 late accounts filing penalties issued of which only 943 were successfully challenged and withdrawn (source: www.gov.uk/government/uploads/system/uploads/attachment_data/file/638401/Companies_House_Management_Information_2016-17.xlsx).

As discussed in chapter 4, members may bring actions through the court against the company or the directors for unfair prejudice or derivative action claims.

As noted in chapter 2, these prosecution and liability provisions in the Act are supplemented by the CDDA1986. Under CDDA1986 depending on the section the prosecution is brought under, the court may or will make a disqualification order that prohibits that person from being a director, liquidator or administrator of a company, a receiver or manager of a company's property, or being in any way involved in the promotion, formation or management of a company for a maximum period of 15 years (CDDA1986 ss. 1–6 and 10).

Companies may be fined by Companies House for late submission of their financial statements. With limited exceptions, companies are automatically fined according to a sliding scale (see Table 5.2). It must be noted that the onus is on the directors to deliver accounts to Companies House within the specified time. 'Deliver' means the receipt of accounts acceptable for registration.

	Private companies	Public companies
Up to one month late	£150	£750
Up to three months late	£375	£1,500
Up to six months late	£750	£3,000
More than six months late	£1,500	£7,500

Note: Where accounts are delivered late in consecutive periods the fine is doubled for the second period.

Table 5.2 Accounts late filing penalties

The issue of a late filing penalty against a company does not prohibit a prosecution being brought against the director(s) personally for failing to submit accounts on time.

If it appears to the Registrar that a company has failed to file either a document amending the Articles, or an amended copy of its Articles the Registrar can give notice to the company requiring the delivery of the missing documents. If the company fails to deliver the documents within 28 days, it is liable to a fine of £200 (CA2006 s. 27).

Stop and think 5.4

Although there is provision in the Act for a company to apply for an extension to the filing period in practice such extensions are extremely rare. This is because in most instances the company being unable to file its accounts on time is usually as a result of not starting the process early enough, rather than any genuine exceptional reason withholding production or delivery of the accounts. Such exceptional circumstances would be present if say a sole director shareholder died. In these circumstances clearly, the director cannot sign the accounts, nor can the shareholder appoint a new director as no one can exercise the votes attached to any shares until probate is granted.

Test yourself 5.3

Is it sufficient to post documents to Companies House prior to the expiry of the appropriate filing period?

5. Corporate governance overview

5.1 Background

Although corporate governance as a concept had been in use for many years it rose in prominence following the financial crisis and corporate scandals of the late 1980s and came back to the fore following the global financial crisis 20 years later in 2007–08 and continuing perceived corporate excesses, gender pay gap and diversity in the boardroom and senior management.

A number of reports have been published and have developed into the corporate governance guidance we have today comprising the UK Corporate Governance Code and the UK Stewardship City Code, both of which look at the governance landscape for publicly listed companies and most recently the development of Corporate Governance Principles for large private companies under the chairship of James Wates.

The first of these reports, published in 1992, against a background of a financial crisis and corporate failures, was the report of a committee chaired by Sir Adrian Cadbury: *Report of the Committee on the Financial Aspects of Corporate Governance,* and was generally perceived as a major advance and has forever since been referred to as the Cadbury Report.

A core element of the report was the Governance Code of Best Practice. Compliance with the Governance Code provisions operate under the so-called 'comply or explain' regime, where companies departing from the Governance Code provisions must explain the reasons for non-compliance.

The FRC acts as a focus for considering whether any developments in corporate governance call for further work.

Figure 5.1 shows the development of UK Corporate Governance since 1992.

5.2 UK Corporate Governance Code (2018)

The current version of the Governance Code was published in July 2018 and applies to companies, with a premium listing, and for accounting periods beginning on or after 1 January 2019. The Governance Code is supported by a number of supplemental guides also issued by the FRC.

Compliance with the UK Corporate Governance Code is not intended to be an exercise in 'box ticking', and compliance with certain aspects of the Governance Code may not be appropriate for all companies.

The Governance Code is divided into 5 sections containing 18 main principles together with supporting provisions, as follows:

1. **Board Leadership and Company Purpose**

    A. **A successful company is led by an effective and entrepreneurial board, whose role is to promote the long-term sustainable success of the company, generating value for shareholders and contributing to wider society.**

Year	Corporate governance
1992	*The Cadbury Report:* Financial Aspects of Corporate Governance
	Cadbury Code of Best Practice
1994	*The Rutteman Report:* Internal control and financial reporting – guidance for directors of listed companies registered in the UK
1995	*The Greenbury Report:* Directors' remuneration – report of a study group
	Greenbury Code of Best Practice
1998	The Combined Code on Corporate Governance
	The Hampel Report: Final report – Committee on Corporate Governance
1999	*The Turnbull Report:* Internal Control: Guidance for Directors on the Combined Code
2001	*The Myners Report:* Institutional Investment in the United Kingdom
2003	The Combined Code on Corporate Governance (first update)
	The Tyson Report: Recruitment and Development of Non-Executive Directors
	The Smith Report: Audit Committees – Combined Code Guidance
	The Higgs Report: Independent Review of Non-Executive Directors
2005	Internal Control: Guidance for Directors on the Combined Code
2006	The Combined Code on Corporate Governance (second update)
2008	FRC Guidance on Audit Committees
	The Combined Code on Corporate Governance (third update)
2009	*The Walker Report:* A review of corporate governance in UK banks and other financial industry entities
2010	UK Corporate Governance Code
	UK Stewardship Code
	FRC Guidance on Audit Committees (first update)
2011	FRC Guidance on Board Effectiveness (under review)
	The Davies Review: Women on boards
2012	UK Corporate Governance Code (first update)
	UK Stewardship Code (first update) (under review)
	FRC Guidance on Audit Committees (second update)
2014	UK Corporate Governance Code (second update)
	FRC Risk Guidance
2016	UK Corporate Governance Code (third update) (under review)
	FRC Guidance on Audit Committees (third update)
	The Hampton-Alexander Review: FTSE Women Leaders
2017	*The Parker Review:* A Report into the Ethnic Diversity of UK Boards
2018	Wates Corporate Governance Principles for Large Private Companies
	UK Corporate Governance Code (fourth update)
	Guidance on Board Effectiveness

Figure 5.1 Development of UK corporate governance

B. The board should establish the company's purpose, values and strategy, and satisfy itself that these and its culture are aligned. All directors must act with integrity, lead by example and promote the desired culture.

C. The board should ensure that the necessary resources are in place for the company to meet its objectives and measure performance against them. The board should also establish a framework of prudent and effective controls, which enable risk to be assessed and managed.

D. In order for the company to meet its responsibilities to shareholders and stakeholders, the board should ensure effective engagement with, and encourage participation from, these parties.

E. The board should ensure that workforce policies and practices are consistent with the company's values and support its long-term sustainable success. The workforce should be able to raise any matters of concern.

2. Division of Responsibilities

F. The chair leads the board and is responsible for its overall effectiveness in directing the company. They should demonstrate objective judgement throughout their tenure and promote a culture of openness and debate. In addition, the chair facilitates constructive board relations and the effective contribution of all non-executive directors, and ensures that directors receive accurate, timely and clear information.

G. The board should include an appropriate combination of executive and non-executive (and, in particular, independent non-executive) directors, such that no one individual or small group of individuals dominates the board's decision-making. There should be a clear division of responsibilities between the leadership of the board and the executive leadership of the company's business.

H. Non-executive directors should have sufficient time to meet their board responsibilities. They should provide constructive challenge, strategic guidance, offer specialist advice and hold management to account.

I. The board, supported by the company secretary, should ensure that it has the policies, processes, information, time and resources it needs in order to function effectively and efficiently.

3. Composition, Succession and Evaluation

J. Appointments to the board should be subject to a formal, rigorous and transparent procedure, and an effective succession plan should be maintained for board and senior management. Both appointments and succession plans should be based on merit and objective criteria and, within this context, should promote diversity of gender, social and ethnic backgrounds, cognitive and personal strengths.

K. The board and its committees should have a combination of skills, experience and knowledge. Consideration should be given to the length of service of the board as a whole and membership regularly refreshed.

L. Annual evaluation of the board should consider its composition, diversity and how effectively members work together to achieve objectives. Individual evaluation should demonstrate whether each director continues to contribute effectively.

4. Audit, Risk and Internal Control

M. The board should establish formal and transparent policies and procedures to ensure the independence and effectiveness of internal and external audit functions and satisfy itself on the integrity of financial and narrative statements.

N. The board should present a fair, balanced and understandable assessment of the company's position and prospects.

O. The board should establish procedures to manage risk, oversee the internal control framework, and determine the nature and extent of the principal risks the company is willing to take in order to achieve its long-term strategic objectives.

5. Remuneration

P. Remuneration policies and practices should be designed to support strategy and promote long-term sustainable success. Executive remuneration should be aligned to company purpose and values and be clearly linked to the successful delivery of the company's long-term strategy.

Q. A formal and transparent procedure for developing policy on executive remuneration and determining director and senior management remuneration should be established. No director should be involved in deciding their own remuneration outcome.

R. Directors should exercise independent judgement and discretion when authorising remuneration outcomes, taking account of company and individual performance, and wider circumstances.

The principles and provisions in the Governance Code are supported by the separate guidance contained in 'Guidance on Board Effectiveness' also updated and issued in July 2018. Many of the previous provisions of the Governance Code although still relevant are now well established and are no longer included in the Governance Code but are contained in the guidance instead. The 2018 update to the Governance Code has placed much more emphasis on the principles. Companies must effectively implement and audit compliance with those principles and provisions as well as reporting on how they have implemented principles and provisions, actions taken to change behaviours and the outcome of those changes and their particular impact and benefit to the reporting company.

5.3   The UK Stewardship Code

The current version of the UK Stewardship Code was published in October 2012 and is currently under review with a revised Stewardship Code expected to be published in summer 2019.

The FRC's aim is 'to enhance the quality of engagement between institutional investors and investee companies to help improve long-term returns to shareholders and efficient exercise of governance responsibilities by setting out good practice on engagement with investee companies'.

Like the Governance Code, the Stewardship Code operates on a 'comply or explain' basis, recognising that what constitutes best practice for most institutions may not be appropriate for all.

The Stewardship Code contains seven main principles, as follows:

1. Institutional investors should publicly disclose their policy on how they will discharge their stewardship responsibilities.
2. Institutional investors should have a robust policy on managing conflicts of interest in relation to stewardship and this policy should be publicly disclosed.
3. Institutional investors should monitor their investee companies.
4. Institutional investors should establish clear guidelines on when and how they will escalate their activities as a method of protecting and enhancing shareholder value.
5. Institutional investors should be willing to act collectively with other investors where appropriate.
6. Institutional investors should have a clear policy on voting and disclosure of voting activity.
7. Institutional investors should report periodically on their stewardship and voting activities.

Test yourself 5.4

1. **What is the comply or explain principle?**
2. **What are the five categories covered by the Governance Code?**

6. Mergers, divisions, arrangements and reconstructions

Where a compromise or arrangement is proposed between a public company and its creditors or members in connection with a scheme for the reconstruction of a company this is known as a merger or division depending on the nature of the reconstruction (CA2006 s. 902).

The common feature of these reconstructions is that the consideration for the transfer is satisfied by shares in the **transferee** receivable by the members of the transferor with or without an accompanying cash payment.

transferee
A person acquiring shares by way of transfer.

A merger 'by absorption' means a situation where the undertaking, property and liabilities of one or more public companies are to be transferred to another existing public company while a merger 'by formation' is the same process but where there are two or more transferor public companies and the transferee company is a newly incorporated company, whether public or private (CA2006 s. 904).

A division is a scheme where the undertaking, property and liabilities of the company are to be divided among and transferred to two or more companies each of which is either an existing public company or a newly incorporated company, whether public or private (s. 919).

6.1 Mergers

The legislation regulating mergers between public companies is extremely complex and designed to ensure that the members of all companies involved in the scheme are either provided with copies of or given access to a number of documents and reports to ensure that they have full disclosure of relevant facts.

A minimum set of disclosure documents specified in CA2006 ss. 905 and 908–911 must be made available, either by making them available at the company's registered office or making them available on a website for a period of at least one month prior to any member or class meetings to approve the transaction, and notice must be given to the Registrar of the availability of the draft merger agreement for publishing in the **Gazette**.

gazette
Official publication for formal announcements. Published daily by TSO on behalf of the National Archive.

The members of each class of shares of the merging companies must approve the terms of the scheme by special resolution requiring approval of 75% of the members present, in person or by proxy, at the general or class meeting convened to consider the resolutions.

The directors of each company that is merging must report (i) to their members at the meeting(s) convened to consider the merger arrangements and (ii) to the directors of the other merging companies of any material changes to the property and liabilities of their company between the date the draft terms were approved and the date of the members' meeting(s) (CA2006 s. 911B).

6.2   Divisions

Like the provisions relating to company mergers the provisions relating to the division of a company's property and liabilities among one or more other companies only applies to situations where the company being divided is a public company and the companies acquiring those assets and liabilities are either public companies or newly incorporated companies whether public or private.

The documents listed in CA2006 ss. 920–925 must be made available either by making them available at the company's registered office or making them available on a website for a period of at least one month prior to any member or class meetings to approve the transaction and notice must be given to the Registrar of the availability of the draft division agreement for publishing in the Gazette.

The members of each class of shares of the companies involved in the division must approve the terms of the scheme by special resolution requiring approval of 75% of the members present, in person or by proxy, at the general or class meeting convened to consider the resolutions CA2006 (s. 922).

The directors of each company that is involved in the division must report (i) to their members at the meeting(s) convened to consider the division arrangements and (ii) to the directors of the other companies involved in the division of any material changes to the property and liabilities of their company between the date the draft terms were approved and the date of the members' meeting(s) (CA2006 s. 927).

6.3   Arrangements and Reconstructions

An acquisition of one company by another may be affected by a liquidation under the provisions of IA1986 s. 110 or a scheme of compromise or arrangement under the provisions of CA2006 ss. 895–901.

Alternatively, the offeror company may acquire the undertaking of the offeree company for cash or the issue of shares in the acquiring company. Schemes of arrangement may be useful where it is desired to acquire 100% of the offeree company but, because of the nature of the business, it would not be possible to obtain the required 90% level of acceptances that would enable the offeror company to effect compulsory acquisition (see page 119). The approval of the court is required and consequently the legal advisers of both companies will be involved in settling the necessary documentation.

Meetings to approve schemes of compromise or arrangement are convened under the authority of the court (CA2006 s. 896). Where meetings are to be convened under the authority of the court rather than the directors application must be made to the court setting out the nature of the proposed transaction. The court will provide detailed information on the required content of the notice convening the members' meeting and accompanying circular. The contents of the notice and all accompanying documentation must be approved in its final form before being issued to members. The meeting itself will be managed by the directors and company secretary in the same way as any general meeting and afterwards a report of the meeting and votes cast will be submitted to the court.

Any notice convening a meeting of the members or creditors must be accompanied by a statement complying with the provisions of CA2006 s. 897 explaining the effects of the compromise or arrangement, and in particular any material interests of any director and the impact of the scheme on those interests (CA2006 s. 897).

Provided 75% of the members or 75% of the creditors, by value of claim, approve the terms of the scheme the court may sanction the scheme of compromise or arrangement (CA2006 s. 899).

Test yourself 5.5

What is the benefit of acquiring at least 90% acceptances on a takeover?

7. Takeovers and acquisitions

takeover
The process under which one company acquires control of another usually by acquiring all the shares.

The object of a **takeover** transaction is the acquisition usually by a company (the offeror or acquirer) of the whole or a majority of the issued share capital of another company (the target or offeree). The consideration for the acquisition may be the issue of shares or other securities in the acquiring company, the payment of cash or a combination of the two.

7.1 Types of takeover

The following are the main types of takeover transaction:

- *Share sale agreement* – A formal agreement may be made with the shareholders of the target company. This is used where there is a small number of shareholders. This is the usual type of takeover transaction for private companies. For a private company transaction, it will be necessary to review both the Articles and any shareholder agreements to consider the effect of any pre-emption or any rights requiring a purchaser of a significant block of shares to acquire shares from other members on the same terms.

issued capital
See share capital.

- *Public purchase* – Arrangements may be made to purchase on a public market, blocks of shares in a company in order to build up a sizeable holding, which could form the basis on which to launch a bid for the remainder of the **issued capital**. It is necessary, however, where the target company is a public company, to have regard to the provisions of the City Code on Takeovers and Mergers (the City Code).

- *Takeover offer* – The acquiring company may make a public offer to the shareholders of the company to be acquired by sending documents to its shareholders making an offer to acquire their shares on stated terms.

- *Scheme of arrangement or compromise* – A takeover may be effected under a scheme of arrangement.

7.2 Agreements with individual members

A simple way of effecting a transfer of ownership of a company is by making agreements with individual members. It can be effected merely by the exchange of the consideration for duly executed transfers with the share certificates. Usually, however, a formal agreement is entered into between the parties, which should be drawn up with legal advice. The agreement should cover such matters as full details of the shares to be acquired and the consideration to be paid for them with a time for completion and set out who will be responsible for paying legal costs, duty and any other related expenses.

Often warranties are required from the directors of the offeree company containing financial information about the offeree company, the title to its property, pending litigation, etc., including any changes affecting the company that may have occurred since the date of the last balance sheet.

7.3 Purchases in the market

Arrangements may be made whereby a company obtains a significant proportion of the shares in a publicly quoted company by purchases of the company's shares on the market to which the company's shares have been admitted to trading. Fewer formalities are involved with this type of transaction, but care should be taken to ensure compliance with the rules of the City Code and administered by the **Panel on Takeovers and Mergers** (the Panel). It is also important to remember that when the holding reaches 3% and each whole percentage point thereafter, notice must be given to the company and the FCA within two days as required by DTR. The company receiving the notification is required to inform a regulatory information service.

When calculating the level of holding giving rise to an obligation to notify the company, e.g. 3%, purchases by persons acting in concert with the acquiring person or company must be included in the total, and there is an obligation for such persons to keep each other informed to ensure compliance with the notification requirements. It should also be remembered that the acquisition of certain levels of shareholdings may give rise to an obligation to make a general offer for all the shares of the company, which could also affect the price of the shares.

Panel on Takeovers and Mergers
An independent body (the Panel), established in 1968, whose main functions are to issue and administer the City Code on Takeovers and Mergers (the City Code) and to supervise and regulate takeovers and other matters to which the City Code applies. Its central objective is to ensure fair treatment for all shareholders in takeover bids.

7.4 Public offers

A public offer is a takeover offer made to all the shareholders of a company to acquire all or a proportion of their holdings in the offeree company, either for cash or for shares and/or other securities in the offeror company. This is the usual form of takeover of a publicly traded company.

Public offers involve many more procedural steps than takeovers by agreement with individual members or by limited purchases on a public market. Where the target company is or has recently been a public company it is necessary to ensure strict compliance with the City Code, LR or market rules that apply to the target company.

Private shareholders tend to accept offers early in the process while institutional shareholders will not usually accept the offer until the final few days before the closing date. The Panel requires stringent procedures to be followed to avoid possible double counting of acceptances and purchases of the same shareholding.

The offer may be extended indefinitely, subject to the offer being declared unconditional by the 60th day after the posting of the offer. The offer becomes unconditional when the minimum number of acceptances, usually expressed as a minimum holding of the acquirer, has been reached. This minimum is rarely less than 50% and often set at 75% or even 90%. A 75% level of acceptance gives the acquirer control while a 90% acceptance level allows the acquirer to compulsorily acquire the remaining shares.

7.5   Action following the first closing date of a public offer

Totals of the complete and incomplete acceptances will be calculated, and the board of the offeror company will then consider whether the level of acceptances is such that it may declare the bid to be unconditional or whether it will extend it for a further period. If the level of acceptances is small, the offeror company may decide to extend the period for acceptances and, perhaps, improve the terms of the offer.

Once the offer has been declared unconditional, however, it is necessary to prepare to issue consideration shares and/or to prepare cheques or bank transfer instructions.

Upon an offer becoming unconditional, share options and other employee share incentive schemes may become exercisable.

7.6   Transfers to offeror company

The transfer that is executed by or on behalf of the offeror company covering the shares in respect of which duly executed forms of acceptance and transfer have been received in order to put these shares into the name of the offeror company is known as a 'bulk transfer'. It is used in conjunction with the individual forms of acceptance and transfer for each separate accepting shareholder. The bulk transfer is obviously more convenient than dealing separately with the many individual forms of acceptance and transfer, each of which has been signed by an accepting shareholder and each of which would have to be duly stamped by HMRC before registration.

CREST
Operated by Euroclear UK & Ireland Limited, CREST is the major UK securities settlement system for UK equities, government bonds and a range of other securities, providing simultaneous and irrevocable transfer of cash and securities for all sterling and euro payments and real-time settlement.

The completed forms of acceptance and transfer, together with the covering share certificates and the duly stamped bulk transfer, are lodged with the offeree company.

Acceptances settled through **CREST** have the duty automatically calculated and deducted as the acceptances are processed.

7.7   Takeover Panel and City Code

The Panel is an independent body, established in 1968, whose main function is to issue and administer the City Code and to supervise and regulate takeovers and other matters to which the City Code applies in accordance with the Rules set out in the City Code. It has been designated as the supervisory authority to carry out certain regulatory functions in relation to takeovers pursuant to the Directive on Takeover Bids (2004/25/EC). Its statutory functions are set out in CA2006 ss. 942–965.

In all cases, the Panel's function is to ensure that shareholders are treated fairly and not denied an opportunity to decide on the merits of a takeover, and that shareholders of the same class are afforded equivalent treatment by an offeror. The City Code is not concerned with the financial or commercial advantages of a takeover.

A very important aspect of the City Code is the requirement for a shareholder or group of shareholders (referred to as a concert party) acting together to make a takeover offer if the total voting rights they control reaches 30% or more of the total votes available. This is known as a mandatory offer. It is due to the mandatory offer requirement that major shareholders will often acquire up to 29.9% of a company's shares which is often sufficient to give them effective control but falls short of requiring them to make a mandatory offer. Care must be taken to ensure the holding does not creep to 30% or more. The mandatory offer requirement can be triggered even if the holder has not acquired any more shares in circumstances where a company has undertaken a share buy back and the total number of shares falls resulting in a holding that might have been 29.9% now representing more than 30%. In certain circumstances and with the consent of the Panel and of the independent shareholders a major shareholder can seek dispensation from the mandatory offer requirement provided this is obtained before their holding reaches 30% or more.

The City Code reflects the collective opinion of those professionally involved in the field of takeovers as to appropriate business standards and as to how fairness to shareholders and an orderly framework for takeovers can be achieved.

7.8 Competition and Markets Authority

Regard should be paid to the provisions of Part 3 of the EA2002 affecting takeovers and mergers references to the CMA. The Enterprise Act introduced a new merger regime, with decisions taken in most cases by independent competition authorities against a competition-based test rather than the previous public interest test.

The criteria for a referral to the CMA are (EA2002 s. 23):

◆ the value of the turnover in the UK of the enterprise being taken over exceeds £70 million; or

◆ the merger would result in the creation or enhancement of at least a 25% share of supply of goods or services in the UK.

7.9 Compulsory acquisition

Compulsory acquisition is dealt with in CA2006 ss. 974–987. These sections are designed to protect the rights of the minority to resist compulsory acquisition if they have reasonable grounds to do so and to ensure that they are treated no less fairly than shareholders who have accepted the offer.

The Act provides a procedure for the offeror company to acquire compulsorily certain non-assented minority shareholdings (squeeze-out provisions). If the offeror company has, by virtue of acceptances to the offer, acquired or contracted to acquire not less than 90% in value of the shares to which the offer relates, it may give notice using Form 984 to the holder of any shares that it has not so acquired, or contracted to acquire, that it desires to acquire their shares (CA2006 s. 979). A copy of the notice together with a statutory declaration confirming that the conditions for giving the notice are satisfied must be sent to the offeree company (CA2006 s. 980(4)).

The notice must be issued during the period of not less than three months after the last date for acceptance of the offer but cannot be given later than six months from the date of commencement of the offer (CA2006 s. 980).

Where the acquiring company, having acquired 90% of the shares, does not wish to enforce its right to buy out the minority holders, notice must be given to those holders so that they may exercise their right to be bought out by the acquiring company on the same terms as the offer (sell-out provisions). The notice must be issued within one month of reaching the 90% acceptance level. The non-assenting shareholders can exercise their right to be bought out, provided they give notice within three months of the end of the period for acceptance under the offer or, if earlier, within three months of the date of the notice issued by the company pursuant to CA2006 s. 984(3) (CA2006 s. 984).

Compulsory acquisition under CA2006 s. 979 may be impossible where a company has numerous untraceable shareholders.

7.10 Stamp duty exemptions

Takeovers (and schemes of arrangements) are sometimes arranged in such a way that there is exemption from stamp duty on the transfer of shares to the offeree company. These exemptions are usually only available where the 'takeover' relates to a restructuring of a company or group of companies and where ultimate ownership does not change as a result of the acquisition. Under FA1986 s. 77, exemption from stamp duty may be claimed under circumstances where there has been no change in ultimate ownership.

Stop and think 5.5

Care must be taken when buying shares not to create a concert party as a result of discussions being held with other shareholders.

In 2018 following a long legal process David King via Laird Investments (Proprietary) Limited (Laird) was forced to make a mandatory takeover offer for Scottish football club Rangers in accordance with Rule 9 of the City Code. This related to an original series of share purchases made by a Trust in which Mr King and his family were interested, amounting to only 14.5% of Ranger's shares purchased in 2014 and 2015. Mr King

was found to have been acting in concert with three other shareholders who between them held 19.4% of Ranger's shares and accordingly the purchases by the Trust took the concert party's holding to a little over 34%.

Test yourself 5.6

1. The City Code applies to what type of company?

2. What is the significance of a share offer being conditional on reaching acceptance of 50%, 75% or 90% of the issued shares?

8. Culture and corporate behaviours

A key building block for ensuring good corporate governance practices within a company is to 'set the tone from the top'. Although the phrase was used previously it was included within the preface to the Governance Code for the first time in the 2014 update. It noted the importance of boards not only setting standards of behaviour but also of acting in accordance with those standards themselves. This leadership in turn will assist in the prevention of misconduct and unethical practices necessary to the delivery of sound long-term success.

8.1   Setting the tone from the top

The intention is to create a corporate culture where all employees have ownership and responsibility. A key feature to creating this corporate culture is the senior executive team not only sponsoring key governance policies but being seen to follow them and being role models. The culture of automatically doing the right thing because it is the right thing to do needs to pervade at all levels of an organisation to be effective.

Corporate culture although delivered through actions and deeds must be underpinned through relevant and appropriate policies together with implementation and refresher training.

8.2   Policies

Diversity & Discrimination

For an organisation to truly succeed all its employees should have a working environment that promotes equality, respect and dignity and where there is a zero tolerance for unlawful or unfair discrimination against employees including contractors, applicants or visitors.

Discrimination can take many forms including harassment, victimisation, intimidation and bullying whether verbal or physical.

Whistle-blowing

The Employment Rights Act 1996, as amended, gives employees the right to take a case to the employment tribunal in circumstances where they have been victimised at work or have lost their job as a result of whistle-blowing.

It is important for a potential whistle-blower to understand that their complaint must be about a matter in the public interest and not a personal grievance. Personal grievances are not covered by whistle-blowing protection even if disclosed via a company's whistle-blowing process.

Although it is not a legal requirement for a company to have a written whistle-blowing policy, having one clearly demonstrates the company's commitment to encourage employees to inform senior managers of wrongdoing taking place within the workplace.

Remuneration

Quoted companies are required to adopt a remuneration policy concerning the remuneration of their directors. This remuneration policy must be approved by shareholders at least every three years and those directors approving payments outside of the approved policy may be liable to repay those amounts.

The Governance Code recognises that remuneration committees should set the remuneration of the executive directors in order to promote the long-term success of the company and that transparency of the key elements of directors performance-related pay is essential. It also notes that they should be sensitive to pay and conditions elsewhere in the group but falls short of recommending that salary increases should be consistent at all levels within a company.

Employment handbook

Companies are not required to have an employment handbook and can place every item within the employment contracts of the employees. However, this does mean that any proposed change in even the most minor element is a variation to the contractual terms that will require each employee to agree to in order to apply to them. In even a medium-sized business it is quite possible that some employees will not consent with the result that different rules will apply to different employees.

To avoid this problem companies will usually place administrative rules such as grievance procedures, process to request holidays, notification of sickness absence etc. within a standalone employment handbook which can be updated from time to time without needing employee consent. The employment contract would only contain those significant contractual terms such as salary and bonus entitlement, holiday entitlement, sick pay entitlement, pension entitlement etc.

9. Company insolvency, dissolution and restoration

9.1 Introduction

A company becomes insolvent when it is unable to pay its debts as they fall due. Once this stage has been reached, in order to protect the interest of creditors, employees and shareholders, the directors must take steps for the company's affairs to be wound up. Winding up involves the realisation of the company's assets and payments made to creditors in full or partial settlement of amounts owed to them. This process is undertaken on behalf of creditors by a licensed insolvency practitioner, who is appointed as the liquidator of the company.

A company will be deemed to be unable to pay its debts if:

◆ it fails to comply with a statutory demand for a debt in excess of £750;

◆ it fails to satisfy enforcement of a judgment debt;

◆ the court is satisfied that the company is unable to pay its debts as they fall due; or

◆ the court is satisfied that the liabilities of the company exceed its assets.

In circumstances where the directors realise that the company is not yet but will become insolvent, they might wish to appoint an administrator to manage the company until it is able to continue, to be sold or, if all else fails, to be wound up.

9.2 Members' voluntary winding up

A **members' voluntary winding** up is a solvent winding up under which the directors must have prepared a statutory declaration within the five weeks immediately preceding the resolution to wind up that they are of the opinion that the company will be able to pay its debts in full, with interest at the official rate, within a period not exceeding 12 months from commencement of the winding up (IA 1986 ss. 89 and 90). If a director makes such declaration without reasonable grounds and the debts and interest are not paid within the specified period, they are liable to a fine or imprisonment, or both, and the burden of proof or innocence is on the director (IA1986 s. 89(4)).

members' voluntary winding up
Solvent winding up of a company by resolution of its members.

There are detailed rules governing the procedures to follow, priority of claims etc. in a liquidation however, these are for the liquidator to follow and the company secretary need not be concerned with these.

9.3 Creditors' voluntary winding up

This is appropriate where a declaration of solvency cannot be made, and the company is wound up as a **creditors' voluntary winding up**. A meeting of the creditors must be called and held within 14 days after the meeting of the members of the company at which a resolution to wind up is passed (IA1986 s. 98). The liquidation commences at the time of passing the resolution to wind up (IA1986 s. 86).

creditors' voluntary winding up
Insolvent winding up of a company by resolution of its members.

There are detailed rules governing the procedures to follow, priority of claims etc. in a liquidation however, these are for the liquidator to follow and the company secretary need not be concerned with these.

9.4 Winding up by the court

A company may be wound up by the court if:

- the company so resolves by special resolution;

judgment creditor
A creditor who has obtained a court order in their favour.

- a **judgment creditor** or a creditor petitions the court where an amount in excess of £750 has not been paid following written demand for payment (IA1986 s. 123);
- it is just and equitable for the company to be wound up; or
- the company fails to comply with certain statutory requirements, e.g. the minimum number of members (IA1986 ss. 122 and 124).

The usual ground for a petition to the court is the inability of the company to pay its debts. A contributory, the Official Receiver, the Secretary of State, the Bank of England or the Attorney General may present a petition under various statutory provisions even if the company is solvent.

9.5 Liquidator

The liquidator should:

1. take over responsibility for the assets of the company, together with its books and records;
2. take other necessary steps to protect and realise the assets, as indicated above in the case of a creditors' voluntary winding up;
3. disclaim any onerous property or unprofitable contracts (IA1986 s. 178 and IR1986 reg. 4.187–4.194);
4. ensure the winding up order halts any proceedings against the company, except by leave of the court (IA1986 s. 130(2)); and
5. provide the Official Receiver with information, access to books or such other assistance as they may reasonably require.

9.6 Report on conduct of directors

A report must be made immediately to the Secretary of State under CDDA1986 s. 7(3) if, in the winding up proceedings, it appears to a liquidator or the Official Receiver that the conduct of a director of the company is such as to render them unfit to be concerned in the management of a limited company.

In addition, a return must be submitted to the Secretary of State within six months of appointment of the liquidator or the Official Receiver, stating whether or not there is any such knowledge of the conduct of director(s), or if the conduct return will be delayed beyond that date.

On conviction the court may impose a disqualification order of up to 15 years.

9.7   Winding up in Scotland

Certain provisions relating to winding up are peculiar to Scottish law and are described in IA1986 ss. 120–121, 122(2), 142, 157, 161–162, 169, 185, 193, 198–199, 204 and 243.

9.8   Phoenix companies

Directors of an insolvent company cannot be appointed as directors of a company with a prohibited name. A prohibited name is one that is the same as that of the insolvent company, or so similar as to suggest an association with that company.

9.9   Strike off and dissolution

The Registrar of Companies is authorised by CA2006 s. 1000 to remove from the register companies that they believe are defunct – for example, where a company has failed to file accounts and confirmation statements, and no response is received to letters sent to the company's registered office. This process is known as striking off the company following which it is dissolved.

Under CA2006 s. 1003, a private company which is not trading may make a voluntary application to have the company's name struck off the register and the company dissolved. This procedure may not be used if, within three months of the proposed application, the company has changed its name, traded, disposed of property or rights for value, or engaged in any activity other than that required to effect the dissolution or where application for a scheme of arrangement or petition or order under the Insolvency Act has been made.

One of the most common causes for an application for dissolution to be stopped is on application of HM Revenue & Customs. HMRC will object in any circumstances where they believe there is or might be any tax due.

Any person may object to the proposed striking off and dissolution of a company by contacting the Registrar and giving reasons why the company should not be struck off. Additionally the directors may halt the strike off and dissolution process by submitting Form DS02.

Any property or rights held by a company immediately prior to its strike off and dissolution automatically pass to the Crown, the Duchy of Lancaster or the Duke of Cornwall as *bona vacantia* or ownerless assets. The Crown estate to which the assets pass is determined by reference to location of the registered office of the company immediately prior to dissolution. If it is later discovered that a dissolved company held assets it is usually necessary to have the company restored in order to deal properly with those assets.

9.10   Restoration

Under CA2006 ss. 1024–8, application may be made to the Registrar by a former director or member of the company to restore the company to the register under an administrative restoration procedure. The procedure is only available for companies struck off and dissolved by the Registrar under CA2006 ss. 1000 or 1001 and in the circumstances prescribed by CA2006 s. 1025, and it is envisaged that the procedure will be used primarily by companies that were dissolved for default in complying with filing requirements, but which continued to trade at the time of strike off.

A procedure for restoration to the register by way of court order is also provided under CA2006 ss. 1029–32. The procedure is available to companies struck off and dissolved for any reason whether at the instigation of the Registrar, on application by the directors or as a result of formal winding up proceedings.

The Secretary of State may also apply to the court for restoration if this is justified in the public interest.

Applications for administrative restoration must be made within the period of six years from the date of dissolution (CA2006 s. 1024(4)).

Applications to the court must be made:

◈   at any time for the purpose of bringing proceedings against the company for personal injury; or

◈   within the period of six years from the date of dissolution.

The six-year period does not apply in circumstances where an application for administration restoration has been validly submitted and rejected by the Registrar. In these circumstances the application to the court must be made within 28 days of the date of the notice of the Registrars' decision even if the normal six-year period has expired.

All costs of the restoration are met by the applicant including the Government Legal Department's costs, fees payable to the Registrar and any late filing penalties due in respect of accounts. The period when the company was dissolved is ignored for the purposes of calculating the amount of penalties due. It is also necessary to file all accounts and confirmation statements and other changes for the period when the company was dissolved so that there is a continuous record as if the company had never been dissolved.

An office copy of the court order with the court seal impressed must be delivered to the Registrar. The company is regarded as restored when the order is delivered.

Stop and think 5.6

Care must be taken to check that the company does not hold title to any assets before it is struck off. Once dissolved, the company cannot then transfer ownership and it would be necessary to restore the company. Typical assets overlooked are title to properties, trademarks, patents and even bank accounts.

Test yourself 5.7

1. **How long after ceasing to trade can an application for dissolution be made?**

2. **What action might occur if the Registrar believes a company is defunct?**

10. Dormant companies

A **dormant company** is one that has had no significant accounting transactions as defined in CA2006 s. 1169 since the end of its previous financial year or, in the case of a newly incorporated company, since its incorporation. The following transactions are disregarded for the purposes of assessing the company's dormant status:

- payment for shares taken by the subscriber(s) to the memorandum and articles of association;

- fees paid to the Registrar of Companies; and

- civil penalties imposed by the Registrar of Companies (i.e. late filing penalties).

Any other transactions required to be entered in the company's accounting records will disqualify the company from claiming dormant status (i.e. bank interest/charges).

Where a company ceases trading but has cash reserves dormant financial accounts will not be available if the reserves are held on an interest-bearing account. In such circumstances consideration should be given to transferring the funds to a fellow subsidiary or parent in the case of a group company or to a non-interest-bearing account if it is a standalone entity.

dormant company
A company which has not traded or has ceased trading and has no accounting transactions that need to be entered in its financial records.

Test yourself 5.8

Which of these activities disqualifies a company from being able to file dormant company accounts?

1. **A late filing penalty being imposed on ABC Ltd, an authorised insurance company.**

2. **Payment for the amounts due on the subscriber share relating to XYZ Ltd.**

3. **A dividend being paid by a non-trading entity.**

Chapter summary

◆   Matters to consider when incorporating a company

◆   Ongoing obligation to file returns with the Registrar

◆   Offences under the Act

◆   Introduction to corporate governance

◆   Overview of mergers and divisions of companies

◆   Corporate behaviour

◆   Liquidations and winding up

Chapter six
Annual or integrated report

CONTENTS

1. Introduction
2. Role and duties of the company secretary in the annual report cycle
3. Statutory, regulatory and listing requirements
4. Narrative reporting
5. Disclosure of financial statements
6. Legislative and other developments

1. Introduction

All companies regardless of their type and whether trading or not are required to keep accounting records (CA2006 s. 386) and to prepare and publish in respect of each financial period their financial statements. The first such period commences on the date of incorporation and ends on its accounting reference date, which cannot be set for a date more than 18 months after incorporation. In subsequent years, the financial period will be 12 months until the accounting reference date is amended.

By default, a company's first accounting reference date is set as the end of the month of the anniversary of its incorporation. This date however may be extended or shortened to suit the company's trading cycle, to match that of other group entities, to coincide with the tax year or some other date chosen by the directors.

2. Role and duties of the company secretary in the annual report cycle

The production of the annual report as opposed to just the financial statements is very much a joint effort between two or more departments. The financial disclosures clearly are the domain of the finance department.

However, the front end comprising the chair's statement strategic and directors' reports, remuneration report, corporate governance report and the reports of the various committees is most often overseen by the company secretary who will also ensure that overall the necessary statutory and governance disclosures are made either within the various reports or in the notes to the accounts.

It is important that one department or individual is in overall charge of the process and ensures that the various constituent parts come together on time. It is also necessary, particularly where there are a number of contributors, to ensure that the annual report has a consistent style and format throughout. This is not just a question of having consistent fonts and palette of colours, but the style of writing must also be consistent otherwise there is a danger that the final version will look and feel like a number of separate reports rather than a cohesive annual report.

3. Statutory, regulatory and listing requirements

The Act permits companies of different sizes to file accounts appropriate to their size and is divided into the following categories:

- micro-entities;
- small companies;
- medium-sized companies;
- default disclosures for unlisted companies; and
- additional disclosures for listed companies.

3.1 Micro companies

Very small companies referred to as micro-entities or micro-sized companies are able to prepare and file micro-sized company accounts. In addition to the exemptions available to all small companies micro-entities can prepare an **abridged** balance sheet with reduced information.

abridged accounts
A condensed version of the annual accounts which small and medium-sized companies (according to the specified size criteria) are allowed to file with the Registrar of Companies. They may not be used as a substitute for the full annual accounts for the circulation to members.

Eligibility
A company that meets any two of the criteria set out below is a micro-sized company (CA2006 s. 384A(4)).

Threshold	Turnover	Balance sheet total*	No. of employees
Not to exceed	£632,000	£316,000	10

* Balance sheet total means total of fixed and current assets.

Figure 6.1 Thresholds for micro-entity

To be eligible to prepare and file micro-sized company accounts for any given financial year, the company must be or have been micro-sized during one or more of the following financial years:

◆ if the accounts are for the first year, in that year;

◆ for accounts for any other year, in that year and the previous year; or

◆ if the company fails to qualify in the year for which the accounts are being prepared, in the previous year (CA2006 s. 384A).

The following companies are excluded from being treated as micro-sized:

◆ a company excluded from the small companies' regime by virtue of CA2006 s. 384;

◆ an investment undertaking;

◆ a financial holding undertaking;

◆ a credit or insurance institution; or

◆ a charity (CA2006 s. 384B(1)).

A company is also excluded if in relation to that financial year:

◆ it is a parent company which prepared group accounts; or

◆ it is not a parent company, but its accounts are included in consolidated group accounts for that year (CA2006 s. 384A(2)).

Filing requirements

Directors' report	Strategic report	Profit & loss account	Balance sheet	Auditor's report	Notes
✓		✓	✓*	✓**	✓
Optional		Abridged	Abridged		
		Optional			

* Including a note that the accounts have been prepared in accordance with the micro-entity provisions.
** If audited.

Figure 6.2 Content of micro-entity accounts

Micro-entity accounts must be sent to all members and a copy submitted to the Registrar within nine months of the financial year-end. In circumstances where the financial year has been shortened, the filing period is nine months after the end of the shortened period or, if later, three months after the change was registered by the Registrar.

The balance sheet must contain a statement in a prominent position above the director's signature that the accounts have been prepared in accordance with the micro-entity provisions. This statement should appear in the accounts sent to members as well as the copy submitted to the Registrar.

3.2 Small companies

Small companies are able to prepare and file small-sized abridged accounts and may elect not to send their directors' report or profit & loss account to their members and submit it to the Registrar.

Eligibility
A company that meets any two of the criteria set out below is a small company (CA2006 s. 382(3)).

Threshold	Turnover (million)	Balance sheet total* (million)	No. of employees
Individual accounts – not to exceed	£10.2	£5.1	50
Group accounts – not to exceed	£10.2 net or £12.2 gross**	£5.1 net or £6.1 gross**	50

* Balance sheet total means total of fixed and current assets.
** Net means after any set offs or other adjustments for group transactions and gross means without those set offs and adjustments.

Figure 6.3 Thresholds for small companies and small groups

To be eligible to prepare and file small-sized company accounts for any given financial year, the company must be or have been small-sized during one or more of the following financial years:

◆   if the accounts are for the first year, in that year;

◆   for accounts for any other year, in that year and the previous year; or

◆   if the company fails to qualify in the year for which the accounts are being prepared, in the previous year (CA2006 s. 382).

The following companies are excluded from being treated as small-sized if at any time during the financial year, they are:

◆   a public company;

◆   an authorised insurance company, banking company, e-money issuer, MiFID investment firm or a UCITS management company;

◆   a company that carries out insurance market activities; or

◆   a member of an ineligible group (CA2006 s. 384(1)).

A group is ineligible if any of its members are:

◆   a traded company;

◆   a corporate body whose shares are admitted to trading on a regulated market in an EEA State;

◆   a person (other than a small company) authorised under FSMA2000 to carry on a regulated activity;

◆ a small company that is an authorised insurance company, banking company, e-money issuer, MiFID investment firm or a UCITS management company; or

◆ a person who carries on insurance market activity (CA2006 s. 384(2)).

Filing requirements

Directors' report	Strategic report	Profit & loss account	Balance sheet	Group accounts	Auditor's report	Notes
✓	✓	✓	✓*	✓	✓**	✓
Optional	Optional	Abridged	Abridged	Optional		
		Optional				

* Including a note that the accounts have been prepared in accordance with the small companies' regime.
** If audited.

Figure 6.4 Content of small company accounts

Small company accounts must be sent to all members and a copy submitted to the Registrar within nine months of the financial year-end. In circumstances where the financial year has been shortened, the filing period is nine months after the end of the shortened period or, if later, three months after the change was registered by the Registrar.

The balance sheet must contain a statement in a prominent position above the director's signature that the accounts have been prepared in accordance with the special provisions applicable to companies subject to the small companies' regime.

If an abridged balance sheet and/or profit & loss account is prepared this must include a statement on the balance sheet that the members have agreed to the preparation of abridged accounts for this accounting period in accordance with CA2006 s. 444(2A).

If the company has taken advantage of the small companies' exemption in preparing the directors' report it must contain a statement above the director's or company secretary's signature to that effect.

3.3 Medium-sized companies

Medium companies are able to prepare and file medium-sized abridged accounts and may elect not to send their directors' report or profit & loss account to their members and submit it to the Registrar.

Eligibility
A company that meets any two of the criteria set out below is a medium-sized company (CA2006 s. 382(3)).

Threshold	Turnover (million)	Balance sheet total* (million)	No. of employees
Individual	£36	£18	250

* Balance sheet total means total of fixed and current assets.

Figure 6.5 Thresholds for medium companies

To be eligible to prepare and file medium-sized company accounts for any given financial year, the company must be or have been medium-sized during one or more of the following financial years:

◆ if the accounts are for the first year, in that year;

◆ for accounts for any other year, in that year and the previous year; or

◆ if the company fails to qualify in the year for which the accounts are being prepared, in the previous year (CA2006 s. 465).

The following companies are excluded from being treated as medium-sized if at any time during the financial year they are:

◆ a public company;

◆ authorised under FSMA2000 Part 4 to carry on a regulated activity or carry on insurance market activities;

◆ a company that carries out insurance market activities;

◆ an e-money issuer; or

◆ a member of an ineligible group (CA2006 s. 467(1)).

A group is ineligible if any of its members are:

◆ a traded company;

◆ a corporate body whose shares are admitted to trading on a regulated market in an EEA State;

◆ a person (other than a small company) authorised under FSMA2000 to carry on a regulated activity;

◆ a small company that is an authorised insurance company, banking company, e-money issuer, MiFID investment firm or a UCITS management company;

◆ a person who carries on insurance market activity; or

◆ an e-money issuer (CA2006 s. 467(2)).

Filing requirements

Directors' report	Strategic report	Profit & loss account	Balance sheet	Group accounts	Auditor's report	Notes
✓	✓	✓	✓*	✓	✓**	✓
	Abridged	Abridged	Abridged	If appropriate		

* Including a note that the accounts have been prepared in accordance with the medium-sized companies' regime.
** If audited.

Figure 6.6 Content of medium-sized company accounts

Medium-sized company accounts must be sent to all members and a copy submitted to the Registrar within nine months of the financial year-end. In circumstances where the financial year has been shortened, the filing period is nine months after the end of the shortened period or, if later, three months after the change was registered by the Registrar.

Medium-sized companies may omit certain information from the strategic report, including analysis using key performance indicators so far as they relate to non-financial information.

Medium-sized companies preparing accounts under the provisions of the Act rather than under IAS may omit disclosure with respect to compliance with accounting standards and related party transactions from the accounts they send to their members.

3.4 Full accounts

Companies that are not eligible to prepare micro-sized, small company or medium-sized company accounts together with any smaller companies that voluntarily elect not to take advantage of the simplified disclosures available to them must prepare and file full accounts.

Full accounts comprise the following:

Directors' report	Strategic report	Profit & loss account	Balance sheet	Group accounts	Auditor's report	Notes
✓	✓	✓	✓	✓	✓	✓
				If appropriate		

Figure 6.7 Content of full company accounts

Accounts may be prepared either in accordance with CA2006 s. 396, referred to as Companies Act accounts or in accordance with IAS, referred to as IAS accounts (CA2006 s. 395).

Once a company has filed IAS accounts it must continue to prepare and file IAS accounts unless there is a relevant change in its circumstances. A relevant change takes place if the company becomes a subsidiary of a parent company that does not prepare IAS accounts, the company or its parent ceases to have its shares admitted to trading on a regulated market in an EEA state, or the company ceases to be a subsidiary. The directors may also change from preparing IAS accounts other than due to relevant circumstances but only if at least five years has passed since the company last prepared Companies Act accounts (CA2006 s. 395).

Filing requirements

Full company accounts must be sent to all members and a copy submitted to the Registrar in the case of a private company within nine months of the financial year-end and in the case of a public company within six months of the financial year-end. In circumstances where the financial year has been shortened the filing period is nine months or six months as appropriate after the end of the shortened period or, if later, three months after the change was registered by the Registrar.

In addition to sending a copy to its members, a public company must lay its audited accounts before the members in a general meeting within six months of the financial year-end (CA2006 s. 437).

Companies that are eligible to prepare and file small company accounts, dormant companies and subsidiaries are able to take advantage of an exemption from the requirement to have their accounts audited.

Figure 6.8 shows the content requirement of a typical private company preparing full accounts. It must be recognised that the actual content of the accounts of any particular company are driven by the activities of each company as any notes to the accounts are only required to explain particular transactions and if there are no such transactions then that particular note may be omitted.

		Small-sized	Medium-sized	Full accounts
Cover page showing at least company name and registered number		①	①	①
Corporate information		✓	✓	✓
Strategic Report	s. 414			
Fair review of the Company's business		–	✓	✓
Description of the principal risks and uncertainties		–	✓	✓
Directors' report	s. 416			
Directors of the company		✓	✓	✓

		Small-sized	Medium-sized	Full accounts
Recommended dividend		–	✓	✓
Research and development		✓	✓	✓
Future developments		✓	✓	✓
Events since balance sheet date		✓	✓	✓
Foreign branches		✓	✓	✓
Financial instruments		–	✓	✓
Going concern		✓	✓	✓
Directors' liabilities		✓	✓	✓
Political donations (subsidiary companies are exempt)		✓	✓	✓
Shares (public company only)		✓	✓	✓
Disabled employees (only required if more than 250 employees)		–	✓	✓
Employee involvement (only required if more than 250 employees)		–	✓	✓
Statement as to disclosure of information to auditors (if audited)		✓	✓	✓
Re-appointment of auditors (if audited)		✓	✓	✓
Directors responsibilities statement in respect of financial statements		✓	✓	✓
Going concern statement (may be omitted if a separate statement is in the directors' report)		✓	✓	✓
Statement re UK Accounting Standards being followed may be omitted by small and medium-sized companies		–	–	✓
Independent auditor's report (if audited)	s. 423	✓	✓	✓
Income statement/profit & loss account – individual (and group if applicable)	s.404		✓	✓
Statement of changes in Equity		–	✓	✓
Statement of financial position/balance sheet – individual (and group if applicable)	ss. 394, 404(1)	✓	✓	✓
Statement of cash flows – individual (and group if applicable)		–	–	–	✓

		Small-sized	Medium-sized	Full accounts
Notes to the financial statements				
Basis of preparation		✓	✓	✓
Accounting policies – description of material accounting policies only		✓	✓	✓
Turnover and segmental analysis		R	✓	✓
Operating profit		✓	✓	✓
Auditors remuneration (if audited)		R	✓	✓
Exceptional items		✓	✓	✓
Profit/loss on disposal of subsidiary previously acquired		✓	✓	✓
Staff costs	s. 411	✓	✓	✓
Remuneration of directors		✓	✓	✓
Interest payable		✓	✓	✓
Tax		✓	✓	✓
Profit attributable to parent company members (only where parent company P&L account not disclosed with group accounts)		✓	✓	✓
Fixed assets		✓	✓	✓
Intangible assets		✓	✓	✓
Tangible assets		✓	✓	✓
Stocks		✓	✓	✓
Debtors		✓	✓	✓
Creditors: amounts falling due within one year		✓	✓	✓
Creditors: amounts falling due after more than one year		✓	✓	✓
Loans		✓	✓	✓
Obligations under leases and hire purchase contracts		✓	✓	✓
Provisions for liabilities		✓	✓	✓
Allotted and issued share capital		✓	✓	✓
Dividends and other appropriations		✓	✓	✓

	Small-sized	Medium-sized	Full accounts
Reserves	✓	✓	✓
Notes to the cash flow statement	✓	✓	✓
Pensions and other post-retirement benefits	✓	✓	✓
Share based payments	✓	✓	✓
Capital commitments	✓	✓	✓
Contingent liabilities	✓	✓	✓
Off balance sheet arrangements	✓	✓	✓
Guarantees and other financial commitments	✓	✓	✓
Directors' advances, credit and guarantees	✓	✓	✓
Financial instruments	✓	✓	✓
Events after reporting period	✓	✓	✓
Related party transactions	✓	✓	✓
Transition to FRS 102 (first year after transition)	✓	✓	✓

ⓘ   Non statutory
✓   Required
–   Exempt
R   Reduced disclosure available

Notes are only required where there is any information to be disclosed and that assists the reader in understanding the accounts.

Figure 6.8 Content of Financial Statements prepared under FRS 102 for small, medium and full accounts

3.5 Listed companies

For companies with publicly traded shares there are a number of overlapping additional disclosure requirements.

A listed company is one that has securities which are listed in the Official List maintained by the UKLA and are eligible for trading on a regulated market. Additional accounting disclosure requirements are set out in the Listing Rules.

3.6 Definition of quoted company

CA2006 s. 385 defines a 'quoted company' for the purpose of Part 15 (Accounts and Reports) of the Act as a company whose equity share capital has been listed in the UK, officially listed in an EEA State or admitted to dealing on the New York Stock Exchange or Nasdaq.

Accordingly, it can be seen that the definition of a quoted company includes a listed company.

Additional accounting disclosures for quoted companies are included in the Act, Listing Rules and the Disclosure and Transparency Directive.

3.7 Filing obligation of quoted companies

CA2006 s. 447 separates out the specific filing obligations of quoted companies and includes a requirement to file the directors' remuneration report with the Registrar together with the auditor's report on the auditable part of the directors' remuneration report, in addition to the company's annual accounts, the directors' report, the strategic report and any separate corporate governance statement.

3.8 Annual report and accounts

A quoted company must publish its annual financial report within four months of the end of the financial year and ensure that its annual financial reports are freely available to the public for at least 10 years after publication (DTR 4.1.3 and 4).

3.9 Summary information

Companies were previously permitted to circulate summary financial statements in place of their full report and accounts. This has now been withdrawn, and instead companies may issue the strategic report and supplemental material to their members in place of the full statutory accounts. Any member receiving the strategic report and supplemental material may request that the full accounts are sent to them (CA2006 s. 426). Although available to any company preparing unabridged accounts (i.e. not small or medium-sized), the issue of the strategic report and supplemental information is generally only taken up by Listed companies as the full annual report and accounts are also readily available where required.

Quoted companies must include, in addition to the supplemental material set out in CA2006 s. 426A, a copy of that part of the remuneration report which sets out the single total figure table in respect of the remuneration of its directors (CA2006 s. 426A(2)(e)).

3.10 Additional disclosures

The annual financial report of a listed company must include the following additional information (DTR 4.1.5):

- ◆ management report containing (DTR 4.1.8–11):
  - – a fair review of the company's business and a description of the principal risks and uncertainties facing it. The business review must be a balanced and comprehensive analysis of the development and performance of the company during the financial year, and the position of the company at the end of the year. The review must also contain sufficient analysis, using financial key performance and other

key performance indicators including environmental and employee matters, to demonstrate the development, performance and position of the company during the financial year;

– details of any important events since the end of the financial year, likely future development, any activities in research and development, details of any acquisition(s) of own shares and the existence of any overseas branches; and

– in relation to the company's use of financial instruments or where required for the assessment of its assets, liabilities, financial position and profit or loss, details of its financial risk management objectives and policies, and the company's exposure to price risk, credit risk, liquidity risk and cash flow risk.

◆ responsibility statements:

– the annual financial report must include a responsibility statement made by those responsible confirming that, to the best of their knowledge and belief, the financial statements have been prepared in accordance with applicable accounting standards and give a true and fair view of the assets, liabilities, financial position and profit or loss of the company, and that the management report contains a fair review of the information required to be reviewed (DTR 4.1.12).

If the company is required to prepare consolidated accounts, the financial statements must comprise (DTR 4.1.6R):

◆ consolidated accounts prepared in accordance with IFRS; and

◆ parent company accounts prepared in accordance with the law of the country of its incorporation.

If the company is not required to prepare consolidated accounts, its financial statements must comprise accounts prepared in accordance with the law of the country of its incorporation (DTR 4.1.6(2)).

The financial statements must be audited, and the full text of the audit report made public (DTR 4.1.7R).

In addition to the requirements set out in DTR 4.1, listed companies must include in their annual financial report (LR 9.8.4):

◆ a statement of the amount of interest capitalised by the group with an indication of the amount and treatment of any related tax relief;

◆ if the company has published unaudited financial information in a class 1 circular or **prospectus** since its previous annual financial report, it must reproduce that information and explain any variance of 10% or more between any profit forecast or estimate and the actual profit (LR 9.2.18R);

prospectus
Any prospectus, notice, circular, advertisement or other invitation to the public to subscribe for purchase of a company's shares or debentures.

◆ details of any long-term incentive schemes as required by LR 9.4.3R;

◆ details of any arrangements under which a director of the company has waived or agreed to waive any emoluments from the company or any subsidiary undertaking;

- ◆ where a director has waived or agreed to waive emoluments, details of such waiver;
- ◆ in the case of any allotment for cash of equity securities otherwise than to the holders of the company's equity shares in proportion to their holdings and any similar issues of shares in a major unlisted subsidiary, neither of which has been specifically authorised by the company's shareholders:
  - – the classes of shares allotted and for each class of shares, the number allotted, their aggregate nominal value and the consideration received by the company for the allotment;
  - – the names of the allottees, if less than six in number, and in the case of six or more allottees a brief generic description of each new class of equity holder;
  - – the market price of the allotted securities on the date on which the terms of the issue were fixed; and
  - – the date on which the terms of the issue were fixed;
- ◆ where a listed company has listed shares in issue and is a subsidiary undertaking of another company, details of the participation by the parent undertaking in any placing of its shares;
- ◆ details of any contract of significance subsisting during the period under review:
  - – to which the listed company, or one of its subsidiary undertakings, is a party and in which a director of the listed company is or was materially interested; and
  - – between the listed company, or one of its subsidiary undertakings, and a controlling shareholder;
- ◆ details of any contract for the provision of services to the listed company or any of its subsidiary undertakings by a controlling shareholder, subsisting during the period under review, unless:
  - – it is a contract for the provision of services which it is the principal business of the shareholder to provide; and
  - – it is not a contract of significance;
- ◆ details of any arrangement under which a shareholder has waived or agreed to waive any dividends or future dividends; and
- ◆ a statement made by the board:
  - – whether the company has entered into any controlling shareholder agreement required under LR 9.2.2ADR; or
  - – where the company has not entered into an agreement as required under LR 9.2.2ADR:
    - • a statement that the FCA has been notified of that non-compliance in accordance with LR 9.2.23R; and
    - • a brief description of the background to and reasons for failing to enter into the agreement that enables shareholders to evaluate the impact of non-compliance on the company; and

- that:
  - the company has complied with the undertakings in LR 6.5.4R or LR 9.2.2ADR;
  - so far as the company is aware, the undertakings in LR 6.5.4R or LR 9.2.2ADR(1) have been complied with by the controlling shareholder or any of its associates; and
  - so far as the company is aware, the procurement obligation (as set out in LR 6.5.5R(2)(a) or LR 9.2.2BR(2)(a)) included in any agreement entered into under LR 6.5.4R or LR 9.2.2ADR(1) has been complied with by a controlling shareholder; or
- where an undertaking in LR 6.5.4R or LR 9.2.2ADR(1) or a procurement obligation (as set out in LR 6.5.5R(2)(a) or LR 9.2.2BR (2)(a)) included in any agreement entered into under LR 6.5.4R or LR 9.2.2ADR(1) has not been complied with:
  - a statement that the FCA has been notified of that non-compliance in accordance with LR 9.2.24R; and
  - a brief description of the background to and reasons for failing to comply with the relevant undertaking or procurement obligation that enables shareholders to evaluate the impact of non-compliance on the company;
- where an independent director declines to support any of the statements relating to controlling shareholders, the statement must record this fact;
- where a listed company's annual financial report contains a statement relating to non-observance of a controlling shareholder agreement, the FCA may still take any action it considers necessary in relation to the underlying breach by the listed company of LR 9.2.2ADR(1) or LR 9.2.2GR; and
- the listed company's annual financial report must include the information required under LR 9.8.4R in a single identifiable section, unless the annual financial report includes a cross reference table indicating where that information is set out.

A listed company need not include with the annual report and accounts details of waivers of dividends of less than 1% of the total value of any dividend provided that some payment has been made on each share of the relevant class during the relevant calendar year.

In the case of a company incorporated in the UK, the following additional items must be included in its annual financial report (LR 9.8.6R):

- details of all the interests notifiable under MAR 19 of each director of the company as at the end of the financial period, including any changes in the interests between the end of the financial period and a date not more than one month prior to the date of the notice of the AGM; if there have been no changes a statement to that effect (LR 9.8.6A);

- a statement showing, as at a date not more than one month prior to the date of the notice of the AGM:
  - interests in voting shares disclosed to the company; or
  - if no disclosures have been made, a statement to that effect;
- a statement made by the directors that the business is a going concern, together with supporting assumptions or qualifications as necessary, that has been prepared in accordance with *Guidance on Risk Management, Internal Control and Related Financial and Business Reporting* published by the FRC in July 2018 (for financial years beginning on or after 1 January 2019);
- a statement setting out:
  - details of any shareholders' authority for the purchase by the company of its own shares that remains valid at the end of the financial period;
  - in the case of purchases made otherwise than through the market or by tender to all shareholders, the names of sellers of any shares purchased, or proposed to be purchased, by the company during the financial period;
  - in the case of any purchases made otherwise than through the market or by tender or partial offer to all shareholders, or options or contracts to make such purchases, entered into since the end of the financial period; and
  - in the case of sales of treasury shares for cash made otherwise than through the market, or in connection with an employees' share scheme, or otherwise than pursuant to an opportunity which (so far as was practicable) was made available to all holders of the listed company's securities (or to all holders of a relevant class of its securities) on the same terms, particulars of the names of purchasers of such shares sold, or proposed to be sold;
- a statement of how the company has applied the main principles set out in the Governance Code;
- a statement as to whether the company has:
  - complied throughout the accounting period with all relevant provisions set out in the Governance Code; or
  - not complied throughout the accounting period with all relevant provisions set out in the Governance Code and if not, setting out: those provisions it has not complied with; in the case of provisions whose requirements are of a continuing nature, the period within which it did not comply with some or all of those provisions; the company's reasons for non-compliance;
- a report to the shareholders by the board that contains all the matters set out in LR 9.8.8R:
  - the unexpired term of the service contract of any director proposed for election or re-election at the forthcoming AGM; and, if any

director for election or re-election does not have a service contract, a statement to that effect.

Stop and think 6.1

Due to the additional disclosure requirements for a listed company many will start the drafting process many months before the year end and often only a few weeks after the previous AGM.

Test yourself 6.1

1.   **What are the differences between listed and quoted companies?**

2.   **A listed company has additional disclosure requirements, where can these be found?**

4. Narrative reporting

The strategic report, directors report, directors remuneration report and corporate governance statements are sometimes referred to as the front end of the accounts due to their position ahead of the financial information within the annual report and accounts.

The strategic report is a mandatory report (CA2006 s. 414A) and is intended to be used by directors to inform the members of the company and assist them in assessing how the directors performed their duty under CA2006 s. 172.

The directors' report is also a mandatory report and is intended to provide an overview of the company financial position at the end of each financial period and by virtue of being in a prescribed format allow easier comparison over time and as between different companies.

In order to address concerns that directors were unfairly rewarding themselves the government introduced legislation requiring quoted companies to publish details of their directors' remuneration (CA2006 s. 420). The disclosures must follow a prescribed format with the details of the various elements of directors remuneration calculated according to prescribed formulae. This facilitates comparison across years and sectors.

4.1   Strategic report

The directors of a company that is not small must prepare a strategic report to inform its members and help them assess how the directors have performed their duty under CA2006 s. 172 to promote the success of the company for the benefit of all members and in doing so have regard to:

◆   the likely consequences of any decisions in the long-term;

◆   the interests of the company's employees;

◆   the need to foster the company's business relationships with customers and others;

◆   the impact of the company's operations on the community and the environment;

◆   the desirability of the company maintaining a reputation for high standards of business conduct; and

◆   the need to act fairly as between members of the company.

The strategic report should provide members with information that is relevant and helpful to them in assessing stewardship by the directors.

The strategic report of a listed company must include a statement from the directors to explain the main trends and factors affecting the long-term success and future viability of the company (Governance Code provision 1). Governance Code provision 31 goes further requiring boards to explain in the annual report how it has assessed the prospects of the company, over what period it has done so and why it considers that period to be appropriate. The board should state whether it has a reasonable expectation that the company will be able to continue in operation and meet its liabilities as they fall due over the period of their assessment, drawing attention to any qualifications or assumptions as necessary. This statement is referred to as the viability statement, and was originally introduced by the 2014 version of the Governance Code.

The review must be a balanced and comprehensive analysis of the development and performance of the business during the year, and the position of the business at the year-end, consistent with the size and complexity of the business and should be consistent with the other information in the annual report (CA2006 s. 414C(3)).

It should also be specific to the company and explain how any relevant general economic or market factors have a particular effect on the company and the steps being taken to take advantage or mitigate those factors. The strategic report should have a future focus explaining how the information contained in it might affect future periods.

Table 6.1 sets out the minimum content requirement of the strategic report for different types of reporting entity.

Matter	Disclosure requirement	Quoted	Large PIE	Plc	Ltd
Risks and uncertainties (CA2006 s. 414C(2)(b))	A description of the principal risks and uncertainties facing the company, together with an explanation of how they are managed or mitigated.	✓	✓	✓	✓
CA2006 s. 414CB(2)(d)	Where relevant and proportionate, contain a description of the company's business relationships, products and services which are likely to cause adverse impacts on principal risks related to environmental, employee, social, human rights or anti-corruption and anti-bribery matters.	–	✓	–	–
Trends and factors (CA2006 s. 414C(7))	The main trends and factors likely to affect future development, performance or position of the business necessary for an understanding of the development, performance or position of the company's business.	✓	–	–	–
Environmental matters (CA2006 ss. 414C(7) and 414CB(1)(a))	Information about environmental matters (including the impact of the company's business on the environment) necessary for an understanding of the development, performance or position of the company's business.	✓	✓	–	–
CA2006 s. 414CB(2)(b)&(c)	Information should include the company's policies and the effectiveness of those policies and, in the case of a large PIE, any due diligence processes implemented by the company in pursuance of those policies.	✓	✓	–	–
Employees (CA2006 ss. 414C(7), 414C(8)(c), 414CB(1)(b))	Information on the company's employees necessary for an understanding of the development, performance or position of the company's business.	✓	✓	–	–
	Information should include the company's policies and the effectiveness of those policies. For a large PIE, this information should also be included if it is necessary for an understanding of the impact of the company's activities on its employees.	✓	✓	–	–

Matter	Disclosure requirement	Quoted	Large PIE	Plc	Ltd
Social, community and human rights issues (CA2006 ss. 414C(7), 414CB(1)(c)&(d))	Information about social, community and human rights issues necessary for an understanding of the development, performance or position of the company's business.	✓	–	–	–
	For a large PIE, this information should also be included if it is necessary for an understanding of the impact of the company's activities on social issues or respect for human rights.	–	✓	–	–
	The information should include the company's policies and the effectiveness of those policies and, in the case of a large PIE, any due diligence processes implemented by the company in pursuance of those policies.	✓	✓	–	–
Anti-corruption and anti-bribery matters (CA2006 s. 414CB(1)(e))	Information on anti-corruption and anti-bribery matters necessary for an understanding of the development, performance and position of the company's business, or of the impact of its activities.	–	✓	–	–
	The information should include a description of the policies pursued by the company in relation to anti-corruption and anti-bribery matters, any due diligence processes implemented by the company in pursuance of those policies and a description of the outcome of those policies.	–	✓	–	–
Absence of information (CA2006 s. 414C(7))	Identify matters on which the company has provided no disclosures and if the company has not provided information on environmental matters, employees or social, community and human rights issues, state which kinds of information is not included in the strategic report.	✓	–	–	–
Absence of policies (CA2006 s. 414CB(4))	If the company does not pursue policies in relation to environmental matters, employees, social matters, respect for human rights, or anti-corruption and anti-bribery matters, the strategic report must provide a clear and reasoned explanation for not doing so.	–	✓	–	–

Matter	Disclosure requirement	Quoted	Large PIE	Plc	Ltd
Business model (CA2006 ss. 414C(8)(b), 414CB(2)(a))	A description of the company's business model.	✓	✓	–	–
GC2018 prov. 1	A statement setting out the long-term viability of the company.	✓			
Strategy (CA2006 s. 414C(8)(a))	A description of the company's principal objectives and the strategies for achieving those objectives.	✓	–	–	–
Performance (CA2006 s. 414C(3)(a) & (b))	A fair, balanced and comprehensive review of the development, performance and position of the company's business, consistent with its size and complexity, which informs members about how the directors have performed their duty under CA2006 s. 172.	✓	✓	✓	✓
CA2006 s. 414CZA	Unless the company qualifies as medium-sized a section 172(1) statement describing how the directors have had regard to the matters set out in CA2006s. 172(1)(a) to (f) when performing their duty under CA2006 s. 172 (for financial years beginning on or after 1 January 2019).	✓	✓	✓	✓
CA2006 ss. 414C(12) and 414CB(5)	References to, and additional explanations of, amounts included in the company's annual report.	✓	✓	✓	✓
KPI (CA2006 s. 414C(4)).	An analysis using financial KPIs.	✓	✓	✓	✓
	Large companies must also (where appropriate) use non-financial KPIs in their analysis.	✓	✓	✓	✓
CA2006 s. 414CB(2)(e)	A description of the non-financial KPIs that are relevant to the company's business.	✓	✓	✓	✓
	As well as providing an analysis using KPIs, the reasons for them being key must be given, that they are properly defined and, where relevant, they are reconciled to the amounts included in the financial statements.	✓	✓	✓	✓

Matter	Disclosure requirement	Quoted	Large PIE	Plc	Ltd
Employee diversity (CA2006 s. 414C(8)–(10))	A quantitative analysis of employee diversity.	✓	✓	✓	✓
	For the purpose of this disclosure a senior manager is an employee who has responsibility for planning, directing or controlling a significant part of the activities of the business or, in consolidated accounts, who was a director of a subsidiary included in the consolidation.	✓	✓	✓	✓
Other information of strategic importance (CA2006 s. 414C(11))	Any information otherwise required to be included in the directors' report, if it is considered to be of strategic importance to the company.	✓	✓	✓	✓

Table 6.1 The strategic report

The directors may exclude and not disclose information if, in their opinion, disclosure would be seriously prejudicial to the interests of the company.

The strategic report must be approved by the board of directors and signed on their behalf by a director or the company secretary (CA2006 s. 414D(1)). Every copy of the strategic report that is by or on behalf of the company must state the name of the person that signed the report (CA2006 s. 433). The copy of the directors' report that is delivered to the Registrar must be signed and have the name of the person that signed the report stated under their signature (CA2006 ss. 445(5), 446(3), 447(3)).

4.2 Directors' report

The directors' report is also a mandatory report and is intended to provide an overview of the company's financial position at the end of each financial period and by virtue of being in a prescribed format allow easier comparison over time and as between different companies.

Under CA2006 s. 415, directors of a company, other than one qualifying as a micro-entity, must prepare a directors' report for each financial year.

As noted above, listed companies are required to make additional disclosures under the Listing Rules and Governance Code.

Table 6.2 sets out the directors' report disclosure under the Act.

Reference	Disclosure requirement	Quoted	Large/ medium- sized	Small
CA2006 s. 236	Details of qualifying indemnity provided for directors	✓	✓	✓
CA2006 s. 416(1)	Names of directors holding office at any time during the financial year	✓	✓	✓
CA2006 s. 416(3)	Amount of any proposed dividend	✓	✓[3]	✓
CA2006 s. 418(2)	Directors' statement on information provided to auditors	✓	✓	✓[4]
CA2006 s. 419(1)	Approval by and signature on behalf of the board	✓	✓	✓
CA2006 s. 419(2)	Statement of use of small companies' exemptions	✓	✓[5]	✓
Sch 7.1A [1]	Identification of any directors' report disclosures that have instead been made in the strategic report	✓	✓	✓
Sch 7.3(2) & 4(1) Sch 5.2(2) & 3(1)[2]	Information on political donations and expenditure in excess of £2,000 in aggregate for the group headed by the company. Only applies to parent companies	✓	✓	✓
Sch 7.6(1)(a)	Financial risk management objectives and policies	✓	✓	✓
Sch 7.6(1)(b)	Information on exposure to price risk, credit risk, liquidity risk and cash flow risk	✓	✓	✓
Sch 7.7(1)(a)	Post balance sheet events	✓	✓	✓
Sch 7.7(1)(b)	Likely future developments in the business of the company	✓	✓	✓
Sch 7.7(1)(c)	Research and development	✓	✓	✓
Sch 7.7(1)(d)	Existence of branches	✓	✓	✓
Sch 7.9	Acquisition of own shares	✓	✓	✓
Sch 7.10(3) Sch 5.5(3)	Policy regarding the employment of disabled persons, if company has more than 250 employees	✓	✓	✓
Sch 7.11 and 11A[6]	If the company has an average of more than 260 employees a statement detailing the steps taken to engage with employees and how the directors have taken employees interests into regard and the effect this has had	✓	✓	✓

Reference	Disclosure requirement	Quoted	Large/ medium-sized	Small
Sch 7.11B and 11C[6]	If the company satisfies two out of three size criteria, a statement detailing the steps taken to engage with suppliers, customers and others in a business relationship and how the directors have taken suppliers, customers and others interests into regard and the effect this has had	✓	✓	
Sch 7.13(2) & 14	Detailed information on capital structure, listed company only	✓	✓	✓
Sch 7.15–19	Greenhouse gas emissions information	✓	✓	✓

[1] Sch 7 refers to Schedule 7 The Large and Medium-sized Companies and Groups (Accounts and Reports) Regulations 2008 (SI 2008/410)
[2] Sch 5 refers to Schedule 5 The Small Companies and Groups (Accounts and Directors' Report) Regulations 2008 (SI 2008/409)
[3] Except a company that would qualify as small if not a member of an ineligible group (CA2006 s. 415A)
[4] If audited
[5] Only applies to a large or medium-sized company that would qualify as small if not a member of an ineligible group (CA2006 s. 415A)
[6] Only applies to financial years beginning on or after 1 January 2019

Table 6.2 Directors' report disclosures

The directors' report must be approved by the board of directors and signed on their behalf by a director or the company secretary (CA2006 s. 419(1)). Every copy of the directors' report that is signed by or on behalf of the company must state the name of the person that signed the report (CA2006 s. 433). The copy of the directors' report that is delivered to the Registrar must be signed and have the name of the person that signed the report stated under their signature (CA2006 ss. 444A(3), 445(5), 446(3), 447(3)).

4.3 Directors' remuneration report

CA2006 s. 420 requires the directors of quoted companies to prepare a remuneration report in respect of each financial year. Failure to comply constitutes an offence punishable by a fine.

For listed companies, the reporting requirements for directors' remuneration fall into three categories:

Companies Act requirements
The requirements are set out in regulation 11 and schedule 8 of the 2008 Regulations.

The provisions in the Act were expanded by provisions introduced by sections 79–82 of the Enterprise and Regulatory Reform Act 2013 with regard to payments to directors of quoted companies. Most recently the Companies (Miscellaneous Reporting) Regulations 2018 (C(MR)R2018) (SI 2018/860) have further amended the Act and the 2008 Regulations. In particular C(MR)R2018 regs. 15–19 add additional disclosure requirements for the directors' remuneration report for financial periods beginning on or after 1 January 2019.

The 2008 Regulations specify the extent to which the directors' remuneration report should be subject to audit. The 'auditable' part of a directors' remuneration report is the part containing the information required by paragraphs 4 to 17 of Part 3 of Schedule 8 to the Regulations, which includes the amount of each director's emoluments and compensation in the relevant financial year, and details on share options, long-term incentive schemes and pensions.

Listing Rule and Governance Code requirements
Although the Listing Rules do not stipulate that the following statements must be disclosed in the remuneration report, that is where they are usually disclosed. The following details are required:

◆ long-term incentive schemes as required by LR 9.4.3R;

◆ arrangements under which a director of the company has waived or agreed to waive any emoluments from the company or any subsidiary undertaking; and

◆ if a director has agreed to waive future emoluments, details of such waiver together with those relating to emoluments which were waived during the period under review (LR 9.8.4(4)–(6)).

Where a remuneration consultant is appointed the consultant should be identified in the annual report alongside a statement about any other connection the consultant has with the company or individual directors (Governance Code provision 35).

There should be a description of the work of the remuneration committee in the annual report, including:

◆ an explanation of the strategic rationale for executive directors' remuneration policies, structures and any performance metrics;

◆ reasons why the remuneration is appropriate using internal and external measures, including pay ratios and pay gaps;

◆ a description, with examples, of how the remuneration committee has addressed the factors in Governance Code provision 40 (executive director remuneration policy and practices);

◆ whether the remuneration policy operated as intended in terms of company performance and quantum, and, if not, what changes are necessary;

◆ what engagement has taken place with shareholders and the impact this has had on remuneration policy and outcomes;

◆   what engagement with the workforce has taken place to explain how executive remuneration aligns with wider company pay policy; and

◆   to what extent discretion has been applied to remuneration outcomes and the reasons why (Governance Code provision 41).

Best practice

There are a number of best practice guides issued by various investor representative bodies including:

◆   Investment Association Guidelines on Responsible Investment Disclosure (2007);

◆   Investment Association Principles of Executive Remuneration (2017);

◆   ABI/NAPF Best practice on Executive Contracts and Severance (2008);

◆   Investment Association Principles of Executive Remuneration (2017);

◆   PIRC Shareholder voting guidelines (2017); and

◆   ISS UK & Ireland Proxy Voting Guidelines (2018).

The directors' remuneration report is usually made up of three components: an annual statement by the chair of the remuneration committee; an annual report on remuneration (Implementation Report); and a remuneration policy (Remuneration Policy).

Each part is subject to different shareholder voting requirements. The Implementation Report must be put to an advisory shareholder vote, at the general meeting at which the financial report is to be received, by ordinary resolution (CA2006 s. 439). In contrast to the Implementation Report, the Remuneration Policy is subject to a binding shareholders' vote, at least once in every three years, as an ordinary resolution (CA2006 s. 439A).

The statement by the chair of the remuneration committee must include a summary of:

◆   the major decisions on directors' remuneration;

◆   any discretion which has been exercised in the award of directors' remuneration;

◆   any substantial changes relating to directors' remuneration made during the year; and

◆   the context in which those changes occurred and decisions have been taken (2008 Regulations sch. 8, para. 3).

Table 6.3 sets out the disclosure requirements of the Implementation Report section of the directors' remuneration report.

Reference	Disclosure requirement
2008 Regulations sch. 8, para 3	A statement from the chairperson of the remuneration committee, which will summarise major decisions on directors' remuneration, substantial changes relating to directors' remuneration and the context changes occurred and decisions were taken
2008 Regulations sch 8, paras 4–12	A report for each person who was a director during the period (set out in a prescribed tabular form), outlining payments to each director and providing a single figure for remuneration for each director
2008 Regulations sch 8, para 13	Total pension entitlements
2008 Regulations sch 8, para 14	Scheme interests awarded during the financial year
2008 Regulations sch 8, para 15	Payments to past directors
2008 Regulations sch 8, para 16	Payments for loss of office
2008 Regulations sch 8, para 17	Statement of directors' shareholding and share interests
2008 Regulations sch 8, para 18	Performance graph and table
2008 Regulations sch 8, para 19	Percentage change in remuneration of director undertaking the role of CEO
2008 Regulations sch 8, para 19A– 19F	If the company has on average 250 employees or more ratio details of the pay of the CEO to the average pay of all UK employees during the same period calculated by one of the three prescribed methods together with an explanation of which method was used, and why it is appropriate to use that method
2008 Regulations sch 8, para 20	Relative importance of spend on pay
2008 Regulations sch 8, para 21	Statement of implementation of remuneration policy in the following financial year
2008 Regulations sch 8, para 22	Consideration by the directors of matters relating to directors' remuneration
2008 Regulations sch 8, para 23	Statement of voting at general meeting

Table 6.3 Implementation report disclosures

The second part of the report, the Remuneration Policy, is separate to the Implementation Report. The latter will be forward-looking and provide information on remuneration and potential payments (including exit payments) for each director.

Chapter 4A of part 10 of the Act stipulates that no remuneration or payment for loss of office can be paid unless they are consistent with the approved policy. On approval of a new or amended policy the previous policy ceases to have effect and accordingly any provisions being carried over from a previous policy must be restated in the new policy to be effective (2008 Regulations sch. 8 para. 24(3)).

When considering the adoption or amendment of the executive director remuneration policy and practices, the remuneration committee should address the following factors within the policy:

- clarity
- simplicity
- risk
- predictability
- proportionality
- alignment to culture (Governance Code provision 40).

Table 6.4 sets out the disclosure requirements for the Remuneration Policy section of the directors' remuneration report.

Reference	Disclosure requirement
2008 Regulations sch 8, para 25	Future policy table
2008 Regulations sch 8, para 29	Approach to recruitment remuneration
2008 Regulations sch 8, para 30	Service contracts
2008 Regulations sch 8, para 33	Illustrations of application of remuneration policy
2008 Regulations sch 8, para 35A	For directors' performance targets covering more than one year an indication of the maximum remuneration receivable assuming share price appreciation of 50% during the performance period and details of the basis of the calculation used (for financial years beginning on or after 1 January 2019)
2008 Regulations sch 8, para 36	Policy on payment for loss of office
2008 Regulations sch 8, para 38	Statement of consideration of employment conditions elsewhere in the company
2008 Regulations sch 8, para 40	Statement of consideration of shareholder views

Table 6.4 Remuneration policy disclosures

Where a company's Implementation Report is voted down, the Remuneration Policy must be put to shareholders, to vote on at the next AGM (CA2006 s. 439A(2)(a)).

For years where a Remuneration Policy is not being put forward for voting on, it may be omitted from the directors' remuneration report for that financial year. However, details should be included as to when the last policy was approved and where a copy of the policy may be found, for example, on the company's website (2008 Regulations sch. 8, para. 1).

Guidance on the new regime was published by the GC100 in September 2013 and updated in 2016. Investor bodies such as the IA and NAPF have also updated their guidance.

4.4 Auditor's report

The purpose of the statutory audit is to provide an independent opinion to the members on the truth and fairness of the financial accounts and some sections of the narrative reports, whether the financial accounts have been properly prepared in accordance with the Act, and to report by exception to the members on the other requirements of company law such as where, in the auditor's opinion, proper accounting records have not been kept. As has been considered in previous chapters the directors are responsible for managing the affairs of the company and the audit assists the members, the owners of the business, in assessing the directors' stewardship. The audit focuses in particular on the directors' fiduciary responsibilities.

Other stakeholders have an interest in the audit and there is a clear public interest, however it is necessary not to lose sight of the fact that the purpose of a statutory audit, as defined in the Act, is that it is conducted for the benefit of the members. Customers, employees, suppliers and others that the company interacts with, as well as prospective investors and the public at large, often rely on the comfort provided by the auditor's opinion. However, these non-member interests, important as they are, are only consequential to the primary purpose of the statutory audit.

All companies' financial accounts must be audited unless the company is exempt from audit:

- as a small company (CA2006 s. 477);
- as a dormant company (CA2006 s. 480); or
- as a qualifying subsidiary (CA2006 s. 479A).

The auditor's report must include:

- the identity of the company the subject of the audit;
- a description of the annual accounts being audited (including the period covered by those accounts);
- a description of the financial reporting framework used in the preparation of the accounts;
- a description of the scope of the audit and confirmation of the auditing standards followed; and

◆   a clear statement of whether in the opinion of the auditor, the accounts:

  –   give a true and fair view;

  –   have been properly prepared in accordance with the relevant financial reporting framework; and

  –   have been prepared in accordance with the requirements of the Act (and, where applicable, Article 4 of the IAS Regulation) (CA2006 s. 495).

The auditor's report must:

◆   be either unqualified or qualified;

◆   include a reference to any matters to which the auditor wishes to draw attention by way of emphasis without qualifying the report;

◆   include a statement on any material uncertainty relating to events that may cast significant doubt about the company's ability to continue to adopt the going concern basis of accounting; and

◆   state the auditor's place of establishment.

CA2006 s. 496 requires that the auditor must state whether based on the work undertaken in the course of the audit:

◆   the strategic report (if any) and the directors' report are consistent with the accounts and have been prepared in accordance with applicable legal requirements;

◆   they identified material misstatements in the strategic report (if any) and the directors' report; and

◆   if applicable, give an indication of the nature of any such misstatement.

The auditors of a quoted company must include details on the auditable sections of the directors' remuneration report and whether in their opinion the directors' remuneration report has been properly prepared in accordance with the Act (CA2006 s. 497).

The audit report must be signed by the auditor or in the case of a joint audit by both auditors and state the name of the auditor(s). Where the auditor is a firm the audit report must be signed by the senior statutory auditor or in their own name on behalf of the firm (CA2006 s. 503).

4.5   Report to the audit committee

Article 11 of the Audit Regulation introduces a new requirement for the auditors to provide a detailed audit committee report, which must include:

◆   identification of the audit partner(s) responsible for the audit;

◆   if some of the audit work has been undertaken by another statutory auditor that is not a member of the same network, or has used the work of external experts, a statement of that fact and that the auditor has received confirmation from the other auditor or external expert regarding their independence;

- a description of the scope and timing of the audit;

- a description of the methodology used, including which balance sheet items have been directly verified and which have been verified based on system and compliance testing, any substantial variation in the weighting of system and compliance testing should be explained, even if the previous year's statutory audit was carried out by another auditor;

- the quantitative level of materiality applied, including qualitative factors considered, to perform the statutory audit for the financial statements as a whole and, where applicable, the levels for particular transactions, balances or disclosures;

- any significant deficiencies in the audited entity's or, in the case of consolidated financial statements, the parent undertaking's internal financial control and/or accounting systems;

- any significant matters identified during the audit involving actual or suspected non-compliance with applicable laws, regulations or the articles of association, considered to be relevant in order to enable the audit committee to fulfil its tasks;

- any significant difficulties or matters encountered in the course of the statutory audit and that were discussed, verbally or in writing, with management; and

- any other matters arising from the statutory audit that in the auditor's professional judgement, are significant to the oversight of the financial reporting process.

A listed company must ensure that the auditors review each of the following before the annual report is published (LR 9.8.10):

- the statement by the directors that the business is a going concern;

- the parts of the statement relating to corporate governance that relate to the following provisions of the Governance Code: principle M, provisions 6, 24–27, 30, 31 and guidance note 63; and

- any statements relating to corporate governance made in compliance with DTR 7.2.5 and 7.2.6 and whether DTR 7.2.2, 7.2.3 and 7.2.7 have been complied with.

4.6 Committee reports

For a listed company, the work of the audit, nomination and remuneration committees should be explained in the annual report (Governance Code provisions 27, 31 and 41).

Shareholders, both current and prospective, as well as analysts value the role of the audit committee and are comforted by the work they undertake. This reliance requires appropriate disclosure in the annual report, which should include:

- disclosures on significant issues;

- aspects of the audit that the committee paid particular attention to;

◆   actions taken to verify and monitor audit independence; and

◆   details of the audit tender, when relevant.

By their nature, nomination committees do not tend to have a regular cycle and often deal with ad hoc events though there are some continuing projects such as succession planning. Where there have been director appointments during the year, disclosure of the process and selection criteria will help with transparency surrounding director appointments.

It is now unusual to have a separate remuneration committee report as the work of the remuneration committee is included within the directors' remuneration report as discussed above.

5. Disclosure of financial statements

5.1   Availability of annual accounts and reports

Section 430 requires quoted companies to make available, on their website, their annual accounts and reports until annual accounts and reports for the next financial year are made available on the website.

A listed company must ensure that its financial statements are publicly available for a period of at least 10 years (DTR 4.1.4) .

The annual accounts and reports must be made available as soon as reasonably practicable, on a website that is maintained by or on behalf of the company, and that identifies the company in question. Access to the website must be available to all members of the public and not just to members of the company, continuously and free of charge. Any member or holder of debentures of a quoted company is entitled to be provided, on demand and without charge, with a single copy (in addition to any copy they might be entitled to under s. 423) of the following documents:

◆   last annual accounts;

◆   last directors' remuneration report;

◆   last strategic report;

◆   last directors' report; and

◆   auditor's report on the accounts (s. 432).

5.2   Filing requirements

Registrar
Companies must deliver a signed copy of their accounts, which need not be full accounts, whether audited or not, to the Registrar as follows:

◆   private companies within nine months of the year-end (CA2006 s. 442);

◆   public companies within six months of the year-end (CA2006 s. 442).

In the case of a financial year that is not 12 months, there are different provisions.

If the company's first accounting period is longer than 12 months, the period allowed for filing the accounts ends on the date nine or six months (as appropriate) after the first anniversary of the company's incorporation or, if later, three months after the end of the accounting reference period.

If the accounting period is shortened, the period allowed for filing the accounts is nine or six months, as applicable, or, if later, three months after the date of notice under CA2006 s. 392 shortening the accounting period (CA2006 s. 442).

Unlimited companies, other than those which are subsidiaries of limited companies, do not need to file their financial statement with the Registrar (CA2006 s. 448).

FCA

A listed company must publish its financial statements within four months of the year-end (DTR 4.1.3).

If a listed company makes a preliminary statement of its annual results, which must be approved by its auditors, this must be made as soon as practical after the statement has been approved by the directors (LR 9.7A1).

Test yourself 6.2

1. **Do micro and small companies need to file their profit and loss account with the Registrar?**

2. **Which legislation governs the content of corporate governance statements for listed companies?**

6. Legislative and other developments

6.1 Integrated reporting

Overview

Over recent years there has been a realisation that the proper recognition of the opportunities and risks facing directors in the achievement of the businesses long-term objectives requires much better and fuller explanation than can be achieved through the generally narrow focus of the annual report and accounts on financial results, measures and performance indicators.

Integrated reporting provides a framework for the reporting by companies on their business model and operational processes and priorities.

Purpose

The focus of integrated reporting is to provide a clear, cohesive and concise narrative of the corporate strategy, the significant key practical opportunities and risks that are being faced daily by management in pursuing that strategy and the financial measures and metrics to support that narrative.

Integrated reporting provides an opportunity for the directors to demonstrate clearly the fullest possible overview of the business' value creation strategy, the impact of current and anticipated macro and micro economic events, providing details of the measures in place, being put in place or available to be put in place to preserve or grow value.

Good integrated reporting will allow investors and in particular investment fund managers and advisers to gain better and easier insight into the company's culture and philosophy to create and preserve investor value. This better understanding in turn should lead to a reduction in the disconnect between investors' stated investment objectives and the corporate strategies and objectives of the companies they invest in together with a better alignment of the interpretation of the financial results with achievement of the long-term business strategy.

Implementation

Integrated reporting needs to deliver a wider range of information than the historic financial statements, in a concise manner that identifies the dependencies between:

◆   corporate strategy, business model and business environment;

◆   historic financial performance presented by reference to the business strategy, strategic objectives for those years, collectively and independently, and the business environment; and

◆   challenges, risks and opportunities encountered during those periods, the effect these had on performance, and strategic changes resulting from those challenges and opportunities.

Unlike classic financial reporting, there is no template that all companies can follow and instead the IIRC issued a discussion paper setting out five guiding principles and six content elements for integrated reporting as set out below.

Strategic focus and how that will create and grow sustainable value

Inter-connection between business model, external factors, resources, and relationships

Assessment of future prospects and uncertainties

Relationships with key stakeholders

Concise, reliable, material information to assess prospects of achieving the strategic goals

- Business overview and business model
- Operating environment, risks and opportunities
- Strategic objectives and road map to achievement
- Governance structure and oversight, board disclosures, remuneration
- Review of performance, qualitative and quantitative measures to achieve strategic objectives
- Future prospects, opportunities and challenges to be faced to achieve corporate strategy in the short, medium and long-term

Figure 6.9 Guiding principles and content elements for integrated reporting

6.2 BEIS

In March 2018 BEIS issued a consultation paper seeking views on proposals to improve corporate governance in firms that are in or approaching insolvency as well as the wider corporate governance framework.

It published its response to the consultation and details of proposed legislative changes in August 2018, including the following:

Insolvency measures:

◆ taking forward measures to ensure greater accountability of directors in group companies when selling subsidiaries in distress;

◆ legislating to enhance existing recovery powers of insolvency practitioners in relation to value extraction schemes; and

◆ legislating to give the Insolvency Service the necessary powers to investigate directors of dissolved companies when they are suspected of having acted in breach of their legal obligations.

Corporate governance measures:

◆ strengthen transparency requirements around complex group structures;

◆ enhance the role of shareholder stewardship;

◆ strengthen the UK's framework in relation to dividend payments; and

◆ bring forward proposals to improve boardroom effectiveness.

Chapter summary

◆ Different types of accounts available

◆ Accounting disclosures for listed companies

◆ Narrative reporting requirements

◆ Publications of financial statements

◆ Future developments in reporting, insolvency and corporate governance

Chapter seven
External audit

CONTENTS

1. Introduction
2. Roles and responsibilities of the company secretary in the external audit process
3. Independence of external auditors
4. Appointment of auditors
5. Rotation of auditors
6. Termination of auditors' appointment
7. Role of external auditors

1. Introduction

All companies, annual accounts must be audited (CA2006 s. 475) unless the company qualifies as exempt from audit:

1. as a small company (CA2006 s. 477);
2. as a subsidiary company (CA2006 s. 479A); or
3. as a dormant company (CA2006 s. 480).

The auditor's primary function is to report to the company's members on the statutory accounts prepared by the directors in accordance with CA2006 ss. 394 or 399, for individual company accounts and group accounts respectively (CA2006 s. 475).

Article 25a of the Statutory Audit Directive seeks to clarify the scope and purpose of the statutory audit. In particular, it notes that the statutory audit does not contain any assessment of the future viability of the company nor any judgement on current or future efficiency or effectiveness of the management.

The directors of a company that is exempt from audit may still chose to have the accounts audited. The members holding between them at least 10% in nominal value of the company's share capital, or for a company without shares 10% of the membership, may require an audit to be carried out (CA2006 s. 476). Any notice must be given during the period commencing at the start of the financial year the notice relates to and one month before that financial year ends.

2. Roles and responsibilities of the company secretary in the external audit process

Interaction with the auditor will be primarily with the finance function of a company but the company secretary may well be requested to assist with any non-financial queries and requests for information.

2.1 Access to documents

A company's auditor has the right enshrined in the Act to information in connection with the exercise of their duties and this includes the following:

◆ the right of access at all times to the company's books, accounts and records (CA2006 s. 499(1)(a));

◆ to require from the company's directors and officers such information and explanations as the auditor thinks necessary (CA2006 s. 499(1))(b);

◆ every UK incorporated subsidiary undertaking and their auditors must provide the auditors of the parent company such information and explanations as those auditors may reasonably require (CA2006 s. 499(2));

◆ a parent company, having an overseas subsidiary undertaking shall, if its auditors require, take all such steps as are reasonably open to it to obtain from the subsidiary such information and explanations as its auditors may reasonably require (CA2006 s. 500);

◆ an auditor is entitled to receive all notices and other communications relating to any general meeting (CA2006 s. 502(2)); and

◆ an auditor is entitled to attend general meetings of the company and has the right to speak on any business of the meeting that concerns them as auditor (CA2006 s. 502(3)).

The auditor will generally request copies of the minutes of meetings of directors, committees of the directors and members from the company secretary covering the period from the commencement of the financial year being audited up to the current date. The company secretary may well also be requested to review and obtain a director's signature on the auditor's formal engagement letter, provide details of any related parties and complete directors' remuneration disclosures.

It is an offence (punishable by fine and/or imprisonment) for an officer of the company, in conveying information and explanations required by the company's auditors, to make a statement that they know contains misleading, false or deceptive information (CA2006 s. 501).

If the company is a quoted company, the auditor must also report on the auditable parts of the remuneration report and state whether, in their opinion, the directors' remuneration report has been properly prepared in accordance with the Act (CA2006 s. 497). Any queries the auditor has with the remuneration report will most likely be directed to the chair of the remuneration committee through the company secretary.

The auditor must also report on the corporate governance statement and state in the audit report whether, in their opinion, the statement is consistent with the accounts (CA2006 s. 497A). Any queries the auditor might have with the corporate governance statements are likely to be directed to the company secretary in the first instance.

For accounting periods beginning on or after 1 January 2019, the directors of large companies are under a new obligation to provide details and evidence of how the directors have complied with their obligations under CA2006 s. 172. Such evidence will largely come from the directors' minutes, board packs and from discussion with the company secretary as there may well be examples of how directors fulfilled aspects of their s. 172 obligations but which have not been specifically minuted.

Test yourself 7.1

1. **Which documents and records are auditors entitled to have access to?**

2. **What are the three categories of companies that can claim exemption from audit?**

3. **Is an audit intended to provide reassurance as to the future prospects of the company?**

3. Independence of external auditors

The auditor's objective is to obtain reasonable assurance that the financial statements, prepared by company management, are free from material misstatement, whether due to fraud or error, and to issue a report to the company's members that includes the auditor's opinion in this regard.

Reliable company financial statements are key to the efficient and effective operation of capital markets. While directors are responsible for the accuracy of the financial statements and ensuring transparency of disclosures, auditors have a parallel responsibility to ensure the quality of the audit, and auditor independence is a key foundation on which that quality is built.

Being able to review the accounts objectively in order to obtain the required level of assurance requires that the auditor is independent of management and other business relationships that might cause them to lose that objectivity.

The Act reinforces this, and CA2006 s. 1214 requires that a person may not be appointed as a statutory auditor in respect of a company if the proposed auditor is:

◆ an officer or employee of the company;
◆ a partner or employee of the auditor or any associated undertaking, where the auditor is a company or a partnership;
◆ an officer or employee of an associated undertaking of the company; or
◆ a partner or employee of an auditor being a natural person, or a partnership of which such a person is a partner in a business directly or indirectly with the company or an associated undertaking of theirs.

An associated undertaking means in relation to a company being audited:

◆ a parent undertaking or subsidiary undertaking of the audited person; or
◆ a subsidiary undertaking of a parent undertaking of the audited person.

If once an audit has commenced the auditor becomes prohibited from acting as auditor of the company by virtue of the provisions of CA2006 s. 1214 they must immediately resign as auditor and give written notice to the company that they have resigned due to lack of independence (CA2006 s. 1215).

3.1 Non-audit services

The extent to which audit firms can undertake non-audit services to the same company without prejudicing their independence has been the subject of considerable debate over the years and is regularly revisited following high-profile accounting irregularities. In such circumstances, the quality of the audit is often called into question. Typically, the accusation is made that the auditors have allowed inappropriate accounting treatments because their independence has been compromised by the non-audit fees payable to them and/or that they are auditing their own work.

The professions believe that independence can best be guaranteed by applying a framework of principles rather than through rule-based legislation which can be adhered to while at the same time ignored in practice. This approach is very similar to the accountancy principle of substance over form. The accountancy bodies believe that a blanket prohibition on the provision of non-audit services to audit clients is not in the best interests of the client, does not ensure auditor independence and requires the audit firm to undertake additional assurance work to understand transactions to maintain the quality of their audit. The principles-based approach they argue recognises the reality that the auditor is not wholly independent of their client, but that the threats to independence must be acknowledged and actively mitigated to ensure that the risk is at an acceptably low level.

The argument against allowing audit firms to provide non-audit services is that auditor independence will inevitably be compromised by self-interest, self-review, being in an advocacy position, over-familiarity or intimidation.

Under the pan-European Statutory Audit Directive as amended by the Amending Directive and the Audit Regulation an auditor of a Public Interest Entity (PIE) is prohibited from undertaking certain specified non-audit services for their audit clients.

Article 5 of the Audit Regulation contains a list of non-audit services that must not be provided by the statutory auditor.

These prohibited services include:

1. tax services relating to: preparation of tax forms, payroll tax, customs duties identification of public subsidies and tax incentives unless support from the statutory auditor or the audit firm in respect of such services is required by law, support regarding tax inspections by tax authorities unless support from the statutory auditor or the audit firm in respect of such inspections is required by law, calculation of direct and indirect tax and deferred tax or provision of tax advice;

2. services that involve playing any part in the management or decision-making of the audited entity;

3. bookkeeping and preparing accounting records and financial statements;

4. payroll services;

5. designing and implementing internal control or risk management procedures related to the preparation and/or control of financial information or designing and implementing financial information technology systems;

6. valuation services, including valuations performed in connection with actuarial services or litigation support services;

7. legal services, with respect to: the provision of general counsel, negotiating on behalf of the audited entity or acting in an advocacy role in the resolution of litigation;

8. services related to the audited entity's internal audit function;

9. services linked to the financing, capital structure and allocation, and investment strategy of the audited entity, except providing assurance services in relation to the financial statements, such as the issuing of comfort letters in connection with prospectuses issued by the audited entity;

10. promoting, dealing in, or underwriting shares in the audited entity; and

11. human resources services, with respect to: management in a position to exert significant influence over the preparation of the accounting records or financial statements which are the subject of the statutory audit, where such services involve searching for or seeking out candidates for such positions or undertaking reference checks of candidates for such positions, structuring the organisation design or cost control.

Where an auditor provides non-audit services that are not prohibited, they must assess whether the provision of those services will have any effect on their audit independence.

Non-audit fees

In addition to the restriction on the types of non-audit services an audit firm may supply to a PIE there is also a restriction on the relative fees payable to the audit firm for audit and non-audit services. This cap on non-audit fees is set out in Article 4 of the Audit Regulation. The cap is expressed as a ratio to the audit fee and is that the auditor may not undertake non-audit services where the fee exceeds 70% of the average audit fees in the previous three consecutive financial years.

The Statutory Auditors and Third Country Auditors Regulations 2016 SI 2016/649 (SATCAR2016) require subsidiaries that are audited by an auditor other than the auditor of the consolidated group accounts to make a disclosure in the notes to their own accounts, as their audit and non-audit fees will not have been disclosed in the consolidated disclosure in the group accounts.

Stop and think 7.1

Audit independence is such a vitally important concept that when it is the auditors themselves who breach the rules, the penalties are quite severe. In 2018, KMPG and one of their audit partners were severely reprimanded and fined £2.1 million and £46,800 respectively by the FRC for breaching the ethical standards which led to a loss of independence in their audit of Ted Baker plc.

This happened as KPMG, the long serving auditors of Ted Baker plc undertook some non-audit services but failed to recognise that the rise in the quantum of the fees for that non-audit work from up to 20% of the audit fee to more than 200% of the audit fee breached their audit independence and could lead to a lack of objectivity or integrity as the audit would require them to self-review the firm's own work.

There was no suggestion that the audit was compromised or that there was any lack of objectivity or integrity but the penalties were levied due to the breach of a fundamental audit safeguarding standard.

Test yourself 7.2

1. **What type of individual or firm cannot be appointed as a company's auditor?**

2. **There are a number of non-audit services that auditors are prohibited from providing to a PIE, name five of them.**

3. **What is the ratio of permitted audit non-audit services fees for public interest entities?**

4. Appointment of auditors

SATCAR2016 Reg. 12 provides that any contractual clauses that restrict the choice of auditor have no legal effect. If a PIE has an audit committee it is required to state that no such clause has been imposed on it (CA2006 ss. 485A(5)(c)(ii) and 489A(5)(C)(ii)). PIEs must report to the FRC any third party attempt to impose such a clause or otherwise influence auditor choice.

4.1   Private company that is not a PIE

Unless the directors have reasonable grounds for believing that the company will qualify from exemption to appoint auditors, auditors must be appointed, for their first audited financial year, before the end of the period allowed for sending accounts to members or, if earlier, the date the accounts were sent to members. For subsequent years, the auditors must be appointed or reappointed within the period of 28 days commencing on the deadline for sending accounts to members or, if earlier, the date the accounts were actually sent to members. This period is known as the 'period for appointing auditors' (CA2006 s. 485).

The directors may appoint the first auditor to the company. The directors may also appoint an auditor following a period during which the company was exempt from audit or to fill a casual vacancy caused by the resignation or death of the previous auditor (CA2006 s. 485(3)).

In the normal course of events the directors will make the initial appointment of an auditor and the appointment is confirmed annually either by the members in general meeting or by there being no objection to the appointment automatically continuing in cases where no general meeting is held.

If a private company, which is not exempt, fails to appoint an auditor in accordance with CA2006 s. 485, the Secretary of State may appoint an auditor to fill the vacancy (CA2006 s. 486). In circumstances where auditors have not been appointed, the company must give notice to the Secretary of State within seven days of the expiry of the period allowed for appointing auditors.

An auditor can only be appointed to a non-PIE private company pursuant to CA2006 ss. 485 or 486, and may be deemed to be reappointed under CA2006 s. 487.

Where no auditor has been appointed by the end of the next period allowed for appointing auditors, the auditor in office immediately before that time is deemed to have been reappointed unless:

◆   their appointment was made by the directors;

◆   the company's Articles require actual reappointment;

◆   deemed reappointment is prevented by members under CA2006 s. 488;

◆   a resolution to reappoint the auditors is lost; or

◆   the directors have resolved that no auditor should be appointed for the financial year in question.

Pursuant to CA2006 s. 488, members holding between them at least 5% of the total voting rights may prevent the deemed reappointment of an auditor by giving notice in writing to that effect to the company before the end of the accounting reference period immediately prior to the time when the auditor would otherwise be deemed to be reappointed.

4.2 Public company that is not a PIE

Other than in the case of a dormant company, all public companies must appoint auditors. For their first financial year, auditors must be appointed before the meeting at which accounts are laid before the members (CA2006 s. 489(1)). The first auditors would usually be appointed by the directors, but can be appointed by the members if the directors fail to do so (CA2006 s. 489(3) and (4)).

For subsequent years, the auditors must be appointed or reappointed at the conclusion of the meeting at which the accounts for the previous financial year are laid before the members (CA2006 s. 489(2)).

The directors may also appoint an auditor following a period during which the company was exempt from audit or to fill a casual vacancy caused by the resignation or death of the previous auditor (CA2006 s. 489(3)).

If a public company fails to appoint an auditor in accordance with the provisions of CA2006 s. 489, the Secretary of State may appoint an auditor to fill the vacancy. The company must give notice to the Secretary of State within seven days of the conclusion of the meeting at which the previous accounts were laid before the members (CA2006 s. 490).

An auditor can only be appointed as auditor of a non-PIE public company pursuant to CA2006 ss. 489 and 490.

The appointment of an auditor to a public company does not automatically renew and their appointment ceases at the conclusion of the meeting at which the accounts are laid before the members, unless they are reappointed (CA2006 s. 491).

4.3 Audits of a PIE

The Statutory Audit Directive applies to PIEs, statutory auditors and audit firms. The Statutory Audit Directive was implemented in the UK through Parts 16 (Audit) and 42 (Statutory Auditors) of the Act and through a number of statutory instruments.

The Statutory Audit Directive was also implemented in the UK through the introduction of DTR 7.1.

The Statutory Audit Directive has been amended by an Amending Directive and also by the Audit Regulation both of which were implemented by SATCAR2016.

A PIE is defined in CA2006 s. 519A as a company, which meets at least one of the following criteria:

◆ an issuer with any transferable securities admitted to trading on a regulated market;

◆   a credit institution; or

◆   an insurance undertaking.

AIM and NEX Growth Market are not regulated markets and accordingly companies whose shares are traded on those markets will not be PIEs unless they are also a credit institution or insurance undertaking.

It should be noted that the definition of a PIE refers to transferable securities rather than equity shares and accordingly the issuers of listed debt instruments are covered by the legislation even if their equity shares are not listed and traded.

4.4 Appointment of auditors by a PIE

There was concern that, among other matters, there was a general lack of competition in the provision of audit services to the largest businesses and that audit firms might become complacent over time and lose vigilance or objectivity in undertaking their work. The UK had already introduced measures to restrict the appointment of auditors following an investigation and finding of the Competition and Markets Authority. The Audit Directive introduced pan-European legislation restricting the length of auditor appointments to PIEs for financial years beginning on or after 17 June 2016.

The Statutory Audit Directive has introduced mandatory audit firm rotation under which the same audit firm cannot be reappointed without a tender of the audit provision of audit services at least once every 10 years and cannot be appointed if they have continuously held the office of auditor for a period of 20 years.

If an audit tender process has not been carried out in the previous 10 years before the appointment by a PIE of an auditor, the audit committee, or directors where there is no audit committee, must undertake a public tender process in accordance with Article 16(3) of the Audit Regulation implemented by CA2006 ss. 485A, 485B, 489A and 489B. CA2006 ss. 485A and 485B apply to private companies and CA2006 ss. 489A and 489B apply to public companies. Article 16(3) sets out a detailed tender process to be followed by the audit committee. If the company does not have an audit committee, the directors must carry out the tender process and it is for the directors to decide how to carry out that process.

Whether carried out by the directors or an audit committee the opportunity to tender must be extended to at least two audit firms either of which has a reasonable chance of being appointed.

For PIEs that have an audit committee at the conclusion of the tender process the audit committee must make its recommendation to the full board of the preferred top two choices for auditor appointment and formally confirm that the recommendation is free from third party influence or contractual restriction. It is for the board as a whole to decide which of the two auditors to appoint. If the directors disagree with the preferred candidate of the audit committee, the directors must provide reasons.

Small or medium-sized enterprises within the meaning of Article 2(1)(f) the Prospectus Directive or in the case of a public company, a company with a reduced market capitalisation within the meaning in Article 2(1)(t) of the Prospectus Directive are exempt from these provisions.

4.5 Audit tender and maximum engagement period for auditors

The maximum term of office for the auditor of a PIE is the longer of:

◆ 10 years from the first day of the first financial year in respect of which the auditor was appointed (CA2006 ss. 487(1C)(a) and 491(1C)(a));

◆ 20 years from the first day of the first financial year in respect of which the auditor was appointed, provided that a tender process has been held for at least one financial year which begins every 10 years in that period (CA2006 ss. 487(1C)(b) and 491(1C)(b)); or

◆ such other period not exceeding 20 years beginning with the first day of the first financial year in respect of which the auditor was appointed and ending on the last day of the relevant 10-year period (CA2006 ss. 487(1C)(c) and 491(1C)(c)).

This means that PIEs must undertake a tender for their audit services at least every 10 years, with no auditor being able to hold office for more than 20 years, unless extended by up to a further two years by the FRC in exceptional circumstances (CA2006 ss. 487(1C) and 491(1C)). An extension cannot be granted if it would result in a period of office that exceeds 22 years.

The auditor of a PIE is not eligible for reappointment if within the previous four years they, or a member of the same network of auditors, have ceased to be auditor having held the appointment for the maximum engagement period (CA2006 ss. 487(1E) and 491(1E)).

In addition to audit firm rotation, audit partners are also required to rotate so that no audit partner is responsible for an individual PIE for more than seven years from their first appointment and cannot be reappointed for a further three years. There should also be gradual rotation for senior personnel involved in the statutory audit. The maximum period of appointment of an audit partner is lower than the period allowed for in the EU Directive as the FRC exercised the member state option to have a shorter period.

There are transitional provisions relating to the mandatory audit firm rotation requirements, as follows:

From 17 June 2020
Where a PIE has been receiving audit services from the same auditor for 20 or more consecutive years at 17 June 2016, it will no longer be able to reappoint that auditor;

From 17 June 2023

Where a PIE that has been receiving audit services from the same auditor for more than 11 but less than 20 consecutive years at 17 June 2016, it will no longer be able to reappoint that auditor.

4.6   Appointment of a partnership as auditor

Unless there is a clear statement to the contrary, the appointment of a partnership as auditor is an appointment of the partnership and not the individual partners (CA2006 s. 1216). Where the partnership ceases, the appointment is treated as having been extended to:

◆ any person who succeeds to that partnership having previously carried it on in that partnership and is an eligible person; or

◆ any partnership eligible and that succeeds the partnership that has ceased. A partnership is treated as succeeding another partnership only if the partners are substantially the same or if the new partnership takes over substantially the whole of the business of the previous partnership.

A partnership established under the laws of England and Wales or Northern Ireland, or any other country where partnerships do not constitute a legal person, ceases whenever there is not only a change on a dissolution, but also a change in partners. Partnerships established under the law in Scotland do constitute legal persons and do not cease on a change of partners.

Many firms of auditors have incorporated as either limited companies or limited liability partnerships. As corporate bodies, these firms have legal personality and it is the corporate body that is appointed. Where a partnership ceases, wherever established, and no person or firm succeeds the appointment, the appointment may be extended by ordinary resolution of the members to any person or firm succeeding to the business of the previous firm or such part of the business as comprised the appointment (CA2006 s. 1216(5)).

4.7   Exempt companies

A company that is exempt from having its accounts audited is also exempt from the obligation to appoint auditors. It should be noted, however, that a private company becoming exempt from the audit requirement does not automatically terminate the appointment of existing auditors, and in such circumstances the directors should resolve that no auditors be appointed for the financial year (CA2006 s. 487(2)(e)).

Certain transactions, such as the giving of a solvency statement on a proposed reduction of capital, require the company's auditor to confirm that the statement made by the directors is reasonable. For an audit exempt company this will necessitate the appointment of an auditor even though an audit of the financial statements is not required.

4.8 Auditor Remuneration

Remuneration of auditors appointed by the directors must be fixed by the directors. Remuneration of auditors appointed or reappointed by the members must be fixed by the members or in such other manner as the members may decide (CA2006 s. 492). In practice most companies seek authority from their members to authorise the directors to determine the remuneration of the auditors. For a public company, this resolution is usually combined with the resolution reappointing the auditors for the coming year when the current accounts are laid before the members.

The amount of the auditors' remuneration in their capacity as auditors, including any expenses, must be disclosed in the accounts (CA2006 ss. 493 and 494). Remuneration includes any cash value of any benefits in kind given to the auditors. In addition to remuneration for audit services, companies are required to disclose amounts paid to auditors and their associates for non-audit services such as financial or taxation services. Companies qualifying as small companies are exempt from these obligations to disclose auditors' remuneration and non-audit remuneration, and parent companies qualifying as medium-sized are exempt from the obligation to disclose non-audit remuneration (Companies (Disclosure of Auditor Remuneration and Liability Limitation Agreements) Regulations 2008 (SI 2008/489) (C(DARLLA)R2008) regs. 4–6).

4.9 Auditor liability

Except in specified circumstances there is a general prohibition on companies providing any form of liability limitation or other protection to their auditor (CA2006 s. 532). There are two exceptions to this general rule:

◆ A company may indemnify their auditor against any liability incurred (CA2006 s. 533):

– in defending proceedings (whether civil or criminal) in which judgment is given in favour of the auditor or they are acquitted; or

– in connection with an application under CA2006 s. 1157 in which relief is granted to the auditor by the court.

◆ A company may enter into a liability limitation agreement to limit the amount of liability owed to a company by its auditor in respect of any negligence, default, breach of duty or breach of trust, occurring in the course of the audit of accounts provided it (CA2006 ss. 534–8):

– relates to only one financial year; and

– is authorised by ordinary resolution of the members of the company. A private company may waive the requirement for the agreement to be approved.

Under CA2006 s. 538 and C(DARLLA)R2008 reg. 8 if a company enters into a limitation of liability agreement with its auditor the financial accounts to which the agreement relates must contain a disclosure of the principal terms of the agreement and the date of approval of the resolution approving the resolution or in the case of a private company the resolution waiving the need for such a resolution.

4.10   UK's competent authority

The FRC has been designated as the UK's competent authority and is given ultimate responsibility for regulatory tasks under the Statutory Audit Directive. The FRC continues to be the standard setting body for auditors and is to conduct inspections, investigations and disciplinary cases in relation to the audits of PIEs. The FRC can delegate tasks to recognised supervisory bodies. Amendments to Schedule 10 of the Companies Act 2006 set out the conditions that bodies must fulfil to qualify as recognised supervisory bodies.

Test yourself 7.3

1.   **Can anyone be appointed as a company auditor?**

2.   **Can the liability of the auditor be limited?**

3.   **How many consecutive years can an auditor be appointed to a PIE?**

5. Rotation of auditors

5.1   Audit partner

Although the Act does not place any restrictions on the period that one audit engagement partner has with a particular company, the Auditing Practices Board (APB) recognises that long association of engagement and other key partners as well as senior staff can pose a threat to the auditor's objectivity and independence.

The APB regularly reviews and updates its ethical guidance to auditors covering among other matters the period during which any partner or senior member of staff is associated with the same audit client.

Generally, it is for audit firms to establish their own procedures and maximum period of association with the same audit client. However, the APB notes that any association of 10 years or more needs careful consideration given as to whether it is probable that an objective, reasonable and informed third party would conclude the integrity, objectivity or independence of the firm or covered persons are compromised.

However, for a PIE, the APB recommends that the maximum period a key audit partner is responsible for carrying out the statutory audit should cease after a period of not more than five years and that a further period of five years should elapse before they participate again in that statutory audit. This period may be extended in exceptional circumstances at the request of the audit client and agreed by the audit firm in order to ensure the quality of the audit but the audit firm should implement additional measures to safeguard independence of the audit process.

5.2 Audit firm

Except for a company that is a PIE there is no maximum length of appointment of their auditor and the same firm may be appointed indefinitely, one year at a time.

PIE audit engagement periods are discussed above.

Stop and think 7.2

In the lead up to and following implementation of the Audit Directive a number of FTSE100 companies had to replace their auditors with companies such as Tesco and BAE each having had the same audit firm for more than 30 years.

Test yourself 7.4

1. **What does audit partner rotation guard against?**

2. **Do all companies need to change their audit firm regularly?**

6. Termination of auditor's appointment

The appointment of an auditor may be terminated by resignation of the auditor, removal by the members or on application to the court or by not being re-appointed by the members.

6.1 Resignation of auditors

An auditor may resign their office by giving notice to the company, with the notice taking effect on the date it is given or such later date as may be contained in the notice (CA2006 s. 516).

If the company is a PIE the notice has no effect unless it is accompanied with a statement setting out the reasons for their resignation and any matters connected with their resignation that they wish to be brought to the attention of the members or creditors of the company.

If the company is not a PIE the auditor must send a statement to the company setting out the reasons for their resignation unless (CA2006 s. 519):

◆ either:
  – in the case of a private company, at the end of a period for appointing auditors;
  – in the case of a public company, at the end of an accounts meeting;

◆   or:
   –   the auditor's reasons for ceasing to hold office are all exempt reasons; and

   –   there are no matters connected with the auditor's ceasing to hold office that the auditor considers need to be brought to the attention of members or creditors of the company.

The exempt reasons for an auditor's resignation are set out in CA2006 s. 519A(3) as follows:

◆   the auditor is ceasing to carry out statutory audit work within the meaning of the Act;

◆   the company is, or is to become, exempt from audit under CA2006 ss. 477, 479A, 480 or 482;

◆   the company is a subsidiary undertaking of a UK parent undertaking and:
   –   the parent undertaking prepares group accounts; and

   –   the auditor is being replaced as auditor of the company by the auditor who is conducting, or is to conduct, an audit of the group accounts; or

◆   the company is being wound up under IA1986 or I(NI)O1989, whether voluntarily or by the court, or a petition for the winding up of the company has been presented and not finally dealt with or withdrawn.

Where the auditor of a company that is not a PIE is required to make a statement but the auditor considers that neither the reasons for their resignation nor any other matters need to be brought to the attention of the members or creditors their statement should include a statement to that effect.

A resigning auditor of a company that is a PIE who makes a statement that they consider should be brought to the attention of members and creditors of the company may lodge a requisition calling on the directors to convene a general meeting of the company to consider the explanation of the circumstances connected with their resignation. The directors must convene this meeting within 21 days of the deposit of the requisition, to be held on a date not more than 28 days from the date of the notice convening the meeting (CA2006 s. 518). In addition, the auditor's statement must be sent to the members of the company with the notice of the meeting. If the statement is received too late for this to be done, the auditor may require that the statement be read out at the meeting. The statement need not be sent if, on the application of the company, the court is of the opinion that the provisions are being used by the auditor to secure needless publicity for defamatory matter.

Notwithstanding their resignation, the auditor is entitled to receive notice and to attend and speak at the meeting convened at their requisition or at any general meeting at which their term of office would otherwise have expired or at which it is proposed to fill the casual vacancy caused by their resignation (CA2006 s. 518(10)).

Accordingly, where an auditor of a PIE resigns during the year, notice of the next general meeting at which accounts are laid before the members must be sent to the previous auditor, and the appointment of auditors to fill the casual vacancy will require special notice to be given to the company, usually by a director.

6.2 Rights of auditors who are removed or not reappointed

Where a resolution is to be proposed at a general meeting or by written resolution for removing an auditor before the expiration of their term of office, or for appointing as auditor a person other than a retiring auditor, the following requirements must be adhered to:

- Copies of the special notice or of the written resolution must be sent as soon as practical by the company to the person proposed to be appointed as auditor and to the retiring auditor, as appropriate (CA2006 ss. 514(3), 515(3)).
- The auditor proposed to be removed or not reappointed may make representations in writing to the company on the proposed resolution and may ask the company to circulate that representation to the shareholders of the company (CA2006 ss. 514(4), 515(4)).
- The company must comply with that request. If it is too late to include the representation with the notice of the meeting, a note that a representation has been made should be included and a copy of the representations should then be sent to all the shareholders entitled to receive notice of the meeting (CA2006 ss. 514(5), 515(5)).
- If the representation is received too late to be circulated to shareholders, or if the representation is not sent out, the auditor concerned may require the representation to be read out at the meeting (CA2006 s. 515(6)).
- The auditor proposed to be removed or not reappointed is also entitled to receive notice of, and to attend and speak at, the general meeting at which the resolution for their removal or non-reappointment is to be considered.

The representations need not be sent out or be read at the meeting if, on the application of either the company or any other person claiming to be aggrieved, the court is satisfied that the rights conferred on the auditor proposed to be removed or not reappointed are being abused to secure needless publicity of a defamatory nature (CA2006 ss. 514(7), 515(7)). In these circumstances, the court may also direct that the company's costs in making the application be met in whole or in part by the auditor.

6.3 Company's obligation on cessation of auditor's appointment

A PIE and any other company receiving a statement from an auditor ceasing to hold office which contain reasons or matters that the auditor wishes to bring to the attention of the members or creditors must within 14 days of receipt of the statement either:

- send a copy of the statement to every person entitled under CA2006 s. 423 to receive a copy or the audited accounts; or
- apply to the court for an order that it need not do so.

If application is made to the court, the company must notify the auditor of the application. The court may reject the statement made by the auditor and order costs against the auditor in full or in part. Within 14 days of the judgment, the company must send a statement of the court's decision to those persons entitled to receive copies of the audited accounts. If the court upholds the auditor's statement, the company must issue the statement to those persons entitled to receive copies of the accounts within 14 days of the court's decision, including the auditor (CA2006 s. 520).

6.4   Auditor notification to Companies House and appropriate audit authority

If the auditor is not notified within 21 days that an application is to be made to the court, pursuant to CA2006 s. 520(2)(b) they must send a copy of their statement to the Registrar within the next seven days. If an application to the court is made and rejected, the auditor must send a copy of their statement to the Registrar within seven days of being notified of the court's decision by the company (CA2006 s. 521).

If an auditor sends a statement under CA2006 s. 519 to the company, they must at the same time send a copy of their statement to the appropriate audit authority (CA2006 s. 522).

6.5   Company notification to appropriate audit authority

Under certain circumstances, a company is required to notify the relevant audit authority that their auditor has ceased to hold office as auditor. The relevant audit authority will be either the auditor's recognised supervisory body or the FRC if the company is a PIE.

Figure 7.1 sets out the various options and conditions for deciding whether a notification is required and if so to which audit authority.

Stop and think 7.3

Once a company ceases to require an audit it is rare for the audit firm to continue as auditor and they are usually happy to resign not only as their audit services are not required but also partly due to the increased regulatory burden on audit firms in terms of record keeping in respect of audit clients.

Test yourself 7.5

1.   **When does an auditor of a PIE need to make a statement if they cease to hold office as auditor?**

2.   **Who are the relevant audit authorities?**

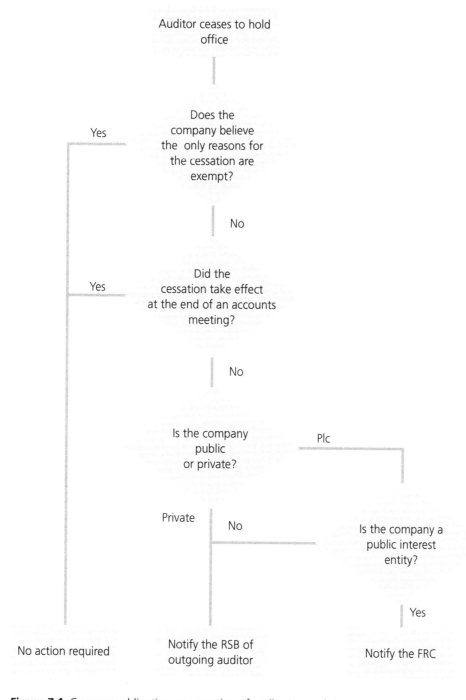

Figure 7.1 Company obligation on cessation of auditor's appointment

7. Role of external auditors

The auditor's objectives are to obtain reasonable assurance about whether the financial statements, prepared by the company's directors, overall are free from material misstatement, whether due to misunderstanding, error or fraud, and to issue a report to the members of the company.

Audits are carried out in accordance with International Standards on Auditing (UK) (ISA (UK)) and although reasonable assurance is intended to provide a high level of assurance, it is no guarantee that the audit will detect a material misstatement when it exists. Misstatements in the financial statements can be caused by error or deliberate fraud. ISA(UK) 2006 explains that in general, misstatements, including omissions, are considered to be material if, individually or in the aggregate, they could reasonably be expected to influence the economic decisions of users taken on the basis of the financial statements.

During the course of an audit, the auditor exercises professional judgement and should maintain professional scepticism throughout the audit.

At the conclusion of the audit, the auditor must make a report to the company's members (CA2006 s. 495). For private companies, the audit report must be sent to members in accordance with CA2006 s. 423; for public companies, the audit report must be laid before the members in general meeting in accordance with CA2006 s. 437.

7.1 Duties of auditor

In carrying out an audit of a company's accounts, an auditor must carry out sufficient investigations so that they can form an opinion as to whether:

◆ adequate accounting records have been maintained;

◆ the accounts are consistent with the accounting records; and

◆ in the case of a quoted company, the auditable part of the directors' remuneration report is consistent with the accounting records (CA2006 s. 498).

If, in the opinion of the auditor, one or more of these statements cannot be made, that fact must be stated in their report to members.

If the auditor does not obtain all the information or explanations they require, this fact must be stated in their report.

If the accounts do not contain the details of directors' remuneration, pensions and/or compensation for loss of office required by CA2006 s. 412, or, in the case of a quoted company, the details required by CA2006 s. 421 relating to the auditable part of the directors' remuneration report, the missing information must be contained within the auditor's report (CA2006 s. 498(4)).

If the directors have prepared accounts taking advantage of the regime available to small companies and, in the opinion of the auditor, the company does not qualify as a small company, this fact must be stated in the auditor's report (CA2006 s. 498(5)).

If the company is required to prepare and include in the directors' report a corporate governance statement in respect of the financial year and has not done so the auditor must state this fact in the audit report (CA2006 s. 498A).

7.2 Auditor's right to information and access

An auditor of a company enjoys certain statutory rights to information in connection with the exercise of their duties and they include a right of access at all times to the company's books, accounts and records (CA2006 s. 499(1)(a)). In addition to this right of access to the books and records the auditor can require individuals connected with the company to provide information or explanations necessary for the purposes of undertaking the audit. These individuals include:

- any officer or employee of the company;
- any person holding or accountable for any of the company's books, accounts or vouchers;
- any subsidiary undertaking of the company which is a body corporate incorporated in the United Kingdom;
- any officer, employee or auditor of any such subsidiary undertaking or any person holding or accountable for any books, accounts or vouchers of any such subsidiary undertaking (CA2006 s. 499(1)(a) and (2)).

A parent company, having a subsidiary undertaking that is not a body incorporated in the UK shall, if its auditors require, take all such steps as are reasonably open to it to obtain from the subsidiary, its officers, employees and auditor, and any person holding or accountable for any books, accounts or vouchers of any such subsidiary undertaking such information and explanations as the parent company auditors may reasonably require (CA2006 s. 500).

It is an offence (punishable by fine and/or imprisonment) for an officer of the company, in conveying information and explanations required by the company's auditors, to make a statement that they know is misleading, false or deceptive in a material particular (CA2006 s. 501).

The auditor is entitled to attend any general meetings of the company and to receive all notices and other communications relating to any general meeting. They may also speak on any business of the meeting that concerns them as auditor (CA2006 s. 502).

7.3 Auditor's report to members

The auditor is required to report to the members on their audit of the financial statements of the company (CA2006 s. 495).

The report of the auditor must include an introduction identifying the company, a description of the accounts including the financial year they cover and the financial reporting framework applied, together with a description of the scope of the audit work carried out and the accounting standards adopted.

The audit report must state clearly whether, in the auditor's opinion, the accounts (s. 495):

1. have been properly prepared in accordance with the relevant financial reporting framework;

2. have been prepared in accordance with the requirements of the Act and, where relevant, the IAS Regulations; and

3. have given a true and fair view:

    (a) in respect of the balance sheet of the state of affairs of that company at the end of the financial year;

    (b) in respect of the profit and loss account in respect of the financial year; and

    (c) in respect of group accounts of the state of affairs of the group at the end of the financial year, the profit and loss account of the company for the year, and any undertakings included in the consolidation as they affect the members of the company.

The auditor's report must:

◆ be either unqualified or qualified;

◆ include a reference to any matters to which the auditor wishes to draw attention by way of emphasis without qualifying the report;

◆ include a statement on any material uncertainty, if any, relating to events or conditions that may cast significant doubt about the company's ability to continue to adopt the going concern basis of accounting; and

◆ identify the auditor's place of establishment.

The auditor must state in accordance with CA2006 s. 496 in their report whether, in their opinion, based upon their work undertaken during the course of the audit:

◆ the information given in the strategic report (if any) and the directors' report for the financial year for which the accounts are prepared is consistent with those accounts, and any such strategic report and the directors' report have been prepared in accordance with applicable legal requirements; and

◆ in the light of the knowledge and understanding of the company and its environment obtained in the course of the audit, they have identified material misstatements in the strategic report (if any) or the directors' report, and if applicable, give an indication of the nature of each of the misstatements referred to above.

If the company is a quoted company, the auditor must also report on the auditable parts of the remuneration report and state whether, in their opinion, the directors' remuneration report has been properly prepared in accordance with the Act (CA2006 s. 497).

Where the company prepares a separate corporate governance statement in respect of a financial year, the auditor must include a statement in the audit report:

- whether, in their opinion, based on the work undertaken in the course of the audit, the information given in the statement in compliance with DTR 7.2.5 and 7.2.6:
    - is consistent with those accounts; and
    - has been prepared in accordance with applicable legal requirements;
- whether, in the light of the knowledge and understanding of the company and its environment obtained in the course of the audit, any material misstatements have been identified in respect of the disclosures made pursuant to DTR 7.2.5 and 7.2.6 and, if applicable, give an indication of the nature of each such misstatement; and
- whether, in their opinion, based on the work undertaken in the course of the audit, DTR 7.2.2, 7.2.3 and 7.2.7 have been complied with, if applicable (CA2006 s. 497A).

7.4 Report to PIE audit committees

Article 11 of the Audit Regulation introduces a new requirement for the auditors of a PIE to provide a detailed audit committee report which must include:

- the identify of the audit partner(s) responsible for the audit;
- if some of the audit work has been undertaken by another statutory auditor that is not a member of the same network, or has used the work of external experts, a statement of that fact and that the auditor has received confirmation from the other auditor or external expert regarding their independence;
- a description of the scope and timing of the audit;
- a description of the methodology used, including which balance sheet items have been directly verified and which have been verified based on system and compliance testing, any substantial variation in the weighting of system and compliance testing should be explained, even if the previous year's statutory audit was carried out by another auditor;
- the quantitative level of materiality applied, including qualitative factors considered, to perform the statutory audit for the financial statements as a whole and, where applicable, the levels for particular transactions, balances or disclosures;
- any significant deficiencies in the audited entity's or, in the case of consolidated financial statements, the parent undertaking's internal financial control and/or accounting systems;
- any significant matters identified during the audit involving actual or suspected non-compliance with applicable laws, regulations or the articles of association, considered to be relevant in order to enable the audit committee to fulfil its tasks;

◆ any significant difficulties or matters encountered in the course of the statutory audit and that were discussed, verbally or in writing, with management; and

◆ any other matters arising from the statutory audit that in the auditor's professional judgement, are significant to the oversight of the financial reporting process.

7.5 Signing of audit report

The auditor's report must state the name of the auditor and be signed and dated (CA2006 s. 503).

In the case of an auditor who is an individual, the report must be signed by that individual. In the case of an auditor that is a firm, the report must be signed by the senior statutory auditor in their own name on behalf of the firm.

The senior statutory auditor is the person identified by the audit firm as such in relation to that particular audit, and must in their individual capacity be capable of being appointed as auditor of the company (CA2006 s. 504).

Subject to CA2006 s. 506, every copy of the audit report that is published must state the name of the auditor and, where appropriate, the name of the senior statutory auditor (CA2006 s. 505). CA2006 s. 506 provides a limited exemption allowing the name of the auditor to be omitted if there are reasonable grounds to believe that the auditor or anyone associated with the auditor is at risk of violence or intimidation. Where advantage of the exemption is taken, the company must give notice to the Registrar stating:

◆ the name and registered number of the company;

◆ the financial year of the company to which the report relates; and

◆ the name of the auditor and, if applicable, the name of the person who signed the report as senior statutory auditor.

Test yourself 7.6

1. **Who is the audit report prepared for?**

2. **Is the audit process expected to uncover all errors or fraud?**

Chapter summary

◆ Interaction between the company secretary and the external auditors

◆ Importance of audit independence

◆ Process for appointment, resignation or removal of auditor

◆ Role of external auditors

Chapter eight
Securities exchange listing regime

CONTENTS

1. Introduction
2. Listing requirements
3. Ongoing reporting, filings and compliance
4. UK corporate governance code
5. UK stewardship Code
6. Insider dealing
7. Dematerialisation

1. Introduction

A Listed company is one whose shares have been admitted to the Official List maintained by the FCA in accordance with FSMA2000 s. 74. Once listed, a company will apply for its shares to be admitted to trading on a regulated market. The largest regulated market operating in the UK is the London Stock Exchange's (LSE) Main Market. Companies with shares admitted to trading on a public market are most often referred to as listed companies. Although there are alternatives to trading shares on the LSE's Main Market this chapter will refer to the processes for admission and continuing obligations for companies admitted to trading on the Main Market. These alternative markets include Euronext London and NEX Exchange.

This chapter looks at the procedure for listing a company's shares, the additional regulatory requirements to be adhered to, the types of public issue available to listed companies, the role of the exchanges as secondary markets and the admission and disclosure standards required of issuers and their major shareholders.

2. Listing requirements

2.1 Listing and the FCA

The FCA, under the guise of the UKLA is the UK 'competent authority' and exercises its powers under three EU directives and FSMA2000 regulating the admission of securities to official listing in the UK (see Figure 8.1).

EU legislation: Prospectus Directive, Transparency Directive – applies in the UK via the Prospectus Rules and the Disclosure and Transparency Rules			European Securities and Markets Authority (ESMA) – informal guidance
EU legislation: Market Abuse Regulations – applies directly across all EU States			
UK legislation: Financial Services and Markets Act 2000			UKLA – formal guidance
Listing Rules	Prospectus Rules	Disclosure and Transparency Rules	

Figure 8.1 Regulatory regime for Listed companies

As the competent authority, the FCA establishes the listing rules for admission of securities to listing, the continuing obligations of the issuers of those securities and the enforcement of those continuing obligations.

Applications for admission to listing (i.e. for securities to be admitted to the Official List) must be made to the FCA, and a separate application must be made to a regulated market such as the LSE for those securities to be admitted to trading on the Main Market. The procedures for seeking and maintaining a listing are set out in the Listing Rules, issued by the FCA.

These rules and the codes are not technically 'law'. The sanction for their breach is disciplinary action against the company and, ultimately, removal from the Official List so that among other matters the company's share price is no longer quoted and the shares no longer tradeable on an exchange. Breaches of the Listing Rules are within the scope of civil prosecution, and the FCA has power to impose unlimited fines on companies, directors or other individuals breaching the rules.

Listing principles
The FCA has established a number of principles applicable to all listed companies together with additional principles applicable to premium listed companies as shown in Table 8.2.

Principle	Description
Listing Principle 1	A listed company must take reasonable steps to establish and maintain adequate procedures, systems and controls to enable it to comply with its obligations.
Listing Principle 2	A listed company must deal with the FCA in an open and co-operative manner.
Premium Listing Principle 1	A listed company must take reasonable steps to enable its directors to understand their responsibilities and obligations as directors.
Premium Listing Principle 2	A listed company must act with integrity towards the holders and potential holders of its premium listed securities.
Premium Listing Principle 3	All equity shares in a class that has been admitted to premium listing must carry an equal number of votes on any shareholder vote. In respect of certificates representing shares that have been admitted to premium listing, all the equity shares of the class which the certificates represent must carry an equal number of votes on any shareholder vote.
Premium Listing Principle 4	Where a listed company has more than one class of securities admitted to premium listing, the aggregate voting rights of the securities in each class should be broadly proportionate to the relative interests of those classes in the equity of the listed company.
Premium Listing Principle 5	A listed company must ensure that it treats all holders of the same class of its premium listed securities and its listed equity shares that are in the same position equally in respect of the rights attaching to those premium listed securities and listed equity shares.
Premium Listing Principle 6	A listed company must communicate information to holders and potential holders of its premium listed securities and its listed equity shares in such a way as to avoid the creation or continuation of a false market in those premium listed securities and listed equity shares.

Table 8.2 Listing and premium listing principles

2.2 Regulatory regime

As noted above the offer for sale of shares in listed companies is subject to the legislation set out in FSMA2000 and the Listing Rules issued by the UKLA, derived in turn from and supported by EU legislation. Trading of those shares on the Main Market of the London Stock Exchange is subject to the Stock Exchange Rules. Figure 8.1 shows the relationship between the EU and UK legislation applicable to UK listed entities.

The regime is supervised by the FCA, to which most of the powers of the Secretary of State under the FSMA2000 have been transferred. The main feature of this regime is that, subject to certain exceptions, only authorised or exempt persons may carry on a regulated activity (FSMA2000 s. 19).

Regulated activity

Regulated activities are defined in FSMA2000 ss. 21 and 22 and Sch 2. In particular, it must be noted that financial promotion and investment activity includes giving any form of investment promotion and advice and investment management, as well as undertaking securities transactions as broker-dealer and/or principal within the UK. While new share issues are an obvious example, company secretaries need to be particularly careful when assisting employees with employee share options schemes to ensure that they are not inadvertently giving investment advice.

Stop and think 8.1

Company secretaries of listed companies operating employee share schemes must be very careful not to induce employees to take up options or other forms of share ownership as these could easily fall foul on the restricted activities of financial promotion or investment activity.

A person carrying on a regulated activity who is not authorised or not exempted commits an offence (FSMA2000 s. 20). Agreements made in respect of the regulated activity may be unenforceable by the unauthorised person (FSMA2000 ss. 26–28), and they may be made subject to a restitution order.

Authorised persons

The status of being an authorised or exempt person is conferred on application to the FCA by an individual or firm. Members of professional bodies such as solicitors and accountants are usually authorised by their professional body.

Premium and standard listing

The provisions for listing and the continuing obligations applicable to any particular company will depend on whether a premium or standard listing is sought. A premium listing is only available for equity shares of commercial companies, closed-ended investment funds and open-ended investment companies that meet the full set of requirements for a premium listing set out in LR 1.5.1 G(3).

The additional provisions applicable to premium listed companies, which go further than the minimum EU listing requirements, are intended to provide extra investor protection and promote investor confidence in the LSE as an investment exchange enhancing the LSE's reputation as a premier international capital market. The additional premium listed requirements are often referred to as 'super equivalent' requirements.

2.3 Eligibility

The eligibility requirements apply to all applicants seeking listing and admission to trading of their shares. In many cases these requirements must be adhered to on a continuing basis once listing and admission is granted. LR 2 sets out the requirements applicable to all applications supported by LR 6 and 14 applicable to premium and standard listings respectively.

Table 8.3 sets out the main criteria applicable to standard and premium listings.

Criteria	Premium Listing	Standard Listing
Transferability of shares	Shares must be fully paid and freely transferable (LR 2.2.4R)	Shares must be fully paid and freely transferable (LR 2.2.4R)
Market capitalisation on listing	Expected minimum market capitalisation of £700,000 (LR 2.2.7R(1))	Expected minimum market capitalisation of £700,000 (LR 2.2.7R(1))
Prospectus or listing particulars required	Prospectus or listing particulars required for admission (LR 2.2.10R, LR 2.2.11R, LR 3.3.2R(2) and FSMA s. 85), prospectus or listing particulars must be approved by the FCA (LR 2.2.10R, LR 3.3.2R(2) and FSMA s. 85)	Prospectus or listing particulars required for admission (LR 2.2.10R, LR 2.2.11R, LR 3.3.2R(2) and FSMA s. 85), prospectus or Listing particulars must be approved by the FCA (LR 2.2.10R, LR 3.3.2R(2) and FSMA s. 85)
Financial information to be provided in prospectus/listing document	Must have published or filed accounts that cover at least the last three years ending no more than six months before the date of the prospectus and have been independently audited and reported on by the auditors without modification (LR 6.2.1R(1)) *	Audited information covering the last two financial years (or such shorter period as the issuer has been in operation) and the audit report for each year must be disclosed in the prospectus (PR 3.1)
Trading record requirement	At least 75% of the issuer's business must be supported by a historic revenue earning record covering the period for which the audited accounts are required (LR 6.3.1R)	No trading record requirement
Control of assets requirement	The issuer must control the majority of its assets and have done so for at least the period for which the audited accounts are required (LR 6.1.4R(2))	No control of assets requirement
Independent business requirement	The issuer must carry on an independent business as its main activity (LR 6.4.1R)	A listed company must carry on an independent business at all times (LR 9.2.2A)
Controlling shareholder	An issuer with a controlling shareholder must demonstrate that it can carry on an independent business as its main activity (LR 6.5.1R) and must have a controlling shareholder agreement in place (LR 9.2.2AD)	An issuer with a controlling shareholder must demonstrate that it can carry on an independent business as its main activity and must have a controlling shareholder agreement in place (LR 9.2.2AB, LR 9.2.2AD)

Criteria	Premium Listing	Standard Listing
Control of business	The issuer must demonstrate that it exercises operational control over the business it carries on as its main activity (LR 6.6.1R)	The issuer must demonstrate that it exercises operational control over the business it carries on as its main activity (LR 9.2.2IR)
Working capital statement	'Clean' working capital statement required (LR 6.7.1R)	Working capital statement required (LR item 3.1, Annex III, PR 3.1)
Constitution to provide for pre-emption rights on new issues of shares	Shareholders must have pre-emption rights (LR 6.9.2R)	No pre-emption rights requirement
Restriction on amount of warrants or options	Warrants or options to subscribe for equity shares must not exceed 20% of the issued equity share capital at the time of issue of the warrants or options, excluding employee share schemes (LR 6.8.1R)	No restriction on amount of warrants or options
Free float requirement	25% minimum free float for each class of shares (LR 6.14.2R)	25% minimum free float for each class of shares (LR 14.2.2(3)R)
Adviser requirement	Sponsor required (LR 8.2.1R(1))	No adviser requirement

Table 8.3 Principal listing criteria

2.4 Listing process

Although the final version of the listing application is required to be submitted to the UKLA 48 hours prior to the proposed listing date in practice draft versions of the documentation, and in particular any prospectus or listing particulars, will have been submitted and discussed with the FCA over a period of many weeks and sometimes months to ensure that everything is in order.

The formal listing applications are made to the issuer management team at the FCA by submitting final versions of the following documents two business days prior to the application date (LR 3.3.2R):

◆ Application for Admission of Securities to the Official List.
◆ One of:
  – prospectus or listing particulars approved by the FCA;
  – prospectus approved in another EAA State;
  – a circular published in connection with the application; or
  – supplemental prospectus or supplemental listing particulars.
◆ Written confirmation of the number of shares to be allotted.

◆ If a prospectus or listing particulars are not required a copy of the announcement detailing the number of shares to be issued and the circumstances of their issue.

On the day of the application hearing, the following are required to be submitted, if relevant:

◆ shareholder statement if the class of shares is to be listed for the first time; or

◆ completed pricing statement where an issue of new shares comprising a placing, open offer, vendor consideration placing, offer for subscription or an issue out of treasury.

Provided all the documents can be approved, the requirements of the Listing Rules met, and the necessary fees paid the FCA will announce its decision to admit the securities via a market announcement and admission becomes effective at this time.

2.5 Types of public issue

There are several methods by which securities may be floated, including the following.

◆ **Capitalisation issues (or bonus issues):** The directors of a company may arrange for fully paid shares of the same class to be allotted free of charge to existing holders in proportion to their holdings, following the capitalisation of the company's existing reserves. This may be undertaken where the company's share price has risen to a level that is reducing the liquidity of the shares. The share price will fall approximately in line with the ratio of new shares issued.

bonus issue
Issue of additional shares to existing shareholders, in proportion to their current holding, already paid up in full out of the distributable reserves of the company.

◆ **Exchanges and conversions:** New securities may be listed as the result of existing securities being exchanged for, or converted into, new securities.

◆ **Exercise of options or warrants:** Securities may carry rights for the holder to subscribe cash for further securities or options may be issued offering the holder the right to acquire securities for cash during a specified period at a stated price, which are issued when the rights are exercised.

◆ **Intermediaries offers:** An intermediaries offer is a marketing of new securities to 'intermediaries' for them to allocate to their own clients, principally private client investors.

◆ **Introductions:** This is where existing securities are listed for the first time.

◆ **Offers for sale or subscription:** The company issues a prospectus in the form of listing particulars inviting application for its shares from investors. An offer for subscription is in the form of new securities issued directly by the company to the applicants. An offer for sale relates to new or existing securities, which are first acquired by an issuing house, which then offers the securities for sale to the public by issuing listing particulars and inviting applications.

◆ **Open offers:** Essentially this is the same as a rights issue; however, the benefit of the right is not permitted to be traded.

- **Placings:** As in an offer for sale, securities are subscribed or purchased by the sponsoring firm of stockbrokers or issuing house, but these are then 'placed' with investment clients, a proportion also being sold through the market.

- **Rights issues:** This is where a company offers new shares to its existing shareholders in proportion to the number of shares they already hold. The rights issue may be underwritten (see below) so that the company is assured of raising the full amount of the working capital it requires. The right to the new shares can itself be traded.

- **Vendor consideration issues:** A company that acquires a business or other assets may issue securities to the vendor instead of, or in addition to, cash.

- **Other issues:** Securities issued in circumstances other than those described above may be listed, provided the relevant conditions are fulfilled. Shares issued under employees' share schemes are a common example.

- **Underwriting:** Although not a type of issue, companies will often use underwriting to ensure the success or at least the minimum amount required is raised. Where a share issue involves the need for potential investors to apply for shares, take up their rights in a rights issue etc. there is always a risk that investors do not subscribe for 100% of the shares on offer. Companies will mitigate this risk by entering into underwriting agreements with specialist financial institutions who guarantee to take up any unsold shares in return for a fee typically between 3% and 7% of the issue price. Any shares they acquire will subsequently be sold in the market.

2.6 Role of the advisers

If not already appointed companies considering a listing of their shares either must or should consider the appointment of a range of advisers, including the following.

Sponsor

A sponsor is mandatory for a premium listed company and recommended for a standard listed company (LR 8.2.1R). Where appointed, the sponsor acts as the link between the company and the FCA, UKLA and the LSE.

Corporate broker

The broker acts as a link between the company and investors following listing and admission to the market. Most brokers retain analysts who will issue research notes on companies, and it is important to select a broker with analysts that have appropriate expertise in the company's sector.

Many firms can act as both sponsor and broker, and this may be appropriate. However, one firm acting in both capacities can cause difficulties where the sponsoring arm has information that, if passed to the broking arm, would put them in the position of not being able to trade in the company's shares, as they would be in possession of price-sensitive information which would give them an unfair advantage when trading shares.

The broker will also actively market the shares to secure the success of the issue. This process is often referred to as book building. During the book-building phase, non-binding commitments to invest are obtained for an aggregate amount of money, as until the last day of any offer, the actual share price will not be known.

Financial public relations consultants

Although some companies will already retain a firm of advertising and marketing consultants, it is advisable to retain a firm of specialist financial PR consultants. Financial PR consultants play a crucial role in raising and maintaining a company's profile during the book-building and fund-raising phases leading up to and after flotation and maintaining awareness of the company to maintain liquidity once the initial flurry of activity associated with the float has subsided. Financial PR consultants will also ensure, in conjunction with the company lawyers, that statements issued by the company comply with FSMA2000 and UKLA disclosure requirements.

Lawyers

Typically, there will be two firms appointed, the first advising the company and the second advising the sponsor. The company's lawyers will often lead the process of drafting documents in conjunction with the sponsor and with all other interested parties commenting on those drafts.

The company lawyers will also undertake verification. This is the process under which factual statements within the documents are verified to prove that they are based on fact. Verification is a painstaking task requiring companies to search their archives for old documents, agreements, research notes, etc. Verification is essential to ensure that statements made by directors are true and that potential investors can rely on these statements. Directors carry personal liability for false and misleading statements in prospectuses or listing particulars.

Reporting accountant

Although this is a separate and distinct function from that of the company auditor, the reporting accountant is often the company auditor, albeit staffed from the corporate finance department rather than the audit department. The reporting accountant's role is to review the company's financial history, accounting systems and internal controls, and to prepare a report for the benefit of potential investors.

Depending on the nature of the transaction, there are three forms of report that might be required.

1. A long form report is a detailed analysis of past financial performance and management structures, strengths and weaknesses. The long form report is not published but is provided to both directors and the sponsor and is used to draft the prospectus.

2. The short form report, as the name implies, is an abridged version of the long form report and is reproduced in the prospectus.

3. The last report that is usually prepared where additional funds are being raised is a working capital report for the sponsor, covering the period 12–

24 months following admission. This is to provide comfort to the sponsor that the company will have sufficient working capital for the period covered by the report, assuming any funds to be raised are actually raised. Additionally, although it is preferable to raise slightly more funds than are required, raising surplus capital has a detrimental effect on share price.

Share registrars

Whether the shares are to be listed and traded on the Main Market or another market, the company will need to retain the services of a CREST compliant share registrar to maintain the share register and is required in order to facilitate electronic share trading and settlement via CREST.

It is the share registrar that will maintain the register of members, preparing mailing lists whenever documents are required to be issued to members, as well as processing dividend and other payments to members as required.

Other advisers

Additional advisers that may be required include surveyors to value properties and other material assets, security printers for the secure and rapid turnaround of any prospectus or offer documentation, insurance brokers and trademark and patent attorneys.

2.7 Prospectus Rules

The Prospectus Rules derive from European legislation and implement the Prospectus Directive. The Prospectus Regulations 2005 (SI 2005/1433) required EU States to draw up rules for the contents, approval and publication of prospectuses issued in respect of public offers of securities. In the UK, this was delegated to the FCA.

The Prospectus Rules came into force on 1 July 2005 and are set out in the FCA Handbook and updated periodically. The rules cover the format and detailed content of a prospectus, the period during which a prospectus remains valid and the manner in which a prospectus must be published. They reiterate the general rule that a person may not make an offer of securities to the public, or seek admission to trading on a regulated market, unless a prospectus has been prepared, approved by the FCA and published.

What is an offer to the public?

Under the Prospectus Rules, there is an offer to the public if there is a communication to any person that presents sufficient information on the transferable securities to be offered and the terms on which they are offered to enable an investor to decide to buy or subscribe for the securities in question. The definition is very broad and can include offers by private companies.

The communication may be in any form and by any means and includes placing through financial intermediaries.

There are a number of exemptions for small offers or to a restricted group of potential investors.

Exemptions

The key exemptions from the requirement to publish a prospectus under the prospectus regime are:

◆ offers addressed to fewer than 150 people (other than qualified investors) in any 12-month period per EEA state;

◆ offers to 'qualified investors' only – i.e. broadly institutions and companies that are not SMEs; and SMEs and individuals who register as qualified investors, based on certain conditions;

◆ offers to persons outside the UK (although local laws would then apply);

◆ the minimum subscription per investor is at least €100,000, or equivalent;

◆ where the denomination of the securities is at least €100,000, or equivalent; or

◆ offers where the total consideration for securities in any period of 12 months is under €8 million or equivalent.

Prospectus contents

Under the Prospectus Rules, companies may choose to prepare a single document or a three-part prospectus containing a registration document containing details of the issuer, a securities note containing details of the shares being offered and a summary document.

As noted above it is extremely important that the prospectus contents are verified as directors carry personal liability for false or misleading information set out in the prospectus.

The single document is the most common form of prospectus while the three-part document is most useful for frequent issuers as the registration document remains valid for up to 12 months.

A single document prospectus must contain the following sections, and in this order (PR 2.2.10):

◆ a clear and detailed table of contents;

◆ a summary containing, on the front page, a prescribed 'health warning' which conveys concisely, in plain English and in an appropriate structure, the key information relevant to the securities that are the subject of the prospectus and which, when read with the rest of the prospectus, is an aid to investors considering whether to invest in the securities. The Amending Directive requires summaries to be prepared in a common format set out in five mandatory sections in the following order:

    (i)   introduction and warnings;

    (ii) issuer and any guarantor;

    (iii) securities;

    (iv) risks; and

    (v) offer;

◆ the risk factors linked to the issuer and the type of security covered by the issue; and

◆ the specific information on the issuer and securities required by the various schedules to, and 'building blocks' set out in, the Prospectus Rules. Although there are a large number of these 'building blocks' for the majority of ordinary share based offers the following will be required:

- registration document containing:
  - details of those responsible for the document;
  - risk factors specific to the issuer or industry;
  - information about the issuer;
  - business overview;
  - organisation structure;
  - property, plant and equipment;
  - operating and financial review;
  - capital resources;
  - research and development, patents and licences;
  - significant trends;
  - profit forecasts and estimates;
  - information on the directors and senior managers;
  - remuneration and benefits;
  - board practices;
  - employees;
  - major shareholders;
  - related party transactions;
  - financial information covering the three previous financial years;
  - legal and arbitration proceedings;
  - additional information; and
  - display documents;
- share security note:
  - risk factors specific to the securities;
  - working capital statement;
  - capitalisation and indebtedness;
  - material conflicts of interests post offer;
  - reasons for the offer and use of proceeds;
  - details of the securities to be offered;
  - terms and conditions;
  - admission to trading and dealing arrangements;
  - selling shareholders;
  - expenses of the offer; and
  - dilution.

Prospectus approval

The draft prospectus must be submitted to the UKLA, part of the FCA for approval (PR 3.1.1R).

Where the issuer does not already have listed shares and had a prospectus approved by the FCA, the completed Form A, the relevant fee, and drafts of all other documents referred to above must be submitted to the FCA at least 20 working days before the intended approval date.

In cases where the issuer is already listed and had a prospectus approved by the FCA, the completed Form A, the relevant fee and drafts of all other documents referred to above must be submitted to the FCA at least 10 working days before the intended approval date.

In either case, final versions of any draft documents must be submitted to the FCA before midday on the proposed approval date.

2.8   LSE as secondary market

As a primary market the LSE provides companies with cost efficient access to some of the world's deepest and most liquid pools of capital.

Once shares have been issued the LSE provides fast and efficient trading of listed shares admitted to trading on its Main Market. This secondary market is important as it allows investors to realise their investment at a time of their choosing and as a result making the availability of capital on the primary market more attractive to investors.

Dealings on the LSE are conducted in accordance with the rules, regulations and usages of the LSE and the conduct of business rules of the FCA (or a self-regulatory organisation (SRO), as appropriate).

Trading systems

The LSE operates various trading services to enable trading in constituent company shares.

◆   *SETS* (or the 'Order book') – SETS is the LSE's premier electronic trading service that combines electronic order-driven trading with integrated market maker liquidity provision, delivering guaranteed two way prices.

◆   *SEAQ* – SEAQ is the LSE's non-electronically executable quotation service that allows market makers to quote prices in a number of fixed interest securities.

◆   *SETS Intra-day Auction* – this scheduled daily SETS intra-day auction is a midday price forming auction mechanism for trading larger sized orders.

◆   *SETSQX* – SETSqx (Stock Exchange Electronic Trading Service – quotes and crosses) is a trading service for securities less liquid than those traded on SETS. SETSqx combines a periodic electronic auction book with standalone non-electronic quote driven market making. Electronic orders can be named or anonymous and for the indicated securities order book executions will be centrally cleared.

2.9 Admission and disclosure standards

A company whose securities are admitted to trading on the LSE's Main Market must also comply with the continuing obligations contained in the Exchange's Admission and Disclosure Standards. For the moment, these replicate the general disclosure obligations contained in the Listing Rules. Accordingly, compliance with the Listing Rules should also ensure compliance with the LSE Standards.

The LSE has adopted these Standards to enable it to enforce its market supervision function. The company services team at the LSE processes applications for admission to trading and deals with all other aspects of the LSE's relationship with companies. The team does not review draft prospectuses, listing particulars or any other circulars. These reviews are carried out by the FCA.

Eligibility criteria

1. An application for admission to trading of any class of securities must relate to all securities of that class, issued or proposed to be issued or further securities of a class that is already admitted, issued or proposed to be issued.

2. The company must be in compliance with the requirements of any securities regulator by which it is regulated and/or any stock exchange on which it has securities admitted to trading.

3. In the case of transferable securities, all such securities must be freely negotiable.

4. Securities that are admitted to trading by the LSE must be capable of being traded in a fair, orderly and efficient manner.

5. The LSE may refuse an application for the admission if it considers that the applicant's situation is such that admission of the securities may be detrimental to the orderly operation or integrity of its markets, or the applicant does not or will not comply with the standards or with any special condition imposed by the LSE.

6. Companies must confirm that they meet the criteria and requirements of the market to which they are applying.

Settlement

To be admitted to trading, securities must be eligible for electronic settlement.

Communication

Companies must provide details of a contact within their organisation who will be responsible for communications between the LSE and the company. A company may wish to use a designated representative.

Issuers must ensure that all information provided in connection with admission to trading is accurate, complete and not misleading, and must be open and honest in all dealings with the LSE.

2.10 Disclosure and Transparency Rules

All listed companies are required to ensure that they have adequate procedures, systems and controls to enable them to comply with their obligations (Listing Principle 1). This is expanded upon in Premium Listing Principle 6 that premium listed companies must communicate information to holders and potential holders of its premium listed securities and its listed equity shares in such a way as to avoid the creation or continuation of a false market in those premium listed securities and listed equity shares.

The disclosure regime for listed companies is set out in the Market Abuse Regulations (MAR 16–19) and in DTR 4 & 6. The specific obligations are discussed in more detail in section 3 below.

Companies should have a framework for the control of **inside information** and establish effective arrangements to restrict access to inside information to those persons who require access to perform their job. Under MAR 17 companies must publish 'inside information', via an RIS, that directly concerns them as soon as possible and must post and keep on its website, for five years, copies of all inside information publicly disclosed (MAR 17(1)).

Such a framework is likely to include establishing and implementing a clear written procedure, systems and controls and a policy for the handling and disclosure of inside information. In addition to having these written procedures, it is important to train and update relevant officers and employees on the procedures for handling inside information.

As a minimum it is recommended that companies should have a disclosure manual and a checklist for identifying inside information and consider establishing a disclosure committee to review and monitor the company's compliance with its disclosure obligations. Use of a disclosure committee should ensure that decisions are made by those with sufficient understanding of the company's obligations, particularly where disclosure is to be delayed and to ensure a consistent approach is employed to disclosure obligations and any announcements required.

inside information
Is information that is precise, has not been made public, relates directly or indirectly to the company and if made public is likely to have a significant effect on the price of the company's shares or securities (that is information that a reasonable investor would be likely to use as part of the basis of their investment decisions).

Stop and think 8.2

As can be seen from the content requirement and list of documents required for a listing, the whole process often takes more than one year to complete and has a significant drain on the executive directors' time as well as a financial cost should the listing process be stopped late on in the process.

Test yourself 8.1

1. **What are the two market functions provided by the LSE?**

2. **Why are applications to both the UKLA and LSE required to list on the Main Market?**

3. Ongoing reporting, filings and compliance

There are a number of additional reporting, disclosure and other obligations placed on listed companies from a number of sources including the Act, the Listing Rules, the Disclosure and Transparency Rules and the Market Abuse Regulations.

3.1 Financial

Accounting reference date
A listed company must make a market announcement via an RIS as soon as possible, of any change in its accounting reference date and confirmation of the new accounting reference date (LR 9.6.20R).

Annual report and accounts
A listed company must publish its annual financial statements within four months of the end of the financial year and ensure that copies of its annual report and accounts are freely available on request for a period of at least 10 years from their original publication (DTR 4.1.3R and 4.1.4R).

As discussed in chapter 6, listed companies are required to include additional information and disclosures in their annual accounts and any interim accounts.

Auditor's report
The report of the auditors of a listed company must include details on the additional auditable sections of the annual report (LR 9.8.10R):

◆ the statement by the directors that the business is a going concern;

◆ the parts of the statement relating to corporate governance that relate to the following provisions of the 2016 Governance Code: C1.1, C.2.1 and C.2.3 and C3.1 to C3.8 (Governance Code principle M, provisions 6, 24–7, guidance 63); and

◆ any statements relating to corporate governance made in compliance with DTR 7.2.5 and 7.2.6 and whether DTR 7.2.2, 7.2.3 and 7.2.7 have been complied with.

Directors' remuneration report
CA2006 s. 420 contains the directors' duty to prepare a remuneration report. The duty applies to every person who was a director of the listed company

immediately before the period for filing the accounts, and failure to comply constitutes an offence punishable by a fine.

The Large and Medium-sized Companies and Groups (Accounts and Reports) (Amendment) Regulations 2013 (SI 2013/1981) specify the extent to which the directors' remuneration report should be subject to audit. The 'auditable' part of a directors' remuneration report is the part containing the information required by paragraphs 4 to 17 of Part 3 of Schedule 8 to the Regulations, which includes the amount of each director's emoluments and compensation in the relevant financial year, and details on share options, long-term incentive schemes and pensions.

A listed company must put a resolution, at the same meeting convened to receive the annual accounts, approving the directors' remuneration report. The resolution is an advisory one and, if lost, does not invalidate the payment of directors' remuneration (CA2006 s. 439).

In addition to the usual obligation to file the various reports and financial statements making up the annual report and accounts, listed companies have a specific additional obligation to file their remuneration report with Companies House together with the auditor's report on the auditable parts of the directors' remuneration report (CA2006 s. 447).

Directors' report
The directors of a listed company must also disclose details on the acquisition of their own shares in their directors' report.

Dividends
A listed company must make a market announcement via an RIS as soon as possible after the directors have approved any decision to pay a dividend or other distribution including the following details:

- net amount payable per share;
- payment date;
- record date; and
- any foreign income dividend election and any income tax treated as paid at the lower rate and not repayable (LR 9.7A.2R).

Publication of financial statements
CA2006 s. 430 requires listed companies to make available, on their website, their annual accounts and reports until annual accounts and reports for the next financial year are made available on the website.

A listed company must forward to the FCA for publication through the document viewing facility a copy of its financial statements and issue an announcement via an RIS that the accounts have been made available and where they may be viewed (LR 9.6.1R, LR 9.6.3R).

Resignation of auditors

An auditor of a listed company on ceasing to hold office, for any reason, is required to deposit, at the company's registered office, a statement of the circumstances connected with their ceasing to hold office. This statement is required even if there are no circumstances connected with their resignation that they consider need to be brought to the members attention. Auditors leaving listed companies will always be required to make a statement of the circumstances (CA2006 s. 519).

In addition to filing a copy of the auditor's resignation with Companies House, companies that constitute major audits are required to notify the FRC. The notification must include the statement of circumstances from the auditor if they consider there are matters to be brought to the attention of members, or, if there are none, the company must itself state why the audit appointment has terminated (CA2006 s. 523(2)).

Figure 8.4 shows the correct notification procedure under different scenarios.

Rights of members to raise audit concerns

CA2006 527(1) permits the members of a listed company, either holding between them 5% of the total voting rights or from at least 100 members holding on average shares with a nominal paid-up capital of £100, to require the company to publish, on a website, a statement setting out any matter relating to the audit of the company's accounts that are to be laid before the next accounts meeting, or any circumstances connected with a departing auditor of the company since the previous accounts meeting, that the members propose to raise at the next accounts meeting of the company.

Summary financial information

Companies may circulate the strategic report and supplemental material to their shareholders in place of the full statutory accounts. Any shareholder receiving the strategic report and supplemental material may require that the full accounts be sent to them (CA2006 s. 426).

Any strategic report and additional material provided to members must disclose (LR 9.8.13) earnings per share, and the content of the strategic report and additional information set out in CA2006 s. 426A.

3.2 Issues of securities

Whenever a listed company issues more securities, those new securities must be listed and admitted to trading. Many companies, especially those with active employee share schemes, regularly issue new shares. To ease the administrative burden, companies may choose to submit block listing information. Under this process, a pool of shares is effectively pre-listed and admitted to trading; this is known as a block listing. Following the initial application, companies submit block listing returns every six months, setting out details of the amount of the pool that has been drawn down and issued.

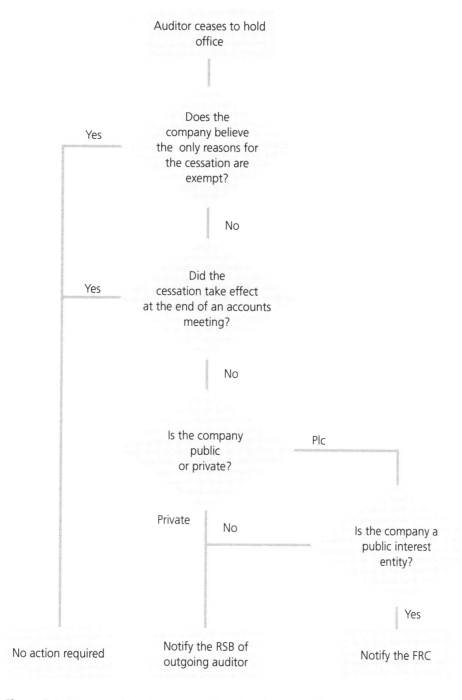

Figure 8.4 Company obligation on cessation of auditor's appointment

3.3 Constitutional changes

Any changes to a company's constitution or its officers will require notification to the market. These changes can include:

- the appointment, resignation or removal of directors or auditors;
- change of company name or accounting reference date;
- results of resolutions at meetings of the members;
- any material change to the company's trading prospects; or
- corrections or confirmation of market expectations, where different from previously published information or guidance.

3.4 Disclosure of inside information

MAR implemented a common EU approach for preventing and detecting market abuse and ensuring a proper flow of information to the market and introduced a significant increase in the record keeping and reporting requirements.

The primary obligation of companies under MAR relates to the control and disclosure of inside information and dealing by PDMRs (MAR 17–21). Investments firms have additional responsibilities to monitor and report investment transactions and suspicious activities for the prevention of market manipulation and other fraudulent activity.

MAR and DTR
MAR works in tandem with DTR and these have been updated to reflect changes introduced by MAR. DTR 4 and 6 apply to listed shares on an RIE while DTR 5 applies to companies with shares listed on an RIE or on a prescribed market.

The ability to share inside information with those owing a duty of confidentiality can only be relied on where the recipient needs that information to provide services or advice to the company (DTR 2.5.7). Where a selective disclosure has been made, a holding announcement should be prepared for release as soon as possible in the event of a leak (DTR 2.6.3). Any holding announcement should contain as much detail on the subject matter as possible, the reasons why a fuller announcement cannot be given and an undertaking to announce further details as soon as possible (DTR 2.2.9).

Under MAR 17:

- Companies must publish 'inside information', via an RIS, that directly concerns them as soon as possible and must post and keep on its website, for five years, copies of all inside information publicly disclosed (MAR 17(1)).
- Disclosure of inside information may be delayed if (MAR 17(4)):
  - immediate disclosure is likely to prejudice the company's legitimate interests;
  - delayed disclosure is unlikely to mislead the public; and
  - the company can ensure the information remains confidential until it is disclosed.

◆   Where a disclosure has been delayed the company must notify the FCA of that fact immediately after the information has been disclosed and provide an explanation if requested.

Inside information is information that is precise, has not been made public, relates directly or indirectly to the company and if made public is likely to have a significant effect on the price of the company's shares or securities (that is information that a reasonable investor would be likely to use as part of the basis of their investment decisions) (MAR 7(1)(b) to (d)).

Other than in situations where the recipient owes a duty of confidentiality where a company or a person acting on its behalf discloses inside information to a third party in the normal course of employment or profession there must also be complete public disclosure of that information simultaneously in the case of a planned disclosure or as soon as possible in the case of a non-intentional disclosure (MAR 17(8)).

Companies should have a framework for the control of inside information and establish effective arrangements to restrict access to inside information to those persons who require access to perform their job. A company should maintain insider lists in relation to employees and advisers with access to inside information (MAR 18).

Companies must have deal specific or event-based insider lists and may have a permanent insider list. To be entered on a permanent insider list the individual will be assumed to have access to all inside information at all times. As a result, any permanent insider list is likely to be very short.

Deal specific or event-based insider lists must be kept in electronic form, must adhere to the format laid down by the regulations, must be retained for five years and must be capable of being produced to the FCA as soon as possible on request (MAR 18(1)(c), 18(3) and 18(5)).

The minimum content for the insider lists is:

◆   identity of each person with access to the information;
◆   reason why the person is on the insider list;
◆   date and time that person obtained access to the information; and
◆   date on which the insider list was drawn up.

Companies are required to keep their insider lists up to date. The list must also contain:

◆   date and time of any change in the reason for inclusion on the insider list;
◆   date and time any new person is added to the insider list; and
◆   date and time when a person ceases to have access to inside information.

All insiders must acknowledge in writing their legal and regulatory duties and that they are aware of the sanctions applicable to **insider dealing** and unlawful disclosure of inside information (MAR 18(2)).

insider dealing
Buying or selling shares on the basis of an unfair advantage derived from access to price-sensitive information not generally available. Insider dealing is a criminal offence.

Disclosure committee

Although not mandatory companies are recommended to establish a disclosure committee in particular to manage the process where disclosure is being delayed. There must be a formal internal process and clarity on who is responsible for taking decisions on disclosure or delaying disclosure of inside information.

Companies are expected to have in place appropriate procedures and arrangements ensuring the process for delaying disclosure of inside information is managed effectively and documented. This includes an effective level of organisation and process to assess whether information is inside information and whether disclosure is permitted to be delayed, including appointing persons within the issuer responsible for taking the relevant decisions. Ongoing monitoring is essential during the period of delay to ensure that the conditions for permitting the delay and assessing the continuing confidentiality of the information are being fulfilled.

3.5 PDMR/PCA dealing

A PDMR is a natural or legal person in an issuer who is either of the following (MAR 1(13) and (25)):

◆ a member of the administrative, management or supervisory body of that entity; or

◆ a senior executive who is not a member of the administrative, management or supervisory body of that entity, but who has regular access to inside information relating directly or indirectly to that entity and the power to make managerial decisions affecting the future developments and business prospects of that entity.

DTR 3.1.2 notes that an individual may be a 'senior executive' irrespective of the nature of any contractual arrangements between the individual and the issuer, and notwithstanding the absence of contractual arrangements, provided the individual has regular access to inside information relating, directly or indirectly, to the issuer and has power to make managerial decisions affecting the future development and business prospects of the issuer.

Accordingly, the classification of individuals as PDMRs will vary from company to company and PDMRs might not be directors of the company.

Person closely associated (PCA)

A PCA includes (MAR 3(1)(26)):

◆ spouse or partner considered equivalent to a spouse under national law of the PDMR;

◆ dependent children of the PDMR;

◆ a relative of the PDMR who has shared the same residence for at least one year; and

◆ any legal person, trust or partnership, the managerial duties and responsibilities of which are carried out by the PDMR or PCA and:

    – is directly or indirectly controlled by the PDMR or PCA;

- is established for the benefit of the PDMR or PCA; or
- whose economic interests are substantially the same as the PDMR or PCA.

Disclosure of PDMR share transactions

MAR 19 contains details of the requirement for PDMRs to notify any transactions in shares undertaken by themselves or their PCAs.

In addition to notifying the company, PDMRs are now also required to notify the FCA of any transactions (MAR 19(1)).

There is a prescribed template for the PDMR disclosure to the FCA (MAR 19(6)) and this may be completed and submitted online from the FCA website (https://marketoversight.fca.org.uk/electronicsubmissionsystem/MaPo_PDMR_Introduction).

Notifiable transactions must be disclosed within three business days:

◆ by the PDMR or PCA to the FCA and the company; and
◆ by the company to the market via an RIS (MAR 19(2) and (3)).

Companies must notify their PDMRs in writing of their obligations under MAR 19 and draw up a list of their PDMRs and PCAs (MAR 19(5)).

PDMRs must notify their PCAs in writing of their obligations under MAR 19 and keep a copy of that notification (MAR 19(5)).

Notifications by PDMRs need not be made until the aggregate of all transactions in any calendar year exceeds €5,000 although notifications below this limit may be made on a voluntary basis (MAR 19(8)).

Closed periods

A PDMR must not for themselves or for a third party, directly or indirectly, conduct any transactions in the financial instruments of the company during a closed period (MAR 19(11)).

A closed period is the period of 30 days prior to an announcement of the company's full or half-year financial report. For this purpose, a preliminary announcement of full year results will count as an announcement of the full year results, provided the announcement contains all the key information expected to be included in the full year-end report.

Under MAR, there is no such prohibition on trading in the period prior to the announcement of quarterly results or trading updates however any transactions might well constitute insider dealing.

3.6 Major shareholders dealing disclosure requirements

Disclosure of interests in voting rights

The provisions relating to notification of shareholdings are set out in DTR 5.

The general principle behind DTR 5 is to identify who is controlling the way in which voting rights are exercised and to disclose this to the market.

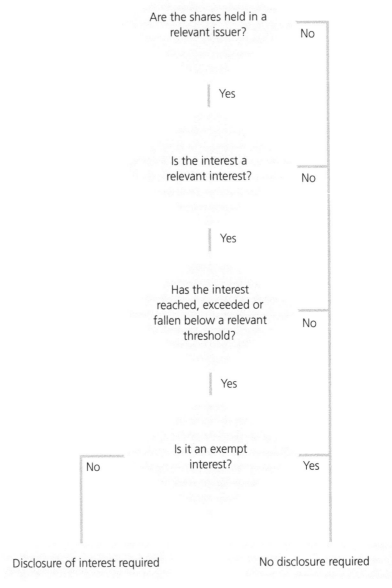

Figure 8.5 DTR5 disclosure obligation

Figure 8.5 will assist in establishing whether a notification obligation under DTR5 exists.

Relevant issuer
The interest in voting rights must relate to shares of a 'relevant issuer'. For the purposes of disclosure of interests in UK companies this means:

◆   any issuer whose shares are admitted to trading on a regulated market whose home state is the UK, i.e. premium and standard listed companies; and

◆   shares of an issuer whose shares are traded on a regulated or prescribed market. This brings exchange regulated markets such as AIM within the scope of the obligation to notify interests in shares (DTR 5.1.1R).

Relevant interest

Under DTR 5 a person will have a 'relevant interest' if they directly or indirectly hold:

◆   shares in a relevant issuer to which voting rights are attached (DTR 5.1.1R and DTR 5.1.2R);

◆   any qualifying financial instruments which result in an entitlement to acquire, on their initiative alone, under a formal agreement, existing shares in a relevant issuer to which voting rights are attached (DTR 5.3.1R); and/or

◆   any financial instruments which (i) are referenced to shares in a relevant issuer (other than a non-UK issuer); and (ii) have a similar economic effect to, but which are not, qualifying financial instruments.

Financial instruments having similar economic effect are instruments that do not give a legal right to acquire shares, but which have a similar effect in practice.

Where voting rights are held by a third party with whom a person has an agreement which obliges them to adopt, by concerted exercise of the voting they hold, a lasting common policy towards the management of the issuer in question all parties to the agreement must comply with the general notification obligation.

Where voting rights are held by a third party under an agreement which provides for the temporary transfer for consideration of the voting rights then both the person who acquires the voting rights and who is entitled to exercise them under the agreement and the person who is temporarily transferring the voting rights must comply with the general disclosure obligation.

Notification thresholds

A person may have a notifiable interest if the percentage of voting rights which they hold directly or indirectly as a shareholder reaches, exceeds or falls below:

◆   the thresholds of 3, 4, 5, 6, 7, 8, 9 and 10% and each 1% threshold thereafter in the case of a UK incorporated issuer; or

◆   the thresholds of 5, 10, 15, 20, 25, 30, 50 and 75% in the case of a non-UK issuer (DTR 5.1.2R).

The thresholds may be passed as the result of either an acquisition or disposal of shares or financial instruments or an event changing the total breakdown of voting rights of the issuer such as a reduction of capital or issue of shares other than to existing shareholders.

Listed companies are required to notify their total voting rights, if there have been any changes, at the end of each calendar month (DTR 5.6.1R). A person's interest in shares is calculated by reference to the information disclosed by the issuer in accordance with DTR 5.6. 1R (in each case rounding down the subsequent percentage interest to the whole number (DTR 5.1.1R(6)).

Where a person is a direct or indirect holder of voting rights under DTR 5.12 or DTR 5.2.1R and/or holds qualifying financial instruments the person must aggregate their holding to establish whether a disclosure obligation arises. If the total is greater than 3% in the case of a UK issuer, or 5% in the case of a non-UK issuer, then an obligation arises (DTR 5.7.1R).

Under DTR 5, a person is required to aggregate their holdings with those of any undertakings under their control (DTR 5.2.1R(e) and DTR 5.2.2R(1)).

A person will be considered to control an undertaking where:

- they hold the majority of the voting rights;
- they can appoint or remove the majority of the board; and
- they have the power to exercise dominant influence or control, or are a member of the undertaking and control alone, pursuant to an agreement with other shareholders or members, a majority of the voting rights in the undertaking.

Exemptions

The obligation to notify an interest does not apply to certain holdings:

- shares acquired for the sole purpose of clearing and settlement within a settlement cycle;
- shares held by a custodian or nominee in their role as custodian or nominee provided they can only exercise the voting rights under written instruction;
- interests of market makers where their interest is less than 10%;
- interests of credit institutions or investment firms where the shares are held within the trading book and the holding does not exceed 5%; and
- interests held by a collateral taker provided the collateral taker has not declared an intention to exercise the voting rights.

Disclosure obligations for investors

The notification must be made by the interested person, or a person delegated by them, so as to be received by the issuer as soon as possible and, in any event, no later than two trading days after the interested person becomes aware, or should have become aware, of the notifiable interest (or is informed of a change in the total voting rights of the issuer (DTR 5.8.3R).

Form of notification to the issuer

Notification to listed companies must be made using the standard form provided by the FCA for this purpose (Form TR-I), available on the FCA website (DTR 5.8.10R).

Filing of information with the competent authority

A person making a notification to an issuer must, if the notification relates to shares admitted to trading on a regulated market in the UK, at the same time electronically file a copy of the notification with the FCA (DTR 5.9.1R). This obligation does not, therefore, apply in respect of issuers listed on AIM.

Contents of disclosures of interests in shares

The notification given pursuant to DTR 5.1.2R must include:

◆   the resulting situation in terms of voting rights;

◆   the chain of controlled undertakings through which voting rights are effectively held (if applicable);

◆   the date on which the threshold was reached or crossed; and

◆   the identity of the shareholder (even if that shareholder is not entitled to exercise the voting rights under the conditions laid down in DTR 5.2. 1R) and of the person entitled to exercise the voting rights on behalf of that shareholder (DTR 5.8.1R).

Test yourself 8.2

Which of the following transactions will trigger a notification obligation under DTR?

a   **Sale of shares taking a holding from 5.9% to 5.1%.**

b   **Purchase of shares taking holding from 3.9% to 4.1%.**

c   **Company purchasing and cancelling shares held by shareholder A resulting in shareholder B's holding increasing from 2.9% to 3.0%.**

d   **Sale of shares taking a holding from 5.1% to 4.9%.**

4. UK corporate governance code

As discussed in chapter 5, the Governance Code is a guide to best practice. It is accepted that compliance with the Governance Code best practice may not be appropriate to all companies and that variations due to size, mix of shareholdings, industry etc. are perfectly acceptable. Compliance with the code is not intended to be an exercise in 'box ticking'. Listed companies should either illustrate how they implement the principles and/or explain any departures from the provisions including a justification of why their practice is best suited to the particular needs of their company.

This comply or explain approach is fundamental to the integrated reporting approach considered in chapter 6. Effective application of any of the principles should be supported by quality reporting of the provisions and conversely any departure from the principles or provisions should be reported with equal quality to explain why that departure is appropriate as necessary.

The Governance Code, updated in July 2018, has been significantly revised and condensed with much more focus on the principles, which emphasise the importance of good corporate governance on long-term sustainable success.

To assist directors in their application of the Governance Code the FRC has published the following guidance:

◆ Guidance on Board Effectiveness (updated July 2018);

◆ Guidance on Audit Committees (updated April 2016);

◆ Guidance on Risk Management, Internal Control and Related Financial and Business Reporting (published September 2014);

◆ Guidance on the Strategic Report (published July 2018); and

◆ Corporate Culture and the Role of Boards (published July 2016).

5. UK stewardship code

The UK Stewardship Code (Stewardship Code) was first published by the FRC in July 2010 replacing the Institutional Shareholders Committee guidance 'The Responsibilities of Institutional Shareholders and Agents: Statement of Principles', originally published in 2002. The current version was last updated in 2012. The FRC has announced that the code is to be revised in 2019.

The FRC's aim is 'to enhance the quality of engagement between institutional investors and investee companies to help improve long-term risk adjusted returns to shareholders'.

Like the Governance Code, the Stewardship Code operates on a 'comply or explain' basis, recognising that what constitutes best practice for some institutions may not be appropriate for all.

Monitoring of investee company performance should not rest with the fund management industry, but is equally the responsibility of pension fund trustees, investment managers and asset owners. Good corporate governance is not the sole preserve of company management but requires active engagement on the part of their major shareholders to guide the strategic planning of the executive directors and to hold the directors to account in respect of their actual performance in achieving those corporate goals.

UK authorised asset managers are required by the FCA's conduct of business rules to publish a statement of commitment to the Stewardship Code or explain why it is not appropriate to their business. These compliance statements are useful to third parties be they investee companies, assets owners seeking new assets managers to manage their investment portfolios and assets managers seeking better clarity on the expectations of current and potential clients.

Signatories to the Stewardship Code are expected to publish on their website a statement that:

◆ describes how the signatory has applied each of the seven principles of the Stewardship Code and discloses the specific information requested in the guidance to the principles; or

◆ if one or more of the principles have not been applied or the specific information requested in the guidance has not been disclosed, explains why the signatory has not complied with those elements of the Stewardship Code.

Test yourself 8.3

What is the purpose of comply or explain?

6. Insider dealing

6.1   Criminal Justice Act

Dealing in shares on a regulated market while in possession of price-sensitive information (insider dealing) is a criminal offence. The legislation is contained in Part V of the Criminal Justice Act 1993 (CJA1993).

Three offences were introduced by CJA1993 s. 52:

1. dealing in company securities while in the possession of inside information;
2. encouraging another person to deal while in possession of inside information; and
3. disclosing information other than in the proper performance of an office, employment or profession.

The insider must either know that they possess inside information or knowingly acquire inside information from an inside source. It is no longer necessary for the insider to be connected with the particular company; a person can be an insider simply by having access to inside information. Accordingly, the husband or wife of a director could be convicted if using inside information passed on by their spouse, and any friends could also be guilty of an offence if they dealt in shares on the basis of inside information gained directly from the director or indirectly from the spouse or some other third party.

The definition of 'securities' has been expanded and now covers not only shares, debentures and debt securities, but also their derivatives (CJA1993 s. 54 and Sch. 2).

Similarly, the definition of 'dealing' has been expanded. Although deals of a purely private nature even on the basis of inside information will not normally be covered by the legislation, any transactions on a regulated market (e.g. the Stock Exchange) and any deals undertaken via professional intermediaries whether or not through a regulated market will be covered (CJA1993 s. 55).

The inside information must be specific, relate to the company whose securities have been dealt and must not be public knowledge. It must also be shown that if that information were to have been made public, it would have had a significant effect on the price of the securities concerned. There is, unfortunately, no definition or guidance as to the meaning of 'significant' in the legislation (CJA1993 s. 56).

The defences against a charge of insider dealing are set out in CJA1993 s. 53 and include that the person:

◆ did not expect the dealing to result in a profit attributable to the information being price-sensitive;

◆ had reasonable grounds for believing that the other party to the deal was also in possession of the information; and

◆ would have dealt irrespective of whether or not they had been in possession of the price-sensitive information.

It should be emphasised that the provisions contained in the CJA 1993 are lengthy and complex, and many companies issue detailed notes of guidance for their directors and senior executives.

6.2 Proceeds of Crime Act 2002

The Proceeds of Crime Act 2002 (POCA2002) sets out the legislative powers under which criminally obtained assets may be confiscated together with related powers to support that activity. The purpose of the legislation is primarily to deny criminals the use of the assets they have acquired illegally, to recover those assets to their legitimate owners and to disrupt and deter criminal activity.

For companies the key provisions relevant to them are contained in POCA Part 7 which sets out the money laundering legislation. Although applicable to all companies POCA places additional obligations on those supplying regulated, accounting, legal or money transfer services to report suspicion of money laundering activities to the authorities.

The definition of money laundering is very widely drawn, and covers assets as well as money.

A person will commit money laundering if they:

◆ conceal, disguise, convert or transfer criminal property or remove it from the UK;

◆ enter into or become involved with an arrangement which they know or suspect facilitates the acquisition, retention, use or control of criminal property; or

◆ acquire, use or have possession of criminal property.

As money laundering includes the possession of criminal property many criminals will find themselves convicted of money laundering in circumstances where it is not possible to prove that they committed the original act of theft.

Regulated businesses and certain professional firms must establish appropriate procedures and training to ensure they recognise suspicious activity but also have an internal process to report those suspicions. Businesses covered by the legislation are required to nominate a money laundering reporting officer (MLRO) to whom employees must report their suspicions. Having reported their suspicions employees need take no further action and it is for the MLRO to decide whether the matter is notifiable or not. Where a report has been made the business must ensure that they do not tip off their client/customer of their suspicions. In certain circumstances, the business cannot continue to provide the service without clearance from the authorities.

Stop and think 8.3

In October 2018, the former CEO and COO of Afren plc received custodial sentences for fraud and money laundering offences. The pair decided to secretly increase their income after shareholders rejected their £6.6 million and £3.8 million salary packages in 2013.

They recommended that the Afren board agree to a $300 million payment to Oriental Energy Resources Ltd, the company's oil field partner in Nigeria. Unknown to the Afren board, the pair had struck a side deal with Oriental, which led to 15% of the $300 million being paid out to a Caribbean shell company controlled by the defendants.

7. Dematerialisation

The Central Securities Depositaries Regulations (CSDR), legislation emanating from the EU, came into force in 2014. One of the far-reaching implications for the UK and Irish listed markets was the requirement to introduce full stock market dematerialisation by 2023. In plain English, this means the elimination of paper share certificates and all shares in listed companies being held in electronic form.

The ICSA Registrars Group published a paper proposing a way forward in December 2014 and this has formed the basis of discussions with government officials. However, following the decision of the UK to leave the EU the government have announced a pause in implementing dematerialisation of the share register until after Brexit.

7.1 Current proposals

The ICSA Registrars Group proposed model retains much of the existing structure of the share register currently in operation. The proposed model conforms to the following industry-agreed principles:

- Shares must be registered.
- Dematerialisation must produce benefits.
- Any book entry model adopted must be the best for each market.
- Shareholder rights must be protected.
- Issuer rights must be protected.
- The structure must be efficient.
- Benefits must outweigh costs and costs should be apportioned in a fair and balanced way.

◆ A logical and measured transition plan must be followed.

◆ The market should consider all dematerialisation options, providing they meet the principles outlined.

Among the benefits of dematerialisation, the following have been identified:

◆ Increased security.

◆ Transfer of off-market transactions can be undertaken much quicker.

◆ No indemnities for lost share certificates.

Chapter summary

◆ Overview of the process for listing and admission to trading

◆ Continuing obligations of listed companies

◆ Corporate governance and stewardship responsibilities of listed companies and institutional investors

◆ Criminal liability for abusing inside information relating to a company

◆ Proposed removal of paper share certificates for listed companies

Chapter nine
Maintenance of records

CONTENTS

1. Introduction
2. Statutory registers
3. Location of records and registers
4. Access to records and registers
5. Minute books
6. Meeting materials/board papers
7. Financial records
8. Corporate records
9. Retention periods for documents and registers

1. Introduction

The importance of maintaining statutory registers and other records cannot be overemphasised however, especially for small private companies, the statutory records are often overlooked and can lead to nasty surprises. Of all the registers, the register of members is vitally important to show who actually owns shares in the company as to be a member requires both consent from the individual and their details being entered in the register of members.

This chapter looks at the obligations on directors and companies to keep specified records, the location of those records and those who have the right to access those records.

2. Statutory registers

Companies must maintain specified registers containing details of their officers, owners and other information as shown below. These registers must be kept up to date and details of changes to certain of these registers notified to Companies House. These registers, often referred to as the statutory registers or statutory books, must be kept available for inspection or for copies to be taken or supplied to any members and in some cases by members of the public.

The statutory registers must be kept either at the registered office or single alternative inspection location or, at the option of the company, some of the registers may be held on the central register (see section 3.2 below).

Companies are required by the Companies Act to keep the following registers, documents and books:

◆ register of members – CA2006 ss. 114 & 128D;

◆ register of directors – CA2006 s. 162;

◆ register of directors' residential addresses – CA2006 s. 165;

◆ directors' service contracts – CA2006 s. 228;

◆ directors' indemnities – CA2006 s. 237;

◆ books containing minutes of directors' meetings, resolutions in writing of directors and decisions of a sole director – CA2006 s. 248;

◆ register of secretaries – CA2006 s. 275;

◆ books containing minutes of company meetings, resolutions in writing of members and resolutions of a sole member – CA2006 s. 355;

◆ accounting records – CA2006 s. 386;

◆ contracts for purchase of own shares – CA2006 s. 702;

◆ documents for purchase of own shares out of capital – CA2006 s. 720;

◆ register of debenture holders, if any – CA2006 s. 743;

◆ register of people with significant control – CA2006 ss. 790M & 790Z;

◆ report to members of investigation by public company into interests in its shares – CA2006 s. 805;

◆ register of interests in voting shares disclosed to a public company – CA2006 s. 808; and

◆ register of charges – CA2006 s. 859Q.

Other legislation also requires companies to keep documents and records including:

◆ certificates of employer's liability insurance;

◆ accidents in the workplace;

◆ PAYE, VAT and corporation tax records; and

◆ complaint handling records – certain FCA regulated firms.

2.1 Which statutory registers must be kept

Directors
The register of directors must contain for each current and former director:

1. Name and former name. Former names need not be disclosed if not used in business or not used in the previous 20 years. Maiden names need not be disclosed.

2. Service address. This can be an office or residential address. An office address is recommended to mitigate against identity theft. The address

in the register of directors, which must be available for public inspection should be the same as on the central register maintained at Companies House. In the case of a corporate appointment the address should be the registered or principal office.

3. Country of residency. For a corporate appointment this is the country of registration and registration reference (in the case of an EAA registered company) or the legal form, law by which governed and the register on which the registration is entered, if any.

4. Nationality.

5. Business occupation, if any.

6. Date of birth.

7. Date of appointment.

8. Date of termination of appointment, if relevant.

Directors' residential addresses
As a fraud prevention measure the publicly available directors' register contains details of a director's service address. While this can be the director's usual residential address it is now more commonly the registered or head office address. The company must however also maintain a register of the usual residential address of each director, and any changes in it.

As a measure to assist companies prevent personal identity theft this register is not required to be available for inspection.

Secretaries
Where the company has appointed a company secretary their details must be entered in the register of secretaries. The content of this register is very similar to the register of directors with the exception that the nationality and occupation are not required. Company secretaries register a service address but there is no requirement for a separate register or disclosure of their usual residential address.

Members
All companies must maintain records of their members and any changes in the information.

The precise information will vary slightly depending on the type of company and category of membership but in general the register of members will contain:

◆ full name and address of each member;

◆ date of becoming a member;

◆ any acquisition or disposal of shares; and

◆ date of cessation of membership.

Companies may also need to keep additional information such as bank mandate details for payment of dividends. Such additional information should not be kept in the register of members, which is open for inspection by anyone but should be kept securely.

Where a company trades overseas and has a substantial number of shareholders in that overseas country, consideration should be given to establishing a branch register in terms of CA2006 s. 129.

A branch register should not be confused with a register of depositary receipts under which securities representing shares are traded on overseas stock exchanges.

It is not possible to establish a branch register in all countries and CA2006 s. 129(2)(b) contains details of those countries where a branch register may be established, as follows:

- Bangladesh
- Cyprus
- Dominica
- The Gambia
- Ghana
- Guyana
- The Hong Kong Special Administrative
- Region of the People's Republic of China
- India
- Ireland
- Kenya
- Kiribati
- Lesotho
- Malawi
- Malaysia
- Malta
- Nigeria
- Pakistan
- Seychelles
- Sierra Leone
- Singapore
- South Africa
- Sri Lanka
- Swaziland
- Trinidad and Tobago
- Uganda
- Zimbabwe

When a branch register is established, notice of its location or any change in its location must be given to Companies House on Form AD06. A duplicate branch register must be kept at the same place as the main register and is treated as part of the main register for all purposes.

Only individuals or legal entities should be registered as members. Holders of an office can be registered provided it is a public office such as the Official Receiver.

Names of English partnerships, trusts, share/investment clubs or settlements must not be registered as the holders of shares as they have no legal capacity and accordingly valid instructions cannot be given. Scottish partnerships may be registered as, unlike English partnerships, these have legal capacity. If documentation is received to register shares in the name of a trust or partnership, it should be rejected. In such circumstances, the shares should be registered in the names of two or more of the partners or trustees. It is usual for the number of joint holders of shares to be restricted to a maximum of four.

The register of members of a company may be kept in manual form, either as bound or loose-leaf books, or may be kept on computer, whether on a simple spreadsheet or database, or using specialised share registration systems.

The register of members must be kept either in the registered office of the company or at the SAIL address.

Where a register of members is held electronically it must be capable of being viewed on screen and as a hard copy print out in order to satisfy the obligation to permit inspection of the register of members and also provide copies of the register upon request (CA2006 ss. 116, 117).

2.2 CREST

CREST is the electronic settlement system used by UK regulated markets, which enables digital settlement of securities, including delivery of the shares being traded. CREST is operated by Euroclear UK & Ireland Ltd.

Where a company's shares have been admitted to CREST, the register of members is split in two, with CREST being responsible for an uncertificated, dematerialised, electronic sub-register, enabling electronic transfer of title on settlement and the company or its share registrar being responsible for the certificated register. An individual member may have two accounts: one certificated and the other uncertificated. Movements between the uncertificated accounts and from uncertificated to certificated accounts (stock withdrawals) are authorised by electronic messages. A movement from a certificated account to an uncertificated account (stock deposit) is a paper-based transaction.

CREST preserves much of the 'name on register' aspects of the former system, although it is more difficult to identify shareholders as more members move to holding shares through nominees.

Stop and think 9.1

CREST settlement is only required for those companies with their shares listed on a public market and almost all of these companies use a share registrar. In practice, most company secretaries only need a high level overview of the operations of CREST as the day-to-day matters will be taken care of by their share registrar.

Test yourself 9.1

What is the difference between a CREST stock deposit and stock withdrawal?

Charges
Prior to 6 April 2013, companies had to keep full details of all charges against their assets.

The amended procedure is that the mortgage register is maintained on the central register kept at Companies House and there is no requirement for companies to keep their own register of charges except where there were any pre-existing charges and there is a requirement to keep this historic register updated with details of any changes to those charges. Accordingly, for these companies they will have a split register with older charge information kept by the company and newer charge information kept by Companies House.

Copies of charges (and any amendments) and instruments creating a charge must be made available for inspection at either the company's registered office or its SAIL address (CA2006 ss. 859P and Q).

Debentures

Even in circumstances where a company has issued debentures there is no obligation to maintain a register, but this is convenient. Where a register is kept it must comply with the requirements set out in CA2006 ss. 743–748. These requirements broadly mirror the rights to request a copy of the register of members and the obligation of the company to ensure that the request is made for a proper purpose.

People with significant control

Introduced in 2016 by SBEE2015 the majority of companies are now required to maintain a register of **persons with significant control (PSC)** – the PSC register. This is intended to be a register of the natural person(s) who ultimately control the company rather than the register of members which only records the identity of the registered members rather than beneficial ownership.

A PSC is anyone in the company who meets at least one of the conditions set out in the Register of People with Significant Control Regulations 2016 (SI 339/2016). Some companies will have no PSCs while others may have several. Most companies will have one PSC reflecting that the majority of companies have a sole shareholder.

A PSC is a person who:

◆ holds, directly or indirectly, more than 25% of the shares;

◆ holds, directly or indirectly, more than 25% of the voting rights;

◆ holds the right, directly or indirectly, to appoint or remove a majority of directors;

◆ otherwise has the right to exercise, or actually exercises, significant influence or control over the company; or

◆ has the right to exercise, or actually exercises, significant influence or control over the activities of a trust or firm which is not a legal person, the trustees or members of which would satisfy any of the four conditions above.

Accordingly, where a company has a corporate shareholder it is necessary to move up the chain of ownership until the ultimate owner is identified. The identity of all individuals exercising control over 25% or more of the ownership or voting rights of the company or the right to appoint directors must be disclosed.

person with significant control (PSC)
An individual owning or exercising control over 25% or more of a company's equity shares or voting rights.

Other than a company that is exempt, all companies must have a PSC register and it can never be blank so that in circumstances where there is no PSC that fact must be recorded.

Where the company has identified a potential PSC or is seeking clarity on the PSC for a group entity then those details must be recorded. There is a comprehensive schedule detailing the permitted statements that may be made depending on the stage of the enquiries into establishing the identity of PSCs.

Although in general, it is details of individual ownership that must be recorded in the PSC Register there are two other types of entity that are permitted. Accordingly, there are three types of ownership structure whose details must be entered into a company's PSC register.

The categories are individual, registrable relevant legal entity (RLE) and other registrable person.

The information to be registered about each category of ownership is as follows:

- For an individual person, the following must be recorded:
  - the date the individual became a registrable person;
  - full name, country/state of residence;
  - nationality;
  - service address;
  - usual residential address (this is not shown on the public record);
  - date of birth (only the month and year is shown on the public record); and
  - the nature of their control over the company.
- For an RLE (such as a company):
  - the date that they became a registrable RLE;
  - corporate name;
  - address;
  - legal form of the corporate body;
  - governing law under which the RLE was registered;
  - place of registration (if applicable);
  - registration number (if applicable); and
  - the nature of their control over the company.
- For another registrable person (such as a corporation, sole trader or local authority):
  - date on which they became a registrable person in relation to the company in question;
  - name;
  - principal office;
  - the legal form of the person;

- the law by which they are governed; and
- the nature of their control over the company.

Listed companies, but not their subsidiaries, are exempt from the requirement to keep a PSC register as they and their shareholders are already under an obligation to disclose interests in shares in excess of 3% under DTR 5.

Interests in voting shares of a public company

All public companies have authority under the Act, which is often supplemented and expanded upon in the Articles of traded companies, to require members to disclose information on the beneficial ownership of the shares and whether they or the beneficial owner are a member of a 'concert party' in respect of the shares (CA2006 s. 793).

Where a company makes any such enquiries, they must keep a register containing the date of the request and any information disclosed in any reply. This register must be kept pursuant to CA2006 s. 808, and as a result is commonly referred to as 'the section 808 register'. The register must be kept at either the registered office or the SAIL address.

Format of registers

There is no prescribed format in the Act and the statutory registers may be kept in hard copy or soft copy. Where hard copy is used this can be in the form of pre-printed 'statutory books' with manual entries or registers created using a word processing or other software application and then printed out as required. Provided the registers contain the prescribed information the format is of no consequence.

There are several statutory records and company secretarial software applications available, which can be used to create and maintain statutory register information. However, companies can commission their own bespoke applications or utilise a word processing or spreadsheet application to maintain the registers. The commercial applications tend to be favoured by groups as changes of address for one director can be easily replicated across all group companies and the necessary statutory forms generated or filed directly from the application. Use of these entity management applications is considered in chapter 10.

Whatever form the statutory records take they must be secure, confidential and any none-prescribed information must comply with data protection requirements. The statutory registers, if not kept in hard copy, must be capable of being made available for inspection and for copies to be taken.

Stop and think 9.2

It is a sad fact, but maintenance of statutory books is often ignored or poorly and only partially undertaken by many companies and their professional advisers. This might be understandable if all companies had many changes to be reflected in the registers, but this is not the case.

The overwhelming majority of companies once the statutory registers have been written up following incorporation might never need to update them until the company is sold or even dissolved or liquidated.

Ask many directors to see their statutory registers and many will assume you are referring to their accounting records or produce copies of their confirmation statements secure in the belief that this proves their directorship or ownership of the company.

Quite often this issue only comes to light in the context of a business sale when the buyer's solicitors ask to inspect the statutory registers. If the registers do not exist or, as is often the case, are blank then the company must reconstitute the statutory registers as soon as possible. Alternatively, the registers may not have been updated post incorporation. For most of the registers this is not an issue. However, if the register of members is incorrect or contain names of trusts or settlements then rectification by the court is required which is both time consuming and expensive.

Directors should therefore ensure the company's statutory registers are up to date and that they have been properly maintained at all times. If a company sale is contemplated this is an area that should be corrected at an early stage and not left to an embarrassing discovery at the completion meeting.

Test yourself 9.2

1. Must the statutory records be kept at any specific location?

2. Must the statutory books be books or are other formats permitted?

3. Why must directors provide both a service address and residential address?

3. Location of records and registers

Until 1 October 2008, the statutory registers and any records that had be to kept available for inspection had to be kept at the company's registered office. On 1 October 2008, the SAIL address was introduced that allowed companies to nominate an alternative address for some of their registers. There can only be one alternative address and this has to be in the same country as the registered office.

On 30 June 2016, another alternative was introduced for private companies which may now elect to hold some of their statutory registers on the central register maintained by Companies House. This option was introduced as a deregulating measure aimed primarily at the high number of sole director/ shareholder companies.

3.1 Registered office

All companies must have an address at which legal documents can be served (CA2006 s. 86). This is known as the registered office. On incorporation, the first registered office will be the address detailed on Form IN01. Any change in registered office must be notified to Companies House on Form AD01 to be effective. The registered office must be situated in the country of registration (CA2006 s. 87).

The registered office address must be shown on the company's business stationery, emails and its website(s) (CA2006 s. 82).

3.2 SAIL address

Any company may elect to hold one or more of the following registers at a SAIL address. Where this option is taken up notification must be given to Companies House, using Forms AD02 and AD03 so that anyone wishing to inspect the registers will know which address to attend. Once a company has used a SAIL address for any particular register notification of any changes to that address must be notified to Companies House even where the records have been moved back to the registered office.

The following registers may be held at the SAIL address (CA2006 s. 1136):

- register of members;
- register of directors;
- directors' service contracts;
- directors' indemnities;
- register of secretaries;
- register of people with significant control;
- records of resolutions, etc.;
- contracts relating to purchase of own shares;
- documents relating to redemption or purchase of own shares out of capital by private company;
- register of debenture holders;
- report to members of outcome of investigation by public company into interests in its shares;
- register of interests in shares disclosed to public company; and
- instruments creating charges and register of charges.

Due to the logistics involved in maintaining a large share register and the need to synchronise the register with the electronic settlement system, CREST, companies with shares traded on a public market in almost all cases appoint an external share registrar to maintain their register of members. As a result, the viewing facility available at the share registry will have to be the company's SAIL address and the remaining statutory registers must be available for inspection at the registered office.

3.2   Central register

Introduced by SBEE2015 from 30 June 2016 private companies can elect to hold five of the statutory registers on the central register maintained by the Registrar of Companies at Companies House. This facility although available to all private companies is principally a deregulating measure intended for use by those single member sole director companies where there are few if any changes to the registered information during the life of the company.

The registers that may be kept on the central register are the:

- register of directors;
- register of directors' usual residential addresses;
- register of secretaries;
- PSC register; and
- register of members.

The main disadvantage of taking advantage of this facility, is the availability of the directors' and shareholders' private residential addresses on the public record. The Companies (Disclosure of Address) (Amendment) Regulations 2018 amended CA2006 s. 1088 and extends the availability of withholding residential addresses where registers are held on the central register. Any person can apply to have this residential address information suppressed on the public record. Individuals must opt in to take advantage of the suppression and provide a communication address for use by the Registrar. The only exception is where the registered office is also a residential address.

Companies wishing to take advantage of this option to keep their registers on the central register do so by opting in to the service by giving notice to the Registrar in respect of each register they wish to hold on the central register. From the time of the election there is no need for the company to update the historical registers it kept until such time as it opts out.

If a company opts out of keeping the registers on the central register it simply files notice and then takes responsibility for maintaining the registers itself. There is no requirement to re-create the records relating to the period the registers were held on the central register as those records will remain on the central register as a permanent part of the statutory registers of the company.

Table 9.1 sets out the various alternative locations available to companies for holding their statutory records and registers.

Record	Registered office	SAIL address	Central Registry (private companies only)
Register of members	✓	✓	✓
Historic register of members	✓	✓	
Register of directors	✓	✓	✓
Register of secretaries	✓	✓	✓
Register of directors' residential address	✓	✓	✓
Register of charges	✓	✓	
Register of interests in voting shares	✓	✓	
Register of debenture holders	✓	✓	
PSC register	✓	✓	✓
Historic PSC register	✓	✓	
Company minutes and resolutions	✓		
Directors minutes and resolutions	✓		
Accounting records			
Directors' service contracts	✓	✓	
Directors' indemnities	✓	✓	
Contracts for purchase of own shares	✓	✓	
Documents re purchases of shares out of capital	✓	✓	
Report into ownership of own shares	✓	✓	

Table 9.1 Locations where statutory records and registers may be kept

Stop and think 9.3

Private companies taking advantage of the option to hold their statutory registers on the central register will often disclose their directors' and members' private residential address information inadvertently not realising that the individuals must opt in to the service to suppress that information.

4. Access to records and registers

As noted above, the Act stipulates not only where the statutory registers must be held but also contains provisions regarding their inspection. Inspection of all the registers is free to members and in the case of the historic register of charges, free to creditors. Anyone else may be required to pay a fee.

The register of directors' residential addresses is not available for public inspection.

4.1 Location

Unless the company has elected to hold some of or all of their registers on the central register all the registers that must be kept available for inspection must either be held at the registered office or SAIL address. Where any particular register is not kept at the registered office notice must be given to Companies House providing details of the SAIL address on Form AD02 and the registers that are kept there on Form AD03.

4.2 Inspection

In person
Private companies must make their company's records available for at least two hours between 9 am and 3 pm on a working day. In addition, any person wishing to inspect any of the records must give due notice of their intention to inspect the records giving the date and time of their proposed visit. Due notice is:

◆ at least two working days if the notice is given within the notice period of a general meeting or the circulation period of a written resolution; or

◆ at least 10 working days in all other cases.

Public companies must make their company records available for inspection between 9 am and 5 pm on every working day for anyone who visits the appropriate address. The person wishing to inspect the records of a public company need not give any prior notice.

Right to request copies
Any member or other person may, as an alternative to requesting to inspect a register, request that a copy of the register be sent to them.

The requester may request that the copy be sent to them in hard copy or electronically but, in the case of an electronic copy, cannot specify the particular format to be used.

Requests to inspect the register of members or the PSC register must be accompanied by a statement identifying the person requesting the information and the purpose for which they require the information. If the company does not believe that the request is being made for a proper purpose, application may be made to the court for a direction either to supply the information or to order the company not to comply with the request. Any application to the court must be made within five days of the request being made. Due to the short timescale and costs involved in making an application to the court this is seldom used.

Fees

Depending on whether the requester is a member or not and the particular register involved the company may be entitled to charge a fee to inspect or be provided with copies of the register or documents requested.

A company may charge a fee of £3.50 per hour or part thereof during which the register(s) is/are inspected. This fee may be charged for inspections by non-members of the registers of: members, register of interests in shares and register of debenture holders.

The fee payable, by both members and non-members, to be provided with a copy of the register of debentures, register of interests in voting shares, register of debenture holders or register of members is on a sliding scale depending on the number of entries in the register as set out in Table 9.2.

No. of entries in register	Fee
First 5	£1.00 each
Next 95 entries or part thereof	£30
Next 900 entries or part thereof	£30
Next 99,000 entries or part thereof	£30
Remainder of the register	£30

Table 9.2 Fees to inspect registers and documents

A fee of 10 pence per 500 words, or part thereof, may be charged for the provision of copies of the following documents plus the reasonable expenses of delivering the copies to the requestor:

◆   directors' service contract (CA2006 s. 229(2));

◆   directors' qualifying indemnity provisions (CA2006 s. 238(2));

◆   resolutions and proceedings at meetings (CA2006 s. 358(4)); and

◆   report under s. 805 into share ownership (CA2006 s. 807(2)).

Stop and think 9.4

Although very rarely exercised in practice, other than for the inspection of register of members of traded companies anyone can walk into the registered office or, if relevant, the SAIL address and request to see a company's statutory books and certain records and without notice in the case of a Plc.

Since, as previously considered, many private companies fail to keep their statutory registers up to date, if at all, it is just as well that requests to inspect them are so rare.

During 30 years as a company service provider, providing a registered office to many hundreds of companies, the author can only recall one instance where a former director arrived unannounced to inspect the statutory registers of a company!

Test yourself 9.3

1. What is the fee to obtain a copy of the register of members for a company with 500 shareholders?

2. Can a request for a copy of a register specify that the information is to be provided in the form of an Excel spreadsheet?

5. Minute books

Companies are required by CA2006 s. 248 to maintain minutes of all meetings of the directors and for these to be available for inspection by any director. This requirement relates to all formal directors' meetings or meetings intended to approve a directors' resolution. Informal gatherings or executive management meetings are not formal directors' meetings and although it may be desired to keep a record of decisions and actions there is no requirement to minute those meetings. There is no provision or right for the members to have access to minutes of the meetings of the directors. The taking of minutes, and their maintenance and safekeeping, is one of the core duties of the company secretary.

Companies are required by CA2006 ss. 355 and 359 to keep records of:

◆ all resolutions passed by members other than at general meetings;

◆ minutes of all proceedings of general meetings;

◆ details of decisions of sole members; and

◆ class meeting minutes, resolutions and decisions.

This requirement relates to all members' meetings or decisions of members. Informal gatherings are not formal members' meetings and there is no requirement to minute those meetings. Members have the right to have access to minutes of the meetings, and written resolutons of the members. The taking of minutes, and their maintenance and safekeeping, is one of the core duties of the company secretary.

5.1 Where kept

There are no statutory provisions nor any reference in the Model Articles as to where copies of directors' minutes should be kept, and it is for each company to decide for itself. Security of the minutes is one of the responsibilities of the company secretary and the original hard copy signed minutes are often kept securely with other sensitive documents under the control of the company secretary.

The records of members' general meetings, class meetings, decisions, resolutions and decisions of any sole member must be kept available for inspection at either the company's registered office or its SAIL address. Where the records have not always been kept at the registered office, the company must notify the Registrar of the location where these records may be inspected.

Directors', members' and class minutes and records must be kept for a minimum of 10 years from the date of the meeting, resolution or decision (CA2006 ss. 248(2) and 355(2)).

5.2 Security

Other than a requirement to keep minutes of meetings there is no further obligation imposed on companies. As a result the minutes may be kept in any format, hard copy or electronic, and in the case of hard copy minutes kept in any way.

The type of minute book kept by the company will depend on the size and procedures of the company concerned. For private companies, they may be kept in bound books, either hand-written or with typed sheets of paper pasted into the bound book with the pages serially numbered. It may be convenient for the minutes to be numbered consecutively from number 1 upwards throughout the book. Thus, in the first minute book, the minutes would be numbered 1.1, 1.2, 1.3, etc., in the second minute book, they would be numbered 2.1, 2.2, 2.3, etc.

Larger public companies generally use loose-leaf minute books. Again, it is recommended that the pages are numbered serially, and the minutes numbered consecutively. Some companies also maintain an index at the back of the minute book giving reference to the items covered by the minutes. The company secretary must decide whether the time spent in indexing the minutes will serve any useful purpose.

Minutes of general meetings should be kept separate from board minutes since members have a right to inspect the minutes of general meetings but not of board meetings (CA2006 s. 358).

However the minutes are kept they must be kept securely with restricted access as the directors' minutes in particular may contain sensitive information.

Larger businesses will circulate a pack of information to support the agenda and provide background information on the topics for discussions. Although these packs do not form part of the minutes, they should be retained as they are frequently referred to in the minutes and will also provide evidence of the verification, due diligence and factors taken into consideration by the directors when deciding on any particular course action. Like the minutes these board packs contain confidential and sensitive information and must be kept securely.

5.3 Directors

As noted above other than the requirement in CA2006 s. 248 to keep minutes of the proceedings of directors for at least 10 years, there are no other statutory provisions regarding where or how they should be kept.

The type of minute book kept by the company will depend on the size and procedures of the company concerned. For private companies, they may be kept in bound books, either hand-written or with typed sheets of paper pasted into the bound book with the pages serially numbered. It may be convenient for the minutes to be numbered consecutively from number one upwards throughout the book. Numbering minutes is useful if it is likely that previous minutes will be referred to in future meetings as it will be possible simply to cross-refer to the reference rather than to the date and subject matter.

Larger public companies generally use loose-leaf minute books. Again, it is recommended that the minutes are numbered consecutively. Some companies also maintain an index at the back of the minute book giving reference to the items covered by the minutes. The company secretary must decide whether the time spent in indexing the minutes will serve any useful purpose.

The Act is a little unclear as to whether the requirement to record and minute meetings of the directors extends also to meetings of committees of the directors. This requirement is however often contained in the company's Articles and as a matter of good practice meetings of committees of the directors should be minuted and a proper record maintained.

5.4 Members

Like minutes of meetings of the directors, the directors have freedom to decide how the minutes of members' meetings should be kept together with the content and style of those minutes.

The type of minute book kept by the company will depend on the size and procedures of the company concerned. For private companies, they may be kept in bound books, either hand-written or with typed sheets of paper pasted into the bound book with the pages serially numbered. It may be convenient for the minutes to be numbered consecutively from number one upwards throughout the book.

Larger public companies generally use loose-leaf minute books. Again, it is recommended that the minutes are numbered consecutively. Some companies also maintain an index at the back of the minute book giving reference to the items covered by the minutes. The company secretary must decide whether the time spent in indexing the minutes will serve any useful purpose.

Minutes of members' meetings tend to much briefer than directors' minutes with the content often restricted to a record of whether the resolutions were approved or not, possibly with details of the votes cast for and against, although that is not a requirement, with little if any record of any discussions or questions put by members to the directors.

5.5 Access rights

Directors do not have any specific statutory right of access to minutes of directors' meetings. They do however exercise the authorities of the company and accordingly have the general right and are entitled to have access to any records they wish to view, for as long as they remain a director and this will extend to minutes of meetings.

Members and class members have no right of access to minutes of meetings of the directors.

Members and class members have the right to inspect the members' and class minutes and records free of charge. If they require copies of any of the records there is a fee payable (CA2006 ss. 358(3), 358(4) and 359).

Auditors have a general right of access to all the company's books and records and this extends to minutes and records of proceedings of both directors' and members' meetings (CA2006 s. 499(1)).

Various regulatory bodies have the right to either request that various documents are provided to them, including minutes of meetings of the directors or members and some may have the right to undertake searches for those documents. Such bodies include inspectors or competent persons appointed by BEIS, HMRC, FCA, CMA or the Takeover Panel.

Stop and think 9.5

In circumstances where a company finds itself under investigation either due to insolvency or breach of rules or legislation the investigating body will invariably call for the minutes and records of directors' meetings to gauge the actions, or inaction, of the directors in respect of the matter under investigation. It can be seen that the content and detail of the minutes can have a significant bearing on such investigations as directors may find it difficult to introduce evidence of satisfactory oversight if there is no mention of that activity at any board meeting.

Test yourself 9.4

1.   Should minutes of all meetings involving directors be minuted?

2.   Can directors' and members' minutes be kept together?

3.   How long must a company keep its original minutes of meetings?

6. Meeting materials/board papers

All meetings share a number of fundamental characteristics. There must be proper notice of the meeting issued to all persons entitled to attend, an agenda, usually forming part of the notice, together with any accompanying documentation required to consider the topics of the meeting.

6.1   Directors

There are no statutory provisions relating to the manner in which boards must hold their meetings and it is up to each board to decide what is appropriate for itself both in terms of length of notice and frequency of meetings.

Traded or larger companies and those with external directors will most often have a schedule of agreed meetings dates arranged many months in advance.

Smaller, usually private, companies may only hold an annual directors' meeting to approve formally the annual financial accounts, together with any ad hoc meetings that might be required from time to time.

6.2   Board papers

There is no formal requirement to circulate an agenda however this is very useful to provide structure to the meeting and provide an opportunity for directors to consider issues in advance. The agenda will most often be accompanied by additional supporting reports, research, third party advice etc. For long reports, it is helpful to ensure that these also contain a brief (ideally one-page) summary.

For meetings with a full agenda it can also be helpful for the agenda to indicate if the matter for discussion requires a decision or is an update or for information only. This assists the chair in ensuring that appropriate discussion time is allocated to each item on the agenda.

The board papers should be issued sufficiently in advance of the meeting to allow directors the opportunity to read and consider the information and seek additional clarification if required. For many companies sufficient notice is usually one week however invariably this shortens to the Friday prior to the meeting. Board papers should be forwarded securely whether by recorded delivery, courier or secure email. There are a number of software applications and online portals used for the secure exchange of board papers and these are considered in more detail in chapter 10.

At the conclusion of the meeting itself the company secretary should ensure that any spare copies of the board papers, any notes, flip charts etc. are removed from the meeting room and securely destroyed.

A copy of the board papers should be retained either with the minutes or separately. This is particularly important if there is a subsequent review of the decision to demonstrate the information that was available to the directors and the factors taken into consideration by them when making their decision.

6.3　Members

Members communications

Communications with members are much more structured and there are many provisions in the Act and each company's Articles governing the notice periods, content of notices, rights to speak, appointment of proxies and voting at members' meetings.

Companies by default will communicate with their members in hard copy with electronic communications only permitted if the members consent or are deemed to have consented. Even in circumstances where a member has consented to receiving communications electronically, they are still entitled to request a hard copy of any communication.

Whether the communication is issued in hard copy or electronically or a mixture of the two, the same information must be provided to all members. The requirements for notice periods, content of notices, rights to speak, appointment of proxies and voting at members' meetings is considered in chapter 14.

Companies need to ensure that their members' address information is kept up to date so as to ensure, as far as possible, that members' communications are sent to the correct address. The legality of a meeting where notice of a meeting is not sent with sufficient notice or sent to an address it knows or ought to know is wrong, can be called into question. If the meeting has not been convened correctly due to improper notice any resolutions approved by that meeting may be declared void. Accidental omission to send a notice does not invalidate the meeting.

Stop and think 9.6

In *Bradman v Trinity Estates plc [1989] BCLC 757*, **notices of a meeting were posted during a postal workers' strike to shareholders living outside London but delivered by courier to those with addresses in London. The only members of the company who attended the meeting were those living in London whose notice had been delivered by courier. The court refused to accept the usual concept that notice is deemed to have been delivered 48 hours after posting.**

The company should keep all papers circulated with notices convening a members' meeting with the minutes of the meeting or separately.

Access rights

Members have no statutory right to access historic copies of circulars etc. however they must be sent those documents in respect of any meetings they are entitled to attend.

Listed companies must publish notice of general meetings via an RIS and accordingly the historic record of general meeting notices and accompanying circulars is available for as long as the company remains listed.

As noted previously auditors have a general right of access to all of a company's records and reports.

Test yourself 9.5

1. **Directors have no statutory right to access board papers, why is this?**

2. **Is there any statutory requirement to retain notices of either directors' or members' meetings?**

7. Financial records

As noted in section 8.4, all companies are required to keep accounting records.

The volume and detail of accounting records kept will vary considerably from company to company. In addition, some companies may retain their records largely in manual hard copy form while others will retain theirs largely if not entirely in electronic form only.

At is simplest form a company's accounting records will comprise bank statements, accounts ledgers, details of suppliers showing who the supplier is, invoices received and paid, details of customers also showing invoices issued and paid and a schedule of assets showing amounts paid and details of any depreciation, etc.

7.1   What accounting information needs to be maintained?

The accounting records that each company must keep must be sufficient to:

◆   show and explain company transactions;
◆   disclose with reasonable accuracy, at any time, the financial position of the company; and
◆   enable the directors to prepare accounts and financial statements required by the Act (CA2006 ss. 386, 387).

These accounting records are likely to include the following details as a minimum:

◆   all items of income and expenditure;
◆   assets purchased outright or leased by the company;

- stock the company owns at the end of each financial year;
- the stocktakings used to work out the stock figure;
- contractual company liabilities such as bank borrowing, rental and lease payments, directors' loans;
- day-to-day trading amounts owed to or due to the company for the supply or receipt of goods and services; and
- details of PAYE, VAT and corporation taxes paid, payable or refundable.

Financial records must be kept in order to prepare annual accounts and company tax returns including bank statements, receipts, petty cash books, orders and delivery notes. Invoices, contracts, sales books and till rolls should also be kept.

Companies registered as employers must also keep PAYE records to complete annual PAYE returns, calculate PAYE and NICs and show employees are receiving all statutory pay to which they are entitled.

7.2 Where kept

A company's accounting records must be kept either at the company's registered office or at such other place as the directors think appropriate and must be available for inspection by any officer of the company at any time (CA2006 s. 388(1)).

7.3 Retention periods

A company's accounting records must be kept for a minimum period of three years in the case of a private company and six years in the case of a public company (CA2006 s. 388(4)).

In practice, many private companies also keep their records for a minimum of six years as this is the period during which HMRC are able to investigate the company's tax affairs after the submission of the relevant tax return.

7.4 Inspection

The directors have a general right to access all the records of the company, have the right to inspect the accounting records at any time and also have an obligation to prepare accounts based upon those records (CA2006 ss. 386–8).

Auditors have a general right of access to all the company's books and records and to make enquiries for the purposes of their audit (CA2006 s. 499(1)).

Various regulatory bodies have the right to request that various documents are provided to them. Some of these may also have the right to undertake searches for those documents. Such bodies include inspectors or competent persons appointed by BEIS, HMRC, FCA, CMA and the Takeover Panel.

Members have no right of access or inspection of a company's accounting records.

8. Corporate records

There are a number of documents that a company must prepare and retain and in certain cases have available for inspection by members and/or the general public.

8.1 Directors' service contracts

A director's employment contract is often referred to as a service contract.

Companies are required at all times to keep copies of directors' service contracts available for inspection by members, free of charge, at either their registered office address or its SAIL address (CA2006 s. 228) and must be kept for a minimum of 12 months following termination of the contract.

8.2 Directors' indemnities

Where a company maintains a directors' indemnity insurance policy this must be noted in the directors' report and a copy of the policy must be kept available for inspection by members, free of charge, at either its registered office address or its SAIL address (CA2006 s. 237) and must be kept for a minimum of 12 months following expiry of the indemnity period.

8.3 Minutes

Minutes of meetings of the directors and of the members and any class meetings must be kept by the company for a minimum of 10 years (CA2006 ss. 248, 355).

The minutes of meetings of the members or class meetings must be kept available for inspection by members, free of charge, at the registered office address or the SAIL address (CA2006 s. 358).

8.4 Accounting records

All companies must keep accounting records. While the Act does not stipulate the form of those records, they must be sufficient to:

◆ show and explain company transactions;

◆ disclose with reasonable accuracy, at any time, the financial position of the company; and

◆ enable the directors to prepare accounts and financial statements required by the Act (CA2006 ss. 386, 387).

A company's accounting records must be kept either at the company's registered office or at such other place as the directors think appropriate and must be available for inspection by any officer of the company at any time (CA2006 s. 388(1)).

A company's accounting records must be kept for a minimum period of three years in the case of a private company and six years in the case of a public company (CA2006 s. 388(4)).

In practice many private companies also keep their records for a minimum of six years as this is the period during which HMRC are able to investigate the company's tax affairs after the submission of the relevant tax return.

8.5 Contracts for purchase of own shares

Where a company purchases its own shares pursuant to authority given under CA2006 ss. 693A, 694 or 701, a copy of the purchase contract or a written memorandum of its terms if the contract is not in writing must be kept by the company for a period of at least 10 years from the date the contract completed or the date on which the contract otherwise determines (CA2006 s. 702).

The contract or memorandum of written terms must be kept at the company's registered office address or its SAIL address and must be kept available for inspection, free of charge by any member in the case of a private company and by any person in the case of a public company (CA2006 s. 702(6)).

8.6 Documents for purchases out of capital

Where a private company purchases it own shares out of capital pursuant to authority given under CA2006 s. 709 copies of the directors' statement and auditor's report must be kept available for inspection for a period of five weeks following the earlier of publication of the Gazette notice required by CA2006 s. 719(1) or newspaper advertisement or individual notice to creditors required by CA2006 s. 719(2). The documents must be kept available for inspection, free of charge by any member or creditor, at the registered office address or SAIL address (CA2006 s. 720).

8.7 Report to members of investigation by public company into interests in shares

If a public company has been requested to investigate the ownership of some of its own shares pursuant to CA2006 s. 803 any report and any interim reports must be kept for a period of six years from the date the report was first published (CA2006 s. 805).

The copies must be kept at the registered office address or SAIL address, and must be available for inspection by members free of charge.

Stop and think 9.7

In the same way that a natural person keeps their personal documents at their home address companies are required to do the same. Many companies however use a third party address, typically their lawyer or accountant, as their registered office and it would be inconvenient to keep the records duplicated at their registered office address. In recognition of this companies may alternatively keep their records available for inspection at their SAIL address which can be a trading address.

Companies with shares traded on a public market and using the services of a share registrar will need to carefully consider where they locate their registered office as their SAIL address will need to be at the office of the share registrar in order to satisfy the obligation to keep the register of members available for inspection at either the registered office or SAIL address.

Test yourself 9.6

1. Companies must keep accounting records with sufficient detail to enable the directors to assess what?

2. For how long must companies keep minutes of meetings of their directors and members?

3. Do a company's members have to pay a fee to inspect the registers or documents that must be available for their inspection?

9. Retention periods for documents and registers

The company secretary is often responsible for exercising control over the company's policy regarding the filing and retention of documents. The period for which documents should be retained depends on the nature of the document. Retention periods are often a balance of a company's desire to keep data relating to its business and the requirement under data protection legislation not to keep personal data for longer than is strictly necessary.

Case law has demonstrated the necessity for companies to have an effective document retention policy that is relevant to their business, is adhered to by all parts of the business and that where litigation is anticipated prompt action is taken to ensure documents are not destroyed either deliberately or in accordance with the normal operation of the policy.

Table 9.3 sets out suggested retention periods for common documents.

Statutory records	Retention period
Certificate of incorporation	Original to be kept permanently
Certificate to commence business	Original to be kept permanently (public company)
Articles of association	Original to be kept permanently
Seal book/register	Original to be kept permanently
Registers other than register of members	Original to be kept permanently
Register of members	Current members permanently, former members 10 years

Statutory records	Retention period
Meeting records	
Minutes of general and class meetings, written resolutions	Originals to be kept permanently for meetings held prior to 1 October 2007
	Ten years after meeting for meetings held after 1 October 2007
Directors' minutes	Originals to be kept permanently for meetings held prior to 1 October 2007
	Ten years after meeting for meetings held after 1 October 2007
Circulars to shareholders including notices of meetings	Master copy to be kept permanently
Accounting and financial records	
Annual report and accounts	Signed copy to be kept permanently (a stock of spare copies should be maintained for up to five years to meet casual requests)
Accounting records required by the Companies Acts	Six years for a public company
	Three years for a private company
Taxation returns and records, internal financial reports, statements and instructions to banks and Customs and Excise returns	Six years
Tax returns	Permanently
Expense accounts	Seven years
Share registration documents	**Refer to Articles, but typical periods are**
Forms for application of shares and transfer, renounceable letters of acceptance and allotment, renounceable share certificates, request for designation or re-designation of accounts, letters	Ten years from date of registration
Powers of Attorney and indemnity for lost certificates	Ten years after cessation of membership to which power relates
Dividend and interest bank mandate	Two years after registration forms
Cancelled share or stock certificates	One year after cancellation
Changes of address	Two years
Any contract or memorandum to purchase the company's own shares	Ten years
Report of an interest in voting shares	Six years for investigations requisitioned by members

Statutory records	Retention period
Register of interest in shares when company ceases to be a public company	Six years

Property records	
Deeds of title, patent and trademark records	Permanently
Leases	Twelve years after lease has terminated
Agreements with architects, builders, etc.	Six years after contract completion

HR records	
Staff personnel records	Seven years after employment ceases
Patent agreements with staff	Twenty years after employment ceases
Applications for jobs	Up to twelve months
Payroll records, medical records, accident books	Twelve years
Employment agreements	Permanently
Time cards and piecework records	Two years
Salary registers, wages records, industrial training records	Six years

Pension records	
Trustees and rules (pension schemes), trustees' minute book, pension fund annual accounts and Inland Revenue approvals, investment records, actuarial valuation records, contribution records	Permanently
Records of ex-pensioners	Six years after cessation of benefit pension scheme investment policies

Insurance records	
Group health policies, group personal accident policies	Twelve years after final cessation of benefit
Public liability policies, product liability policies, employers' liability policies	Permanently
Sundry insurance policies	Three years after lapse
Claims correspondence, accident reports and relevant correspondence	Three years after settlement
Insurance schedules	Ten years

Statutory records	Retention period
Other records	
Vehicle registration records, MOT records	Two years after disposal of vehicle certificates and vehicle maintenance
Certificates and other documents of title	Permanently or until investment disposed of
Trust deeds	Originals to be kept permanently
Contracts with customers, suppliers or agents, licensing agreements, rental and hire purchase agreements, indemnities and guarantees	Six years after expiry

Table 9.3 Suggested document retention periods

Chapter summary

◆ Requirement to make and keep minutes of meetings

◆ Board packs and general meeting circulars

◆ What corporate records are required, where they should be kept and who has the right of access

◆ How long must corporate records be kept

Chapter ten
Company secretarial software

CONTENTS

1. Introduction
2. Evaluation of needs for company secretarial software
3. Implementation of appropriate software
4. Security issues
5. Potential uses and benefits of company secretarial software
6. Ongoing maintenance and updates

1. Introduction

Over recent years there has been an expansion in the availability of software applications designed to assist company secretaries. These can be divided into four broad categories:

- form filing and online filing packages;
- statutory register maintenance;
- minutes and resolution generation applications; and
- group structure overview.

In addition, there are packages that combine two or three of these categories into one application as well as packages providing complete entity management solutions and platforms or online portals which in addition to the core company secretarial requirements comprise a database for keeping a wide variety of information including GDPR records, data protection registration and trade mark renewal information, advisers etc.

For the purposes of the following sections, it is assumed that an entity management application is the preferred option. However, similar stages of assessment and implementation will apply to a greater or lesser extent to any software acquisition and deployment project.

As companies grow, whether through organic growth or by acquisition, this is often (especially in the case of M&A growth) accompanied by an increase in the number of subsidiaries within a group. While the number remains modest maintaining these records using a manual system, hard copy or electronic, supplemented with utilising the Companies House online web portal for submitting forms remains a practical answer to maintaining the corporate records.

However, as the number of group companies starts increasing and the range of 'group' information required to be kept track of increases, such as tax reference numbers, GDPR registration and renewals, trade mark and patent registrations etc., manual systems are quickly overwhelmed. Group record keeping can soon become a governance problem as information and requests are received and processed in different ways and the records of when actions were taken, by whom and when the renewal is due is also undertaken by different members of staff in different ways, with different descriptions and sometimes different documents and spreadsheets.

Online submission of forms and documents and acknowledgement or rejection of those filings is facilitated via the Companies House XML Gateway. In addition to all the forms available to be filed using Companies House own WebFiling facility, companies developing their own software can submit additional types of company accounts as well as incorporation documents. Software filing uses XML while accounts submission uses iXBRL. A technical interface specification giving detailed information for software developers is available via email from Companies House.

In addition to purchasing an existing product or developing an in-house solution, an online filing account is required to use software to file information.

2. Evaluation of needs for company secretarial software

As with any major purchase, a significant software or application system should not be chosen lightly, and it is important to assess in advance exactly what the objective is. The first stage is to understand what the current system delivers, the areas of weakness and the wish list the users, or end recipient(s) of the system output, would like to see.

The process of establishing the businesses requirements is often poorly combined with establishing standard operating procedures and practices. Both elements are important but all too often the desire to adopt standard processes obscures the underlying business requirements and can lead to poor choices being made further along in the process. However, the business requirements should be a framework from which the standardised procedures and practices are based rather than the goal itself.

These business requirements should be documented in a structured and methodical way, with prioritisation of current and future needs and differentiation between needs and wants are important areas to focus on. This process is particularly important for a non-IT department setting out its requirements to the IT or purchasing department that will be responsible for identifying and undertaking the initial assessment of potential solutions.

Application sellers can also use this documentation to match their functionality against, highlight any areas where any bespoke needs might be required and introduce additional complimentary processes within their product of which the end users might not be aware.

There are many different ways of identifying and documenting business requirements including:

◆ **Focus groups within the company:** a group of users that perform specific duties and tasks that can be polled to ascertain their duties, functions and system interactions within the company.

◆ **Interviews:** an account of what is currently being done to support the business.

◆ **Interface analysis:** an examination as to inputs, outputs and intermediary steps that may be required for the system to function and define interoperability to existing systems.

◆ **Surveys:** an internal account from different points of view as to how operations and processes actually happen.

◆ **Observation:** this refers to walking around and drawing your own conclusions as to how things are done.

Figure 10.1 gives an overview of the process for establishing the business requirement to be used to assess potential software solutions against.

The business requirements document should include all processes that are or might be carried out whether that is daily, weekly, quarterly or on an ad-hoc basis.

Documenting the current processes should be relatively straightforward however the business requirements should also look forward and try and capture new

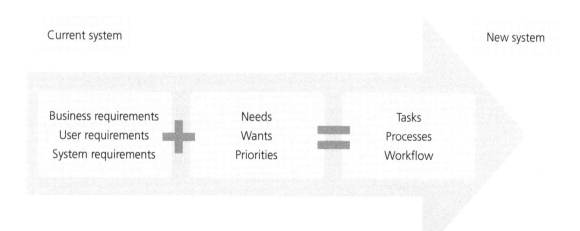

Figure 10.1 Overview of process to document business requirement

functions that might be required in the future or additional processes that the new software solutions will facilitate.

To avoid unnecessary confusion, it is important to ensure that those tasked with documenting the processes, especially those involved at the periphery understand the purpose of the exercise as otherwise critical processes might be omitted in error or additional features not requested at an early stage. At best, such omissions can cause delay and increased costs and at worst can cause a new software solution to represent a backward step in terms of a department's operational efficiency, effectiveness or capability. This is more of a potential risk where a large amount of bespoke work is required rather than in a case where an off the shelf solution is adopted with minimum tailoring required.

In addition to ensuring that all current processes, however rarely occurring, are captured it is also important to distinguish between a need rather than a want. Needs are key to ensuring the platform is able to provide the full range of current activities and must have priority over wants.

The process of documenting the business requirements and existing, potential or actual business needs and wants, is susceptible to scope or requirement creep.

Once your business requirements document is finalised the next stage is the creation of a tender document which potential vendors will use to demonstrate how their solution/platform matches the required business processes and identifies any configuration or additional development work that might be required.

The choice of preferred software vendor is equally important to the successful implementation of a software solution. Factors to consider include the following.

Flexibility
You need a supplier that will adapt to your changing business model, not a supplier that is only interested in providing their standard product with no system tailoring. This flexibility does however require balancing with the cost both financial and in time required to develop a bespoke solution.

Helpfulness
By contrast to the need to be flexible a supplier that is only interested in supplying additional modules such as incorporations or validating data with Companies House without demonstrating statutory register reports which should be at the core of the system is probably not too interested in building a long-term partnership. Once your order has been secured they will be off to the next customer.

Knowledge
Does this supplier know which legal requirements and technology solutions work in your industry? If you have to stop a conversation to correct a salesperson then it is possible that the supplier is not necessarily an expert in the systems you require, but perhaps the entity management solution is part of a larger package.

There is a danger where your requirements are not the primary focus of the supplier that when legislation or form designs change these may not be as high a priority for them as they are for you.

Foresight

Try to find out what the supplier's main areas of development are. If these match your own expectations for the application, you will benefit from their main focus and area of interests and expertise. However, if their main focus is on expanding the capability of the platform for say international governance and your group is entirely UK centric this may not be the best fit for you. Ask if there are any major system upgrades in the pipeline possibly requiring greater hardware performance than the existing platform. You do not want to go through the expense of implementing a new platform only to discover in 12 months that a substantial new investment in the latest upgrade for both software and hardware is required to take advantage of their latest system enhancements.

Support

Tech support is crucial during the early stages of a relationship with a new vendor. For the first few months of transition, your vendor should provide staff training to your business's employees and back-end support to your IT department to prevent any serious delays in your operations.

Accountability

In a perfect world, new applications and platforms will integrate seamlessly with your existing IT estate. In reality things are rarely that simple and you need to have the confidence that your supplier will be on hand to assist with the necessary tweaks to iron out these integration issues without wanting to charge extra. The chances are they will have experienced the same or similar integration issues with previous customers.

Security

Entity management solutions and platforms handle very sensitive commercial as well as personal data and it is important that the supplier of choice is fully committed to providing assurance of security controls and practices ideally through third-party certifications and audits.

Asking the right questions of your potential suppliers is important, but also ensuring that your company's own IT resources are engaged at an early stage and have the capacity to assist with the implementation will reap great benefits longer term.

Stop and think 10.1

Whether a general upgrading of an existing platform or the first-time adoption of a digital solution replacing largely manual processes is being considered, getting the right platform is key, getting the best known or the one preferred by most employees does not necessarily deliver the solution the business requires.

3. Implementation of appropriate software

Having chosen the application of choice the next phase is implementation and transfer of the existing records from whatever format they are currently held in onto the new database. During the lead-up to the go-live date, it is sensible to ensure that the existing data is accurate and up to date and that any data that is no longer required can be deleted or marked for archiving in accordance with the company's data retention policy.

Where data currently resides in manual records, it will be necessary to develop a plan to create the new database and populate it with the necessary entity data. Many of the entity management platforms are able to populate the basic company data directly from the Companies House database, which greatly assists it setting up the core information. Unfortunately for other records that may be spread across a number of departments, these will require manual entry and there needs to be a methodical and systematic approach to entering the data ensuring consistency of data entry as well as a verification phase.

As part of the assessment phase, the software supplier should have reviewed the existing datasets and established which, if any of the digitally held records, could be imported directly into the new database.

Where the new platform is replacing an existing database, the software supplier will have mapped the existing dataset and imported the existing data into the new database with the result that the new database will, in most cases, be operational 'out of the box'. Inevitably, the new platform will have additional functionality and additional data points that can be utilised and there will need to be a methodical and systematic approach to entering this data ensuring consistency of data entry as well as a verification phase.

Employees that will be using the new platform will require training on the new system. Often introductory training can be undertaken in advance of implementation to demonstrate the layout, menu systems etc. followed up by detailed sessions once the platform has been deployed and live data added.

Unless the new platform requires new hardware, it is common (if not desirable) to retain the previous platform at least in the short term with older archived records remaining on that system, pending deletion in due course, rather than loading historic information on now-defunct entities onto the new platform.

Once the data, both old and new, is captured in the new system, ideally there should be a validation process to ensure the data is accurate and error free. As the amount of data companies and especially groups hold grows, managers and strategic planners need access to accurate, insightful and timely data.

It is important to recognise that, as with all databases, the Achilles heel to the ability to generate meaningful, accurate and pertinent information in a timely manner is the accuracy and completeness of the underlying dataset. Inevitably, over time the accuracy of the database will degrade. GIGO (garbage in, garbage out) may be an acronym that has been in use for as long as computers have been used, but it remains as true today as when it was first used. In computer science, GIGO describes the concept that flawed, or nonsense input data produces nonsense output or 'garbage'. The principle also applies more generally to all analysis and logic, in that arguments are unsound if their premises are flawed.

The deployment of a new platform is an ideal opportunity to bring the database back to its ideal state and to complete all those little administration tasks that have been on the 'to do when quiet' list longer than anyone cares to remember. Whatever method, operational processes and templates are used to ensure data consistency the key to delivering a truly enabling platform is being able to deliver the right data to the right people at the right time.

Once managers and senior executives across the company or group know they can rely on the data that their entity management platform delivers, they can perform their job functions with confidence. Creating a single, trustworthy source of data truth is a key function of any entity management platform.

An entity management platform must provide data that is:

◆ accurate

◆ secure

◆ accessible.

In this context accessibility refers to system access being tiered and segmented with access to different levels or types of report, input and editing rights being granted according to function and seniority of the user.

Test yourself 10.1

1. **Which gateway is used to software file at Companies House?**

2. **In addition to an appropriate software package what else is required to software file?**

3. **What is GIGO?**

---

4. Security issues

In a world of cyber attacks, phishing and hacks ever increasing data security is an absolute priority with any entity management platform which when used to their fullest extent will hold both personal information on a group's most senior employees as well as confidential information and essential calendar reminders for key business renewals.

Even systems with more limited capabilities such as form filing software have the ability to save and keep copies of forms created and many of these will also contain personal information. While much of this might not be so sensitive especially as the forms created are to be placed on the public record some forms do contain confidential information, such as residential addresses of directors and members.

Even where the personal data is available on the public record, GDPR considerations require the company to keep that data secure.

Hand in hand with the requirement to keep data secure and prevent data loss is the equally important need to keep the data secure from unauthorised access, tampering and falsification of the data whether from external or internal sources. In many ways the internal threat from a disaffected member of staff can be more difficult to protect against as they are already, to a large extent, inside the security wall. The usual IT security techniques of ensuring the appropriate access levels, restricting the ability to make changes to the data and regular password refreshes will go a long way to mitigate against this risk. Other measures are to generate reports of changes to sensitive data and while not stopping the fraudulent activity reviewing changes to the information filed at Companies House and elsewhere will at least alert the company at an early stage that there is a problem.

Companies House have introduced their PROOF system to guard against unauthorised filings of certain changes such as director changes or change of registered office unless those changes are submitted electronically. The protection gained from this process will be worthless if the fraudster can simply tamper with the electronic registers maintained by the company and use the application to change both the company's registers and also the information at Companies House.

5. Potential uses and benefits of company secretarial software

The corporate secretariat sits at the centre of any organisation and is usually the resource owner of an entity management platform which has maintenance of the core statutory records and automating compliance obligations at its heart. Complimentary to this role is the necessity to identify and prevent legal, governance and compliance risks. One easy way to help accomplish this is to adopt and enforce standard processes and documentation, automating existing manual processes and introducing effective control and monitoring processes to both check that tasks are completed on time but also to check that nothing unexpected has changed. Entity management systems have evolved over the years to streamline, automate, improve accuracy and speed up the delivery of managing company and in particular group regulatory and compliance requirements. These changes combined with the relative rise in the profile of the governance aspects of the corporate secretariat compared to the traditional compliance role have enabled corporate secretariats to contribute to strategic initiatives.

As organisations continue to focus on how to grow their business effectively and globally, many are increasingly growing through M&A, adding subsidiaries, adding new products and services, or venturing into new markets. For organisations to support these high-growth initiatives properly, they require a robust corporate governance platform to make sure this growth is coupled with good governance practices. Effective corporate governance means having specific rules, controls, policies and resolutions in place to dictate corporate behaviour; good governance is nothing more than using the right information and controls to direct an organisation effectively and to make decisions.

Using a well thought-out and easy to use entity management platform allows the corporate secretariat to provide all relevant departments with real-time access to entity- and subsidiary-related information in a secure manner. The entity management platform becomes the single respected and trusted source of corporate records, which in turn facilitates compliance and governance risk mitigation through standard processes and procedures, and to keep data accuracy and data relevance as high as possible.

At its core an entity management platform should assist the efficiency of the corporate secretariat by both increasing the throughput of compliance work and also by automatically tracking compliance deadlines ensuring as far as possible 100% on time completion of regulatory, governance and compliance tasks.

The pace of legislative and regulatory changes continues in spite of the many red tape initiatives by successive governments. Entity management platforms can assist tracking which, if any, entities in a diverse group will need to address changes such as the introduction of disclosure of gender pay gap information, ensuring all relevant companies have a modern slavery statement through to tracking the requirement to undertake an audit tender process or payment practices disclosures – and these are just changes affecting UK companies!

6. Ongoing maintenance and updates

In many ways, the hard work commences as soon as the implementation and data verification phase is completed and signed off.

The database accuracy has the potential to degrade as soon as everyone believes it has entered a steady state. It is vital that all departments using the platform provide information on changes needed simply to keep the existing dataset up to date, but there will also be new entities being incorporated or acquired on a regular basis for some groups. By utilising one central database and system that those other departments use, there is a better chance of the information being captured even if not directly by the corporate secretariat.

In addition to ensuring the accuracy of the dataset, it is vitally important that there are regular programme updates reflecting changing legislation and best practice.

Stop and think 10.2

The corporate secretariat of a large insurance group once commented that their main problem with keeping the group entity structure up to date was persuading the various departments, be they legal, finance or business development, actually to tell them when they had incorporated new companies. The first indication was often a reminder from Companies House to file the first confirmation statement!

Chapter summary

◆ Benefits of entity management platforms

◆ Process of evaluating new platforms for upgrades or first time deployment

◆ Security considerations

◆ Benefits to be gained from a good entity management platform

◆ Implementation is just the start and the database must be kept up to date

Chapter eleven
Minutes and minute books

CONTENTS

1. Introduction
2. Required information in minutes
3. The six 'C's
4. Proof of existence of an organisation and its historical development
5. Record of decisions made and actions taken
6. Demonstration of due diligence on part of decision-makers
7. Legal evidence in support of actions taken
8. Records retention
9. Risk management – protecting the organisation

1. Introduction

The importance of proper record keeping in general and minutes of meetings of the directors and members, especially of directors' meetings, cannot be overemphasised. At best it might prove difficult to demonstrate appropriate governance on an important issue and at worst it might invalidate subsequent event(s).

While some acts of directors can subsequently be ratified if there has been a change of directors that may not be possible. Alternatively, the failure to properly authorise and record one decision may have a consequential effect that invalidates another decision that cannot be ratified either at all or with sufficient speed to meet a pressing deadline.

2. Required information in minutes

Companies are required to keep minutes of meetings of their directors (CA2006 s. 248) or general meetings of their members (CA2006 s. 355(1)(b)), written resolutions of the members (CA2006 s. 355(1)(a)) or decisions of any sole member (CA2006 s. 355) or sole member of a class (CA2006 s. 359).

It is clear from the legislation that it is essential that a proper record is kept of all decisions of the members and directors of the company and that there can be no doubt as to the veracity of the minutes and consequently of the decisions taken unless a contrary position can be proved. This requirement for proof goes beyond any suggestion or the recollection of those present as actual proof is required to overturn any minuted decisions.

The Act is not entirely clear if the provision to record and keep minutes of meetings of the directors extends also to meetings of committees of the directors. Some company Articles may have an explicit requirement to keep committee meeting minutes and it certainly is good practice to do so.

As with the organisation and holding of meetings of the directors or the members the Act gives directors much more freedom to govern their own affairs to suit their own purposes. Consequently, the Act makes no provision for directors to take decisions by written resolution and any such authority will derive from the Articles or under common law.

The Act and the Articles are silent on the detail of what constitutes minutes and it is for each company to decide for themselves the style, content and format of the minutes. On the face of it taking minutes should be a simple task to prepare a synopsis of the discussions held and to record decisions made at the meeting. Unfortunately, meetings, especially directors' meetings, are rarely that straightforward.

The company secretary needs to have a sixth sense to interpret the mood of the meeting and the individuals present and the near invisible body language intended to indicate the detail of the minutes required or even whether minutes of the discussion are required at all. It is all too common after five minutes of feverish writing on the part of the company secretary on a sensitive subject for the main speaker to add the words 'and none of this is for the minutes...'. It is very rare indeed for the other directors present, or any of them, to disagree with that assertion.

It can be very useful for the company secretary to have a pre-meeting with the key directors, as this will often enable the company secretary to include in the minutes those key items that the director did not mention at the meeting but are known to all present and are important to be recorded as part of the decision-making process. The art of deciphering what was understood to be said rather than the words that in reality were said is one of the key differences between a good minute taker and someone who merely transcribes what was said.

There will be routine departures from the pre-agreed running order of the agenda with disproportionate time spent discussing minor matters while the main topic of the meeting is relegated to a brief discussion as those present prepare to leave the meeting. There will be many occasions where a new topic is introduced, discussed at length but which no one present wants to be recorded.

Minutes of meetings of the directors recorded and retained in accordance with CA2006 s. 248 and authenticated by the chair of the next directors' meeting are evidence (in Scotland sufficient evidence) of the proceedings of the meeting (CA2006 s. 249(1)). Provided the minutes have been properly recorded then until the contrary is proved the meeting is deemed duly held and convened, the proceedings to have taken place and any appointments made at the meeting are deemed valid (CA2006 s. 249(2)).

Where the decisions are taken by written resolution there will of course be no minutes but instead one or more copies of the resolutions signed by the directors to signify their consent. By their nature such written resolutions only contain details of the decisions to be approved and may also contain a briefing of the relevant subject matter. Written resolutions do not however contain any discussion of the subject matter as there is no forum for any such discussion.

2.1   Static data

The content requirement of minutes is not set out in the Act nor in the Articles, but the following are generally agreed as best practice for directors' minutes:

◆ company name and registered number (registered number is useful where the company subsequently changes its name);

◆ place, date and time the meeting commenced;

◆ attendees (indicating which part of the meeting was attended by those not present for the whole meeting);

◆ identity of the person chairing the meeting;

◆ confirmation that a quorum is present;

◆ declaration of any specific potential conflicts of interest in matters to be discussed or changes of general potential conflicts of interest; and

◆ time meeting closes.

For members' meetings, it is not necessary for those present to declare any conflicts of interest. Additionally, particularly for meetings with large numbers of members present it is not necessary to identify in the minutes everyone that is present with some companies referring to the attendance list and others noting the number of members present. Others might simply refer to a quorum of members being present.

The time the meeting starts and ends is not absolutely necessary; however, it can prove useful where a sequence of meetings are being held to demonstrate the order of those meetings.

2.2   Variable data

Variable data includes:

◆ matters brought forward and action points from previous meeting(s);

◆ review and approval for signature of minutes of the previous meeting;

◆ synopsis of discussions on matters on agenda, actions points, decisions made;

◆ matters to be carried forward and action points; and

◆ any other business not on the agenda.

Of these items of variable data, the synopsis of the discussions and decisions made is the most important. As considered in more detail in the next section the minutes need to strike a balance between including a full note of the discussion and the contribution of each speaker and the need for the minutes to be a concise record of proceedings.

Stop and think 11.1

Where the matter under discussion is contentious personal feelings can come to the fore and the language of the meeting change to be of a more personal nature and quite possibly contain forceful language. At such times the speakers might indicate to the minute taker that they want specific phrases included word for word. In reality and once tempers have cooled this is of course the last thing that they would wish to see recorded for posterity and the company secretary will most often use their discretion and take extra care to choose appropriate wording and possibly a briefer note.

3. The six 'C's

In addition to the six Cs discussed below, one of the areas where there is little if any guidance on is the process of actually taking notes during the meeting. Every person who takes notes of meetings has their own method for doing so. The only common feature of the various techniques is that it is usually impossible to take a verbatim record. Some people use short hand or their own version of shorthand others write long form notes to act as an aide-memoire while others precis the discussions in real time. Whichever method is used the key is to ensure that from these notes the minutes can be written and that no key discussions, actions or decisions are omitted.

Minutes are intended to allow someone who was not at the meeting to understand the reasoning behind each decision made without any additional input.

The six Cs of good communication are a useful guide to keep in mind when preparing and reviewing draft minutes.

Clarity
Minutes should be clear. Ideally, sentences should deal with single topics and each paragraph convey a clear message. The reader should not need to make assumption or read between the lines to understand the discussion or decision.

Meeting discussions can on occasion get heated and passions can run high. These emotions have no place in the minutes and the language of the minutes should be calm and neutral.

Coherence

A coherent minute is one that is written logically and with a consistent tone and flow and with all ancillary points linked to the main topic. Discussions at meetings can often get side tracked to other unrelated topics. If these are not part of the meeting, then there is no need to record them.

If, however, an action point or decision was made on the secondary issue, it may be preferable for this to be minuted, but in a section of its own rather than being intertwined with the matter originally under discussion even though in reality that is what happened.

Conciseness

Minutes should be a concise record of the meeting. While nothing material should be omitted, the company secretary will win no friends by padding out the minutes or repeating the same point several times – even if that actually happened during the meeting.

When writing the minutes, it is good to keep in mind whether or not what was said makes any difference to the overall discussions and whether it will add anything to the reader of the minutes in a month or a year or more. If the answer is not then it can safely be left out.

Consistency

Minutes that are written in a consistent style and tone will be much easier to read and be understood. This consistency should apply not just to individual meetings but to all the minutes. The meetings themselves may have a very different feel depending on the topic under discussion but the minutes should be free of emotion and emotive language impartially reflecting the discussion.

Consistency of style should apply not just to the minutes of each meeting but a consistent style for all meetings of that type. This makes the reading and understanding of the minutes in the context of previous or subsequent meetings much easier.

Board minutes and committee minutes will often have a similar style whereas minutes of general members' meetings tend to have a completely different, briefer and more formal style.

Completeness

Each section of the minutes should be complete showing the discussion and the decision reached, whether that is that the item was approved, not approved, deferred pending additional clarity or results of some testing until a later date, simply noted or some other result.

During a meeting, it may not always be clear what the result of the discussion has been and the company secretary should always seek clarification from the chair of the meeting.

For some meetings there is what can feel like a constant string of attendees coming and going which can be difficult to keep track of especially if the meeting carries on during these changeovers. Far better to prepare an attendance sheet before the meeting starts listing all those expected to be in attendance. As people arrive, they can be requested to sign in and note the time of their arrival and departure. Alternatively, if details of when each person arrived is not necessary the company secretary can simply tick off attendees as they arrive.

Correctness

Minutes that are correct in terms of the language, technical terms, grammar and spelling, will be much easier to understand and allow the reader to concentrate on the meaning of the message rather than the message itself.

Spelling and grammatical errors have no place in the minutes. Not only does this present a sloppy approach, but it deflects from the purpose of the minutes. It is strange how directors reviewing minutes may spot and comment on small typos, but completely overlook that a decision has been incorrectly recorded or an action attributed to the wrong person.

Stop and think 11.2

Good minute taking is often referred to as an art rather than a science and one that many, especially directors, do not fully understand or appreciate. As a general rule of thumb minutes of meetings of directors will often take two or three times as long to prepare as the meeting itself lasted. A speedier turnaround is of course possible, but the casualty will most often be accuracy and conciseness.

Test yourself 11.1

1. **Is it acceptable for minutes of members and directors to simply record decisions?**

2. **Is it necessary to record attendees at directors' meetings?**

4. Proof of existence of an organisation and its historical development

Companies are occasionally asked to prove that they exist and that directors or others have due authority to undertake certain specific actions. The existence of a company can be verified by way of providing copies of the Articles and Certificate of Incorporation. Authority to contract on behalf of the company may be inferred from any directors' authority matrix but otherwise will usually require an extract from the relevant board minute. Such extracts from board minutes may be certified as true copies by the company secretary.

The minute books of any company provide a historical record of significant events and decisions in a company's development over the years. The style and detail of the minutes as much as the content itself will reflect the stage of the company evolution.

Directors and company secretaries change over time with the result that minutes of meetings provide the only long-term first-hand account of what took place at meetings. Consequently it is extremely important that these are accurate and that the directors present review the minutes as there may not be anyone who was actually at the meeting to provide any explanations or clarity if the minutes subsequently are required as proof that a particular decision was made or more likely to provide evidence as to why it was made and the factors considered in reaching the decision.

5. Record of decisions made and actions taken

Minutes should record decisions reached, both in favour or against each individual matter brought to the board for a decision and include sufficient detail of the discussion to allow someone, not present at the meeting, upon reading the minutes to gain an insight into the reasons leading up to that decision and the key factors taken into consideration. It is important for the minutes to reflect not only the actions of the board but the context so that there is no uncertainty that it was done properly and that the directors discharged their duties to act in the best interests of the members but also with due regard to other stakeholders. In the interest of brevity, background information need not be repeated in detail in the minutes where that information is also provided in the board papers.

Where action points are recorded, it is useful to keep a record of these separately, including detail of the person the action had been assigned to and the target completion date, if known. This schedule can then be circulated to those tasked with any actions immediately after the meeting has closed and before the minutes are circulated. There may also be action points for persons who are not directors and who should not receive a copy even of only part of the minutes.

6. Demonstration of due diligence on part of decision-makers

As discussed above, minutes should always include sufficient detail of the discussion on any matter discussed to provide the reader with an accurate picture of all relevant factors giving rise to the decision. Simply recording any discussions may not however provide sufficient detail and background to the decision, in particular for listed or regulated companies, where the directors are often required to be able to demonstrate that they have fulfilled their duties to challenge decisions and consider their overriding duties to members and other stakeholders. Accordingly, the style and detail of minutes will also be influenced by the business and sector of the organisation.

The importance of accurate minute taking as well as the content of board papers is likely to come into focus with the introduction of the 's. 172 statement' as required by CA2006 s. 414CZA in strategic reports and for larger companies to report on their engagement and how they have had regard to the interests of members, employees, customers and suppliers. It is likely to see pressure for further evolution in the content of minutes towards more expansive minutes with particular emphasis on these reporting requirements.

For many companies, however, the board meeting may not be the forum where such directors' duties are best exercised. Directors that ensure that any regulatory or statutory duties are considered at an early stage and before the matter comes to the board for final review are no less diligent than those directors that raise such issues at a board meeting. Far better that the directors should exercise those duties to ensure that such considerations are built into the core values of the business and the decision-making process rather than being considered at the final approval process.

Although minutes can, and should, facilitate regulatory oversight this is not the purpose of the minutes and so they should not be written with that goal in mind, and regulators should use the minutes in conjunction with other evidence and not as the only or primary source of confirmation of due process.

There is also the danger that if minutes are to be used as the primary source of evidence of proper oversight by individual directors that either discussions at board meetings become muted as individuals do not wish too great a detail within the minutes or that unnecessary questions are asked in order that the minutes record challenge by individual directors.

Test yourself 11.2

1.   **Why should a record of votes for and against resolutions be maintained?**

2.   **What is the purpose of keeping directors' minutes?**

7. Legal evidence in support of actions taken

Accuracy in minutes writing is essential, since the minutes become the definitive record of the proceedings at a board meeting and of those who attended.

Evidential status is given to minutes of general meetings made under CA2006 s. 255 and signed by the chair as a correct record (CA2006 s. 356). These provisions are replicated for written resolutions of the members by CA2006 s. 382(A). Such minutes, unless there is evidence to the contrary, indicate that:

- the meeting they relate to is deemed duly held and convened;
- all proceedings at the meeting are deemed to have taken place; and
- all appointments made at the meeting are deemed valid.

Similarly to members' minutes, the minutes of meetings of the directors kept in accordance with CA2006 s. 248 and signed by the chair as a correct record are also given evidential status (CA2006 s. 249) and, unless the contrary is proved:

- the meeting they relate to is deemed duly held and convened;
- all proceedings at the meeting are deemed to have taken place; and
- all appointments made at the meeting are deemed valid.

This evidentiary status is not afforded to written resolutions of the directors, as there are no provisions in the Act specifically authorising the directors to make use of written resolutions unlike the position with written resolutions of members. As there is no provision for written resolutions there are consequently no provisions requiring copies of written resolutions to be kept and accordingly CA2006 s. 249 makes no mention of granting evidential status to directors' written resolutions.

By contrast the Model Articles Ltd and Guar reg. 15 do require copies of unanimous or majority decisions of the directors to be retained and this clearly also includes written resolutions.

If the minutes are retained in electronic form, they must still be authenticated by the chair of the meeting to be treated as evidence in proceedings. Alternatively, where the minutes are signed in hard copy and then scanned with the original being destroyed for those minutes to be accepted as evidence the British Standard code of practice for legal admissibility of information stored electronically should be followed.

Where a company is involved in a court case, the advice provided by its lawyers enjoys legal privilege. Care must be taken in circumstances where a court case is being considered at a directors' meeting to ensure that any privileged legal advice reflected in the minutes is clearly identified as privileged in order to avoid accidental disclosure. The minutes generally and any decisions taken based on the advice will not have legal privilege. Depending upon the specific circumstances the company secretary should consider clearly identifying those parts of the minutes that may be privileged or keeping privileged sections together in an annex to the main minutes.

Stop and think 11.3

Minutes that are properly authenticated and kept are evidence that the meeting took place and that the business set out in the minutes was undertaken.

If, however, the minutes are not properly authenticated or kept no such evidential status is conferred.

This is demonstrated in the case of *POW Services v Clare (1995) 2 BCLC 435*. In this case, the minutes were held not to be valid, as it was not possible to determine who had chaired or signed the minutes, and the minutes had never been entered in the minute books kept by the company.

8. Records retention

As noted in chapter 9, companies must keep minutes of meetings of both members and directors for at least 10 years, for meetings held after 1 October 2007 (implementation of the Act) (CA2006 ss. 248(2) and 355).

The minute retention period set out in the Act only applies to meetings held after 1 October 2007. For any meetings held before this date the retention period set out in CA1985 continues to apply. Under the CA1985, minutes of meetings of the members and of the directors have to be kept permanently.

In practice, the majority of companies retain all their minutes as part of the permanent record and do not take advantage of the availability of destroying historic minutes.

It is recommended that the notes taken by the minute taker are securely destroyed once the final version of the minutes has been agreed. Although some minute takers keep their notes there is a potential danger here as the notes would be discoverable in any legal proceedings and the meaning of the notes is often less clear than the agreed minutes leading to questions of which is the 'correct' record.

There is a similar danger with directors' notes, whether in hard or soft copy or annotated with board portal applications, and draft versions of the minutes, particularly in the regulated sectors. Individual directors may wish to retain any notes in order to demonstrate their oversight of specific issues that may not have been specifically included in the minutes or not in sufficient detail. It is for each board to reach its own policy in this regard and there may also be a requirement to reflect the practice within the corporate document retention policy.

Where minutes are created and retained in electronic form, they must still be capable of being reproduced in hard copy form (CA2006 s. 1135(2)). This requirement will apply not only at the point when the minutes are first stored in electronic form but for at least the 10-year period following the date of the meeting. As technology advances and systems are upgraded to the latest versions it will be essential to ensure that historic minutes are capable of being reproduced in hard copy as well as the records being readable on the new platform being used.

8.1 Security of documents

However the minutes and other board papers are stored they must be kept securely with access limited to those that require access. Board papers will contain sensitive information and for a listed company very possibly price sensitive information as well as confidential information.

Security is required not only to keep the content of minutes secure but also to guard against falsification of the minutes and to facilitate its discovery in any legal proceedings. As noted before the Act is silent on the format of the minute books and many companies use loose-leaf minute books. Their use was criticised by a judge in an action in 1936 as he observed that anyone wishing to do so can readily remove pages and insert replacement altered pages. Accordingly, although loose-leaf minute books are not barred it is important to ensure their security and to be able to demonstrate that no one was able to tamper with the minutes.

Companies that keep hard copy minutes and board packs will most likely keep these in a lockable, often fireproof, cupboard or filing cabinet. Where electronic copies are retained these will often be on a secure board portal or a restricted network drive.

Distribution of board packs in advance of the board meetings possesses the greatest security risk. There are a number of board meeting applications for the secure compilation, dispatch and retention of board papers as well as secure email applications. Where hard copy packs must be issued these are often delivered by courier rather than relying on ordinary postal delivery services.

Although companies are permitted to keep their minutes, of both directors' and members' meetings, in any way that they chose, it should be noted that the authenticity of the minutes can be questioned if they are not kept securely. There have been a few court cases where minutes have been rejected due to their insecurity including where minutes were kept in a loose-leaf minute book but could easily have been tampered with, as they had not been kept securely.

Whatever method is used to keep minutes, the following safeguards will provide additional security against tampering and falsification:

◆ Sequential numbering of all paragraphs.

◆ The chair to both sign the last page but also sign or at least initial each page.

◆ Hard copy minute books to be kept in lockable cupboard with restricted access.

◆ Where loose-leaf binders are used these should be lockable.

◆ To mitigate against the insertion of new text, minutes should be printed single spaced, no spaces between paragraphs and the signature of the chair on the line immediately following the last paragraph.

◆ Using special security printed and possibly numbered paper for the copy of the minutes to be signed. This does of course present an additional security risk, as the paper must also be kept securely.

Test yourself 11.3

1. **What are the differing minute retention periods for meetings held before or after 1 October 2007?**

2. **What are the dangers of not keeping minute books secure?**

3. **How long must a company keep its original, authenticated minutes?**

9. Risk management – protecting the organisation

As has been discussed already directors have an obligation to act in the best interests of the company's members and in exercising that duty must also have regard to the often-competing interests of employees, customers, suppliers and others having a business relationship with the company.

Managing risk in today's business environment is no easy task, and few commentators would argue that effective risk management and risk mitigation are fundamental components in the directors' arsenal to preserve value and assist value creation for a business. The risks associated with effective record keeping and information management have unfortunately not necessarily always been recognised by those charged with risk management although that has changed in recent years.

Within the context of risk management and mitigation, effective record keeping and document management are essential tools available to directors to demonstrate good governance and need not be an administrative burden or time-consuming task. In the longer term, good document management systems and processes bring far greater benefits than problems.

For company secretaries, good records and document management processes should be applied to the good maintenance and storage of statutory, financial, legal, commercial and other business records.

One of the drivers among larger traded companies for the rise in the use of corporate board portals was document security. Historically board packs were posted or couriered to each director if they were not based in the same office as the company secretary. Obviously, there are clear security concerns with such a process. The rise in the capacity of internet connections means that sharing even very large document files is fairly straightforward. In addition, many of the board portal applications include a number of security features especially for portable devices such as tablets and laptops such that if the device is lost or stolen the portal application can remotely delete any information transferred via the portal.

As noted above, one of the keys to good minutes is accuracy. Using exemplary document management processes, allowing ready access to the minutes on any given subject matter are however of little practical assistance if the minutes themselves do not accurately record the reasons for business decisions. The contrary position is equally true in that having properly drafted, accurate, detailed yet concise minutes clearly setting out the decision-making process are no use if the filing system in use is so poor as to make the minutes inaccessible.

Organisations are increasingly moving to keeping all their records electronically whether on commercially available or bespoke systems or simply by scanning original documents and destroying the originals, with only a limited number of hard copy originals being retained in the long-term. Whatever system is used to keep the records it is important to ensure that they are kept securely, confidentially and tamper proof.

As noted in chapter 9, all companies are required to keep their accounting records for a minimum period of three years in the case of a private company and six years in the case of a public company (CA2006 s. 388(4)). This requirement extends to much more than simply a copy of the published annual report and accounts but also the working papers, original ledgers, purchase and sales invoices and expense receipts, etc.

The same process should be employed with retained commercial agreements. While a copy or original of the final signed agreement must of course be kept it is also sensible to retain copies of notes of any negotiations, exchanges of correspondence and any legal advice obtained to guard against any potential litigation where the contract may be unclear and the original intent not obvious without reference to supporting documents.

Many companies have learned the hard way of the need to plan for the likelihood of the unthinkable happening and the need for effective contingency plans to ensure the business survives the event. The impact of record keeping risks cover the full range of commercial risks including economic and financial losses, reputational damage, injuries and delays. Record keeping risks also include the failure by a listed company to share or publish price sensitive inside information, as well as the more usual examples of breaches of information security.

With every year that passes, greater regulatory and compliance requirements have been imposed on companies in all aspects of business, from compliance with GDPR designed to restrict data disclosure, Listed Rule compliance designed to increase transparency and disclosure of information and increased reporting on environmental standards and carbon footprints. There is plenty of evidence that organisations are failing to meet this rising challenge of records management leading to own goal data breaches such as the classic 'leaving a laptop in a public venue' as well as the all-too-familiar cyberattacks against even the largest of companies.

Although increasing in recent years the role of chief information officer remains relatively rare and, when created, is most often seen as a technical IT systems role and not a content management role.

Managing record keeping risks is harder than ever before. Technology improvements have made it both easier, and harder. Technology makes it easier to copy electronic information, distribute and move it, while simultaneously making it more fragile, harder to preserve and protect from obsolescence.

As a result and with little over-all co-ordination records management responsibility is devolved across several departments each with their own, sometimes contradictory, records management policies and practices including the company secretary, IT, legal, finance, operations manager, HR and business development.

Ownership and control of records management should be clearly assigned, with particular regard for privacy protection and information security.

Stop and think 11.4

Breaches of information policies carry great reputational risks as well as the risks of regulatory fines as seen in the 2016 cyberattack against Tesco Bank which was fined £16.4 million by the FCA for failing to exercise due skill, care and diligence in protecting its personal current account holders against a cyberattack.

The data breach need not necessarily be against the company as seen in the 2017 data breach, which landed Equifax Ltd with a £500,000 fine for failing to protect the personal information of up to 15 million UK citizens.

The ICO investigation found that, although it was the information systems of its US parent, Equifax Inc., that were compromised, Equifax Ltd was responsible for the personal information of its UK customers. The UK arm of the company failed to take appropriate steps to ensure its American parent, which was processing the data on its behalf, was protecting the information.

Chapter summary

◆   Requirement to take and keep minutes of meetings of all types

◆   How to write good minutes

◆   Evidential status of minutes and source of historical information on a company

◆   Accessing company minutes

◆   Obligation to keep minutes, differing provisions for CA1985 and CA2006

◆   Risk management in the context of corporate records and minutes

Chapter twelve
Oversight by regulators

CONTENTS

1. Introduction
2. Governance practices – processes and procedures
3. Assessment of performance in carrying out governance responsibilities
4. Protection of stakeholders
5. Investigation powers of regulators

1. Introduction

All companies and especially those that have raised finance from external third party sources must ensure that their internal governance and compliance controls are appropriate. This means not only adopting relevant policies for the effective operation of the board and senior managers and decision-makers but at every level of the organisation. These policies must be implemented, monitored and regularly updated reflecting not only changes in best practice but also changes to the company.

Directors and a small group of investors guilty of insider trading, thousands of small investors losing everything, bribery of politicians and long-lasting damaging effect on the national economy might seem a familiar tale from the 2008 global financial crisis. However, in truth, this is a description of the South Sea Bubble from almost 300 years earlier.

After the initial outrage and prohibition on companies being formed without a Royal Charter, a consequence of the collapse of the South Sea Company and others was the creation of a new legal system to govern companies. In particular, measures intended to protect investors from the worst excesses of directors were included in the Joint Stock Companies Act of 1852, which is the foundation of the system of modern company law we have today.

2. Governance practices – processes and procedures

Move forward 300 years, and the government and regulators are still grappling with the consequences of perceived corporate governance failures such as seen with the recent collapse of Carillion plc, BHS Limited and House of Fraser Limited. While poor corporate governance will not have been the underlying cause of their collapse there is little doubt that better corporate governance processes are likely to have enabled the respective boards to have been in a better position to recognise, understand and act upon the warning signs earlier and possibly before the tipping point to failure occurred. Unfortunately, even the very best of corporate governance processes and practices cannot overcome a board that makes and sticks to a poor corporate strategy.

As seen in chapter 2, the UK company law model has at its heart a unitary board where directors have collective responsibility. Collective responsibility works best where no individual or group of directors become so powerful as to stifle debate and accountability from the remaining directors. This is also true at the various management levels. Accordingly, it is necessary, for listed companies, for there to be transparency in the whole appointment process for directors including the recruitment process, selection criteria and disclosure of the reasons the chosen candidate was better than their rivals for the role. Hand in hand with this transparency in the recruitment process are effective corporate governance processes and practices embedded within the management and oversight structures to provide appropriate checks and balances.

For sole director/shareholder companies corporate governance may seem unnecessary. While this is true in the sense that directors' and shareholders' interests are clearly aligned, corporate governance is best practice guidance covering several areas and some of these, with suitable adjustment, will be of benefit to even the smallest of organisations.

As discussed in chapter 5, in the UK, one of the more advanced countries in terms of promoting systems of corporate governance, the requirements are set out in the UK Corporate Governance Code most recently updated in 2018.

The first version of the UK Corporate Governance Code was produced in 1992 by the Cadbury Committee. It defined corporate governance as follows:

> Corporate governance is the system by which companies are directed and controlled. Boards of directors are responsible for the governance of their companies. The shareholders' role in governance is to appoint the directors and the auditors and to satisfy themselves that an appropriate governance structure is in place. The responsibilities of the board include setting the company's strategic aims, providing the leadership to put them into effect, supervising the management of the business and reporting to shareholders on their stewardship. The board's actions are subject to laws, regulations and the shareholders in general meeting.

Boards should comprise a balance of executive and independent members to provide the necessary checks and balances and scrutiny of management decisions and strategy. The balance of executive to independent directors is for each board to consider; however, generally speaking, the wider the ownership of the company and the larger the organisation the greater the importance of ensuring there are independent voices on the board.

First issued in 1999 and most recently updated in 2015, the OECD: Principles on Corporate Governance sets out six key principles. The principle on responsibilities of the board recommends the following:

◆ Board members should act on a fully informed basis, in good faith, with due diligence and care, and in the best interest of the company and the shareholders.

◆ Where board decisions may affect different shareholder groups differently, the board should treat all shareholders fairly.

◆ The board should apply high ethical standards. It should consider the interests of stakeholders.

◆ The board should fulfil certain key functions:

  – reviewing and guiding strategy, plans of action, risk management policies and procedures, annual budgets, business objectives, monitoring corporate performance and overview of capital expenditure, acquisitions and divestments;

  – monitoring the effectiveness of corporate governance practices;

  – responsibility for recruiting, setting salaries and other benefits and monitoring performance of the senior executives, replacing under-performing executives and ensuring appropriate succession planning is implemented;

  – establishing a framework to ensure the interests of executive directors and senior managers are aligned with the longer-term interests of the company and its shareholders;

  – ensuring a transparent board nomination and election process;

  – monitoring and managing potential conflicts of interest;

  – maintaining the integrity of accounting and financial systems; and

  – implementing an appropriate process for the timely disclosure and communication of information and in particular price sensitive information.

◆ The board should be able to exercise objective independent judgement on corporate affairs.

  – Consideration should be given to ensuring there is an appropriate balance of non-executive directors to provide independent oversight especially where there is potential for conflicts of interest.

  – Boards should assess whether additional board committees are required to support the board in key areas.

  – Boards must ensure that all directors are not over committed by taking on too many other directorships.

  – Regular board evaluations should be undertaken.

- To fulfil their responsibilities, board members should have access to accurate, relevant and timely information.
- In circumstances where employee board representation is required the representative must be supported in their role including providing access to information and training in order that the representative can effectively represent their constituency and is enabled to make a positive benefit to the board and its decision-making processes as a whole.

Written corporate governance policies ensure that organisations are run in a transparent, ethical manner, promoting good business practices. Corporate governance policies, formulated by the board and management and made available to all stakeholders, should address some or all of the following:

- election of directors to the board;
- the proportion of executive, non-executive and independent non-executive directors and diversity policy for board appointments;
- disclosure of information on finance and operations;
- composition and independence of audit, nomination, remuneration, risk and disclosure board standing committees;
- senior executive remuneration below board level;
- board meetings and operations;
- dividend policy;
- matters reserved for the board;
- delegated authority; and
- whistle-blowing.

Stop and think 12.1

Poor corporate governance combined with poor decision-making or cutting corners often contributes to corporate failure or scandal and leads to much greater losses than the original 'savings'.

In 2014, it emerged that Tesco, due to a failure of senior managers to correct accounting irregularities, had overstated its profit by over £250 million and which ultimately wiped £2 billion off Tesco's share price and led to the three men being prosecuted by the Serious Fraud Office.

3. Assessment of performance in carrying out governance responsibilities

Although most boards would not even question the business need and benefits of annual employee appraisals and target setting this is not the case when the topics of director and board evaluation, effectiveness and target setting are raised.

To borrow a sporting phrase, having a team composed of top-class individual players does not usually make the best team. The same is equally true for a board of directors. One of the key skills of the chair of a board and to a lesser extent of the company secretary is knowing how to ease and assuage the ego of individuals, usually the best at their job within the company, in order to maximise the usefulness and decision-making of the collective board.

3.1 Board performance and evaluation

It is a recommendation of the Governance Code that boards of the FTSE350 companies undertake an independent board evaluation exercise at least once every three years complemented by formal and rigorous annual evaluation of the performance of the board, its committees and individual directors (Governance Code principle L, provision 21).

Board evaluation can take many forms from completing standard questionnaires through to formal party interviews and observation at a board meeting. Accordingly, the Governance Code requires listed companies to provide details of the externally facilitated board evaluation undertaken (Governance Code principle L, provision 21).

The support and engagement of the chair of the board is often key to a productive evaluation exercise. Board evaluation, in whatever form, should be overseen by the chair of the board and facilitated by the company secretary with or without external support.

Board evaluations are often comprised of two distinct areas: the structure of the board in terms of composition and procedures and secondly the behaviour and activities of the directors individually and collectively. Individual evaluation should demonstrate whether each director continues to contribute effectively.

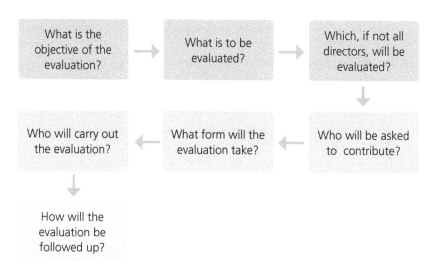

Figure 12.1 Board evaluation structure

The fundamental key to an evaluation exercise is for the board to understand what the purpose of the evaluation is expected to achieve. Figure 12.1 sets out the key questions a board should ask itself when considering an evaluation exercise.

One key question often heard from directors is why an external evaluation is required. A good independent external evaluator can provide useful insight and comparison to how other boards operate and how other boards have dealt with similar issues. The external viewpoint can be challenging as well as beneficial. Boards collectively and individually, just like individual employees being appraised, do not like hearing that they could do better while hearing that they are doing well in other areas is a boost.

Four of the main reasons cited for undertaking board evaluations are:

1. to address a specific need identified by the board;
2. a requirement to benchmark board performance externally;
3. to ensure the board is as effective as it can be; and
4. directors observing the benefits flowing from previous board evaluations.

Whatever the driving force behind the decision to undertake a board evaluation exercise, all directors need to support the process and the following points should be considered:

◆ Without a clear objective any evaluation will be muddled and disjointed with directors and other contributors potentially all approaching the evaluation with a different personal agenda.

◆ The evaluation needs to have a clear focus.

◆ Not all directors need to be evaluated on all occasions. There might be a focus on the non-executives, executives, chair, senior independent directors, etc.

◆ While the evaluation will routinely be of director performance by other directors, it may also be appropriate to consider how others that regularly take part in board meetings view proceedings.

◆ The format of the evaluation can often be decided by the budget assigned to the project, although with larger FTSE100 companies budgetary concerns will be less of a constraint.

◆ The Governance Code recommends that FTSE companies undergo external evaluation at least every three years but it is open to the board to undergo external evaluation more frequently.

◆ There are as many arguments for as there are against internal or external facilitated evaluations, with external facilitators and commentators often both citing the same criteria but with the opposite benefit or pitfall, as shown in Table 12.1.

◆ Possibly the most important consideration is what will be done with the results of the evaluation, how much detail will be reported in the annual report, what actions and follow-up will there be.

		Pro	Con
Cost	Internal	Cheaper	Saving money is not the goal of board evaluation
	External	Expertise is expensive	Expense of hiring external consultant
Ease of undertaking	Internal	Quicker as no need to bring external consultant up to speed	An internal evaluator is likely to require more time to conduct research, asses different types of evaluation and the time to write the report will be competing for their time with their normal daily duties
	External	Whilst company specific knowledge will be poor, an expert external evaluator is likely to be able to conduct their research, interviews and complete their report quicker as that is their sole focus	Time required to brief external consultant on company and industry issues/practices
Expertise	Internal	High degree of company and industry knowledge	Lack of evaluation expertise
	External	Expert board evaluators with lots of experience	Potential lack of company or industry specific factors
Objectivity	Internal	An internal evaluator might already know what types of common issues to ignore as not being relevant to their board	An internal evaluator is likely to have pre-conceived ideas and lack of objectivity
	External	External evaluators should not have pre-conceived ideas or any agenda to pursue and will be seen as independent	An external evaluator may need to ask a broader range of questions in order to identify areas of concern or where improvement can be made
Focus	Internal	Issues may well already be known to the evaluator saving time in trying to establish the problems and concentrating on finding solutions	Internal evaluator may not be able to bring external experience to bear
	External	May identify issues that internal evaluators are unaware of or have discounted through familiarity	More difficult for an external evaluator to identify key relevant issues and might suggest solutions that are not appropriate or relevant to the company's situation

Table 12.1 Internal v external board evaluation

Board evaluation can have significant benefits for the board, individual directors as well as the company and ultimately shareholders and other stakeholders. One of the main objectives of board evaluation is to enable the board to identify barriers that stop them being as effective as possible and through identification of the problems developing processes and strategies to mitigate or remove those barriers.

Figure 12.2 sets out some of the other benefits to the board.

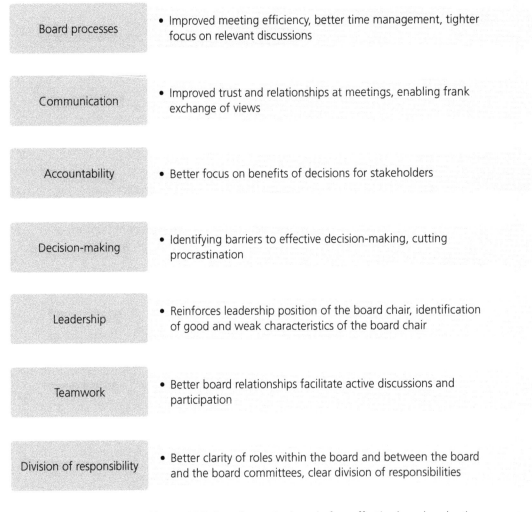

Board processes	• Improved meeting efficiency, better time management, tighter focus on relevant discussions
Communication	• Improved trust and relationships at meetings, enabling frank exchange of views
Accountability	• Better focus on benefits of decisions for stakeholders
Decision-making	• Identifying barriers to effective decision-making, cutting procrastination
Leadership	• Reinforces leadership position of the board chair, identification of good and weak characteristics of the board chair
Teamwork	• Better board relationships facilitate active discussions and participation
Division of responsibility	• Better clarity of roles within the board and between the board and the board committees, clear division of responsibilities

Figure 12.2 Benefits to the board of an effective board evaluation process

Board evaluation should not be seen as a stand alone exercise but part of the process of continual improvement required across all levels of a successful business. Once a board evaluation has been completed, the results must be reviewed by the board and its recommendations acted upon. Listed companies should outline the evaluation process and any recommendations made in their annual report and report back progress on implementing those recommendations in the following year's report.

Stop and think 12.2

Board evaluation is an essential element in the checks and balances of a good board to ensure that the board is operating efficiently and effectively. Failure to ensure a good working board and that no one director is dominating the board, whether deliberately or not, can contribute to a failure to challenge decisions properly. This was seen very clearly with the board of the charity, Kids Company. The charity had many high-profile backers, including the government; however, the charity's board failed to adequately address risk, steer strategy and keep the executives accountable. The situation was heightened by the dominant personality of the CEO and founder, which contributed to a lack of internal challenge and holding to account.

Test yourself 12.1

1. **How often should listed companies undertake a board evaluation?**

    i) **Internally**

    ii) **Externally facilitated**

2. **Must every director be evaluated every year?**

3. **Should evaluations follow the same format and cover the same topics each year?**

4. Protection of stakeholders

As seen in chapter 2, company directors have a number of statutory, fiduciary and common law duties and responsibilities. Under normal circumstances their overriding duty is to manage the company for the benefit of its members as a whole.

The directors do need to consider the impact on other stakeholders, but those interests do not take precedence over the interests of the members except in circumstances where a winding up or compromise with creditors is being contemplated.

Although 'stakeholders' as a concept in company law has only really come to prominence during the comprehensive company law review process that culminated with the Companies Act 2006, anyone with an economic interest in the company is clearly a stakeholder, but there are others too. Stakeholders often have different and sometimes competing interests in a company. Stakeholders can be divided into the following broad categories:

◆ members;

◆ directors;

◆ creditors;

◆ suppliers;

◆ local community;

◆ employees (present and former);

◆ the environment; and

◆ the government.

The main protection for many of those groups is contained in CA2006 s. 172, supported to some extent by specific provisions in the Insolvency Act 1986 and other legislation. CA2006 s. 172, however, does note the primacy of directors acting in the interests of the company's members as a whole but that they should 'have regard' to the interests of other stakeholders.

The importance given to the requirements of CA2006 s. 172 has been brought into sharp focus following the 2018 updating of the Governance Code as well as the report of the Wates Committee and their principles of governance for large unlisted and private companies.

When the original Cadbury Code was published, the focus of corporate governance was very much about holding the directors to account for protection of investors. This led to the Code primarily being applied against publicly owned companies as private groups where the directors were directly answerable to either only one shareholder or a small number of shareholders who did not need any additional protection. Over the years, the focus of corporate governance in general, reflected in updates to the Governance Code, has widened to include additional stakeholder groups relevant to both publicly owned and privately owned companies.

There are six principles, set out below, which together with accompanying guidance were published in December 2018.

The six Wates principles are as follows:

1. **Purpose:** An effective board promotes the purpose of a company, and ensures that its values, strategy and culture align with that purpose.

2. **Composition:** Effective board composition requires an effective chair and a balance of skills, backgrounds, experience and knowledge, with individual directors having sufficient capacity to make a valuable contribution. The size of a board should be guided by the scale and complexity of the company.

3. **Responsibilities:** A board should have a clear understanding of its accountability and terms of reference. Its policies and procedures should support effective decision-making and independent challenge.

4. **Opportunity and risk:** A board should promote the long-term success of the company by identifying opportunities to create and preserve value and establishing oversight for the identification and mitigation of risks.

5. **Remuneration:** A board should promote executive remuneration structures aligned to the sustainable long-term success of a company, taking into account pay and conditions elsewhere in the company.

6. **Stakeholders:** A board has a responsibility to oversee meaningful engagement with material stakeholders, including the workforce, and have regard to that discussion when taking decisions. The board has a responsibility to foster good stakeholder relationships based on the company's purpose.

In conjunction with these reports being issued the government published C(MR)R2018 which bring in a number of new reporting obligations including a requirement for all companies that do not qualify as small or medium-sized to include a 'section 172 statement' in their strategic report setting out details of how the directors have demonstrated their duties under CA2006 s. 172 (CA2006 s. 414CZA).

In addition, the largest of companies having either more than 2,000 employees or turnover in excess of £200 million and a balance sheet total of more than £1 billion will be required to make a new corporate governance statement under amendments made to the 2008 regulations Sch. 7, reg. 26 as follows:

1. The directors' report must include a statement (a 'statement of corporate governance arrangements') which states:

    (a) which corporate governance code, if any, the company applied in the financial year;

    (b) how the company applied any corporate governance code reported under sub-paragraph (a); and

    (c) if the company departed from any corporate governance code reported under sub-paragraph (a), the respects in which it did so, and its reasons for so departing.

2. If the company has not applied any corporate governance code for the financial year, the statement of corporate governance arrangements must explain the reasons for that decision and explain what arrangements for corporate governance were applied for that year.

Of all the groups of stakeholders, members are the best protected other than once a company reaches the position where insolvency is very likely or that tipping point has been exceeded. Not only are companies managed for their express benefit, but as discussed, they can also bring action for unfair prejudice or a derivative action claim.

Employees have additional protection in terms of other legislation including general redundancy rules and TUPE regulations as well as priority of payment of unpaid wages in insolvent liquidations.

Directors' protection is largely afforded by virtue that they are responsible for managing the affairs of the company and are best placed to take mitigating action. Although exposed to potential legal action by members directors can protect themselves, except in instances of fraud and deliberate wrong-doing, by taking out indemnity insurance (at the cost of the company).

Creditors' main protection comes from their ability to withhold future services pending payment for past services, being able to sue the company to make settlement and that in the event of a winding up assets are applied to meet their debts. The priority of payments in a liquidation does not, unfortunately, favour the majority of day-to-day trading creditors, suppliers, etc. who are on the whole unsecured.

The need to consider the impact of the company's operations on the local community and the environment highlight the need to have a thought-out corporate social responsibility policy. These duties also highlight the balance to be struck between members and stakeholders and that the balance need not be restricted to purely financial or economic factors.

As noted above, although directors are required to have regard for these other stakeholders the section had little 'real bite' as, if the directors take no account of their interests, they have no right of action under CA2006 s. 172 and it is left to the Insolvency Service to bring an action.

Stop and think 12.3

In practice, legal action by shareholders against companies and executives is rare and expensive. In a long-running dispute with Lloyds Banking Group plc (LBG) a group of about 6,000 investors brought a £550 million claim action against LBG and certain directors in connection with its fateful takeover of HBOS at the beginning of the financial crisis in 2009. At the time of writing, millions of pounds have been spent by both sides, 10 years have elapsed and judgment is still awaited from the trial judges following conclusion of the trial.

Test yourself 12.2

1.   **What are the two main options available to members under the Act to take action against directors?**

2.   **Of whose interests should directors be most mindful?**

5. Investigation powers of regulators

As considered in chapter 9, all companies are required to allow access to the company's statutory records and certain specified documents on request by individuals and organisations. Certain organisations – principally BEIS and the Insolvency Service – have the power to investigate a company's affairs. Although they have the power to investigate very few office holders, including investigators for most government departments, have the right of entry to business or residential premises. Where a warrant to enter and search premises is given, this is valid only if served by a police officer.

5.1   Department for Business, Energy and Industrial Strategy investigations

When the Companies Act legislation was reviewed almost all of the provisions of CA1985 were repealed and either replaced by amended provisions or were replicated in CA2006. The exception to this general rule is that the investigation provisions were retained and remain in force as the Companies Act 1985. All companies are regulated by BEIS, which has authority, given by these retained provisions, CA1985 ss. 431–53 as amended by CA2006 ss. 1035–9, to investigate companies. Investigations can be made in a variety of ways although there are levels of investigation common to all investigations. The Secretary of State for BEIS will either appoint inspectors, usually an accountant and a barrister, with power to examine witnesses under caution, or require the production of documents and records for examination by BEIS officials.

Power of entry

Inspectors appointed by the Secretary of State under CA1985 ss. 431, 432 or 442 to enquire into the affairs of a company or to investigate company ownership have no right of entry or right to undertake a search of business or other premises without a search warrant. They may however require the company and any officers or agents, past and present, to produce documents and to be questioned by the inspectors. For the purposes of investigations, an agent includes the company's bankers, solicitors and auditors.

If a request for the production of documents is ignored, in part or in full, or if there are reasonable grounds for believing that documents exist but which have not been produced application may be made by the inspectors to a justice of the peace to issue a warrant under CA1985 s. 448 for the entry and search of premises.

A warrant issued under CA1985 s. 448 authorises a police officer and any named persons with them to:

◆   enter the specified premises;

◆   search and take possession of documents appearing to be relevant;

◆   take copies of any such documents; and

◆   require explanations concerning the documents from any persons in the premises.

There are six categories of inspection:

1. appointment of inspectors to investigate the affairs of the company;
2. investigations into ownership of company;
3. investigations of directors' share dealings;
4. production of documents;
5. investigations to assist overseas regulatory authorities; and
6. investigations under FSMA2000.

Power to investigate the affairs of a company

Appointment of inspectors by the Secretary of State can be requested by the company itself, by a minimum of 200 shareholders or, if the company does not have a share capital, by not less than one-fifth of the company's members (CA1985 s. 431). Such applications are, however, very rare.

The usual process for the initiation of an investigation is for the Secretary of State to appoint inspectors to investigate the affairs of a company, if the court by order declares the affairs should be investigated, if it appears to them that there are circumstances to indicate that:

◆   the company's affairs are or have been undertaken with intent to defraud creditors, or the creditors of another person, for fraudulent or unlawful purpose or in such a way that is unfairly detrimental to some part of its members;

◆   any act or intended act or omission or intended omission whether by or on behalf of the company would be prejudicial to some part of the members, or that the company was formed for any fraudulent or unlawful purpose;

◆   persons forming the company or connected with its management have in that regard been guilty of fraud, misconduct or misfeasance towards the company or its members; or

◆   the members have not been given information concerning the affairs of the company that they might reasonably expect.

The terms of appointment will determine the form of report required from the inspectors and may stipulate that the report will not be made public: (CA1985 s. 432(2A)).

Inspectors appointed under CA1985 s. 431 or 432 to investigate the affairs of a company have power to extend their investigation to any subsidiary or holding company without the need for any specific appointment by the Secretary of State (CA1985 s. 433).

Once inspectors are appointed under CA1985 ss. 431 and 432, it is the duty of all officers and agents of the company and of any person who is or may be in possession of information or documents relating to the company under investigation to:

◆ produce to the inspectors all documents of or relating to the company in their custody or power;

◆ attend before the inspectors when required, inspectors may examine any person on oath and may administer an oath accordingly; and

◆ give all assistance in connection with the investigation that they are reasonably able to give (CA1985 s. 434, as amended by CA2006 s. 1038).

The right to silence has been excluded and the inspectors may compel a witness to answer questions; any answers may be given in evidence against that person. Where a witness refuses to answer any question or refuses to assist in the investigation, the inspectors may certify that fact to the court. On enquiry, the court may punish the person as if they are guilty of contempt of court (CA1985 s. 436).

The inspectors report to the Secretary of State on the conclusion of their investigation. The publication of the inspectors' report is at the discretion of the Secretary of State and it is the policy of the BEIS to publish a report only if it is in the public interest (CA1985 s. 437).

If matters have come to light during the course of an investigation that suggest that a criminal offence has been committed, those facts are referred to the appropriate prosecuting authority. Once referred, the inspectors need take no further action (CA1985 s. 437(1B)).

If there is evidence to suggest that civil proceedings ought to be brought, in the public interest, by any company, the Secretary of State may bring such proceedings in the name of and on behalf of the company and will indemnify the company for the costs of such action (CA1985 s. 438).

The expenses of an investigation under CA1985 ss. 431 or 432 will be borne by BEIS, who may recover those costs, or part of them, from any person convicted as a result of the investigation. Where the appointment was made at the request of shareholders, the company may be liable for some or all of the costs (CA1985 s. 439).

Power to investigate ownership
If it appears to the Secretary of State that there are good reasons for doing so, inspectors or BEIS officials may be appointed to investigate the true identity of those financially interested in the success or failure of a company or able to control or materially influence its management (CA1985 ss. 442 and 444(1)).

The terms of appointment may limit the investigation to matters connected with specified shares or holdings. Such investigations are usually used to investigate the circumstances where there is a potential takeover and there are circumstances to suggest the existence of undisclosed arrangements or undertakings between groups of shareholders (CA1985 s. 442(2)).

Inspectors appointed under CA1985 s. 442 have the same powers as inspectors appointed under CA1985 ss. 431 and 432. As noted above, such powers are, however, restricted to those persons who are or have been or appear to be or have been interested in the shares or debentures, together with those other persons it appears to the inspectors possess information relevant to their investigation (CA1985 s. 443).

Where the matter to be investigated does not require the appointment of inspectors under CA1985 s. 442, the Secretary of State may require the production of documents or information concerning present or past interests in shares or debentures from any person they reasonably believe might have it (CA1985 s. 444(1)). Any person failing to provide the information or supplying false information is liable to fine, imprisonment or both (CA1985 s. 444(3)).

Production of documents

The majority of investigations initiated by BEIS do not require the appointment of inspectors. Instead, the Secretary of State may, if they think there are good reasons, give a direction directly to the company or any person requiring the production of specified documents and records or to provide information. Alternatively, rather giving the direction directly the Secretary of State may authorise an inspector to require the company or any person to produce specified documents and evidence or to provide information (CA1985 s. 447).

The power to require the production of documents extends to the taking of copies and requesting explanation of any matter in those documents from any person. Failure to produce the documents or provide an explanation without good reason is an offence under CA1985 s. 447(6). Making false or reckless statements is an offence under CA1985 s. 451. Documents can be withheld if they are covered by professional privilege (CA1985 s. 452).

Overseas regulatory authorities

BEIS was given power under CA 1989 ss. 82–91 to assist overseas authorities investigating UK companies. The power permits investigation, interviews under oath and seeking documents and records. In deciding whether to provide assistance, regard must be given to whether reciprocal assistance would be forthcoming.

5.2 HM Revenue and Customs investigations

HMRC typically investigates tax returns and claims for tax credits and allowances as civil investigations. Criminal investigations are reserved for cases where a strong deterrent message is required or where the severity of the conduct requires a criminal sanction and often relate to schemes attempting to evade excise duty or reclaim VAT.

Criminal investigations

Although HMRC always reserves the right to conduct a criminal investigation, these are usually reserved for the more serious offences or offenders and for the following types of offence:

- organised criminal gangs attacking the tax system or systematic frauds where losses represent a serious threat to the tax base, including conspiracy;

- individuals that hold a position of trust or responsibility;

- where materially false statements are made or materially false documents are provided in the course of a civil investigation;

- where, pursuing an avoidance scheme, reliance is placed on a false or altered document or such reliance or material facts are misrepresented to enhance the credibility of a scheme;

- deliberate concealment, deception, conspiracy or corruption is suspected;

- use of false or forged documents;

- importation or exportation breaching prohibitions and restrictions;

- money laundering offences with particular focus on advisers, accountants, solicitors and others acting in a 'professional' capacity to facilitate the offence;

- repeat offenders, criminal or civil, and continuing unlawful conduct;

- theft, or the misuse or unlawful destruction of HMRC documents;

- assault on, threats to, or the impersonation of HMRC officials; and

- links to suspected wider criminality, whether domestic or international, involving offences not under the administration of HMRC.

To counter the threat to the UK's tax and duty systems posed by criminal activity HMRC uses similar criminal investigation powers available to other law enforcement agencies to enable them to obtain orders requiring the production of documents and information, apply for search warrants and the power of arrest and undertake searches of people and premises following arrests.

In England and Wales HMRC's criminal investigations are governed by the Police and Criminal Evidence Act 1984. In Northern Ireland the authority is contained in the Police and Criminal Evidence (Northern Ireland) Order 1989 and in Scotland the regulations are provided in the Finance Act 2007, the Criminal Law (Consolidation) (Scotland) Act 1995 and the Criminal Procedure (Scotland) Act 1995.

A limited number of HMRC officers have powers of arrest although this power is limited to HMRC offences and is not a general right of arrest.

Direct tax investigations

Generally speaking, HMRC can give notice requiring the production of documents and the provision of information. This must be complied with in a specified period of not less than 30 days. Relevant legislation includes: the Taxes Management Act 1970, s. 20; the Finance Act 1998 para. 27, Sch. 18; the Corporation Tax (Instalment Payments) Regulations 1998, regs. 10, 11 and 12; and the Income and Corporation Taxes Act 1988, ss. 708 and 767A.

HMRC also has power to review company PAYE and NI records. This power is given by: the Income Tax (Employments) Regulations 1993, reg. 53; the Social Security (Contributions) Regulations 2001, para. 26, Part III, Sch. 4; and the Income Tax (Sub-contractors in the Construction Industry) Regulations 1975, reg. 41.

In terms of investigation of National Insurance records, the Social Security Administration Act 1992 s. 110ZA provides broad information-gathering powers of entry at all reasonable times to premises where it is believed either a trade or business or the records of a trade or business are kept. This right of entry is limited to reasonable times, and entry can be refused if the request or time etc. is unreasonable in the circumstances.

HMRC officials have no automatic right of entry. They may, however, obtain a warrant under the Taxes Management Act 1970 s. 20C, signed by a circuit judge, to enter and search premises. The warrant is valid if served by a police officer. To obtain a warrant, the circuit judge must be satisfied that there are reasonable grounds for suspecting that evidence of an offence involving serious tax fraud is to be found on the premises. Certain documents are privileged and cannot be seized. These include personal, medical or religious records, and the property of any tax adviser.

Indirect tax investigations
The Customs & Excise Management Act 1979 and VAT Act 1994 Sch. 11 gave the Commissioners of Customs wide-reaching powers of investigation and information gathering.

HMRC is moving away from the previous system of periodic VAT visits with visits now generated by:

◆   VAT returns showing an unusual level of sales or purchases compared to industry norms;

◆   information received;

◆   information obtained during the course of an inspection of another company's records; and

◆   information from other government departments.

Unannounced visits do still take place and HMRC officers have the right of entry to premises to inspect records at any reasonable time. The right of entry to inspect records however, does not permit a search for records to be undertaken. Visits are usually by appointment and the HMRC officer has the right to call for any books and records. Where the visit is by appointment and the business owner is therefore on notice of the visit, they are obliged to answer the officer's questions. This is not the case for unannounced visits.

Where there has been an unannounced visit, and, for genuine business or personal reasons, it is inconvenient, the officer(s) can be asked to leave. If the officer(s) insist(s) on their right of entry, they should be given access to a clear room and should be accompanied at all times. They should not be given uncontrolled access to business records.

5.3 Financial Conduct Authority and Prudential Regulation Authority

The powers of the FCA and the PRA to gather information and carry out investigations are set out in Part XI of the FSMA2000.

Production of documents

The FCA has authority under FSMA2000 s. 165 to require or to give an officer of the FCA authority to require the production of specified documents and information or documents and information of a specified description from:

- an authorised or formerly authorised person;
- a person connected with an authorised person;
- the operator, trustee or depository of an open-ended investment company;
- a recognised investment exchange; and
- a recognised clearing house.

Following the financial crisis, FSMA2000 was extended to give similar authority to the PRA to require the production of documents or information in connection with financial stability of one or more aspects of the UK financial system (FSMA2000 ss. 165A and 165B).

Instead of requiring the production of documents, the FCA may require that an authorised, formerly authorised or connected person commission and provide a report into any relevant matter (FSMA2000 s. 166). Although the report is commissioned, and paid for, by the person or organisation under review the FCA may direct and control the scope of the investigation, the length of the investigation, the conduct of the investigation and how the investigation is to be reported upon. Authorised persons and firms are required to co-operate with any person writing the report. The persons nominated to provide the report are referred to as skilled persons and as a consequence these reports are often referred to as a 'skilled person report'.

For more serious matters, the FCA has power to appoint a competent person to conduct a general investigation into the business or ownership or control of an authorised person or appointed representative (FSMA2000 s. 167). Written notice of the appointment of an investigator must be given to the person or firm under investigation. The competent person appointed to carry out the investigation may be an employee of the FCA or some other person engaged for that purpose (FSMA2000 s. 170).

Under FSMA2000 s. 168, the FCA may appoint a competent person to conduct an investigation where it appears there are circumstances to suggest that a specific contravention or offence may have taken place. Such specific investigations would include breaches of the general prohibition to provide investment advice, breaches of any rules or regulations made under the FSMA2000, commission of misleading statements and practices in terms of FSMA2000 s. 397, market abuse in terms of FSMA2000 s. 188, insider dealing in terms of the CJA1993 or suspected breach of the money laundering regulations.

FSMA2000 s. 169 extends the authority of the FCA to enable it to investigate authorised persons and firms operating in the UK on behalf of an overseas regulator.

The power of investigators appointed by the FCA varies depending under which provisions of FSMA2000 they have been appointed.

Investigators appointed under FSMA2000 s. 167 have power to require persons to attend before them and answer questions, provide information and to provide documents. This power is restricted to information relevant to the investigation and to the person under investigation or a connected person of that person (FSMA2000 s. 171).

Investigators appointed by the FCA under FSMA2000 s. 168 have additional powers set out in FSMA2000 ss. 172 and 173. These powers do not apply in all cases and care must be taken to establish the appropriate power in any given case. Generally, the investigators' powers of interview and information gathering are extended to persons not under investigation themselves but who might have any relevant documents or information.

Investigators appointed by the FCA or the Secretary of State under FSMA2000 s. 175 have power to compel the production of relevant documents from any person, together with any explanation of the document where needed. Where an individual does not possess a document or fails to produce it they may be required to state, to the best of their knowledge, where that document is. Confidential banking documents may be withheld without the consent of the person to whom they relate, unless their disclosure has been specifically authorised by the FCA or the Secretary of State.

Where any person fails, without good reason, to comply with a request made under Part XI of the FSMA2000 to provide information or to produce documents, that fact may be certified to the court. On enquiry, the court may punish the person as if they were guilty of contempt of court (FSMA2000 s. 177). A person who recklessly provides false or misleading information or who falsifies, withholds or destroys any documents or information is guilty of an offence and, on conviction, is liable to a fine of up to £5,000 or up to six months' imprisonment, or both.

Power of entry

An investigator appointed by the FCA under the terms of the FSMA2000 has no right of entry or search; accordingly, entry may be refused. The investigator may, however, obtain a warrant to enter and search premises from a justice of

the peace or, in Scotland, from a sheriff. A warrant to enter and search must
be executed by a police officer. To obtain a warrant, the justice of the peace or
sheriff must be satisfied that there are grounds for believing that:

- a request for the production of documents has not been complied with
  and that the documents are on the premises;

- there are grounds to believe that any request to provide documents found
  on the premises would not be complied with or the documents would be
  moved, altered or destroyed; or

- a serious offence has been or is being committed and that there is
  information or documents on the premises relevant to the offence and that
  a request for their production would not be complied with or might result
  in the documents being removed, altered or destroyed.

5.4 Competition and Markets Authority

On 1 April 2014, the CMA took over all functions of the Competition
Commission and the Office of Fair Trading and their powers of investigation
contained in the CA1998 and the EA2002, respectively. EA2002 ss. 194–201,
224 and 225 set out the investigation and surveillance powers of the CMA.
CA1998 ss. 25–31 set out the additional investigatory powers of the CMA.

Production of documents

EA2002 ss. 193 and 224 give the CMA power to require persons to attend
interviews to answer questions or to provide documents or other written
evidence. The power under EA2002 s. 193 relates to the investigation of cartels;
EA2002 ss. 224 and 225 relate to consumer protection.

CA1998 s. 26 gives power to the CMA to issue a written notice requiring the
production of documents or information. The notice must state the subject
matter and purpose of the investigation, describe the documents or information
(specifically or in general terms) and set out the nature of the offences that may
be committed if the information and documents are not provided. The notice
will also set out the appropriate timescale for the delivery of the documents or
information and the recipient may also be asked to provide an explanation of
any documents delivered either at the same time or subsequently.

Power of entry

EA2002 s. 194 allows the CMA to obtain a warrant from the High Court
(procurator fiscal in Scotland) to allow a named CMA officer to enter premises
and conduct searches for documents or other evidence in connection with
investigations into cartels. This power is for use where the CMA believes that:

- a request for the production of documents has not been complied with
  and that the documents are on the premises;

- there are grounds to believe that any request to provide documents found
  on the premises would not be complied with or the documents would be
  moved, altered or destroyed; or

◆ a serious offence has or is being committed and that there is information or documents on the premises relevant to the offence and that a request for their production would not be complied with or might result in the documents being removed, altered or destroyed.

EA2002 ss. 31, 109 and 176 give the CMA authority to require the production of specified documents or to require individuals to attend interviews and to give evidence. These powers are in respect of the CMA's investigations into mergers and abuse of market dominance.

The CMA has power to launch competition investigations and in carrying out those investigations CMA officials have the power to enter and in some circumstances search premises for relevant documents.

CMA officials have power under CA1998 s. 27 to enter business and residential premises without a warrant and require production of documents or provision of information and to take copies of documents. CA1998 s. 27 does not permit a search of the premises or for forced entry.

Under CA1998 s. 28, CMA officials can obtain a warrant from the High Court or the Competition Authority Tribunal to enter, by force if necessary, business premises and search and take possession of documents. CA1998 s. 28A provides the power of entry and search by warrant in respect of domestic premises.

The CMA has similar powers of entry with or without a warrant where it is acting on behalf of another EU member state. These powers are confirmed by CA1998 ss. 65E–H.

5.5 The Panel on Takeovers and Mergers

The Panel is an independent body, whose main functions are to issue and administer the City Code and to supervise and regulate takeovers and other matters to which the Code applies in accordance with the rules set out in the Code. It has been designated as the supervisory authority to carry out certain regulatory functions in relation to takeovers pursuant to the Directive on Takeover Bids (2004/25/EC).

Its statutory functions and powers are set out in CA2006 ss. 942–965. The rules set out in the Code also have a statutory basis in relation to the Isle of Man, Jersey and Guernsey.

Production of documents

CA2006 s. 947 empowers the Panel to require, by notice in writing, a person to produce specified or described documents and/or to provide in such form or manner as may be specified such information as is specified or described.

The requirement to produce documents or information must be supplied at a specified place and within a reasonable period specified by the Panel and may be required to be authenticated in such manner as the Panel may reasonably require.

The documents or information that the Panel may require are those that they may reasonably require to enable it to exercise its functions (CA2006 s. 947(3)).

The Panel may authorise any person to exercise its powers to require the production of documents or information (CA2006 s. 947(5)).

The Panel or their authorised representative cannot require the production of documents or information in respect of which a claim for legal professional privilege (confidentiality of communication in Scotland) could be maintained in legal proceedings (CA2006 s. 947(10)).

CA2006 s. 948 prohibits the Panel from disclosing documents or information, other than those already in the public domain, provided to it in the exercise of its functions that relate to a private individual during their lifetime or a business for as long as the business continues, without their consent. This protection does not apply to any disclosure made for the purpose of facilitating the Panel of carrying out its functions, is made to a person, is of a description and is in accordance with CA2006 Sch. 2 (CA2006 s. 948(3)).

Right of entry
The Panel and their representatives have no right of entry to premises.

Stop and think 12.4

As a company secretary, you need to be aware of the rights of regulators, HMRC and the police to attend and enter company premises. However, except in the case of small organisations it is quite likely that the company secretary will not be the person opening the door to visitors or possibly even be based in the same office. Accordingly, it is essential that reception staff, office managers etc. are aware of the procedures to follow in the event of a regulatory visit. This will usually involve asking them to wait in a meeting room until a senior manager, company secretary or director is available. In most cases inspectors only have power to request the production of documents and do not have search powers.

Test yourself 12.3

1. In general, how is the power of entry and search granted and who to?

2. Can an HMRC inspector with the power of arrest make an arrest for any criminal offence?

Chapter summary

◆　Corporate governance as a tool to check director excesses

◆　Board and director effectiveness appraisals

◆　Investigation powers of the various government agencies charged with oversight of companies

Chapter thirteen
Regulation and disclosure

CONTENTS

1. Introduction
2. Disclosure requirements for listed companies
3. Link between disclosure, accountability, transparency and trust
4. Data protection
5. Public access to corporate information

1. Introduction

Regulation, disclosure of corporate information and protection of personal information are key requirements of a public company's risk management processes.

In order to ensure that company investors can make investment decisions based upon the same information and that no investors have more information than others, listed and other companies with publicly traded shares are required to publish price sensitive information as soon as possible and to inform their market of any changes to existing forecasts, predications or market expectations.

Public disclosure of information and transparency when dealing with shareholders and potential shareholders, customers and regulators are vitally important to creating and maintaining accountability and trust in company management.

Although all of us readily provide personal information in our daily lives to companies in order to access tier services we expect that they will treat that information carefully and securely.

In this chapter, we will consider the disclosure obligations on listed companies, how disclosure aids transparency, accountability and trust and the obligation of companies to keep personal information secure and the requirement on government bodies to have processes in place to be able to respond to requests for information under freedom of information requests.

2. Disclosure requirements for listed companies

All companies are under an obligation to disclose the following types of information:

◆ constitution and any changes;

◆ directors and company secretaries;

◆ changes of registered details including company name, registered office or SAIL address;

◆ share capital;

◆ accounts;

◆ mortgages and charges; and

◆ persons with significant control.

This information must be notified to the Registrar on the incorporation of the company and whenever there are any changes. Additionally, a confirmation statement, which is a snapshot of this information, must be submitted at least annually (see chapter 5 for more information).

All companies must also comply with the business names disclosure requirements on all their business stationery, invoices, emails etc. requiring disclosure of their registered name, registered office address, place of registration and registered number (see chapter 5 for more information).

In addition to these general disclosure requirements applicable to all companies, listed companies are obliged to make additional disclosures either to complement existing disclosure requirements, such as additional disclosures in their financial statements, or as separate standalone disclosures.

There are different continuing obligations for premium and for standard listed companies. In general, the continuing obligations for a company with a premium listing are more onerous than for a company with a standard listing.

2.1 Companies Act obligations

The Act does not refer directly to listed companies but instead to quoted companies which covers not only listed companies but also companies with equity shares listed in another EEA state or admitted to trading on the New York Stock Exchange or Nasdaq (CA2006 s. 385).

Strategic report

For a quoted company, the strategic report must also include (CA2006 s. 414C (7–10)) information on:

◆ main trends and factors likely to affect future development, performance or position of the company;

◆ environmental matters;

◆ company employees;

- social and community interests;
- the company's strategy;
- the company's business model;
- the genders of its directors, senior managers and employees; and
- those third parties with which the company has contracts or arrangements essential to its business.

The directors may exclude and not disclose information if, in their opinion, disclosure would be seriously prejudicial to the commercial interests of the company.

Directors' report

A listed company's directors' report must also include details of information on the company's capital and holders of securities and agreements in relation to change of control/takeover (2008 Regulations Sch. 7).

The directors of a quoted company must include in the directors' report to the financial statements details of the acquisition by the company of any of its own shares (2008 Regulations Sch. 7.9).

Directors' remuneration report

The directors of a quoted company must prepare a directors' remuneration report which should contain the following sections (CA2006 ss. 420, 421 and 2008 Regulations Sch. 8) including, among other disclosures:

- statement by the chair of remuneration committee;
- single total figure table of remuneration for each director;
- details of any payments to past directors;
- where the directors' remuneration policy is not being put to a resolution at the AGM, performance targets for the financial year;
- details of remuneration committee including an assessment of independence;
- a statement of voting on the remuneration report and remuneration policy in the previous year; and
- a separate section on the remuneration policy.

A quoted company must put a resolution approving the directors' remuneration report. The resolution is an advisory one and, if lost, does not invalidate the payment of directors' remuneration (CA2006 s. 439).

Auditor's report

The auditor's report on the financial statements of a quoted company must include details on the auditable sections of the directors' remuneration report, strategic report, directors' report and the corporate governance statement.

Summary information

Companies are permitted to issue the strategic report and supplemental material to their shareholders in place of the full statutory accounts. Any shareholder receiving the strategic report and supplemental material may require that the full accounts be sent to them (CA2006 s. 426).

Quoted companies must include, in addition to the material set out in CA2006 s. 426A, a copy of that part of the remuneration report which sets out the single total figure table (s. 426A(2)(e)).

Availability of annual accounts and reports

CA2006 s. 430 requires quoted companies to make available, on their website, their annual accounts and reports until annual accounts and reports for the next financial year are made available on the website.

Access to the website must be:

- available to all members of the public, and not just to members of the company;
- throughout the period; and
- free of charge.

Any member or holder of debentures of a quoted company is entitled to be provided, on demand and without charge, with a single copy (in addition to any copy they might be entitled to under CA2006 s. 423) of the following documents:

- last annual accounts;
- last directors' remuneration report;
- last strategic report;
- last directors' report; and
- auditor's report on the accounts (CA2006 s. 432).

Directors' remuneration policy

A quoted company must, at least every three years, put a resolution to the meeting held to receive the annual report and accounts and a resolution to approve the directors' remuneration policy or any revisions to the directors' remuneration policy (s. 439A).

Any changes to the existing, approved, directors' remuneration policy are not effective until approved by the members.

Filing obligation of quoted companies

CA2006 s. 447 separates out the specific filing obligations of quoted companies and includes a requirement to file the directors' remuneration report with the Registrar of Companies together with the auditor's report on the auditable part of the directors' remuneration report, in addition to the company's annual accounts, the directors' report and any separate corporate governance statement.

Notice of general meeting

For traded companies, the notice periods to convene a general meeting are set out in CA2006 s. 307A as follows:

◆ general meetings where specified conditions met: 14 days;

◆ all other general meetings: 21 days.

In order for a general meeting of a traded company to be held on 14 days' notice, the circumstances specified in CA2006 s. 307A must be met. This section was inserted into the Act by the Companies (Shareholders' Rights) Regulations 2009 (SI 2009/1632). These circumstances are as follows:

◆ the meeting is not an annual general meeting (AGM);

◆ members are offered an electronic voting facility; and

◆ a special resolution has been passed to reduce the notice period to 14 days. This must have happened at either the immediately preceding AGM or at a general meeting held since the last AGM.

If all three conditions are met, the notice period will be 14 days. In all other cases, 21 days' notice will be required.

2.2 Listing rules and disclosure and transparency obligations

In order to obtain listed status companies must disclose additional information. Once listed status is granted such companies must ensure that they maintain this level of disclosure by adhering to the listing and premium listing principles together with the various continuing obligations set out in the Listing Rules and the disclosure and transparency rules.

These are divided into the following broad categories:

◆ principles (LR 7); and

◆ continuing obligations:

– suspensions, cancellation and restoration of listing and reverse takeovers (LR 5);

– sponsors (LR 8);

– general obligations – premium listing (LR 9);

– significant transactions (LR 10);

– related party transactions (LR 11);

– dealing in own securities (LR 12);

– general obligations – standard listing (LR 14);

– disclosure and control of inside information (DTR 2);

– transactions by persons discharging managerial responsibilities (PDMRs) and their connected persons (DTR 3);

– periodic financial reporting requirements (DTR 4);

– vote holder and issuer notification rules (DTR 5);

– continuing obligations and access to information (DTR 6);

– corporate governance (DTR 7); and

– primary information providers (DTR 8).

Listing principles

Chapter 7 of the Listing Rules sets out two general listing principles for all companies. In addition, there are six principles applicable to companies with a premium listing as follows:

Principle	Description
Listing Principle 1	A listed company must take reasonable steps to establish and maintain adequate procedures, systems and controls to enable it to comply with its obligations.
Listing Principle 2	A listed company must deal with the FCA in an open and co-operative manner.
Premium Listing Principle 1	A listed company must take reasonable steps to enable its directors to understand their responsibilities and obligations as directors.
Premium Listing Principle 2	A listed company must act with integrity towards the holders and potential holders of its premium listed securities.
Premium Listing Principle 3	All equity shares in a class that has been admitted to premium listing must carry an equal number of votes on any shareholder vote. In respect of certificates representing shares that have been admitted to premium listing, all the equity shares of the class which the certificates represent must carry an equal number of votes on any shareholder vote.
Premium Listing Principle 4	Where a listed company has more than one class of securities admitted to premium listing, the aggregate voting rights of the securities in each class should be broadly proportionate to the relative interests of those classes in the equity of the listed company.
Premium Listing Principle 5	A listed company must ensure that it treats all holders of the same class of its premium listed securities and its listed equity shares that are in the same position equally in respect of the rights attaching to those premium listed securities and listed equity shares.
Premium Listing Principle 6	A listed company must communicate information to holders and potential holders of its premium listed securities and its listed equity shares in such a way as to avoid the creation or continuation of a false market in those premium listed securities and listed equity shares.

Table 13.1 Listing and premium listing principles

Listing suspensions, cancellation and restoration

The FCA can suspend the listing of a company's securities if the smooth operation of the market is or is likely to be at risk or for the protection of investors. During the period of suspension, the company must continue to comply with the Listing Rules (LR 5.1). A company can request that its own shares be suspended. Any such request must be in writing and contain the information set out in LR 5.3 including a clear explanation of the background and reasons for the request.

The FCA may cancel a listing if it is satisfied that there are circumstances that mean that normal trading of the securities is no longer possible (LR 5.2). A common cause for the cancellation of a listing is following a takeover where the number of shares in public hands falls below the 25% threshold requirement set out in LR 6.14.

Sponsors

Premium listed companies are not required to have a sponsor appointed at all times but, generally, only at those times when they need to make submissions to the FCA or guidance is required. The full list of those events that require a sponsor to be appointed are set out in LR 8.2. In practice the majority of premium listed companies will retain the services of a sponsor.

General obligations

- LR 9.2 – *continuing application*

A listed company must, at all times, have its shares admitted to trading on a regulated market operated by a regulated investment exchange (RIE) and must notify the FCA that it has requested an RIE to admit or readmit any shares to trading, requested an RIE to cancel or suspend trading or that its shares have been cancelled or suspended from trading.

At least 75% of the company's business must be independent and controlled by the company.

At least 25% of the issued shares excluding any shares held in treasury must be held by the public.

A listed company with a controlling shareholder must demonstrate that it is able to carry on business independently at all times and must have a controlling shareholder agreement in place and its Articles must allow for the election or re-election of independent directors.

- LR 9.3 – *holders*

A listed company must ensure that a proxy form allows for three-way voting and state that if there is no indication on how the proxy may vote, the proxy shall exercise their discretion as to whether and if so how to vote. Where there are five or more directors to retire by rotation, the proxy form may give shareholders the opportunity to vote on all elections as a whole, in addition to voting on each re-election individually.

Companies must not prevent shareholders from exercising their rights by proxy and must provide all shareholders with either a paper form of proxy or by electronic means.

Where a company has power in its articles of association to impose sanctions on a shareholder for non-compliance with a request for information under s. 793, those powers are restricted to:

◆   any sanction can only be implemented after 14 days' notice;

◆   for shareholdings of less than 0.25%, the sanctions are restricted to prohibition on attending meetings and exercise of voting rights;

◆   for shareholdings in excess of 0.25%, additional permitted sanctions are the withholding of dividend payments and restricting the right of transfer; and

◆   any sanctions imposed must cease to apply within seven days of the information requested being supplied or notice of a sale to an unconnected third party has been made through an RIS or overseas exchange or by the acceptance of a takeover offer.

A company proposing to issue further equity shares or to sell treasury shares must offer them to existing shareholders in proportion to their holding, unless a general disapplication of the statutory pre-emption rights has been given pursuant to CA2006 s. 561 or a rights issue is proposed and the disapplication relates to fractional entitlements and entitlements that are necessary or expedited (i.e. withholding entitlements from overseas shareholders), or where the sale is to an employee share scheme.

◆   LR 9.4 – *documents requiring FCA approval*

Companies must ensure that the terms of any employees' share scheme or long-term incentive scheme are approved by ordinary resolution of shareholders in general meeting before being adopted, other than schemes where all or substantially all employees are eligible to participate on similar terms provided that all or substantially all employees are not also directors.

Companies must not issue options or warrants where the exercise price is less than the market value as determined in accordance with the scheme rules without the prior sanction of shareholders by ordinary resolution in general meeting. This rule does not apply where the grant relates to options or warrants being granted in an employees' share scheme and participation is offered on substantially the same terms to all or substantially all employees, or in circumstances where the grant of options or warrants is pursuant to the issue of replacement options following a takeover or reconstruction.

◆   LR 9.5 – *transactions*

As soon as practical following completion of a rights issue, the company must notify an RIS of the issue price and principal terms of the offer, and the results of the issue including the date and price at which any unsubscribed rights were sold, if any.

Rights issues and open offers must remain open for acceptances for at least 10 business days.

The timetable of an open offer of securities must be approved by the RIE on which the shares are traded. If the terms of an open offer are subject to shareholder approval, the circular relating to the open offer must not imply that the offer gives the same entitlements as a rights issue.

An offer by a listed company by way of open offer, placing, vendor placing, offer for subscription or issues out of treasury must not be at a discount of more than 10% to the mid-market price on the day the announcement of the offer or agreeing the placing takes place. A discount of more than 10% is permitted if the issue is subject to specific shareholder approval or made pursuant to a pre-existing general disapplication of pre-emption rights.

A company undertaking an offer for sale or offer for subscription must ensure that letters of allotment or acceptance are all issued simultaneously and numbered serially. There must be equality of treatment between certificated and uncertificated holdings.

If a listed company issues a circular in connection with a reconstruction or refinancing, the circular must contain a working capital statement drawn up under the provisions of LR 13.3 and on the basis that the reconstruction or refinancing is successful.

◆　LR 9.6 – *notifications*

Companies must forward two copies of all circulars, notices or other documents to which the Listing Rules apply to the FCA for publishing through the document-viewing facility. These copies must be forwarded to the FCA at the same time that they are issued. Other than routine business at their AGMs, companies must forward two copies of all resolutions passed in general meeting to the FCA for publication through the document-viewing facility as soon as possible after the meeting. Companies must notify an RIS when a document is available for viewing on the document-viewing facility, unless the full text of the document is also provided to the RIS.

The FCA must be informed of the following information in relation to changes in capital:

◆　proposed changes to capital structure including any listed debt securities;

◆　number of shares redeemed and the number remaining outstanding; and

◆　details of any extension to the validity of temporary documents of title.

Details of the results of a share issue must be notified as soon as known except that, subject to DTR 2, the announcement may be delayed by up to two business days, to enable underwriting commitments to be taken up or lapse.

An RIS must be notified no later than the end of the business day following the decision or receipt of notice of any change in the board including:

◆　name, position and function of any new director;

◆　resignation, removal or retirement of any director. Notification is not required where a director retires by rotation and is reappointed at a general meeting.

In respect of the appointment of a new director, the following information must be disclosed within five business days of the decision to appoint them:

◆ details of all current directorships of publicly quoted companies held during the preceding five years distinguishing between current and past directorships;

◆ any unspent convictions in relation to indictable offences;

compulsory liquidation
Winding up of a company by order of the winding up court.

◆ details of any receiverships, **compulsory liquidations**, creditors' voluntary liquidations, administrations, company voluntary liquidations or compositions or arrangements with creditors or any class of creditors where the director was an executive director at the time or within 12 months preceding those events;

◆ details of any compulsory liquidations, administrations or partnership voluntary liquidations or compositions or arrangements with creditors or any class of creditors where the director was a partner at the time or within 12 months preceding those events;

◆ details of any receiverships of any asset of such person or partnership in which the director was a partner at the time or within 12 months preceding those events; and

◆ details of any public criticisms of the director by statutory or regulatory authorities and whether the director has ever been disqualified by a court from acting as a director or from fulfilling management duties or conducting the affairs of a company.

When a company changes its name, it must notify an RIS, stating the date on which the change was effective, notify the FCA in writing and forward to the FCA a copy of the certificate of incorporation on change of name.

A company must notify an RIS as soon as possible of any change in its accounting date, including the new accounting reference date. Where the effect of the change is to extend an accounting period to more than 14 months, the company will be required to issue a second interim report. The second interim report should be made up to either the old accounting reference date or a date not more than six months prior to the new accounting reference date.

◆ LR 9.7A – *preliminary announcements*

If a company prepares a preliminary statement of its annual results, the statement must be published as soon as possible after it has been approved by the board. The statement must be agreed with the company's auditor prior to publication.

The statement must include figures in the form of a table, including the items required for its interim report, and must be consistent with the presentation to be adopted in the annual report.

A company must notify an RIS as soon as possible after the board meeting to approve a decision to pay or withhold a dividend or other distribution to shareholders. It must give details of the net amount per share payable, the payment date, record (if applicable) and any foreign income dividend election, together with any income tax treated as payable at the lower rate and not repayable.

◆   LR 9.8 – *annual financial report*

The detailed content requirements for the annual financial report are detailed in chapter 6.

2.3   Market Abuse Regulations and the Disclosure and Transparency Rules

MAR implemented a new approach to market abuse regulation. The previous legislation had been implemented by way of the Market Abuse Directive (MAD), the key difference in the legislative approach being that under MAD EU countries had to implement the terms of the directive under their own legislation which imposed minimum standards and a degree of interpretation. This resulted in the market abuse legislation in each EU country being very different as some countries such as the UK went much further than the minimum requirements. MAR being an EU regulation has introduced a common EU approach with the same rules applying across all EU countries for preventing and detecting market abuse and ensuring a proper flow of information to the market. MAR, which came into force on 3 July 2016, introduced a number of changes to the previous UK disclosure regime. Although overall, the compliance requirements are largely unchanged there has been a significant increase in the record keeping and reporting requirements as well as a shift of responsibilities on to the PDMRs to make the required disclosures.

In the UK, the most visible change for companies was the deletion of the Model Code from the Listing Rules and changes to the disclosure requirements of share dealing by PDMRs.

The primary obligation of companies under MAR relates to the control and disclosure of inside information and dealing by PDMRs (MAR 17–21). Investment firms have additional responsibilities to monitor and report investment transactions and suspicious activities for the prevention of market manipulation and other fraudulent activity.

MAR works in tandem with DTR, and these were also updated to reflect changes introduced by MAR. DTR 4 and 6 apply to listed shares on an RIE (listed companies) only and DTR 5 applies to companies with shares listed on an RIE or on a prescribed market. Accordingly, DTR 5 also applies to companies with shares admitted to AIM or the NEX Growth Market.

DTR 1, 2 and 3 have been deleted and replaced by MAR 16 to 19.

Inside information
◆   Under MAR 17, companies must publish 'inside information', via an RIS, that directly concerns them as soon as possible and must post and keep on their website, for five years, copies of all inside information publicly disclosed (MAR 17(1)).

◆   Inside information is information that is precise, has not been made public, relates directly or indirectly to the company and if made public is likely to have a significant effect on the price of the company's shares or securities (that is information that a reasonable investor would be likely to use as part of the basis of their investment decisions) (MAR 7(1)(b) to (d)).

◆ A short delay may be acceptable in order to provide full clarification, in which case a holding announcement should be issued (DTR 2.2.9).

To facilitate the disclosure of inside information listed companies must have appropriate processes in place to identify inside information (MAR 17(4)).

DTR 2.2 sets out a range of factors that a listed company should consider when assessing whether information constitutes inside information including:

◆ significance of the information relative to the size of the company;

◆ likelihood that an investor will make an investment decision based on this information; and

◆ the company and its advisers are best placed to determine if any specific information constitutes inside information.

MAR 17(1) and (9) – information to be disclosed on website
Disclosure of inside information may be delayed if:

◆ immediate disclosure is likely to prejudice the company legitimate interests;

◆ delayed disclosure is unlikely to mislead the public; and

◆ the company can ensure the information remains confidential until it is disclosed (MAR 17(4)).

Where a disclosure has been delayed the company must notify the FCA of that fact immediately after the information has been disclosed and provide an explanation if requested.

Other than in situations where the recipient owes a duty of confidentiality where a company or a person acting on its behalf discloses inside information to a third party in the normal course of employment or profession, there must also be complete public disclosure of that information simultaneously in the case of a planned disclosure or as soon as possible in the case of a non-intentional disclosure (MAR 17(8)).

Selective disclosure
The FCA guidance in this area is clear that selective disclosure of inside information relating to any matter to any person cannot be justified only on the basis that that person owes the company a duty of confidentiality. The ability to share inside information with those owing a duty of confidentiality can only be relied on where the recipient needs that information to provide services or advice to the company (DTR 2.5.7) or to persons directly involved in the matter such as:

◆ those persons with whom the listed company is negotiating, or intends to negotiate, the listed company's own advisers and the advisers of any party to the matter;

◆ employee representatives, or trade unions acting on their behalf, in any discussions relating to the matter;

- any government department, the Bank of England, the Competition Commission or any other statutory or regulatory body or authority;
- major shareholders of the issuer;
- the issuer's lenders; and
- credit-rating agencies.

However, care must be taken where a wide group of external parties are made aware of inside information on a selective basis as this increases the likelihood of a leak of that information which in turn will trigger full disclosure (DTR 2.5.7–9).

Listed companies must establish effective arrangements to keep inside information confidential and only accessible to those within the company that require access in the exercise of their function within the listed company (DTR 2.6.1).

In any circumstances where disclosure of inside information is delayed whether in connection with a specific non-routine mater or in the period in the immediate run up to an announcement of financial results the company must be able to issue a holding announcement as soon as reasonably practical in the event of any breach of confidentiality or leak of the information or any part of it (DTR 2.6.4).

Listed companies will need to carefully assess situations where there is press speculation or market rumour, whether that speculation or rumour is accurate or not, and make an announcement in circumstances where knowledge of the true position constitutes inside information.

Control of inside information

Companies should have a framework for the control of inside information and establish effective arrangements to restrict access to inside information to those persons who require access to perform their job. A company should maintain insider lists in relation to employees and advisers with access to inside information (MAR 18).

Companies must have deal specific or event-based insider lists and may have a permanent insider list. To be entered on a permanent insider list the individual will be assumed to have access to all inside information at all times. As a result any permanent insider list is likely to be very short.

Deal specific or event-based insider lists must be kept in electronic form, must adhere to the format laid down by the regulations, must be retained for five years and must be capable of being produced to the FCA as soon as possible on request (MAR 18(1)(c), 18(3) and 18(5)).

The minimum content for the insider lists is:

- identity of each person with access to the information;
- reason why the person is on the insider list;
- date and time that person obtained access to the information; and
- date on which the insider list was drawn up.

Companies are required to keep their insider lists up to date and the list must also contain:

◆ date and time of any change in the reason for inclusion on the insider list;

◆ date and time any new person is added to the insider list; and

◆ date and time when a person ceases to have access to inside information.

Prevention of insider dealing

Dealing in shares on a regulated market while in possession of price-sensitive information (insider dealing) is a criminal offence. The legislation is contained in CJA1993 which introduced three offences (CJA1993 s. 52):

1. dealing in company securities while in the possession of inside information;

2. encouraging another person to deal while in possession of inside information; and

3. disclosing information other than in the proper performance of an office, employment or profession.

The insider must either know that they possess inside information or knowingly acquire inside information from an inside source. It is no longer necessary for the insider to be connected with the particular company; a person can be an insider simply by having access to inside information. Accordingly, the husband or wife of a director could be convicted if using inside information passed on by their spouse, and any friends could also be guilty of an offence if they dealt in shares on the basis of inside information gained directly from the director or indirectly from the spouse or some other third party.

The definition of 'securities' has been expanded and now covers not only shares, debentures and debt securities, but also their derivatives (CJA1993 s. 54 and Sch. 2).

Similarly, the definition of 'dealing' has been expanded. Although deals of a purely private nature even on the basis of inside information will not normally be covered by the legislation, any transactions on a regulated market (e.g. the Stock Exchange) and any deals undertaken via professional intermediaries whether or not through a regulated market will be covered (CJA1993 s. 55).

The inside information must be specific, relate to the company whose securities have been dealt and must not be public knowledge. It must also be shown that if that information were to have been made public, it would have had a significant effect on the price of the securities concerned. There is, unfortunately, no definition or guidance as to the meaning of 'significant' in the legislation (CJA1993 s. 56).

The defences against a charge of insider dealing are set out in s. 53 of the CJA1993 and include that the person:

1. did not expect the dealing to result in a profit attributable to the information being price-sensitive;

2. had reasonable grounds for believing that the other party to the deal was also in possession of the information; and

3.   would have dealt irrespective of whether or not they had been in possession of the price-sensitive information.

PDMRs

A PDMR is a natural or legal person in an issuer who is either (MAR 1(13) and (25)):

◆   a member of the administrative, management or supervisory body of that entity; or

◆   a senior executive who is not a member of the administrative, management or supervisory body of that entity, but who has regular access to inside information relating directly or indirectly to that entity and the power to make managerial decisions affecting the future developments and business prospects of that entity.

It can be seen that the designation of a PDMR will vary from company to company and that PDMRs might not be directors of the company.

PCA

A PDMRs PCA includes:

◆   spouse or partner considered equivalent to a spouse under national law;

◆   dependent children of the PDMR;

◆   a relative of the PDMR who has shared the same residence for at least one year;

◆   any legal person, trust or partnership, the managerial duties and responsibilities of which are carried out by the PDMR or PCA;

◆   anyone directly or indirectly controlled by the PDMR or PCA;

◆   anyone established for the benefit of the PDMR or PCA; and

◆   anyone whose economic interests are substantially the same as the PDMR or PCA (MAR 3(1)(26)).

Disclosure of PDMR share transactions

MAR 19 contains details of the requirement for PDMRs to notify any transactions in shares undertaken by themselves or their PCAs.

In addition to notifying the company, PDMRs are now also required to notify the FCA of any transactions (MAR 19(1)).

There is a prescribed template for the PDMR disclosure to the FCA (MAR 19(6)) and this may be completed and submitted online from the FCA website.

Notifiable transactions must be disclosed within three business days:

◆   by the PDMR or PCA to the FCA and the company; and

◆   by the company to the market via an RIS (MAR 19(2) and (3)).

Companies must notify their PDMRs in writing of their obligations under MAR 19 and draw up a list of their PDMRs and PCAs (MAR 19(5)).

PDMRs must notify their PCAs in writing of their obligations under MAR 19 and keep a copy of that notification (MAR 19(5)).

Notifications by PDMRs need not be made until the aggregate of all transactions in any calendar year exceeds €5,000 although notifications below this limit may be made on a voluntary basis (MAR 19(8)).

Closed periods

A PDMR must not for themselves or for a third party, directly or indirectly, conduct any transactions in the financial instruments of the company during a closed period (MAR 19(11)).

A closed period is the period of 30 days prior to an announcement of the company's full or half-year financial report. For this purpose, a preliminary announcement of full year results will count as an announcement of the full year results provided the announcement contains all the key information expected to be included in the full year-end report.

Financial information

Listed companies are required to publish their annual financial report within four months of the end of the financial year to which they relate (DTR 4.1.3). A listed company must ensure that copies of its annual financial reports are available, free of charge, for a minimum period of 10 years following publication (DTR 4.1.4).

The management report comprised in the annual financial report must contain the review of the company's business required by DTR 4.1.8 and 9 as well as the details required by DTR 4.1.11 (see chapter 6 for fuller details)..

The annual financial report must include a responsibility statement made by those responsible confirming that, to the best of their knowledge and belief, the financial statements have been prepared in accordance with applicable accounting standards and give a true and fair view of the assets, liabilities, financial position and profit or loss of the company. It must also confirm that the interim management report contains a fair review of the information required to be disclosed by DTR 4.1.8–11 (DTR 4.1.12).

Listed companies are required to issue a half-yearly financial report covering the first six months of the financial year. The half-yearly report must be published as soon as possible and no later than two months after the end of the period to which it relates. Copies of the half-yearly report must be available to the public for at least 10 years (DTR 4.2.2).

The half-yearly report must include a responsibility statement made by those responsible confirming that, to the best of their knowledge and belief, the financial statements have been prepared in accordance with applicable accounting standards and give a true and fair view of the assets, liabilities, financial position and profit or loss of the company, and that the interim management report contains a fair review of the information required to be disclosed by DTR 4.2.7 and 8 (DTR 4.2.10).

If the half-yearly report has been audited, the auditor's report must be reproduced in full. If the half-yearly report has not been audited, a statement of this fact must be included in the report (DTR 4.2.9).

The responsibility statement must disclose the name and functions of those making the responsibility statement (DTR 4.2.10).

Payments to governments

Companies carrying out business in the extractive or logging of primary forest industries are required to report annually on payments made to governments in each financial year (DTR 4.3A.4). The report must be published within six months of the end of the relevant financial year and the reports must be available free of charge for at least the next 10 years (DTR 4.3A.5 and 6).

A copy of the report must be filed with the FCA by uploading a copy to the National Storage Mechanism (DTR 4.3A.10).

Information requirements

Companies must ensure equal treatment of shareholders and provide all the facilities and information to enable such holders to exercise their rights (DTR 6.1.3 and 4).

Forms of proxy must be available either with the notice of general meeting or following the announcement of the meeting (DTR 6.1.5).

Companies must appoint a financial institution through which shareholders may exercise their financial rights (DTR 6.1.6).

Companies may take advantage of electronic communications, but:

◆ any decision to do so must be taken in general meeting and the use of electronic communication must not be dependent on the location of the shareholder;

◆ identification arrangements must be made to ensure shareholders can exercise their rights and are informed;

◆ shareholders must be contacted in writing to request their consent to the dissemination of information by electronic means; and

◆ shareholders must be able to request information in written form (DTR 6.1.8).

Companies must disclose any changes in the rights attaching to shares (DTR 6.1.9).

Companies must provide information to the holders of loan stock or other debt instruments concerning the place, time and agenda of meetings, total number of shares and voting rights and the right of shareholders to participate in meetings (DTR 6.1.12).

Stop and think 13.1

In recent years the FCA, and previously the FSA, has increasingly been bringing boards to account for breaches of the listing principles rather than specific rule breaches. In part this is due to it being much easier to demonstrate a failure of having appropriate systems of control while a specific rule may not have been breached.

In addition, the fines accompanying the breaches have been increasing dramatically. The table below sets out an overview of some of the more recent instances of prosecutions for breach of Listing Principles, in addition to some specific rule breaches.

Company	Fine	Description
2013 – Nestor Healthcare Group	£175,000	Failing to take adequate steps to ensure that its board members and senior executives complied with the share dealing provisions of the FSA's Model Code
2013 – Lamprell plc	£2,428,300	Significant failings in its systems and controls resulting in Listing Rules and related breaches
2013 – Prudential plc	£30m	Breaching FSA Principles and UKLA Listing Principles
2015 – Reckitt Benckiser Group plc	£539,800	For breaching Listing Rule 9.2.8 (LR 9.2.8R), Principle 1 and 2, Disclosure and Transparency Rule 3.1.4R(2) and DTR 3.1.5R
2015 – Asia Resource Minerals plc	£4,651,200	For breaching Listing Principle 2, Listing Rules 8 and 11 and Disclosure and Transparency Rule 4.
2017 – Rio Tinto plc	£27,385,400	For breaching Disclosure and Transparency Rules

Table 13.2 FCA enforcement actions

3. Link between disclosure, accountability, transparency and trust

Trust can only be accomplished if stakeholders, be they investors, employees, suppliers or customers, believe what they are told by companies and, at least within the context of their contact with the company, understand, if not necessarily agree with, the reasons behind any particular decision that affects them. Clearly, it is impossible and commercially untenable for every single piece of information behind every business decision to be made public.

Transparency refers to the extent to which an organisation's inner workings are observable by an independent third party observer. Transparency relies on a combination of information disclosure, the clarity of the communication and the accuracy of the information.

Information disclosure can be in accordance with a regulatory obligation or the voluntary provision of information.

Disclosure alone is not transparency, however. Whatever the motivation behind any specific information disclosure, the communication of the information needs to be clear and free from jargon. There is nothing to be gained from making regulatory or voluntary disclosure if the content of the communication is incomprehensible to few outside the organisation as a consequence of using industry or company specific abbreviations and terminology. Such poor communication, whether deliberate or not, is highly unlikely to engender any trust in the organisation.

Companies need to be aware of the audience any communication is being issued to, while not losing sight of the other audiences that may also receive that communication, whether directly or indirectly.

The main focuses of company communications are:

◆   investors
◆   employees
◆   customers.

Good-quality informative communications to each of these three groups on a consistent basis will provide long-term benefits for all.

Provided the financial performance meets an investor's criteria, good-quality informative communication may well persuade investors to invest in any future share issues in addition to holding on to their shares in the long-term.

A well-informed workforce is more likely to have a positive attitude towards their employer and this would be expected to increase productivity and decrease employee turnover.

Disclosure is the tool of choice for regulators in their attempts to improve transparency. After all, if we know the facts, we know we are not being misled, a key component in establishing and maintaining trust.

However, proving too much information can result in the core message becoming lost. An example of this was the remuneration disclosure requirements under The Large and Medium-sized Companies and Groups (Accounts and Reports) Regulations 2008 (I 2008/410). In the period following their coming into force corporate disclosures on directors' remuneration, although complying with the requirements of the legislation, were becoming ever more complex, as more and more information was disclosed. Consequently, it was difficult for investors to understand how much a director had actually been paid and perhaps more importantly, how much the directors might be paid in future. There was a wealth of information provided but no overall coherent message and different valuation methods adopted by companies made cross company comparisons, especially on incentive and long-term benefits, impossible. Great disclosure but no transparency.

The Large and Medium-sized Companies and Groups (Accounts and Reports) (Amendment) Regulations 2013 substituted new disclosure requirements, a key component of which is the 'single figure' table for the remuneration of each director and which includes a value placed on share-based payments and pension benefits using calculations prescribed in the legislation. This use of a common calculation makes comparisons across companies more meaningful.

Perhaps a better way to describe the need for relevant disclosure and transparency in the communication of the disclosures is that company should have openness as their guiding principle. Trust relies on both data and intent. A communication is much more likely to be effective if the intention is to inform the reader rather than merely meet a disclosure requirement.

Investors' expectations can have a significant effect on the quality of corporate communications. Investors that are disengaged are not going to bring pressure on company boards to make better information and coherent disclosures. By comparison, engaged investors, actively seeking engagement will bring about fuller disclosures.

At the same time there has been a shift in sentiment among companies and investors concerning a company's involvement with and reporting of social and environmental engagement more usually now referred to as sustainability reporting. Historically seen as non-core activities which added little if any value the rise in sustainability reporting on social and environmental activities particularly where that activity can be shown to be integrated with and delivering part of the company's corporate strategy is an increasingly important aspect of reporting the value drivers within companies. Reporting on these areas is also a key component to fully delivering integrated reporting as considered in chapter 6.

As core engines of corporate growth, employees should not be overlooked or taken for granted. At the same time employees are perhaps the directors' and senior managers' fiercest critics and sometimes the most challenging stakeholders to convince that a change of strategy or operational practice is a positive move. Investors, both current and prospective, will no doubt be delighted to hear that an underperforming company is 'exploring opportunities to move work to jurisdiction with a lower cost base'; the employees, however, will hear the message that their jobs are under threat. When a company announces that it is 'future proofing its IT systems', employees will look at their frozen desktop and think to themselves, 'Really?'

There are of course many benefits of transparency in the workplace and a happy motivated workforce is a key goal of all managers. Job satisfaction does not only flow from job security and being well informed about the direction and strategy that the employer is following. There are other factors including the organisations' environmental policy and philosophy, its charitable works, training schemes and how employees are treated all combine to create the company personality. The best companies successfully combine hardnosed commerciality with being a good employer doing the right thing for their employees.

Transparency is equally important for customers but from a very different perspective. Customers will be naturally attracted to companies demonstrating the same environmental and social ethos that they themselves have. Customers also require clear truthful and understandable information about the items they are purchasing.

In some quarters accountability is taken to mean the attribution of blame and/or a way to shift responsibility of a particular, unexpected or unwelcome outcome. Accountability is however much more than this and is a key part of the risk management process, providing stability to a business and creating the right conditions to promote value-creation.

As discussed in chapter 2, directors of all companies are accountable generally as a board for the actions and decisions of the company and board and also individually for their own actions and decisions. Companies with external investors need to clearly demonstrate how they have exercised the company's and their own power and authority for the benefit of the members and other stakeholders.

Listed company boards in complying with the Governance Code must explain the decision-making processes of the board and that they evaluate their own performance to manage the affairs of the company effectively and efficiently. Directors of listed companies are recommended to offer themselves for re-election by members each year thus providing their shareholders with the means to hold individual directors to account.

For financial years beginning on or after 1 January 2019, directors will need to include additional disclosures on how they have met their duties under CA2006 s. 172 in managing the affairs of the company for the benefit of the members as a whole while also having regard to the interests of employees, suppliers, customers and others with whom the company has a business relationship.

3.1 Clear and concise annual reporting

Over the last few years, the FRC through their financial reporting lab have been reviewing how financial reports can be improved to be presented in a clear and concise way.

The FRC's Clear and Concise initiative's main aim is to ensure that the reports relay relevant information to investors and promote good communication.

Figure 13.1 sets out the timeline for the nine reports issued since 2012 supporting this initiative, some of the early ones have now been overtaken by legislative changes in particular those focused on remuneration and audit committee reporting.

Remuneration reporting   **Strategic report**   **Governance reporting**

	Performance metrics	2018
	Risk & viability reporting	Case study	2017
	Business model reporting	2016
	Disclosure of dividends	2015
	Towards clear & concise	2014
Reporting of pay & performance		Performance metrics	2013
Single figure for remuneration		2012
	clear & concise financial reporting	

Figure 13.1 Clear & concise reporting guidance

Disclosure of dividends

Dividend disclosures are important to companies and investors alike and a key measure by which companies demonstrate their stewardship of the company and by which investors validate their investment case.

Investors have indicated that a good dividend disclosure combined with a description of the dividend policy will cover the following issues:

- Why this policy?
- What will the policy mean in practice?
- What are the risks and constraints associated with this policy?
- What was done in practice to deliver under the policy?

In addition, investors have expressed a preference for the dividend disclosures to be grouped together rather than spread out either in different parts of the annual financial statements or in different communications and announcements.

Business model reporting

A common theme from investors is that business model descriptions require addition information. There is a preference that companies should assume that the reader knows nothing about the company and should provide a comprehensive description of the business model including:

- what the company does;
- key divisions, legal structure and contribution to assets, liabilities and profit;
- key markets;
- its USP;
- key assets and liabilities, relationships and resources including the measures taken to preserve and enhance them;
- key revenue and profit drivers;
- value created for other stakeholders and the benefits this brings to the company; and
- statistics to illustrate relative importance of elements.

Risk and viability reporting

The annual financial statement is the primary source of information on a company for many investors and disclosure of principle risks facing the company and how the company is managing those risks is vital to their understanding of the underlying business. Investors are looking for company specific risks linked to the business model, disclosing how the risks have changed over time and what the impact of risks occurring might be.

The introduction of the viability statement has improved directors' consideration of sustainability and risk resilience. However, that increased awareness has not necessarily been reflected in the viability statement, which too often resembles an extended going concern statement. Investors are looking for information on the sustainability of the company's business model and the company's resilience to the risks it faces. In addition, investors are looking for more information on the prospects and risks over a much longer period even if the viability statement itself is limited to a shorter period.

Performance metrics

Performance of a company is crucial to all investors and although the specific measures key to an investment will vary from one investor to another all investors would agree that a range of measures is required.

Performance measures are essential for companies and directors to demonstrate the value they create and consequently how investors value companies. The performance measures chosen, how they are reported, and whether the information is reported in a way that investors consider to be fair, balanced and understandable are central to this assessment.

From their research the reporting lab have reported that investors prefer a range of measures covering financial measures comprising numbers prepared under recognised defined GAAP methodology together with appropriate non-GAAP defined numbers combined with non-financial measures also being a combination of standard and company specific measures.

Whichever measures are chosen, they should all meet the following principles:

- aligned to strategy;
- transparent;
- in context;
- reliable; and
- consistent.

Stop and think 13.2

For many companies the combination of obligation and desire to provide shareholders, analysts and potential investors with all the information they needed in one place saw the length of annual financial statements grow in size without necessarily improving communications.

HSBC Group was a good case in point, with the 2015 annual report coming in at 500 pages. A year later and after a fundamental review of what the annual report was for, breaking regulatory and environmental, social and governance reports into separate reports more than achieved the initial goal of a 20% reduction in the length of the annual report with the 2016 report being reduced to 282 pages and creating positive feedback from investors.

4. Data protection

2018 saw a significant change to data protection legislation across Europe with the implementation of the pan-European GDPR, supported in the UK by the Data Protection Act 2018 (DPA2018), and the Privacy and Electronic Communications Regulations (PECR). In formulating their data protection policies, practices and procedures public bodies must also be aware of the requirements of the Freedom of Information Act 2000.

4.1 Overview DPA2018

What does DPA2018 do in addition to GDPR?

- Makes UK data protection laws fit for the digital age when an ever-increasing amount of data is being processed.
- Empowers people to take control of their data.
- Supports UK businesses and organisations through this change.
- Ensures that the UK is prepared for the future and in particular makes provision for the data protection regime to continue after Brexit.

DPA2018 provides a comprehensive and modern framework for data protection in the UK, with stronger sanctions for malpractice.

DPA2018 establishes new standards for protecting general data, in accordance with the GDPR, giving people more control over use of their data, and providing them with new rights to move or delete personal data. Exemptions contained in the previous Data Protection Act have been retained ensuring that UK businesses and organisations can continue to support world-leading research, financial services, journalism and legal services.

DPA2018 provides a framework tailored to the needs of our criminal justice agencies and the intelligence services, to protect the rights of victims, witnesses and suspects while ensuring we can tackle the changing nature of global threats.

The main elements of DPA2018 are as follows:

General data processing

- Implements GDPR standards across all general data processing.
- Provides clarity on the definitions used in the GDPR in the UK context.
- Ensures that sensitive health, social care and education data can continue to be processed while making sure that confidentiality in health and safeguarding situations is maintained.
- Provides appropriate restrictions to rights to access and delete data to allow certain processing currently undertaken to continue where there is a strong public policy justification, including for national security purposes.
- Sets the age from which parental consent is not needed to process data online at age 13, supported by a new age-appropriate design code enforced by the Information Commissioner.

Law enforcement processing

- Provides a bespoke regime for the processing of personal data by the police, prosecutors and other criminal justice agencies for law enforcement purposes.
- Allows the unhindered flow of data internationally while providing safeguards to protect personal data.

Intelligence services processing
Ensures that the laws governing the processing of personal data by the intelligence services remain up-to-date and in line with modernised international standards, including appropriate safeguards with which the intelligence community can continue to tackle existing, new and emerging national security threats.

Regulation and enforcement
- Enacts additional powers for the Information Commissioner who will continue to regulate and enforce data protection laws.
- Allows the Commissioner to levy higher administrative fines on data controllers and processors for the most serious data breaches, up to £17 million (€20 million) or 4% of global turnover for the most serious breaches.
- Empowers the Commissioner to bring criminal proceedings against offences where a data controller or processor alters records with intent to prevent disclosure following a subject access request.

Registration regime
From 25 May 2018, the Data Protection (Charges and Information) Regulations 2018 require every organisation or sole trader that processes personal information to pay a data protection fee, unless they are exempt. The fee is collected by the ICO.

The ICO maintains a public data protection register of data controllers, who pay the data protection fee, which is available at https://ico.org.uk/ESDWebPagesSearch.

The data protection fee depends on the size of the company measured in terms of turnover or numbers of staff. There are three different tiers of fees as set out in Table 13.3. An organisation meets the tier test if it meets either of the criteria for that tier.

Tier	Turnover	Number of staff	Fee
Tier 1 - micro organisations	Not more than £632,000	Not more than 10	£40
Tier 2 – small and medium-sized organisations	Not more than £36 million	Not more than 250	£60
Tier 3 – large organisations	More than £36m	More than 250	£2,900

Table 13.3 Data protection fee tiers

PECR sits alongside DPA2018 and GDPR and provides additional protection for individuals in relation to electronic communications which are out of scope of GDPR as follows:

- electronic marketing including marketing calls, texts, emails and faxes;
- use of cookies or similar technologies that track information about website or other electronic service usage;
- security of public electronic communications services; and
- privacy of customers using communications networks or services as regards traffic and location data, itemised billing, line identification services and directory listings.

GDPR has made a number of changes to the operation of PECR. Generally, the existing PECR rules continue to apply with the main change being the adoption of the new GDPR standard of consent. As a result, companies making use of electronic marketing techniques must ensure that these comply with both GDPR and PECR rules.

A key difference between these two sets of sometimes overlapping rules is that PECR apply even in circumstances where personal data is not being processed. Unlike GDPR where the focus is on providing protection to individuals PECR rules give protection to companies as well as individuals.

4.2 GDPR

As noted in section 4.1, GDPR was implemented as pan-European regulation in May 2018 and represents significant advance in data protection legislation fit for modern data uses. Previous legislation, the Data Protection Act 1998 (DPA1998) had been overtaken by advances in technology and the rise of companies such as Facebook and Google and capabilities brought about by big data.

GDPR only applies to personal data and has seven key principles:

1. lawfulness, fairness and transparency;
2. purpose limitation;
3. data minimisation;
4. accuracy;
5. storage limitation;
6. integrity and confidentiality (security); and
7. accountability.

There are no formal fixed rules, but organisations controlling or processing personal data need to design their procedures and policies within the context of the principles and be prepared to justify how adherence to any particular principle is met.

There are very few exceptions to these principles, but among the ones that are permitted are certain activities including processing covered by the Law Enforcement Directive, processing for national security purposes and processing carried out by individuals purely for personal/household activities.

GDPR applies to 'controllers' and 'processors' of personal data. The definitions are broadly the same as under DPA1998 – i.e. the controller says how and why personal data is processed and the processor acts on the controller's behalf.

GDPR places new specific legal obligations on data processors including a requirement to maintain records of personal data and processing activities. Data processors have significantly more legal liability if they are responsible for a breach.

Data controllers are also subject to additional obligations. In particular where a controller uses the services of a third party data processor the data controller must ensure that the service contractor carries out the processing activities in compliance with GDPR whether those activities are carried out within or outside the EU.

As noted above, GDPR applies to 'personal data'. However, GDPR's definition has been much more widely drawn than the previous legislation and makes it clear that any information that identifies a person can be personal data. This wider definition now encapsulates not only email address data as before, but also an IP address. The more expansive definition provides for a wide range of personal identifiers to constitute personal data, reflecting changes in technology and the way organisations collect information about people.

For most organisations, keeping HR records, customer lists, or contact details etc., the change to the definition should make little practical difference.

GDPR applies to the processing of personal data that is:

- wholly or partly by automated means; or
- the processing other than by automated means of personal data which forms part of, or is intended to form part of, a filing system.

Personal data only includes information relating to natural persons who can be:

- identified, or are identifiable, directly from the information in question; or
- indirectly identified from the information in question when combined with other information. A building access system might record the unique reference of an access card each time it is used. On its own, this does not identify any individual but when used in combination with a schedule of access cards issued to individuals becomes personal data.

Simple identification alone is not enough to be covered by GDPR the information must relate to the person in some way such as identifying them as an employee, or resident in a building, member of a club, owner of a vehicle, etc.

Stop and think 13.3

A schedule of employee names and addresses is clearly personal information.

A log recording usage of access cards by reference to their unique issue number for entry or exit from a building on its own is not personal data. However, when combined with the records of which cards are issued to which employee the access log becomes personal data.

Organisations must have valid grounds under GDPR (known as a 'lawful basis') for collecting and using personal data. There are six categories of lawful basis and these are:

Consent
GDPR requires consent to be explicit. Deemed consent, use of pre-ticked check boxes or opt out are no longer permitted options to obtain consent. Organisations will need to ensure their systems can demonstrate how and when explicit consent was obtained in order to justify why they hold data on any individual. Additionally, data subjects have the right to withdraw consent at any time.

Contractual obligations
Any processing of personal data required to fulfil a contractual obligation or in anticipation of a contractual obligation, such as providing a quote, is permitted under GDPR provided there is no alternative way to meet the obligation without requiring the personal data to be processed.

Legal obligations
Processing of personal information is permitted if the organisation undertaking it is doing so in order to meet a legal obligation. For all companies this permitted use applies to maintaining statutory records and filing personal information when filing forms such as the confirmation statement with the Registrar.

Vital interests
This usage has limited practical use in everyday situations as it permits processing of personal data necessary to protect someone's life, who need not be the person whose data needs processing. It is expected that this would only be required in situations involving the emergency services.

Public task
Processing of personal data is permitted by organisations in order to carry out a task in the national interest or the exercise of official authority including administration of justice, exercising the function of the Crown or a government department.

Legitimate interests
This category provides the most flexibility to the data controller or data processor as it permits the processing of data necessary for the legitimate interests of the data controller or by a third party except where the fundamental rights and freedoms of the data subject require the data to be protected. As a result, although providing flexibility it requires the data processor or data

controller to be able to demonstrate and justify the use of that flexibility and how the processing is permitted by GDPR.

Stop and think 13.4

Organisations that collected personal data under any deemed consent process will need to revise their data capture processes and will need to obtain explicit consent from persons they already hold data for.

Test yourself 13.1

1.   **What are the seven GDPR principles?**

2.   **GDPR is supplemented in the UK by which additional legislation?**

5. Public access to corporate information

Under DPA2018, individuals have the right to find out what information the government and other organisations store about them, including:

◆   how the data is being used;

◆   access personal data relating to themselves;

◆   have incorrect data updated;

◆   have data erased;

◆   stop or restrict the processing of that data;

◆   data portability; and

◆   in certain circumstances, object to how that data is processed.

Individuals also have rights in respect of automated decision-making processes and the use of their personal data for profiling.

There is not a prescribed form for individuals to complete instead they simply write to the organisation identifying themselves and ask for a copy of the information the organisation holds about them.

The organisation must provide a copy of the data they hold about you as soon as possible which in most instances is considered to be within one month.

An organisation can take up to three months where the request is particularly complex but in order to take advantage of this extra time must inform the individual within one month and provide details of why the additional time is required.

An organisation is permitted to withhold, without explanation, some or all information if it relates to:

◆ the prevention, detection or investigation of a crime;

◆ national security or the armed forces;

◆ the assessment or collection of tax; and

◆ judicial or ministerial appointments.

Requests for copies of information an organisation holds on an individual are usually provided free of charge however a small fee may be charged if there is a lot of information or it is a complex operation to collate all the information.

5.1 Right to request details of data held by an employer or company

Companies must keep their employees' personal data safe, secure and up to date. An employer is permitted to keep certain personal information about their employees without their consent including:

◆ name and address;

◆ date of birth;

◆ sex;

◆ education and qualifications;

◆ work experience;

◆ National Insurance number;

◆ tax code;

◆ emergency contact details;

◆ employment history with the organisation;

◆ employment terms and conditions;

◆ any accidents connected with work;

◆ any training taken; and

◆ any disciplinary action.

Certain additional personal information on an employee constitutes 'sensitive' personal data and can only be kept and processed with the employees' explicit permission. This type of data includes:

◆ race and ethnicity;

◆ religion;

◆ political membership or opinions;

◆ trade union membership;

◆ genetics;

◆ biometrics, for example if your fingerprints are used for identification;

◆ health and medical conditions; and

◆ sexual history or orientation.

An employee has a right to be told by their employer:

◆   what records are kept and how they are used;

◆   the confidentiality of the records; and

◆   how these records can help with their training and development at work.

If an employee requests details of the information an employer holds about them, the employer has 30 days to provide a copy of that information.

5.2   Freedom of information

The Freedom of Information Act 2000 (FOIA2000) (Scottish public authorities are covered by the Freedom of Information (Scotland) Act 2002) provides public access to information held by public authorities in two ways:

◆   public authorities are obliged to publish certain information about their activities; and

◆   members of the public are entitled to request information from public authorities.

The Act covers any recorded information that is held by a public authority. Public authorities include government departments, local authorities, the NHS, state schools and police forces.

Any natural person or corporate entity can make a freedom of information request and there is no need to provide any reason for the request or the use the information will be put to.

Requesters should direct their requests for information to the public authority they think will hold the information. The public authority that receives the request is responsible for responding.

Public authorities can withhold information where disclosure is prohibited under other legislation. Additionally, information need not be provided that is accessible under other legislation.

A public authority has two separate duties when responding to freedom of information requests:

◆   to tell the applicant whether it holds any information falling within the scope of their request; and

◆   to provide that information.

Public authorities have 20 working days to respond to a request.

For a request to be valid under the Freedom of Information Act, it must be in writing, include the applicant's name and correspondence address and identify the information requested.

Although technically any question posed to a public authority could come within scope of FOIA2000 routine operational queries can be responded to in the usual manner, without recourse to the procedures under FOIA2000.

Chapter summary

◆ Additional disclosures required from listed companies, financial and non-financial

◆ How the manner of disclosures can build trust and accountability

◆ Transparency means the right disclosure not more disclosure

◆ Data protection changes from GDPR

◆ Access to data held by companies on individuals

Part three

Chapter fourteen
Meetings of
shareholders and
members

Chapter fifteen
Meetings of the
board and its
committees

Meetings

Overview

This part examines and considers the plethora of rules and regulations relating to the convening, holding and voting at meetings of members and the paucity of rules and regulations concerned with the convening, holding and voting at directors' meetings.

Chapter 14 examines the detailed rules and regulations in both the Companies Act and each company's articles of association for the holding of and voting at members' meetings. The chapter notes the legislator's view that for private companies written resolutions are likely to become more common and the default method for obtaining members' authority rather than the holding of physical meetings. There is a detailed review of the types of meetings that can be held, the period of notice that must be given and content of the notice convening the meeting. The chapter considers the role of the chair of the meeting and the procedural resolutions available to ensure smooth running of the meeting. Lastly, the meeting considers the right of members to appoint proxies, the mechanisms for voting and the technology now available to facilitate and improve the running of large meetings of many thousands of members as well as differing communication channels available for companies and members.

Chapter 15 explores the procedures for the running of directors' meetings including consideration of who might typically attend these meetings. The chapter considers the right to convene directors' meetings and the length and type of notice required together with associated board papers commonly required. It examines the quorum requirements, the role and duties of the chair, and the use of technology such as telephone and video conferencing to enable attendance remotely. Finally, the chapter considers the voting process and conflicts of interest of directors participating in the meeting.

Learning outcomes

At the end of this part you will be able to:

◆ exercise appropriate judgement to advise the board on the expectations of and compliance with regulatory requirements;

◆ understand that knowing the Articles provisions is key to good meeting management;

◆ discuss the purpose of the different types of general meeting;

◆ explain the role the company secretary has in the organisation, convening, holding and follow-up actions in relation to general meetings;

◆ be able to advise the chair on their responsibility for ensuring the smooth running of the meeting, that all opinions are heard and the use of procedural motions;

◆ explain the process to undertake voting on a show of hands or on a poll and the role of share registrars and scrutineers;

◆ discuss the increase in use of technology in meeting management and holding of virtual/hybrid meetings;

◆ compare and contrast the key differences between general meetings and directors' meetings;

◆ advise the board on the procedures for convening and holding board meetings; and

◆ explain the reasons for having written board policies such as signing authorities, matters reserved to the board and terms of reference for any board committees.

Chapter fourteen
Meetings of shareholders and members

CONTENTS

1. Introduction
2. Member meeting or written resolution
3. General meetings
4. Regulations governing general meetings
5. Role of the company secretary before, during and after the annual general meeting
6. Notice of meetings
7. Quorum, agenda, meeting materials
8. Resolutions
9. Role of the chair
10. Rules of order, standing orders
11. Proxies
12. Polls
13. Attendance
14. Voting
15. Meeting technology
16. Share registrar and role of scrutineer
17. Communication with members and other stakeholders

1. Introduction

As discussed in chapter 1, a company is owned by its members who delegate management to the directors. While day-to-day management decisions are delegated members retain powers to alter the company's constitution or to appoint and remove directors and the auditors. Although most resolutions put before members are recommended and indeed proposed by the directors, members themselves can propose resolutions and pass resolutions without requiring the consent of the directors. This provides members with the necessary tools to remove directors running a company in a way of which they disapprove.

2. Member meeting or written resolution

Although the process to approve resolutions in writing was often contained in a company's Articles the only mechanism in the CA1985 was for members' resolutions to be put before meetings of the members. The CA2006 reversed this position and the presumption is that for private companies written resolutions will be the preferred option, under the detailed provisions in CA2006, with the need to convene physical meetings reserved for the few resolutions that are not permitted to be approved by written resolution or where the number or make-up of members makes obtaining their approval too difficult.

There are no corresponding written resolution powers for members of public companies within the Act. However, under the **duomatic principle** where it can be shown that all members having the right to attend and vote at a general meeting of the company assent to some matter which a resolution approved at a general meeting of the company could carry into effect, that assent is as binding as the resolution in general meeting would be.

2.1   Resolutions in writing

The members of a private company may pass any resolution that could be put to a general meeting by written resolution (CA2006 ss. 282, 283, 288) except for resolutions to:

◆   remove a director under CA2006 s. 168; and

◆   remove an auditor under CA2006 s. 510.

Written resolutions may be proposed by the directors using the procedure set out in CA2006 s. 291 or by the members using the procedure set out in CA2006 ss. 292 to 295 (CA2006 s. 288).

The company must send copies of the proposed resolution to all eligible members at the same time either in hard copy, by electronic means or by using a website (CA2006 ss. 291(2) and (3)). An eligible member is a member entitled to attend and vote at a general meeting (CA2006 s. 289). Alternatively, if it can be accomplished quickly, the same copy can be circulated for signature, but to be valid, all sufficient signatures must be obtained within the 28-day window imposed by CA2006 s. 297. The resolution must be accompanied by a statement informing the members of how to signify consent and the deadline for receipt of consent.

A member signifies their agreement to a written resolution by returning to the company a document in hard copy or electronically, identifying the resolution and signifying their consent (CA2006 s. 296). Once agreement has been conveyed to the company it cannot be revoked (CA2006 s. 296(3)).

A written resolution is approved when the requisite majority of members have signified their agreement, votes being calculated according to the number of shares held by each member (CA2006 ss. 284 and 296).

duomatic principle
The 'Duomatic principle' (called after the case of the same name, *Re Duomatic Ltd [1969]*) provides that where it can be shown that all shareholders having the right to attend and vote at a general meeting of the company assent to some matter which a general meeting of the company could carry into effect, that assent is as binding as a resolution in general meeting would be. This can in some cases obviate the requirement to hold a general meeting to pass a resolution – so long as all the shareholders agree to that resolution.

If agreement has not been given within 28 days from the date the resolution was circulated, it is deemed to have lapsed and any consent given after that date has no effect (CA2006 s. 297).

Copies of written resolutions circulated to members must also be sent to the company's auditor, if it has one (CA2006 s. 502(1)).

Any member or members of a private company together holding not less than 5% of the total voting rights of the company may require the company to circulate a proposed resolution, provided it is a valid resolution, and may also request that a statement of not more than 1,000 words be circulated with the proposed resolution (CA2006 s. 292). The company's Articles may provide for a share ownership threshold of less than 5%.

A company need not comply with such a request if the proposed resolution, on being passed, would be ineffective by reason of inconsistency with legislation or the company's constitution or if it is frivolous, vexatious or defamatory (CA2006 s. 292(2)).

Where a valid request is received, copies of the proposed resolution and any accompanying statement must be circulated to all eligible members at the same time in hard copy, in electronic form or by means of a website within 21 days of receiving the request (CA2006 s. 293).

The persons requesting the circulation of the proposed resolution must meet the cost of circulation, unless the company has previously agreed to do so. The company need not comply with the requisition unless sufficient funds are deposited to meet the expenses in advance of the circulation (CA2006 s. 294).

The company or other aggrieved person may apply to the court for an order not to comply with a request to circulate a proposed resolution and any accompanying statement on the grounds that the rights conferred by CA2006 s. 292 are being abused (CA2006 s. 295).

Stop and think 14.1

Written resolutions work well where a company has only a few, responsive, members. With a large number of members, including some the company may no longer have current address information for, obtaining the requisite majority may be difficult or impossible. A general meeting does not have the same issue as the majority required at a general meeting is of those members actually voting rather than the total membership.

Test yourself 14.1

1. **Can any member request that a resolution be circulated?**

2. **Who has the right to exercise the voting rights on that written resolution?**

3. **On what basis can members of a public company approve a resolution other than at a general meeting?**

3. General meetings

Unlike directors' meetings which are largely left for the directors to determine their own procedures, the Act's requirements for general meetings of members have detailed provisions covering the convening of general meetings, notice of general meetings, proceedings to be followed at general meetings and the voting at general meetings, including provisions for proxies for members unable or unwilling to attend in person.

There are three main types of members' meetings:

- annual general meetings (AGMs);
- general meetings (GMs); and
- class meetings of the holders of a particular class of the company's capital.

3.1 Annual general meetings

Except for a traded company that is a private company, private companies are no longer required to hold an annual general meeting (CA2006 s. 336(1A)).

Any private company required by its Articles to hold an AGM will need to comply with the general provisions on meetings in Part 13 of the Act, together with any more onerous requirements in its Articles.

Members of private companies no longer have the statutory right to demand that the company holds an AGM, except by amending the Articles to require this.

Although not able to demand an AGM be held, members of private companies holding 5% of the voting rights can requisition a general meeting (CA2006 ss. 303–305) and also have the right to requisition a written resolution (CA2006 ss. 292–295).

Every public company and every private company that is a traded company must hold an annual general meeting within the period of six months (nine months for a private traded company) commencing on its accounting reference date (CA2006 s. 336).

The directors have general authority to convene general meetings, including AGMs (CA2006 s. 302). Members may requisition a general meeting but not an AGM (CA2006 s. 303) and the court has power to order a general meeting to be held, including as an AGM.

3.2 Business at annual general meetings

The following is the routine business of an annual general meeting:

- Receiving the report and accounts laid before the meeting, as required by CA2006 ss. 437–8.

◆ The declaration of a final dividend, if any.

◆ The election or re-election of directors. (This will include both the election of directors who have been appointed since the last AGM and the re-election of directors who have retired by rotation, as required by the company's Articles, the Act or the Governance Code.)

◆ The reappointment and remuneration of the auditors.

◆ Quoted companies must put a, non-binding, resolution at the meeting that receives the audited accounts for the approval of the directors' remuneration report (CA2006 s. 439).

◆ Quoted companies must put a resolution at the meeting that receives the audited accounts for the approval of the directors' remuneration policy at intervals of not more than three years or to approve the adoption of a new remuneration policy (CA2006 s. 439A).

Apart from the routine business as noted above other resolutions may be put to the members on any topic but most often these will include:

◆ special resolutions for any proposed alterations to the company's Articles (CA2006 s. 21);

◆ ordinary resolution granting authority to the directors to issue additional shares (CA2006 s. 551);

◆ special resolution to disapply pre-emption rights on the issue of new shares (CA2006 s. 571);

◆ ordinary resolution to authorise the directors to offer shareholders the right to receive new ordinary shares instead of cash for all or part of any dividend; and

◆ ordinary resolution to give general authority to make political donations (CA2006 s. 366).

3.3 Members' right to propose directors at an AGM

Members only have the right to propose a resolution to be put at an AGM to appoint a person as a director if that right is contained in their Articles. There is no such provision in the Act or the Model Articles.

3.4 Class meetings

As the name implies, class meetings are meetings of holders of a certain class of the company's capital and are held in accordance with the Articles of the company or conditions that attach to the shares concerned. Class meetings are required whenever the rights of the holders of the class are to be varied because of some action proposed by the company. Such variations may relate to a change in the voting, dividend or other rights attaching to the class or to changes proposed in a reorganisation of the company's share structure.

Where a class has no rights to vote that refers to the right to vote at a general meeting not to a class meeting.

Subject to any provisions in the company's Articles and the exceptions set out in CA2006 s. 334, the same rules for the holding of general meetings apply to class meetings, with the exception that there is no general power for members of a class to requisition a class meeting (CA2006 ss. 334 and 335).

Test yourself 14.2

1. **Under what circumstances must a private company hold an AGM?**

2. **What additional resolutions would a quoted company routinely add to its AGM notice?**

4. Regulations governing general meetings

The requirement for companies to hold general meetings of members is laid down in the Act and reinforced by the company's Articles. The provisions of the Act cannot be overruled by a company's Articles where the effect would be to deprive the members of any rights provided by statute. However, in instances where the procedure stipulated by the Articles is merely different from the statutory position, the Articles may still prevail.

Table 14.1 sets out the various provisions in the Act and Model Articles relating to the holding of general meetings.

Provision	CA2006 reference	Ltd Model Articles	Plc Model Articles
Convening general meetings	ss.302 - 306		28
Notice of general meetings	ss. 160, 283, 307–313, 325, 337, 360, USR1985 s. 41		
Quorum at general meetings	s. 318	38, 41	30, 33
Proceedings at a general meeting	ss. 319–323, 341–351	37, 39–41, 44, 47	29–33, 36–39
Right to appoint a proxy	ss. 282–284, 324, 331	45, 46	
Use of electronic communications for general meetings	ss. 293, 299 , 308, 309, 333–333A, 430, 1145, sch 5 paras 4 & 9	48	
Voting at general meetings	ss. 282–287, 360A–360B	42, 43, 44	34, 35, 41

Table 14.1 Companies Act provisions relating to general meetings

Stop and think 14.2

The ability to vary the statutory provisions contained in the Act with provisions in the Articles makes it extremely important that the company secretary is aware of the provisions in the company's Articles as otherwise the validity of resolutions can be called into question.

This is particularly true in the case of groups of companies where subsidiaries will often have very different provisions in their Articles resulting in different notice periods and quorums.

5. Role of the company secretary before, during and after the annual general meeting

Although it is the directors that have authority to convene general meetings the actual process of drafting and issuing notices convening the general meeting, ensuring the pre-meeting preparations are carried out, collating proxy forms, drafting a script for use by the chair, ensuring the smooth running on the day of the general meeting and any post-meeting follow-up is usually delegated to the company secretary.

For companies with a large number of members, the venue for their annual general meeting will probably have been fixed several months in advance not only to ensure availability of the venue but also so that the date and place of the meeting can be included in the corporate diary and made available to investors sometimes more than a year in advance.

The following is a checklist of matters to be undertaken by the company secretary convening an AGM of a listed company although the same process, although not every step, would apply for every general meeting.

Company secretary's checklist for listed company AGM

Before the meeting

1. **The AGM must be held no later than six months after the financial year-end (nine months for a private company).**

2. **The resolutions will usually include some or all of to:**

    ◆   **receive and consider the audited final report and accounts;**

    ◆   **approve the remuneration report of the directors;**

    ◆   **approve/amend the remuneration policy;**

- declare a final dividend;
- elect or re-elect directors;
- authorise the directors to fix the remuneration of the auditors;
- authorise the directors to issue additional shares;
- waive pre-emption rights; and
- authorise the payment of political donations.

3. The notice must:
    - state that the meeting is an annual general meeting;
    - specify the date, time and location for the meeting;
    - contain a statement that members are entitled to appoint one or more proxies to attend and vote on their behalf;
    - distinguish between ordinary resolutions and special resolutions;
    - comply with the content requirements of circulars under LR 13; and
    - be dated and signed.

4. The notice and accompanying documents should then be sent 21 days (clear notice – not including the day of posting and day of the meeting) in advance of the meeting, 20 business days for a listed company.

5. The notice should be sent to all eligible members, the auditors and personal representatives of deceased shareholders.

6. If there is any unusual business to be dealt with at the AGM, an explanatory circular should be sent to members.

7. Forms of proxy should be sent with the notice and accompanying documents.

8. Forms of proxy should normally be returned 48 hours before the meeting commences (this period cannot be extended).

9. Notice of a resolution proposing to remove a serving director or auditor or appoint a new auditor must be given 28 days in advance of the meeting.

10. The company secretary will normally prepare a script to cover the running order of events for the chair at the meeting.

11. The company secretary should prepare appropriate wording for procedural resolutions for use by the chair in the event of disruption, too many attendees, adjournment, etc.

Meeting venue

Matters to consider or attend to in connection with the meeting venue:

◆ Make sure venue is booked in plenty of time and visit the venue beforehand.

◆ Estimate how many will attend the meeting.

◆ Ensure that the venue complies with health and safety regulations.

◆ Ensure that you will have access to the room in plenty of time in advance of the meeting to arrange for logistics and setting up of equipment.

◆ How will the room be laid out?

◆ Who will sit at the top table?

◆ Is a stage required for the platform party?

◆ Liaise with share registrar regarding the room layout and in particular member verification area and any audio-visual requirements especially if electronic voting to be used.

◆ Will sound and vision equipment be required?

◆ Is security for the board required?

On the day

1. Ensure copies of all documents, including the agenda, are available.

2. The company secretary, or another appropriate person tasked to do so, will take the minutes of the meeting.

3. The company secretary should bring a copy of the articles of association to the meeting.

4. The company secretary should ensure that the display documents are available at the meeting:

    ◆ financial reports and accounts;

    ◆ register of members; and

    ◆ directors' service contracts or terms of appointment of non-executive directors.

    The directors' service contracts/terms of appointment must be available for inspection by members from 15 minutes before the meeting commences until 15 minutes after the meeting finishes.

5. Unless attendance is being recorded by the share registrars all members should be asked to sign the attendance sheet on their way into the meeting.

During the meeting

1. Ensure a quorum is present and confirm this to the chair to open the meeting.

2. The company secretary should be prepared to read the notice if this is not taken as read.

3. All directors should attend and they should sit on the platform or in the front rows – they should wear name badges.

4. Attendance by other professionals – auditors, scrutineers, registrar, press (if allowed), external auditors, company lawyers etc. is at the discretion of the meeting and they should not be permitted to vote, unless they are also a member.

5. There is no requirement to read the auditor's report but if this is company practice it is usual to restrict this just to the audit opinion paragraphs.

6. For quoted companies, the chair will normally read a statement reviewing the year's affairs as well as a trading update. The text of this update must be released to the Stock Exchange in advance of the statement being read to comply with disclosure requirements.

7. The chair should allow time for members to ask questions during the meeting even where there is a specific Q&A session prior to the formal resolutions being put to the meeting. Members, as a courtesy to others, should state their name before asking their question.

8. The chair should explain the method of voting for resolutions. For larger companies the resolutions are often taken on a poll as a matter of course in which case there is no need for a show of hands. For smaller companies and especially private companies voting on a show of hands is the norm with poll votes being the exception.

9. Ensure that sufficient supplies of ballot papers are available if required.

10. Amending a resolution:

    ◆ An ordinary resolution can only be amended if the amendment is reasonably within the scope of the original. The revised amendment wording must be approved by the meeting before it is then voted on.

    ◆ An amendment cannot be allowed if it is a direct contradiction of the original resolution.

    ◆ A special resolution cannot be amended at the meeting.

11. Polls can be demanded at the meeting in accordance with the Articles. These typically provide for the demand to be made by at least three members present and entitled to vote, members representing at least 10% of the voting rights or members having at

least 10% of the shares with voting rights. The company secretary will often oversee the process, in conjunction with the share registrars, if any.

After the meeting

1.   The company secretary should collect all books and papers left by directors.

2.   Arrange for copies of approved resolutions, that require registration, to be filed on time with the Registrar.

3.   Listed companies must make a market announcement via an RIS of all resolutions, other than ordinary resolutions at an AGM, approved by the shareholders at a general meeting (LR 9.6.18).

4.   Organise the payment of the dividend, if approved, at the meeting.

All proxies are entitled to speak at the meeting including demanding or joining in the demand for a poll vote on any resolution (CA2006 ss. 324 and 329).

Following the meeting the minutes of the meeting should be prepared. It is not usually necessary for these to be sent out in draft to all the directors for comments, since the minutes will usually cover only routine business or such other business as may have been specified in the notice convening the meeting.

Test yourself 14.3

1.   Which documents should be available for inspection by members at an AGM?

2.   Are amendments to resolutions allowed?

3.   Can members ask questions about anything?

6. Notice of meetings

The minimum periods of notice required for general meetings are specified in CA2006 s. 307. These periods cannot be reduced by the company's Articles, although the minimum periods can be extended.

Listed companies are required, where possible, to comply with the Governance Code, which contains a best practice requirement for notice of AGMs to be convened on 20 working days' notice in all cases (Governance Code Guidance para. 36).

Type of meeting	CA2006 notice period	Table A notice period
a. General meeting of a private company – ordinary resolutions	14 days	14 days
b. General meeting of a private company – special resolutions	14 days	21 days
c. Annual general meeting of a public company	21 days	21 days
d. General meeting of a public company (not traded) – ordinary resolution	14 days	14 days
e. General meeting of a public company (not traded) – special resolution	14 days	21 days
f. General meeting of traded public company where consent given	14 days	Refer to (d) and (e) above
g. General meeting of traded public company where consent not given	21 days	Refer to (d) and (e) above
For traded companies the notice periods are set out in CA2006 s. 307A, as follows:		
General meetings where specified conditions met (see below)	14 days	Refer to (d) and (e) above
All other general meetings	21 days	Refer to (d) and (e) above

Table 14.2 Notice periods

In order for a general meeting of a traded company to be held on 14 days' notice, the conditions specified in CA2006 s. 307A must be met. This section was inserted into the Act by the Companies (Shareholders' Rights) Regulations 2009 (SI 2009/1632). These conditions are:

◆ the meeting is not an AGM;

◆ members are offered an electronic voting facility; and

◆ a special resolution has been passed to reduce the notice period to 14 days. This must have happened at either the immediately preceding AGM or at a general meeting held since the last AGM.

If all three conditions are met, the notice period will be 14 days. In all other cases, 21 days' notice will be required.

6.1 Clear days

In all cases, the period of notice is expressed as clear days' notice. This means that the day on which the notice is served and the day on which the meeting is to be held are excluded (CA2006 s. 360). CA2006 s. 1147 also provides that communications sent by a company are deemed to have been received 48 hours after posting or sending by electronic means, excluding any non-working days.

For example, if a private company wishes to hold a general meeting on 17 May, the latest date for posting the notice of meeting would be 1 May. The notice would be deemed to be served on 3 May, and the 14 days counted from 4 May would expire on 17 May.

However, a company's Articles may have a very different definition of clear days and in particular when notice is deemed given.

6.2 Agreement to short notice of meeting

There is a useful concession under CA2006 s. 307(5) in circumstances where it is not possible (or desirable) to give the minimum period of notice required by subsections (1) and (2) of that section or by the Articles under which a general meeting may be held on short notice.

It should be noted that the provision does not allow the complete dispensation of giving notice and notice must still be given to all members, even if it is known that they cannot attend.

The number of members required to give valid consent to short notice is defined in CA2006 ss. 307(5) and (6), which provides that for a private company, the requisite majority to agree to short notice is a majority in number of the members having a right to attend and vote at the meeting, and together holding not less than 90% of the share capital of the company. This 90% limit may be increased by the company's Articles to not more than 95%. This provision protects minority members holding less than 10% of the shares.

For a public company, the percentage required to hold a general meeting on short notice is 95%.

In the case of an AGM, consent must be given by all the members entitled to attend and vote at the AGM (CA2006 s. 337(2)). The form of consent to short notice for an AGM should include, if appropriate, agreement to accept the company's report and accounts (if necessary), even though they were sent to members less than 21 days before the date of the meeting, as required by CA2006 s. 424.

6.3 Entitlement to notice of general meetings

Subject to any provisions in the company's Articles, notice must be given to every member and director (CA2006 s. 310).

Surprisingly, the company secretary has no formal right to receive a copy of the notice or to attend general meetings. Holders of preference shares or non-voting shares will often not be entitled to receive notice of general meetings. In practice, however, and especially in the case of listed companies, notices will usually be sent to every holder of shares or debentures, whether or not the registered address of the holder is in the UK and irrespective of whether the securities held entitle that member to vote at the meeting. This is because, under CA2006 ss. 431 and 432, every member and holder of debentures must be sent a copy of the report and accounts, and the notice of meeting is usually incorporated in this document. It is, however, usual practice to include an explanatory note stating that the notice is sent for information only to debenture holders, who are not entitled to attend and vote at the meeting.

For a class meeting, only the holders of the shares of that class are entitled to notice.

CA2006 s. 313 affords protection to the company in the case of accidental omission to give notice to any person entitled to receive it. Without this if even one member were accidently not sent the notice this would invalidate the proceedings of the meeting and no resolutions 'passed' would be valid.

6.4 Content of notices

The notice must state the time, place and date of the meeting, and the general nature of the business to be transacted (CA2006 s. 311). Where a special resolution is to be proposed, the notice must contain the text of the resolution and must state that the resolution is to be proposed as a special resolution (CA2006 s. 283(6)). Since the directors normally instruct the company secretary to convene the general meeting, the notice is usually signed by the company secretary on behalf of the board.

Listed companies must follow the provisions of the Listing Rules (LR 9.3.6, 7) in regard to proxies, i.e. every member must be given the opportunity to vote for, against or abstain on every resolution included in the notice (the so-called **three-way proxy**).

Every notice must include a prominent statement that makes clear that the member entitled to attend and vote may appoint one or more proxies to attend, speak and vote on their behalf (CA2006 s. 325). A proxy need not be a member of the company. Any provision in the company's Articles requiring proxies to be lodged more than 48 hours (excluding any day that is not a working day) before the meeting is invalid (CA2006 s. 327).

The notice of an AGM of a public company must state that the meeting is to be the AGM (CA2006 s. 337).

three-way proxy
A proxy form, which must be used by a listed company, which allows a member to instruct his proxy to vote for, against or abstain on each resolution.

6.5 Special notice

This must not be confused with notice required of a special resolution. Special notice of certain ordinary resolutions must be given to the company (CA2006 s. 312), as follows:

◆ a resolution to remove an auditor before the expiration of their term of office (CA2006 s. 510); and

◆ under CA2006 s. 168, resolutions:

 – to remove a director before the expiration of their period of office; and

 – to appoint somebody in place of the director removed at the meeting at which they are removed.

Where special notice is required, this must be given to the company at least 28 days prior to the meeting.

The company is required to give notice of the resolutions of which special notice has been given to all members in the notice of meeting or, if not practicable, by advertisement in a newspaper or such other manner allowed by the Articles, not less than 14 days before the meeting (CA2006 s. 312(3)).

Test yourself 14.4

1.   **What does clear days mean?**

2.   **What must a traded company have done to allow members' meetings to be held on 14 days' notice?**

3.   **Do notices of general meetings need to distinguish between ordinary and special resolutions?**

7. Quorum, agenda, meeting materials

The quorum for members' meetings is set out in CA2006 s. 318 and provides that for a company with a sole member, the quorum is one and that in all other cases, subject to any provisions in the company's Articles, two members present in person or by proxy may constitute a quorum.

A company's Articles usually make provision for a procedure to be adopted in the event of a quorum not being present. Where one member appoints two proxies as their representative and they are the only attendees a quorum will not be present as only one member is represented. Additionally where two members appoint the same person as their proxy that one person cannot form a valid quorum as two persons are required (CA2006 s. 318(2)).

Model Articles Plc reg. 33, Ltd reg. 41, require that, if a quorum is not present within half an hour, the chair must adjourn the meeting and must either specify the time and place for the adjourned meeting, or state that the meeting will continue at such time and place as the directors may decide.

If a quorum was present at the start of the meeting, this must be maintained for the meeting to continue. The Model Articles provide that if a quorum ceases to exist after the meeting has commenced then the meeting is automatically adjourned (Model Articles Plc reg. 39, Ltd reg. 39).

Stop and think 14.3

Companies with a small number of members and only regular business to be considered at an AGM can find themselves unable to raise a quorum if no shareholders attend the meeting even if many members have appointed the chair as their proxy.

At a recent meeting, the chair of the meeting was the only member present but also held all the proxy nominations. Fortunately, the Articles allowed proxies to be appointed up to the start of the meeting and so the chair was able to appoint one of the other directors as his proxy in order to satisfy the quorum criteria.

Test yourself 14.5

If one of two members refuses to attend general meetings, can a meeting be held?

8. Resolutions

Members' resolutions are either approved as ordinary resolutions or special resolutions with a different majority required for each.

Unlike written resolutions where the majority required to approve any particular resolution is determined by reference to the total number of shares issued, for a members' meeting the majorities are determined by reference to the total votes held by those attending, either in person or by proxy, and voting on each resolution. As a result, if members present at a meeting do not vote on every resolution those resolutions will have a different majority requirement.

8.1 Ordinary resolutions

A simple majority of those present and voting is all that is required to pass an ordinary resolution at a members' meeting where the vote is undertaken on a show of hands where each member present has one vote.

Examples of this type of resolution include:

- appointment or re-appointment of directors;
- re-appointment of auditors;
- alterations to the share capital under CA2006 ss. 617 and 618;
- a capitalisation of profits;
- the grant of authority for the allotment of securities (CA2006 ss. 550 and 551); and
- subject to provision in the Articles, a resolution authorising the directors to offer shareholders the right to elect to receive new ordinary shares for the whole or part of a cash dividend.

8.2 Special resolutions

The majority required to pass a special resolution is one of not less than 75% of those voting. It is essential that the notice of the meeting states that it is intended to propose a resolution as a special resolution. CA2006 s. 307 provides that 14 days' notice needs to be given of a general meeting at which a special resolution is to be passed. This does not apply to general meetings of traded companies, where 21 days' notice will still be required, unless a resolution reducing the notice period to 14 days has been passed.

The type of business that must be dealt with by a special resolution is specified in the Act and/or the company's Articles. It includes:

- alteration of the Articles (CA2006 s. 21);
- change of name (CA2006 s. 77);
- disapplication of pre-emption rights (CA2006 s. 571); and
- reduction of capital (CA2006 s. 641).

The notice convening the meeting at which a special resolution is to be considered must include the full text of the resolution.

Test yourself 14.6

1. **What is the key difference between an ordinary and a special resolution of the members?**

2. **What advantage does passing a resolution at a meeting have compared to the same resolution circulated as a written resolution?**

9. Role of the chair

The role of the chair at a members' meeting is to ensure that the meeting is properly and fairly conducted, allowing all opinions to be expressed and that the sense of the meeting is properly ascertained and reflected in the minutes.

The company's Articles will usually give the chair specific powers relating to the conduct of meetings including:

- authority to adjourn the meeting;
- rule on points of order;
- decide upon the validity of votes;
- declare the results of resolutions on a show of hands;
- eject members from the meeting for unruly behaviour;
- decide upon the validity of amendments proposed for resolutions; and
- demand a poll.

Model Articles Plc reg. 39, Ltd reg. 31 state that the chair of the board will also be chair for general meetings. If the chair is not present, then another director (e.g. a deputy chair or vice-chair) takes the chair. In the absence of any director, the members present may elect one of their number to take the chair.

Although the chair has authority to adjourn a meeting they would normally do so only with the consent of the meeting. The chair also has no authority to close a meeting before it has concluded all matters on the notice, only the members can do this.

An important role for the chair is to ensure that all points of view are expressed. This after all is one of the objects of holding the meeting.

10. Rules of order, standing orders

As noted above, the chair is tasked with ensuring the sense of the meeting is obtained and that all points of view are expressed. Sometimes certain sections of the members present will try to stop full discussion by making lengthy speeches to try and cause the meeting to run out of time or to stop an alternative point of view being expressed. To counter this the chair may use a particular type of resolution called a procedural motion.

10.1 Procedural motions

Procedural motions are motions that are used to regulate the conduct of the business of the meeting. For the vast majority of routine meetings, they are never used. However, where contentious resolutions are proposed or where there is a vociferous element present, the use of procedural motions can be used to curtail discussion of a particular resolution.

As with many aspects of the legal system, the terminology of procedural motions has not changed over the years, and now sounds arcane and intimidating to those not used to it. There are six common procedural motions:

1. the closure (that the questions be now put);
2. next business (that the meeting proceeds to the next business);
3. previous question (that the question be not now put);
4. postponement (version 1) (that the question lie on the table);
5. postponement (version 2) (that the matter be referred back to…); and
6. adjournment.

10.2 Speaking

All members, proxies and corporate representatives entitled to attend and vote at a members' meeting are entitled to speak at the meeting.

Although those attending have the right to speak, they may be prevented from doing so in order to keep the meeting to a reasonable length or to maintain order. The chair should ensure that all differing opinions on the matter under consideration are expressed and, in doing so, it should not be necessary for every person who wishes to speak to do so if they are simply repeating points made by previous speaker(s).

Traded companies must ensure that all questions put by members attending the meeting and relating to the business of the meeting, are answered. The exceptions to this are in circumstances where to do so would interfere with preparations for the meeting, require the disclosure of confidential information, if the answer has already been provided on a website in the form of an answer to a question or if it is undesirable in the interests of the company or the good order of the meeting for the question to be answered (CA2006 s. 319A).

10.3 Adjournment of general meetings

Although the chair may adjourn the members' meeting without the consent of the members if there is disorder, the power to adjourn a members' meeting usually rests with the members attending, who must give their consent. The Model Articles Plc reg. 33(6) provide that no business at an adjourned meeting shall be transacted other than that which could have been transacted at the original meeting.

If the meeting is adjourned for more than 14 days, fresh notice of at least seven days, specifying the business to be transacted, must be given.

Test yourself 14.7

1. **Can proxies speak at meetings?**

2. **Who has authority to adjourn a general meeting?**

11. Proxies

CA2006 s. 324 gives all members the right to appoint one or more proxies to attend, speak and vote on either a show of hands or a poll. Where a member appoints more than one proxy each proxy must be appointed to exercise the rights attaching to different shares.

A proxy need not be a member of the company. Proxies are appointed for individual meetings or adjournments of it and have no other rights. The notice of a general meeting must state clearly the right of the members to appoint one or more proxies (CA2006 s. 325).

For unlisted public companies and private companies, it is not obligatory to send proxy forms with notices of meetings.

Where proxy forms are issued by the company, they must be issued to all members of the company and not just to those who favour the board (CA2006 s. 326). The company may accept proxy forms lodged at the last minute, provided they are in an appropriate form. It is unlawful for a company to require proxies to be lodged with the company more than 48 hours prior to the time of the meeting (CA2006 s. 327), excluding any days that are not working days. Proxies may be submitted in electronic form, but only to an address supplied by the company for that purpose (CA2006 s. 333). Accordingly, sending a form of proxy by email to the company secretary's normal email address would not constitute a valid proxy.

A traded company must provide an electronic address for the receipt of proxies (CA2006 s. 333A(1)).

11.1 At the meeting

Members who appoint a proxy may still attend the meeting and vote in person; attendance and voting at the meeting effectively revokes the proxy appointment. The right of a person appointing a proxy to attend and vote at a meeting is conditional upon this not being prohibited by the Articles.

Proxies have a statutory right to attend, speak and vote at the general meetings on behalf of the member(s) that has appointed them (CA2006 s. 324) and at any adjournment of that general meeting. Proxies are entitled to demand or join in the demand for a poll on any resolution (CA2006 s. 329). Unless the company has taken advantage of CA2006 s. 322A permitting the lodgement of poll votes in advance, the proxy must attend the general meeting in person in order to vote. The proxy's right to vote upon a show of hands contained in CA2006 s. 285 is subject to any provision in the company's Articles.

11.2 Three-way proxies

Listed companies must issue three-way proxy forms (LR 9.3.6). A three-way proxy includes provision for members to indicate which way they wish the proxy to cast their votes or to abstain from voting in the event of a poll being demanded. It must cover all the resolutions on the notice of meeting. The form must also state that, if it is returned without any indication as to how the proxy shall vote on any resolution, the proxy may exercise their discretion.

The proxy form cannot restrict the member to appointing the chair or another director as their proxy; it must include provision for the member to appoint a proxy of their own choice.

11.3 Form and dispatch of proxy forms

The pattern of voting indicated on returned forms of proxy will show whether or not there is likely to be any contentious business at the meeting.

If there are to be a number of meetings being held on the same day, e.g. a general meeting or a meeting of any particular class of the members, the proxy cards for those meetings are usually different colours, to facilitate sorting.

The address to which proxies are to be returned may be the company's office, which in most companies' Articles is defined as the registered office of the company, or to some other place specified in the notice convening the meeting.

For example, if the share registration work of the company is carried out by a share registrar at a place other than the registered office, the proxies may be sent to the address of the registrar.

Notwithstanding anything contained in a company's Articles or the Model Articles as adopted by the company, proxies may be submitted by an electronic communication to an address notified by the company for that purpose (CA2006 ss. 333 and 333A).

In addition to providing numbered boxes for each resolution, so that the members can indicate with a tick whether they vote for or against a resolution, it is useful for the proxy form to include a phrase to the effect that, on any other business arising at the meeting (including any motion to amend a resolution or to adjourn the meeting), the proxy will act at their own discretion.

11.4 Appointment of a proxy

Except in the case of listed companies, the Act does not stipulate how a proxy is appointed. For listed companies CA2006 s. 327 requires that any proxy appointment is made in writing which for the purposes of the Act means in hard copy or in electronic form. Additionally traded companies must permit the appointment of proxies by electronic means.

Model Articles Plc regs. 38 and 39 require proxy appointments to be in writing and that the company must specify an address in the notice of the meeting for the receipt of proxy appointments delivered in hard copy or electronically. Model Articles Ltd reg. 45 provides for written notice of a proxy appointment but does not specify how the proxy form should be delivered to the company.

11.5 Evaluation of proxies

The proxy forms should be sorted and scrutinised as they are received by the company or its share registrar, to check that they have been properly completed. A running total should be kept of the votes for and against each resolution, as well as open votes, so as to try and identify any resolutions that may have a close vote or even be rejected. If this is the case the board might consider contacting larger shareholders to request that they vote and or ask why they have voted a particular way. If the chair of the company is appointed as the proxy, and there is no direction to vote for or against any or all resolutions, the chair will usually vote in favour of the resolutions. It should be noted that shareholders may limit their proxies to only part of their holdings, and that they can appoint more than one proxy, each proxy appointed covering separate parts of their shareholding.

The proxy form should be signed personally by individual members. Corporate members must complete the proxy card in accordance with their own Articles, and the authority under which it is signed should be lodged with the proxy card if not already registered with the company.

Incorrectly completed proxy forms must be rejected, but if there is time and if the shareholding is substantial, they should be returned for amendment. A proxy may be revoked by the lodgement of a subsequent appointment, provided that the appointment is received by the company in time prior to the meeting.

Pooled nominee accounts can pose particular problems when lodging proxy forms especially for an actively traded stock. Due to the forms of proxy requiring lodgement in advance of the record date and time for when voting entitlement is calculated it is possible that, as a consequence of trading between completion of the instruction and the cut-off, the total votes submitted on a pooled account are greater than the actual holding. This is called over voting. In such circumstances, the company or most likely the share registrar will attempt to contact the registered holder to resolve the issue.

Stop and think 14.4

Where a resolution is contentious, has been requisitioned or subject to pressure from a pressure group it is quite common for those wishing an outcome other than that recommended by the directors to collate completed forms of proxy and to lodge these at the last minute before the cut-off for receipt of proxies. This late delivery is in order to mitigate against those acting for the company from contacting the members to try and persuade them to change the way they have voted. There is also a danger where a pre-completed form is circulated to members for them to sign that the directors might argue that the members were not able to make their own mind up and/or that the forms were not in the form approved by the directors and reject the forms accordingly.

Test yourself 14.8

1. What options does a corporate member have in order to cast their vote at a general meeting?

2. What is the maximum period before a general meeting for the cut-off for the receipt of forms of proxy by the company?

3. How many proxies can an individual member appoint?

12. Polls

A poll is the process by which members vote at a general meeting and the number of votes each member or their proxy can cast is calculated by reference to the number of shares the member held on the record date.

12.1 Demand for a poll

The rules governing the demanding of a poll are laid down in the company's Articles. The provisions of CA2006 ss. 321 and 329 must also be taken into account. CA2006 s. 321 renders void any provision in the Articles excluding the right to call a poll except on the election of the chair or to adjourn the meeting. CA2006 s. 329 ensures that a demand for a poll by a proxy is deemed to be a demand by the member appointing them.

CA2006 s. 321 provides that any provision in a company's Articles is void if it were to exclude the right to demand a poll by:

- not fewer than five members;
- a member or members representing not less than one-tenth of the total voting rights of all the members with the right to vote at the meeting; or
- a member or members holding shares conferring a right to vote at the meeting, being shares on which an aggregate sum has been paid up

equal to not less than one-tenth of the total sum paid up on all the shares conferring that right.

For a demand for a poll to be valid, it must be called before or immediately on the declaration by the chair of the result of the vote on a show of hands.

12.2 When a poll is demanded

When a poll is demanded, the validity of the demand should be checked by confirming that those who have demanded it are, in fact, members and that they hold not less than one-tenth of the total voting rights.

If the company secretary or the share registrar advise that the poll has not been properly demanded, the chair makes a statement to this effect and the meeting carries on from where it left. If the demand for the poll is valid and is not withdrawn, the chair advises the meeting to this effect. If they have not already advised the meeting as to the proxy position when the poll was first demanded, they should now do so. Assuming the poll is not withdrawn, the chair announces the time for holding of the poll, e.g. either immediately, at the conclusion of the meeting or at a later date. It is usual practice for the poll to be held at the end of the meeting. The exception to this general rule is that a poll demanded on a procedural motion such as an adjournment must be taken immediately.

The meeting then proceeds to its next business until the conclusion of business. At the end of the meeting, the chair declares the meeting adjourned if the poll is to be taken immediately or closes the meeting if the poll is to be taken at a later date. Polls are usually only carried out at a later date if new information has come to light during the meeting which it is believed should be shared with the wider membership so that those members not present may vote having considered the new information.

Regardless of whether the poll takes place during the meeting or at its conclusion, the process is the same. The chair, the company secretary or the share registrar should inform the members of the procedure for the poll. It should be made clear that an abstention is not a vote and accordingly has no impact on the approval or disapproval of the resolution.

Ballot papers must be attributed to individual members present at the meeting and indicate how many, if not all of their votes they wish to cast. Completed papers are handed to the company secretary/share registrar/scrutineers. The scrutineers, especially if they are the company's auditors or share registrars, will no doubt have their own instructions for checking ballot papers, verifying holdings and preparing a report and final certificate of the result of the poll for the chair.

Many FTSE100 companies carry out poll votes as a matter of course on all resolutions and increasingly use electronic voting via hand held devices. The process of conducting the poll is exactly the same, except that members cast their votes against each resolution as requested by the chair. Although the vote capture phase might take a little longer than traditional ballot papers the results of the poll are almost instantaneous as the devices are each registered to individual members upon arrival at the meeting serving not only as an attendance record but also to verify entitlement to attend, votes held and negating any proxy appointments previously made. As the votes are captured for each resolution the system automatically includes the proxy votes given to the chair (provided they also vote).

12.3 Publication of results of a poll

Quoted companies that are not traded companies must ensure that when a poll vote is taken, the following information is made available on a website (CA2006 s. 341(1)):

◆ date of the meeting;

◆ text or description of the subject matter of the resolution; and

◆ number of votes cast in favour and against each resolution.

Traded companies must ensure that when a poll vote is taken, the following information is made available on a website (CA2006 s. 341(1A)):

◆ date of the meeting;

◆ text or description of the subject matter of the resolution;

◆ number of votes cast;

◆ proportion of the issued capital represented by those votes;

◆ number of votes cast in favour and against; and

◆ number of abstentions (if counted).

The information must be made available on the website in the case of a quoted company that is not a traded company as soon as reasonably practical and must be retained for a period of at least two years (CA2006 s. 353). A traded company must make the information available within 16 days of the meeting, or the day following the declaration of the result, if later (CA2006 s. 341(1B)).

During the 2018 AGM season for FTSE quoted companies poll votes have become the norm, at least within the larger companies, with 93% of FTSE100, 62% of FTSE250 and 22% of other companies voting by poll only rather than a show of hands.

13. Attendance

13.1 By a corporate member

A member that is a corporate body may be represented at a company meeting by a person appointed as its representative by a resolution of the corporate body's directors under CA2006 s. 323. Following the changes to proxy rights introduced by the Act, the only practical difference between a corporate representative and a proxy is that details of a proxy must be lodged in advance, whereas a corporate representative can bring their letter of appointment to the meeting.

Where shares are held by a nominee in one account for multiple beneficiaries, this can cause problems at a meeting if multiple corporate representatives are appointed without any clear instructions as to the number of votes that each represents.

13.2 By a member that is a natural person

A member that is a natural person simply needs to attend the meeting in person. There is no requirement to pre-register an intention to attend.

For high-profile meetings or where there has been previous attempts to disrupt the meeting proof of identity may be requested in order to gain access to the meeting.

As noted above a member may, if they are unable to attend in person, appoint a proxy to attend, speak and vote on their behalf. Appointment of a proxy does need to be notified to the company in advance of the meeting, and a person appointed as a proxy who simply turns up at the meeting will most likely be excluded, or perhaps allowed to attend but not to speak or vote.

13.3 Disruption

Although all members are invited to attend general meetings members have no automatic right of entry and entry can be refused but only in circumstances where this would be reasonable such as carrying a weapon or offensive placards etc. Members can be ejected from meetings if their behaviour is so disruptive as to make continuing the meeting impossible. Such events are extreme and very much a last resort. Every effort should be made to allow members to raise matters in an appropriate manner.

It is an important aspect of company meetings and indeed encouraged by the Governance Code that members are encouraged to participate in meetings and that the chair is under a duty to ensure that all points of view have the opportunity to be expressed. Accordingly, the chair needs to balance the sometimes competing objectives of maintaining order, discipline and keeping the meeting to the agenda and in a timely fashion, and the need to allow contrary arguments to be expressed and to anticipate, pre-empt and respond to legitimate tactics designed to frustrate the purpose of the meeting.

As with so many aspects of running general meetings, the authority and power of the chair to deal with disruption adequately lies in the Articles of the company.

Test yourself 14.9

1.   Can a member appoint more than one proxy?

2.   Can proxies vote both for and against the same resolution?

3.   If a member's proxy does not attend the meeting, are their votes still counted as recorded on the proxy appointment form?

14. Voting

For the majority of companies, resolutions are put to the meeting for members to vote on by a show of hands. If a resolution is defeated on a show of hands and the chair is aware that there are a substantial number of proxy votes in favour of the resolution, they should demand a poll. CA2006 s. 324A states that the proxy holder must vote as instructed by their appointor. Additionally, the chair of the meeting has a duty to ensure that the sense of the meeting is captured and recorded and a key aspect of this is to ensure that all available votes are cast and counted regardless of their own personal views on the matter.

On a show of hands, every member present in person or by proxy and entitled to vote has one vote only, irrespective of the number of shares held. On a poll, however, the number of shares held determines the number of votes the member may cast either in person or by proxy. In the event of an equality of votes, Articles of older companies often give the chair a casting vote.

The declaration by the chair of whether the resolution has been approved or not, passed with a particular majority (i.e. ordinary or special, 50% or 75%), is conclusive evidence of that fact and the validity of the resolution cannot be questioned later (CA2006 s. 320). An entry in the minutes reflecting that declaration is also conclusive evidence. Once the result is declared it cannot be challenged in the courts even if a mistake has been made with the exception that the court can overrule a vote in circumstances where fraud can be proved.

14.1 Abstaining

The increasing role of corporate governance and the need for members, particularly institutional shareholders, to express their opposition to various aspects of a company's corporate governance performance has seen an increasing use of abstentions on proxy forms. In law, an abstention is not a vote. CA2006 ss. 282(3), 282(4), 283(4) and 283(5), however, state that the majority on a show hands or on a poll is to be calculated by reference to the voting rights of the members who vote, whether in person or by proxy, accordingly abstentions have no effect.

Although acknowledged that an abstention is not a vote in support of a resolution it is equally true that an abstention is not a vote against the resolution either. While it may be true that some members lodge an abstention as some sort of protest others may do so simply to record that they are not persuaded by the arguments for or against a particular course of events.

Stop and think 14.5

In the case of *Second Consolidated Trust Ltd v Ceylon Amalga Tea & Rubber Estates Ltd [1943]*, the chair of a general meeting of the members was successfully prosecuted for failing to call a poll even though he had the power to do so as chair and held sufficient proxy votes to have reversed the result of the vote.

Test yourself 14.10

1. **What, if any, are the practical differences between voting on a show of hands and on a poll?**

2. **Must a chair always call for a poll?**

3. **If an abstention is not a vote, why do some members insist on ensuring their abstention is recorded?**

15. Meeting technology

Although many of the rules of procedures for running and managing general meetings have their roots very firmly in the past, technology has had a big impact on meetings especially with respect to the mechanics of voting, proxy appointment, management of meetings being held in multiple locations and most recently the use of the so-called virtual and hybrid general meetings.

15.1 Electronic voting

Popular among companies where attendance at general meetings is very high as the technology has simplified and become cheaper to employ it is increasingly being used for smaller meetings too. A key benefit to using electronic voting is the speed of being able to declare the results. This is especially relevant in the case of procedural resolutions as everyone present who wishes to vote will need to submit a vote and the process to verify and count paper-based votes of this nature can be very time consuming.

On arrival at the general meeting where electronic voting is to be used, each member will be provided with a voting handset which is registered to their shareholder account so that when they cast their vote the system instantly logs the number of votes for, against or as an abstention.

15.2 Online proxy submission

Like electronic voting, online proxy submission has been possible for a number of years via the CREST settlement system and increasingly directly via the company or its share registrar's website.

CA2006 s. 333A requires a traded company to provide an electronic address for the receipt of any documents or information relating to proxies for a general meeting.

15.3 Audio-visual conferencing

For any general meeting, a fundamental principle is that the members present should be able to see and hear both the chair of the meeting but also any other person speaking, which might include from the floor of the meeting hall. The use of audio-visual links was tested in the courts and its use approved (*Byng v London Life (1989)*). As a result it can be seen that provided members are in each other's presence, even if only electronically, not only need all members present not need to be in the same room but feasibly they can be in different cities or even countries. The biggest drawback to use of audio-visual links is that if they prove unreliable an adjournment or suspension of the meeting is likely to be required in the event of a system failure.

15.4 The electronic or hybrid meeting

A natural extension to the use of audio-visual systems is the use of webcasts broadcast via the internet, allowing members to participate from anywhere in the world.

Although the 2016 AGM of Jimmy Choo plc was held entirely electronically, a more popular choice is a combined physical and electronic meeting or hybrid meeting. In these meetings the board and those members that are able to, meet in one physical location with other members joining the meeting via an online portal which allows them to not only hear and see the meeting presentations but also to put questions to the meeting via their PC, tablet or even smart phone.

Stop and think 14.6

The first electronic annual general meeting was held by Jimmy Choo plc in 2016 by combining existing state-of-the-art meeting management and voting software with a bespoke online portal. The meeting met with the prime motivating factors of engaging with more investors than the company's first physical AGM the year before. A further benefit was a reduced carbon footprint as members and directors did not have to travel to a physical location, saving all parties travel costs and time.

Test yourself 14.11

1. **In order to constitute a valid meeting what must all attendees be able to do?**

2. **How has digital voting promoted the use of poll voting as a matter of course?**

16. Share registrar and role of scrutineer

Traded companies especially those with sizeable numbers on their register of members will often rely on their share registrars to undertake much of the mechanics of registering attendees and counting votes either on a show of hands or conducting poll votes on their behalf usually under the oversight of the company secretary.

Historically some companies used a firm of accountants or auditors to provide scrutiny for the proxy count, although this has largely fallen out of favour.

16.1 Independent proxy report

Members of a quoted company may require the directors to obtain an independent report on any poll taken or to be taken at a general meeting (CA2006 ss. 342–351). To be valid, the request for an independent report must be made by:

1. a member or members together holding not less than 5% of the total voting rights; or
2. not fewer than 100 members each holding shares on which, on average, there has been paid up the sum of at least £100.

The request may be in writing or electronic form, must identify the poll to which it relates, must be authenticated by those making the request and must be received no later than one week after the date on which the poll is taken (CA2006 s. 342).

If an independent report is requested, the directors must appoint an independent assessor. In order to be independent the assessor must not:

◆   be an officer or employee of the company;

◆   be a partner or employee of an officer of the company or an employee or partner of a firm in which that person is a partner; or

◆   have had any role in connection with carrying out the poll vote upon which the report has been demanded (CA2006 ss. 343, 344).

Where appointed in advance of the poll the assessor is entitled under CA2006 s. 348 to be present at the meeting and during the conduct of the poll. Whether the assessor attended the meeting and poll or not the assessor is entitled to have access to the records of the poll and the meeting to which the poll relates (CA2006 s. 349).

The assessor's report must state, in their opinion, whether:

◆   the procedures adopted in connection with the poll were adequate;

◆   the votes cast whether in person or by proxy were fairly and accurately recorded and counted;

◆   proxy appointments were appropriately assessed;

◆   the notice complied with CA2006 s. 325 (statement of right to appoint proxies); and

◆   any company sponsored forms of proxy complied with CA2006 s. 326.

17. Communication with members and other stakeholders

The requirement to communicate with members and other parties in connection with meetings is often limited to issuing the notice of the meeting and any accompanying circular or form of proxy.

The company's auditor is entitled to receive copies of notices of general meetings in order that they speak to the meeting about any proposed resolution that concerns them in their capacity as auditor (CA2006 s. 502(2)).

The company's share registrar will usually be in attendance, in order to provide support to the company secretary.

After the meeting, there is no requirement to provide members with details of the results of the votes on any resolution. Listed companies do however need to make a market announcement of the results of any general meetings.

Chapter summary

◆ Importance of knowing the Articles provisions is key to good meeting management

◆ Different types of general meeting

◆ Company secretaries have a considerable role in convening and running general meetings

◆ Resolutions typically proposed by the directors but members can also propose resolutions

◆ Chair responsible for ensuring the smooth running of the meeting and that all opinions are heard

◆ Procedural motions can be used to assist in regulating meetings

◆ For larger meetings poll voting is taking over from voting on a show of hands

◆ Rise in use of technology in meeting management and holding of virtual/ hybrid meetings

◆ Role of share registrars and scrutineers

Chapter fifteen
Meetings of the board and its committees

CONTENTS

1. Introduction
2. Board meetings
3. Role of the company secretary before, during and after board meetings
4. Delegation of authority and responsibility
5. Reliance on management and advisers
6. Committees – types, purpose and composition
7. Matters reserved for the board
8. Executive discretion
9. Motions and written/circular resolutions
10. Conflicts of interest

1. Introduction

Compared to the plethora of detailed regulations governing the convening, notice periods, proceedings and voting relating to members' meetings the Act and the Articles are very light on the equivalent details for directors' meetings. Instead, directors are very much left to decide for themselves, within broad parameters, the best way to regulate their own meetings.

2. Board meetings

The Act and the Articles are only concerned with formal meetings of the directors most commonly referred to as board meetings. Day-to-day management meetings are not covered by these provisions at all. Model Articles Plc reg. 19, Ltd reg. 16 authorise the directors to conduct their meetings as they see fit. Consequently, unlike general meetings of members there is no formal notice period or format and content requirements for notices convening meetings of the directors.

2.1   Types of meeting

In companies with a mix of executive and non-executive directors, the management of the company is often divided into two or more elements. Formal structured board meetings set corporate strategy and evaluate the performance of the company executives against that strategy and, usually more informal and flexible, executive management meetings where the day-to-day business decisions to implement and deliver the corporate strategy are made and performance measured against a whole array of key performance indicators.

In smaller businesses, and those without non-executive directors, formal board meetings are rarely held with most discussions and decisions being made informally or at management meetings held on an as required basis.

2.2   Management meetings

These will usually be held frequently, often at regular pre-determined intervals such as weekly, fortnightly or monthly. There will be a general agenda with the exact business determined by the actual performance of the various departments or divisions and as a result of usually free flowing discussions around particular issues of current concern.

Any minutes might be limited to action points with little, if any, record of the discussions leading to those decisions or actions.

2.3   Board meetings

These will usually be held at longer intervals than the management meetings. The frequency will depend entirely on the board or chair's preference and the stage of the company's evolution – an early stage company might have more frequent meetings, whereas a much more developed and stable business might only need a light touch approach from the board.

Formal board minutes will be kept, recording not only the decisions but the rationale for those decisions. Historically, board minutes were often written very much as an internal record of business decisions. However, particularly in industries with external regulators, minutes are a primary source of information on the performance of the board and management and minutes are increasingly written with this external audience in mind.

There is no minimum number of board meetings that must be held each year although in practice as a minimum a meeting should be held to approve the financial statements formally, even for dormant companies.

The role of the board of directors varies depending on the size and complexity of the company's business and whether it is a member of a group where subsidiary directors are not so involved in determining group strategy, if at all, or if it is a listed company bringing with it greater focus on corporate governance and investor oversight.

For the vast majority of private companies, formal board meetings are seldom held with any formal resolutions approved as written resolutions. In these circumstances, the management of the company is dealt with on a day-to-day basis by a series of informal discussions between the relevant directors with no formal written record.

Directors must ensure that they are fully aware of all decisions being reached in this informal manner, as they are collectively responsible for the company's activities. Ignorance is no excuse and, as seen earlier, in extreme circumstances can lead to disqualification and personal liability.

Although directors carry collective responsibility for their decisions, formal votes at directors' meetings are rare with most decisions being agreed following sufficient discussion to resolve any uncertainties or concerns. Where unanimity is not possible, the matter will usually be deferred to another meeting to allow the concerns to be addressed.

In the event of a director not agreeing with any decision this should be minuted.

Board meetings are general discussion meetings and, unlike the formal structured nature of members' meetings where formal resolutions are proposed, usually proceed on a less rigid way with projects and reports being brought to the meeting for review and discussion. The chair assesses whether the general view of the meeting should be incorporated into the minutes of the meeting as the decision of the board, either in narrative form or, where appropriate, as a formal resolution. If, however, the views of directors are fairly evenly balanced on the pros and cons of a particular course of action, it may not be appropriate to put the matter to a formal vote.

Although not on the formal agenda for the meeting or indeed any informal agenda, the chair should permit any director or the company secretary to raise at any board meeting any matter concerning the company's compliance with any legal or regulatory requirement.

2.4 Convening directors' meetings

If meetings are not held on fixed dates, the chair will usually instruct the company secretary to convene a meeting. However, any director or the company secretary, at the request of a director, may convene a meeting of the directors. There is no minimum notice period and any reasonable notice may be given. What constitutes reasonable will vary from company to company depending upon the location and availability of each director and the subject matter to be discussed.

For a small company with only two directors in the same office, 30 minutes notice might well be more than sufficient. By contrast, for a multi-national listed company with directors spread across many countries reasonable notice for an urgent meeting could easily be several days while routine meetings will have been agreed and diarised several years in advance.

It must also be remembered that meetings can take place using audio/audio-visual facilities to negate the requirement for all directors to be physically present at the meeting.

The notice of a directors' meeting will usually include the place, date and time for the meeting and an agenda of the general topics to be discussed. The notice can be circulated in any manner appropriate to the company, e.g. verbally, by letter, fax, email or by hand.

The matters to be discussed at a board meeting will naturally depend on the nature of the company's business and the number of directors. According to the size of the company, board papers and reports will either be circulated with the agenda or tabled at the meeting. Where any complex matters are to be considered, it is helpful to the directors, and in particular any non-executive directors, for board papers to be circulated in advance of the meeting.

2.5 Quorum

The quorum for board meetings is set out in the company's Articles and, if these follow the Model Articles, will be two directors (Model Articles Plc reg. 10, Ltd reg. 11) unless the directors decide otherwise. If the company had only two directors and one resigned or died, Model Articles Plc reg. 10, Ltd reg. 11 provide that the sole continuing director may appoint another director. This should be done formally by signing a suitable document, which is inserted in the directors' minute book. Where the number of directors falls below the minimum required by the Articles, the remaining director(s) have no power other than to appoint another director or directors, or to call a general meeting of the members at which another director or directors could be appointed.

It is increasingly common, however, for private companies to incorporate in their Articles a provision vesting all the company's authority in the hands of a sole or surviving director(s), even where their number has fallen below the minimum number stipulated elsewhere.

As noted above, directors' meetings can include participation via audio/audio-visual facilities, and as a result it is not necessary for the quorum to be present in one location.

2.6 Minutes of directors' meetings

As discussed in chapter 11, all companies are required to keep minutes of meetings of the directors (CA2006 s. 248). For meetings held after this provision of the Act came into force, 1 October 2007, the minutes must be kept for a minimum of 10 years. For earlier meetings the provisions of CA1985 s. 382 apply and this provides that minutes of directors' meetings be kept permanently.

The style of minutes varies from company to company and from industry to industry. Historically, board minutes were written very much as an internal record of business decisions. However, particularly in industries with external regulators, minutes are a primary source of information on the performance of the board and management and minutes are increasingly written with this external audience in mind with a greater focus on challenges being raised by specific directors and actions taken to review those challenges.

The importance of accurate minute taking cannot be over emphasised.

The chair, in conjunction with the company secretary, will determine how much of the discussion should be reflected in the minutes and whether in the form of suitable narrative or formal resolutions, action points and follow-up actions.

2.7 Chair

It is for the board members collectively to elect one of their number to act as chair of the board (Model Articles Plc & Ltd reg. 12). For listed companies the Governance Code sets out guidance on the election of a chair to ensure their independence from the executive management team. The Governance guidance on board effectiveness is a useful source of guidance on the role of the chair and although written for the chair of listed companies is applicable to all.

The chair should ensure that all points of view are discussed on any issue while avoiding repetition. Discussion should be pertinent to the matter under consideration and discussion should not be allowed to digress into other areas.

The Articles may give the chair a second or casting vote in the event of an equality of votes (Model Articles Plc reg. 14, Ltd reg. 13). While the use of such a casting vote is entirely at the discretion of the chair, it is suggested that this should only be used to defeat the resolution, on the basis that there is no majority in favour of it. In practice however, it is unusual for decisions of directors to proceed unless there is unanimity or failing that a healthy majority in favour.

Chairing a board is much more than just ensuring the smooth running of directors' meetings. The chair should lead by example demonstrating ethical leadership, providing advice and support to the executive team and especially the chief executive while not straying into executive decision-making.

A good chair will promote good relationships with all directors and senior managers, encouraging them to use all their skills, qualifications and experience to provide an appropriate forum to set and monitor strategy, create value and ensure accountability. The chair is responsible for ensuring the board regularly reviews its own performance collectively and individually and that there are appropriate resources to develop directors. The chair and other independent directors should ensure effective communication with shareholders in general and with the major shareholders specifically, to ensure their views are known to the board.

Stop and think 15.1

An effective chair is crucial to the correct functioning of the board of directors.

A good chair facilitates appropriate consideration of agenda items ensuring sufficient time is allocated and allowing all views to heard with equal weight.

Consider the impact that a domineering outspoken chair might have and the detrimental effect this is likely to have on proper board discussion and evaluation of agenda items.

Test yourself 15.1

1. **How are decisions at board meetings usually decided?**

2. **Who can elect the chair of the board?**

3. **Where are the rules and procedures governing the holding of directors' meetings?**

3. Role of the company secretary before, during and after board meetings

The company secretary usually plays a central role in the preparations for, and management of, board meetings and is responsible for any administration arising from the meeting.

3.1 Preparation for a board meeting

Prior to the board meeting, the company secretary should ensure the following tasks are done.

1. Issue a call for board papers to relevant directors and managers responsible for preparing the reports to the meeting.

2. Send a notice to each director stating the time, date and place of meeting. The notice usually incorporates the agenda but if this is a separate document it should accompany the notice together with the supporting reports and papers.

3. If any of the company's managers are to attend the whole or part of the meeting, e.g. the company's financial controller, they should also be advised of the meeting details and sent a copy of the agenda and supporting papers. If they are to attend only part of the meeting, they should be sent the papers for the relevant items only.

4. It is sensible for the company secretary to ensure that spare copies of the agenda and supporting papers are available at the meeting itself.

5. In preparing the agenda for the meeting, the company secretary should consider those items that come up on a recurring basis, e.g. half-yearly staff report, and if necessary, remind the appropriate department to have the report ready in time for circulation with the agenda. Matters on which no decision was reached at a previous meeting or which were deferred from a previous meeting should also be included in the agenda.

6. Sometimes the supporting papers will incorporate a formal resolution, which the board is to be asked to pass. This will save time when the minutes of the meeting are prepared.

7. Just before the meeting, arrangements should be made to ensure that everything necessary for the meeting is ready in the boardroom. It is also usual to have a copy of the company's articles of association, the Act and

other relevant material in the boardroom, in case it is necessary to refer to them during the meeting.

8. In the case of listed companies, the opportunity is often taken to have schedules of transfers available for inspection by board members. For those companies with an active share register, these summaries will usually be restricted to the largest transfers, as otherwise the reports would be too lengthy to be of any practical use.

3.2 At the board meeting

1. For incorporation in the minutes, take a note of those directors present and report any apologies for absence. Any conflicts of interest should be noted. In practice general interests are noted and updated annually and any changes or new interests in between these annual declarations noted at the next meeting.

2. Ensure that a quorum is present. If any item in which a director has an interest is to be considered, ensure that there will still be an independent, disinterested quorum to deal with it.

3. Take notes during the course of the meeting on any action decided on by the board and of its decisions reached, together with appropriate justification, if necessary. The minutes should not be a verbatim record of what is said; if they were, this could cause complications. Some companies record their meetings to assist the preparation of the minutes. It is recommended that once the minutes of the meeting have been approved any notes or recordings are destroyed.

4. It is usual to note in the minutes the arrival of any director after the proceedings have started or the departure of a director before the meeting has ended.

5. The chair may ask the company secretary to advise on any point of procedure regarding the conduct of the business of the meeting, but it would be appropriate for the company secretary to intervene in the meeting (unless they are themselves a director) only if the board were proposing to do something that was unlawful or contrary to the company's articles of association.

6. If a manager is to be called in for discussion of a specific item, ensure that they are ready to be called when that item is reached on the agenda.

7. If any confidential papers, flip charts or white boards are used during the meeting these should be collected and/or cleared by the company secretary before staff come in to clear the room.

3.3 After the board meeting

1. (*Listed companies*) If the company has made a decision with regard to the payment of a dividend on the company's ordinary shares, yearly or half-yearly accounts have been approved or a decision for the appointment or resignation of a director, an announcement should be released via an RIS (LR 9.7A.2). If necessary, an RIS should also be advised of any decision to make an issue of shares or debentures or to postpone the payment of a preference dividend or of interest (LR 9.6.4, 9.7A.2).

2.   The company's managers should be notified of any action which the board require them to take, e.g. by sending a memorandum or letter to the managers concerned.

3.   Make a note of any item that has been deferred for future consideration to ensure that it is not overlooked.

4.   If the directors have asked for a report on a specific subject to be prepared for their next meeting, ensure that the manager responsible for preparing it is notified.

5.   Prepare the minutes of the meeting, showing the names of the directors present, those whose apologies were noted, and the arrival and departure of any director who was not present at the beginning or end of the meeting.

6.   The procedure to be followed after preparation of the minutes will vary from company to company. However, it is usual to send a copy of the draft minutes to every director present with a request that they return any comments by a given date, following which the minutes can be prepared in their final form for distribution to all directors.

7.   If a director makes a comment about the wording of a particular minute, the alteration should be agreed with the chair, who will then mention the amendment at the subsequent board meeting before signing the minutes. Since the chair has agreed the amendment, it is unlikely that any director present at the subsequent board meeting will object to the alteration. Other than obvious mistakes, alterations should be confined to what was said rather than what any particular director meant to say or, on reflection, would have preferred not to say.

4. Delegation of authority and responsibility

The directors are generally responsible for the management of the business of the company, but the extent of their authority depends on the provisions of the Articles and any overriding provisions in the Companies Act. Model Articles – Plc reg. 3 provides that 'subject to the articles, the directors are responsible for management of the company's business, for which purpose they may exercise all the powers of the company'.

In exercising their responsibility for overall governance the board must ensure that senior executive management establish and maintain adequate systems of risk identification, management and control.

The potential for overlap between the responsibilities and authorities of the board and the executive management team is ever-present. In these circumstances, it is essential that there are clear, documented policies and procedures setting out both those specific decisions and exercise of authority that are reserved to the board to decide upon and those other matters that are delegated to the executive management team. Hand in hand with the delegation of this authority, the board must establish appropriate oversight and reporting processes in order that the board can monitor the actions of the executive management team in the exercise of these delegated responsibilities, as well as establishing appropriate procedures to monitor and evaluate the implementation of the corporate strategy.

A copy of these written procedures should be given to each director. Compliance should be monitored and breaches of the procedures should be considered by the chair and the board.

Delegation of directors' authority must be contained in the company's Articles whether that authority is being delegated to board committees or to senior management (Model Articles Plc & Ltd regs. 5 and 6).

When delegating any of its powers to a committee, the board should establish and approve written terms of reference. These terms of reference should include the following sections:

- membership;
- quorum;
- frequency;
- secretary;
- notice;
- minutes;
- duties; and
- reporting responsibilities.

In addition to board committees, many companies have management committees established under the CEO's remit to assist in implementing the corporate strategy and operational decisions. Most commonly, a CEO will establish an executive committee. The authority of an executive committee flows from the authority of the individual members with no specific authority of its own. Due to the importance of the executive committee, the CEO will often provide a report on its actions to the board.

The members of the executive committee need to have a clear understanding about their power and delegated authority, and which decisions must be referred to the board. Executive committee terms of reference might include:

- purpose and authority;
- membership;
- chair;
- secretary;
- quorum;
- frequency of meetings;
- notice;
- duties:

- preparation of business plans, budgets and company strategies for consideration by the board and, to the extent approved by the board, implementing these plans, budgets and strategies;

- execution of agreed strategies and control of budgets;

- establishment of necessary processes to identify and monitor risks and formulating strategies for managing those risks;

- establishing financial and other reporting mechanisms and systems and control to capture all relevant material information on a timely basis;

- providing the board and its various committees with the necessary information with respect to the company's financial performance, condition and future prospects, to enable the board and its committees to fulfil their governance responsibilities; and

- implementing the company's policies and processes;

◆ reporting.

Although day-to-day responsibility might be delegated to an executive or executive committee ultimate responsibility remains with the board of directors and the directors should ensure that regular updates are provided both at board meetings and, if appropriate, in between, depending on the frequency of those meetings.

As discussed in more detail in chapter 2, while directors are able to delegate authority to committees of the board and to the executive management they cannot delegate their duties under the Act to:

◆ act within their powers (CA2006 s. 171);

◆ promote the success of the company (CA2006 s. 172);

◆ exercise independent judgement (CA2006 s. 173);

◆ exercise reasonable care, skill and diligence (CA2006 s. 174);

◆ avoid conflicts of interest (CA2006 s. 175);

◆ not accept benefits from third parties (CA2006 s. 176); and

◆ declare interests in any proposed transaction or arrangement (CA2006 s. 177).

Stop and think 15.2

For companies with non-executive directors it is essential to ensure that there is documented separation of the roles of the board and executive management to avoid overlapping and potentially conflicting messages emanating from the board and senior management.

5. Reliance on management and advisers

Following further high-profile business failures blamed on poor management, government attention has once again been focused on corporate governance and behaviour of directors.

On 26 August 2018, BEIS published its response to the Insolvency and Corporate Governance consultation, the aim of which was to identify changes that would assist in reducing corporate failure by strengthening corporate governance, stewardship and to improve the insolvency regime.

The reforms announced by the government are intended to ensure that the responsibilities of directors of firms when they are in or approaching insolvency are met and more generally to improve the performance of directors and the effectiveness of the boards of public companies.

In a response to recent high-profile business failures the government is looking at measures to enhance stewardship of the largest companies, through stronger mandates and greater transparency over group structures and dividend policies.

The government also announced that they intend to introduce new legislation to ensure that directors of dissolved companies can be held to account if they have failed to discharge their duties properly.

It is hoped that the reforms will see more failing companies rescued or restructured, that stewardship and transparency of the largest companies is further strengthened and that returns to creditors in insolvency will be higher.

The following proposals for change were announced.

Insolvency proposals:

◆ taking forward measures to ensure greater accountability of directors in group companies when selling subsidiaries in distress;

◆ legislating to enhance existing recovery powers of insolvency practitioners in relation to value extraction schemes;

◆ legislating to give the Insolvency Service the necessary powers to investigate directors of dissolved companies; and

◆ when they are suspected of having acted in breach of their legal obligations.

Corporate governance proposals:

◆ strengthen transparency requirements around complex group structures;

◆ enhance the role of shareholder stewardship;

◆ strengthen the UK's framework in relation to dividend payments; and

◆ bring forward proposals to improve boardroom effectiveness.

New legislation or guidance is expected in these areas.

In general, where a director, acting in good faith, seeks comprehensive advice from either the company's own management or from suitably qualified advisers, and in good faith acts in accordance with that advice, they will have discharged their duties to promote the success of the company (CA2006 s. 172) and their duty to exercise reasonable care, skill and diligence (CA2006 s. 174).

Where a director is professionally qualified, and that qualification is relevant to the matter at hand, the courts will apply more exacting standards of behaviour. For instance, a director and chartered surveyor with many years' experience in commercial property valuation will be expected to have a better understanding of a complex property financing proposal than a colleague on the board whose expertise is in IT. In *Re Peppermint Park Limited (1998) BCC 23*, the judge took account of the directors' relative responsibilities, knowledge and qualifications and the director holding a non-executive role was disqualified for a much lesser period than the director who had effective day-to-day control of the company.

Where directors are not experts in the matter under consideration, it is sufficient that they seek advice from suitably qualified professionals and that they act on that advice. However, directors should not blindly accept advice without reviewing it or challenging it if appears to be at odds with the facts and should attempt to understand the advice and its consequences as far as they are able. Directors are equally liable for their inaction as they are for their actions.

Professional advisers are often invited to attend meetings of the directors, sometimes on a regular basis. Such advisers must take care to restrict their advice to their area of expertise such as accountancy or property transactions. Otherwise, if they provide wide-ranging advice which the directors regularly take or act upon they are likely to become shadow directors.

Of particular concern for regulators will be whether professional advice was truly impartial or whether it was tailored to what the client wanted to hear. All directors and especially non-executive directors should challenge advice in circumstances where a number of professional firms have been approached for the advice or opinion that the executive directors are seeking. If only one out of five advisers provides the 'right' advice this is most likely an indication that their advice is pushing the boundaries rather than an indication that they have some unique knowledge of the issues.

6. Committees – types, purpose and composition

As noted above, boards comprising both executive and non-executive directors will often constitute committees of the board to provide more detailed independent oversight of certain areas. Listed companies are recommended by the Governance Code to establish several standing board committees including audit, remuneration and nominations committees or to explain why these are not appropriate.

Model Articles Plc & Ltd regs. 5 and 6 provide that directors may delegate their powers to committees with such powers as the board may decide. The proceedings of committees will follow those that apply to the board as a whole. In certain circumstances, it may also be desirable that the action taken by a committee should be validated by the directors or by the company in general meeting.

Board committees generally bring four main benefits to the company:

◆ member knowledge specialisation;

◆ committee specialism;

◆ better accountability; and

◆ more time to look into specific matters in more detail.

Certain non-executive directors will have been appointed due to their specialist knowledge which can be exploited by or is essential to the good operation of a committee. A good example of this is the appointment of an experienced accountant, ideally a current or former CFO to head the audit committee. Their specialist knowledge is critical to the proper functioning of the audit committee. Over time, other non-specialist members of committees will build a body of knowledge and be better able to interact with and make a positive contribution to the task of holding the executive team to account. However, this knowledge specialism does need to be monitored, as there is a danger of limiting the input available from those directors not on the committees due to their lack of detailed subject knowledge.

Co-ordinating the board's in-depth review of specialist areas such as remuneration policy, risk management or health and safety allows a better allocation of issues needing to be addressed by the board. This generally enables more efficient and effective working of the board as a whole.

Board committee structure enables improved individual accountability and responsibility of committee members. Many boards comprise 10 or more directors, and time pressures can make it difficult for all directors to contribute on all topics, especially where their views are similar to others. Some non-executives may also feel intimidated by detailed industry knowledge and experience of the executive directors or even the chair. However within the committee structure they are more able to perform their oversight function with more time available, fewer participants and a degree of separation from the executive directors.

Board committees can devote more time to the detail of their area of responsibility than is possible for the full board. While the board makes use of committees to assist in its oversight of their area of interest the full board retains responsibility for and makes the final decisions in all those areas.

For a listed company, a majority of the members of these committees should be independent of the executive team and, especially in the case of the chair of each committee have an appropriate level of qualification and experience. In two significant areas, the remuneration and audit committees, the membership should be entirely independent non-executives to provide, as far as possible, a neutral view to setting the executive remuneration policy and agreeing the scope and terms of the external audit, including the appointment of the external auditor.

The minutes of all meetings of committees of the board (or a written summary thereof) should be circulated to the board prior to its next meeting and the opportunity should be given at that meeting for any member of the board to ask questions which are usually directed to the relevant committee chair.

It is a Governance Code recommendation that the work of the audit, remuneration and nomination committee be contained in the annual financial statements and these normally take the form of a report to the members by each committee chair.

Test yourself 15.2

1. **What is the main risk associated with having professional advisers present at all directors' meetings?**

2. **What do committees of the board, and especially non-executive members contribute to the board?**

7. Matters reserved for the board

For many companies, there is no practical difference between the composition of the senior executive management team and the board of directors. However, in larger companies and especially listed companies, executive directors will very much be a minority on the board of directors and there will be an executive committee below the board of directors which undertakes the day-to-day management of the business and implementation of the strategy agreed by the board of directors.

In exactly the same way that delegation of board authority to its committees must be fully documented the same is true of separation of the roles and responsibilities of the board and executive management. With this division of responsibilities, it is essential that there is a clear demarcation of matters that are the responsibility of the board and those matters delegated to the executive management team.

The directors should identify categories of matters as well as specific items which require the prior approval of the board of directors. The schedule is most often referred to as the 'matters reserved for the board'. The directors should also lay down procedures to be followed in the rare circumstances where a decision is required before the next directors' meeting.

As a basic principle, all material contracts, and especially those not in the ordinary course of business, should be referred to the board of directors for decision prior to the commitment of the company.

The directors should approve definitions of the terms 'material' and 'not in the ordinary course of business'.

Where there is any uncertainty regarding the materiality or nature of a contract, it is best practice for that contract to be brought before the board of directors for consideration.

The ICSA has published a useful generic schedule of matters reserved for the board, as set out in Table 15.1.

Strategy and management

Responsibility for the overall leadership of the company and setting the company's values and standards.

Approval of the group's strategic aims and objectives.

Approval of the annual operating and capital expenditure budgets and any material changes to them.

Oversight of the group's operations ensuring:

- competent and prudent management;
- sound planning;
- maintenance of sound management and internal control systems;
- adequate accounting and other records; and
- compliance with statutory and regulatory obligations.

Review of performance in the light of the group's strategic aims, objectives, business plans and budgets and ensuring that any necessary corrective action is taken.

Extension of the group's activities into new business or geographic areas.

Any decision to cease to operate all or any material part of the group's business.

Structure and capital

Changes relating to the group's capital structure including reduction of capital, share issues (except under employee share plans), share buy backs [including the use of treasury shares].

Major changes to the group's corporate structure, including, but not limited to acquisitions and disposals of shares which are material relative to the size of the group in question (taking into account initial and deferred consideration).

Changes to the group's management and control structure.

Any changes to the company's listing or its status as a plc.

Financial reporting and controls

Approval of the half-yearly report, interim management statements and any preliminary announcement of the final results.

Approval of the annual report and accounts, [including the corporate governance statement and directors' remuneration report].

Approval of the dividend policy.

Declaration of the interim dividend and recommendation of the final dividend.

Approval of any significant changes in accounting policies or practices.

Approval of treasury policies [including foreign currency exposure and the use of financial derivatives].

Approval of material unbudgeted capital or operating expenditures (outside pre-determined tolerances).

Internal controls

Ensuring maintenance of a sound system of internal control and risk management including:

◆ approving the company/group's risk appetite statements;

◆ receiving reports on, and reviewing the effectiveness of, the group's risk and control processes to support its strategy and objectives;

◆ approving procedures for the detection of fraud and the prevention of bribery;

◆ undertaking an annual assessment of these processes; and

◆ approving an appropriate statement for inclusion in the annual report.

Contracts

Approval of major capital projects [and oversight over execution and delivery].

Contracts which are material strategically or by reason of size, entered into by the company [or, in the case of a subsidiary, recommendations for approval] in the ordinary course of business, for example bank borrowings [above £xx million] and acquisitions or disposals of fixed assets (including intangible assets such as intellectual property) [above £xx million].

Contracts of the company [or any subsidiary] not in the ordinary course of business, for example loans and repayments [above £xx million]; foreign currency transactions [above £xx million]; major acquisitions or disposals [above £xx million].

Major investments [including the acquisition or disposal of interests of more than (3)% in the voting shares of any company or the making of any takeover offer].

Communication

Ensuring a satisfactory dialogue with shareholders based on the mutual understanding of objectives.

Approval of resolutions and corresponding documentation to be put forward to shareholders at a general meeting.

Approval of all circulars, prospectuses and listing particulars [approval of routine documents such as periodic circulars about scrip dividend procedures or exercise of conversion rights could be delegated to a committee].

Approval of press releases concerning matters decided by the board.

Board membership and other appointments

Changes to the structure, size and composition of the board, following recommendations from the nomination committee.

Ensuring adequate succession planning for the board and senior management so as to maintain an appropriate balance of skills and experience within the company and on the board.

Appointments to the board, following recommendations by the nomination committee.

Selection of the chairman of the board and the chief executive.

Appointment of the senior independent director to provide a sounding board for the chairman and to serve as intermediary for the other directors when necessary.

Membership and chairmanship of board committees following recommendations from the nomination committee.

Continuation in office of directors at the end of their term of office, when they are due to be re-elected by shareholders at the AGM and otherwise as appropriate.

Continuation in office of any director at any time, including the suspension or termination of service of an executive director as an employee of the company, subject to the law and their service contract

Appointment or removal of the company secretary.

Appointment, reappointment or removal of the external auditor to be put to shareholders for approval in general meeting, following the recommendation of the audit committee.

Appointments to boards of subsidiaries.

Remuneration

Determining the remuneration policy for the directors, company secretary and other senior executives.

Determining the remuneration of the non-executive directors, subject to the articles of association and shareholder approval as appropriate.

The introduction of new share incentive plans or major changes to existing plans, to be put to shareholders for approval.

Delegation of authority

The division of responsibilities between the chairman, the chief executive [and other executive directors,] which should be clearly established, set out in writing and agreed by the board.

Approval of the delegated levels of authority, including the chief executive's authority limits (which must be in writing).

Establishing board committees and approving their terms of reference, and approving material changes thereto.

Receiving reports from board committees on their activities.

Corporate governance matters

Undertaking a formal and rigorous annual review of its own performance, that of its committees and individual directors, and the division of responsibilities.

Determining the independence of non-executive directors in light of their character, judgement and relationships.

Considering the balance of interests between shareholders, employees, customers and the community.

Review of the group's overall corporate governance arrangements.

Receiving reports on the views of the company's shareholders to ensure that they are communicated to the board as a whole.

Authorising conflicts of interest where permitted by the company's articles of association.

Policies

Approval of policies, including:

- code of conduct;
- share dealing code;
- bribery prevention policy;
- whistle-blowing policy;
- health and safety policy;
- environment and sustainability policy;
- human resources policy;
- communications policy [including procedures for the release of price-sensitive information];
- corporate social responsibility policy; and
- charitable donations policy.

Other

The making of political donations.

Approval of the appointment of the group's principal professional advisers.

Prosecution, commencement, defence or settlement of litigation, or an alternative dispute resolution mechanism [involving above £xx million or being otherwise material to the interests of the group].

Approval of the overall levels of insurance for the group including directors' and officers' liability insurance [and indemnification of directors].

Major changes to the rules of the group's pension scheme, or changes of trustees or [when this is subject to the approval of the company] changes in the fund management arrangements.

Any decision likely to have a material impact on the company or group from any perspective, including, but not limited to, financial, operational, strategic or reputational.

This schedule of matters reserved for board decisions.

Table 15.1 Schedule of matters reserved for the board

8. Executive discretion

It is very rare for formal meetings of the full board to take place more often than once a month and in many companies, quarterly board meetings are very common. In such circumstances, authority must be delegated to the executive directors and senior managers to allow them to manage the affairs of the company on a day-to-day basis.

Within the parameters of any delegated responsibilities, the matters reserved for the board and their general duties under the Act to promote the success of the company, executive directors have a fair degree of discretion as to exactly how they exercise those powers.

The delegation of any powers or authorities to executive directors and senior managers should be clearly documented. At the very least, this should be set out in terms of reference for each executive committee an executive sits on and, albeit in a broader view, by each individual's contract of employment with the company. Additionally signing authority schedules should be adopted, although these are often referenced in terms of monetary values of payments or contracts, which are not always relevant for all decisions.

Their duty to act bona fide in the company's interests is primarily a subjective duty but with an objective threshold. Directors must exercise their discretion and powers honestly and sincerely in what they, and not what a court, may consider is in their company's interests.

Where directors act within their delegated authority, the company is bound by those acts and decisions under the normal rules of agent and principal. If a director has not been given executive power by the board or the Articles they have, in principle, no power or right to bind the company. It would not, however, be equitable to allow a company to step away from a contractual arrangement entered into with a third party by a director acting outside their authority. The Act (CA2006 s. 40) provides that the powers of the directors to bind the company shall be deemed free from any limitations in the company's constitution and the validity of such contracts will not be called into question. This protects third parties entering into transactions with the company in good faith where the directors have exceeded their authority. However, directors should be aware that this protection is only for third parties and does not prevent a member of the company bringing a restraining action in respect of an act beyond the directors' authority, unless the act is necessary to fulfil a legal obligation arising from a previous act of the company.

The directors can only be delegated powers of the company that the company actually possesses.

9. Motions and written/circular resolutions

Although there are no provisions in the Act equivalent to those authorising members of a private company from passing resolutions by using the written resolution procedure, Model Articles Plc regs. 17 and 18, Ltd reg. 8 provide that a resolution signed by all the directors entitled to attend a board meeting is as valid and effectual as if passed at a duly constituted board meeting. If convenient, such a resolution could be a single document, which is signed by each director in turn. Alternatively, a separate copy of the resolution could be sent to each director for signature. The document or documents signed by the directors should be inserted in the directors' minute book.

Model Articles Ltd reg. 8 goes further than simply permitting written resolutions, but allows directors of private companies to reach decisions simply by indicating to each other, by any means, that they share a common view. Nowadays such consent might be in the form of an exchange of emails from distant directors and verbal consent from those office-based directors. Model Articles Ltd reg. 15 requires that companies retain a written record of these unanimous decisions and there is no requirement for this to be signed by any director let alone all of them. However, best practice would dictate that the record of the decision is authenticated by the chair or company secretary as an accurate record of the decision.

It is now common practice for companies to adopt Articles allowing directors to conduct meetings by video or telephone, either by a conference facility or by the chair ascertaining the views of the directors individually. In addition, resolutions agreed by facsimile or email are being used, although it is desirable for any written resolution to be signed to provide a permanent record.

10. Conflicts of interest

Directors occupy a position of trust within companies and to provide protection for members there are detailed provisions obliging directors to avoid conflicts of interests generally but that where they do exist to disclose their interest in matters being discussed to prevent abuse of their positions by running the company for their own benefit. In addition, where a director proposes to undertake a transaction with the company there are specific provisions governing how that arrangement must be approved by members together with provisions governing the making of loans by companies to their directors.

Listed company directors are also required to comply with MAR and the Governance Code or explain any departures from the Governance Code as more fully discussed in chapter 8.

10.1 Conflicts of interest

Directors are required to declare any interests that either do conflict or might conflict with the interests of the company. It is most common for directors to declare their general interests on appointment and to confirm these on a regular basis. This could be annually, half-yearly or quarterly, depending on the size and nature of the company. It is also good practice for interests relating to any items of business on the agenda to be declared at the start of the meeting.

Where a director has a significant conflict, or a direct interest, in a proposed transaction this might require approval of the members either by written resolution or at a general meeting. Such transaction will often be seen in property development companies where a director purchases a property built by the company.

10.2 Duty to avoid conflicts of interest

Directors have a duty under CA2006 s. 175 to avoid situations in which they have or might have a direct or indirect interest that conflicts or might conflict with the interests of the company. Of particular importance are conflicts relating to property, information or opportunity, regardless of whether the company could take advantage of such opportunities (CA2006 s. 175(2)).

The duty under CA2006 s. 175 does not apply to:

◆ conflicts arising out of transactions or arrangements directly with the company; or

◆ if the directors authorise the matter.

Where the company is a private company, authorisation may be given by resolution of the directors, provided there is nothing in the company's articles of association that invalidates the authorisation.

Where the company is a public company, authorisation may be given by resolution of the directors, provided there is specific authority in the company's Articles that permits directors to authorise such transactions.

Such authorisation, whether for a private or public company, is only valid if the necessary quorum for a meeting of the directors is present excluding the director with the conflict of interest and without that director voting (CA2006 s. 175(6)).

10.3 Interests in contracts

Avoiding conflicts of interest is not always possible and where a director is directly or indirectly interested in a contract or a proposed contract with the company, they must declare the nature of their interest (CA2006 s. 177). Model Articles Plc reg. 16, Ltd reg. 14 and Table A, reg. 94 impose restrictions on a director in voting on a matter in which they are personally interested.

The type of interest relevant for this purpose is widely defined and includes contracts by the company with any other company of which the director is also a director. However, if the director's interest in a contract arises merely because they are a minor shareholder in another company that is a party to the contract, this would not constitute a declarable interest, provided the shareholding was not material.

A useful procedure for a director to give general notice of interests is given by CA2006 ss. 182–185.

Where notice of an interest is given in writing, it must be given by the director to each other director in hard copy by post or by hand, or by such other means as may be agreed between them. Written notice of an interest is deemed to form part of the proceedings of the next meeting of the directors (CA2006 s. 184).

A director may give general notice, either at a directors' meeting or in writing, of an interest in or with another company, firm or person and that will constitute a declaration of an interest in any future transaction or arrangement with that company, firm or person. Where a significant transaction is being considered with a party in which a director has previously declared a general interest it is recommended that the existence of that interest be brought to the attention of the board.

Where the director required to give a notification is a sole director, such notification must be in writing (CA2006 s. 186).

Material transactions between the company and its directors must be disclosed in the company's accounts. The Act imposes restrictions on substantial property transactions between companies and their directors, as discussed below.

In the case of listed companies, it is usual to find that the Articles include a provision prohibiting the directors to vote on all but a few matters in which they have an interest. Such allowable interests include arrangements for approved pension schemes, and directors' and officers' insurance schemes. Non-disclosable transactions with companies, where the interest is in that company's share capital, are limited to holdings not exceeding 1%.

10.4 Substantial property transactions

A director of a company or of its holding company may not enter into any arrangement to acquire from or transfer to the company a 'non-cash asset' without prior approval of the members by ordinary resolution passed in general meeting (CA2006 s. 190).

The restriction on substantial property transactions extends to persons connected with a director and to shadow directors, and requires that, where a director or connected person is also a director of the holding company, additional approval in general meeting of the holding company is sought.

A 'substantial non-cash asset' is defined in CA2006 s. 191 as any asset of the company if its value is greater than £5,000 and which is also in excess of the lower of 10% of the company's net asset value or £100,000. Transactions exceeding this limit require approval by ordinary resolution of the members either in general meeting or by written resolution.

The net asset value is determined by reference to the most recent statutory accounts or, if there are none, to the company's aggregate called-up share capital.

There are a number of transactions that are exempted from the requirement including:

1. a non-cash asset valued at less than £5,000;
2. an arrangement between a wholly owned subsidiary and either the holding company or a fellow wholly owned subsidiary;
3. an arrangement where the company is being wound up (except a members' voluntary winding up); or
4. in circumstances where the director is acquiring the asset in their capacity as a member of the company and not as a director, i.e. issue of shares pursuant to a rights issue.

While a transaction does not require approval of the members by ordinary resolution, it should be disclosed at a directors' meeting and the circumstances entered in the minute book to ensure that there is no question subsequently raised as to the validity of the transaction and the director held liable, see below.

A transaction approved pursuant to CA2006 s. 190 is likely to be 'material' and will require disclosure in the company's annual financial statements.

The UKLA normally requires that, other than small transactions, transactions between directors and a listed company are the subject of a circular to members and require prior approval of the members in general meeting (LR 11.1 and 11 Annex 1).

Where requirements of CA2006 s. 190 are contravened and a transaction does not receive the necessary approval, the director or connected person and any other directors who authorised such arrangements or transaction are liable to account to the company for any direct or indirect gain made from the transaction, and jointly indemnify the company from any loss or damage resulting from the transaction.

The transaction or arrangement may also be voidable at the instance of the company (CA2006 s. 195(2)).

However, where advance approval was not obtained, the transaction can be affirmed by members in general meeting within a reasonable period thereafter (CA2006 s. 196).

10.5 Loans to directors

A company may not make loans to its directors or connected persons or to directors of its holding company, nor may it give guarantees or other securities for such loans or enter into credit transactions for the benefit of the director, unless it has been approved by members (CA2006 ss. 197–214). Although a loan that is outstanding when a person is appointed as a director is permitted to continue, any additional amounts of principal or rolled-up interest would come within the prohibitions.

quasi-loan
A loan where a company reimburses the director's creditor.

Additional restrictions apply to public companies and companies that are members of a group containing a public company. **Quasi-loans** to directors and loans or quasi-loans to connected persons of directors of such companies are prohibited. A quasi-loan is a transaction under which one party pays a sum for someone else, or agrees to reimburse expenditure incurred by someone else, on the terms that that person will reimburse the person making the payment or where the circumstances give rise to a liability on that person to reimburse the payer.

A director's 'connected persons' are their immediate family members as defined in CA2006 s. 253, including spouse, civil partner, parents, children or stepchildren, but excluding grandparents, grandchildren, siblings, aunts, uncles, nieces and nephews, even if they live at the same address. A connected body corporate is defined in CA2006 s. 254 as any company of which they have at least 20% control or the trustees or any settlement for the benefit of such persons.

The exceptions that apply to a company making loans or quasi-loans to directors or persons connected with them without members' approval are strictly limited and are as follows:

1. An advance of up to £50,000 may be made to a director to enable them to meet expenditure incurred for the purpose of the company or to enable them to perform their duties properly (CA2006 s. 204).

2. Approval is not required where the company meets the expenses in defending an action in connection with an alleged negligence, default or breach of duty or trust, provided the amounts are repayable on conviction, judgment being given against the director or being refused relief (CA2006 s. 205).

3. Approval is not required where the company meets the expenses in defending an action or investigation brought by a regulatory authority in connection with an alleged negligence, default or breach of duty or trust. The company may not fund the payment of any fines imposed on the director personally (CA2006 s. 206).

4.   A loan or quasi-loan is permissible, provided that the amount concerned does not exceed £10,000 (CA2006 s. 207(1)).

5.   A credit transaction for an amount not exceeding £15,000 is permitted (CA2006 s. 207(2)).

6.   A transaction entered into in the ordinary course of the company's business, provided that the value of the transaction and the terms on which it is made are not more favourable than those that would be offered to a person of similar financial status unconnected with the company (CA2006 s. 207(3)).

7.   Special exemptions apply for loans made by money-lending companies (including banks) in the ordinary course of their business, provided the value of the loan and any terms are not different to those imposed to a person not connected with the company but otherwise under similar circumstances (CA2006 s. 209).

The provisions prohibiting unauthorised loans to directors contained in the Act are detailed, and reference should always be made to the legislation in the Act and (if thought desirable) legal advice taken. In particular, care should be taken if reliance is placed on the exemption relating to advances to enable a director to carry out their duties properly, as there is potential for this exemption to be abused.

Chapter summary

◆   Historical growth in the importance of the company secretary

◆   Appointment process

◆   Qualifications

◆   General duties

◆   Relationship with the chair, CEO and other directors and executives

◆   Communications to and by companies

Part four

Chapter sixteen

Shares, share
capital, share
register and debt
capital

Shares

Overview

This part considers the regulatory regime of the securities
industry and a detailed review of the different types of share and
debt capital available to be used by companies raising capital
funds. The chapter examines the different procedures for the
allotment and issue of shares as well as the mechanism available
for the company to buy back its own shares. There is a review of
the role of the share registrar and requirements for maintaining a
share register. It discusses the methods of transfer of ownership
of shares and the type of documents that companies can receive
from members affecting their share ownership. It considers the
processes for the payment of dividends on shares or interests
on loan notes. There is a review of the range of capital events
that companies can undertake and finally consideration of the
features and creation of employee share incentive schemes.

Learning outcomes

At the end of this part you will be able to:

◆ exercise appropriate judgement to advise the board on matters relating to shares and share capital;

◆ understand the roles of the tri-partite bodies overseeing the securities industry;

◆ explain the different rights and privileges that can be attributed to shares;

◆ discuss the role of the share registrar for traded companies and explain the purpose of the various documents that might be lodged by members or others in respect of a member and their shareholding;

◆ advise on the process required to transfer shares;

◆ explain the distribution of profit and capital and the authority required; and

◆ provide an overview of employee share schemes.

Chapter sixteen

Shares, share capital, share register and debt capital

CONTENTS

1. Introduction
2. Regulation of the securities industry
3. Types of share and debt capital
4. Share capital
5. Company share registrar function
6. Register of members
7. Share transfers
8. Transmission of shares
9. Registration of documents affecting title
10. Share certificates
11. Distributions
12. Rights and warrants, debentures and bonds
13. Capital events and role of share registrar
14. Key features and establishment of employee share schemes and their ongoing administration

1. Introduction

A company is owned by its members. Companies without a share capital will have some other method of determining ownership, but the overwhelming majority of companies have a share capital consisting of one or more classes of shares.

Large portions of both the Act and a company's Articles are devoted to ensuring the relationships between the members and each of the directors and the company as well as between members are transparent and free from unfair practices and regulation of the share capital is one such area.

2. Regulation of the securities industry

The regulatory structure of the UK financial services industry was last revised in 2013 to addressed concerns about the robustness of the supervisory system and its resilience to risk. The structure comprises five interacting bodies:

1. The Treasury – tasked with delivering the government's objective to promote stability, fairness, efficiency and competitiveness in financial markets.

2. Bank of England (BoE) – the BoE has specific statutory responsibilities for setting policy – for interest rates, for financial stability, and for the regulation of banks and insurance companies.

3. Financial Policy Committee (FPC) – the FPC is a BoE committee established to identify, monitor and take action to remove or reduce systemic risks with a view to protecting and enhancing the resilience of the UK financial system.

4. Financial Conduct Authority (FCA) – The FCA's strategic objective is to ensure that the financial markets function well while its operational objectives are to protect consumers, protect the financial markets and to promote effective competition for the benefit of consumers.

5. Prudential Regulation Authority (PRA) – a subsidiary of the BoE tasked with enhancing financial stability, promoting safety and soundness of authorised persons and minimising impact of failure.

The structure and interaction of the regulatory responsibilities of these bodies is set out in Figure 16.1.

Larger companies often require additional working capital to fund business acquisitions or to grow their business organically. Although such funding can be provided via bank financing or other forms of debt financing, raising funds through the issue of additional shares remains a popular option. Some companies will have secured early stage funding and having realised their potential need to provide an exit opportunity for those early investors. Without an obvious exit strategy companies may struggle to secure the necessary early stage funding.

Listing the shares and having them admitted to trading on the Main Market of the London Stock Exchange or one of the other public markets provides both a primary market to raise new and replace existing funding by the company and importantly a secondary market where shares may be freely traded.

These markets are highly regulated to ensure that all participants whether providing funding or trading in the company shares do so based on the same information.

Offers of fully 'listed' securities are governed by FSMA2000 and the Listing Rules. These rules and regulations apply to securities that are listed or are the subject of an application for listing or are being offered for sale conditional on their being admitted to listing. Trading on the Stock Exchange is subject to the Stock Exchange Rules.

The regime is supervised by the FCA, to which most of the powers of the Secretary of State under the FSMA2000 were transferred. The main feature

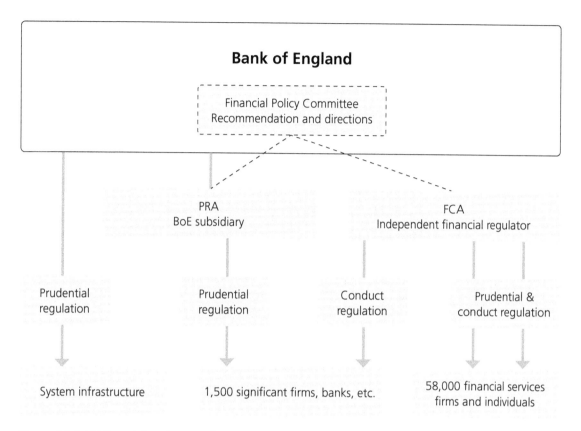

Figure 16.1 UK financial services regulatory structure

of this regime is that, subject to certain exceptions, only authorised or exempt persons may carry on a regulated activity (FSMA2000 s. 19).

2.1   Regulated investment activity

Regulated activities are defined in FSMA2000, ss. 21, 22 and Sch. 2. In particular, it must be noted that financial promotion and investment activity includes giving any form of investment promotion and advice and investment management, as well as undertaking securities transactions as broker-dealer and/or principal within the UK.

2.2   Authorised firms

The status of being an authorised or exempt person is conferred on application to the FCA by an individual or firm. Members of professional bodies such as solicitors and accountants may be authorised by their relevant professional body (FSMA2000 ss. 325–333).

A person carrying on a regulated activity who is not authorised or not exempted commits an offence (FSMA2000 s. 20). Agreements made in respect of the regulated activity may be unenforceable by the unauthorised person (FSMA2000 ss. 26, 27 and 28), and they may be restrained by injunction or be made subject to a restitution order.

2.3 Controlled functions

The FCA supervises the qualification and experience of those persons charged with running or having crucial roles in financial services firms through a process known as controlled functions. Where a firm wishes to employ someone to carry out specified functions, they must seek approval from the FCA in advance. These controlled functions are broadly divided into customer functions and significant influence functions.

The full list of controlled functions is set out in Table 16.1.

While a person may be appointed to more than one controlled function the firms must demonstrate that the individual is capable of managing these multiple regulated functions. Some combinations of roles do however sit better together such that being a company director and having oversight of the firms' systems and controls or compliance function will be easier to justify than say having oversight of compliance and retail mortgage advice.

Significant influence functions	CF 1 Director function
	CF 2 Non-executive director function
	CF 3 Chief executive function
	CF 4 Partner function
	CF 5 Directors of an unincorporated association
	CF 6 Small friendly society function
	CF 8 Apportionment and oversight function (non-MiFID business only)
	CF 10 Compliance oversight function
	CF 10A CASS oversight operation function
	CF 11 Money laundering reporting function
	CF 12 Actuarial function *
	CF 12A With-profits actuary function *
	CF 12B Lloyd's actuary function *
	CF 28 System and controls function *
	CF 29 Significant management function
Customer functions	CF 30 Customer function

Table 16.1 List of FCA-controlled functions

Stop and think 16.1

Careful planning for a change of director holding a controlled function is required as a new director although being able to join the company cannot be formally appointed as a director until authorisation of the FCA is received. Applications for authorisation can take many weeks, especially if the person being appointed has not held a controlled function previously.

Test yourself 16.1

1. **Which organisations have oversight of the UK financial services industry?**

2. **What is the name of the process through which the FCA supervises the employment of financial services professionals?**

3. Types of share and debt capital

All companies need to raise funding at some stage in their development, and there are a number of different ways to secure funding. The main factors which will determine which particular source of funding to use include the following.

	Equity	Debt
What is it?	Equity is funding raised through the issue of shares to private or institutional investors	Debt funding is loans owed by the company towards another party usually institutions but sometime private individuals.
Examples	Shares	Term loan, debentures, bonds, loan notes
Reflects	Ownership	Liability
Term	Long term	Short term
Status of holders	Ownership	Lenders
Risk	High	Lower
Return	Dividend and capital gain	Interest
Nature of return	Variable and irregular	Fixed and regular
Collateral	Not required	Essential to secure loans
Security required	No	Usually

Figure 16.2 Comparison of equity versus debt financing

3.1 Authorised capital

The Act abolished the concept of authorised share capital – the pool of shares both issued and available to be issued to investors. For companies incorporated under the previous Act, the authorised share capital stated in their memorandum continues to act as a ceiling on the number of shares that can be allotted and will be considered as a restriction in the Articles of the company.

3.2 Allotted capital

The Act defines 'allotted share capital' as shares that the company has allotted (CA2006 s. 546(1)(b)). CA2006 s. 558 states that shares are taken as allotted when a person acquires the unconditional right to be included in the company's register of members which is generally accepted to be once the contract of allotment is completed and acceptance of the application notified to the applicant.

Allotted shares includes shares taken by the subscribers on incorporation (CA2006 s. 546(2)).

3.3 Issued capital

Issued capital is the total capital that has been issued and taken up by the members of the company and is expressed by reference to the aggregate nominal value of the shares. Accordingly, a company that issues 250 shares of £1 each has an issued share capital of £250. Provided there are no restrictions in the Articles, a company can increase its issued share capital by allotting new shares.

Stop and think 16.2

Although there is no statutory definition of when a share is issued, it is generally accepted that this is when the shares are allotted and entered in the register of members and this was confirmed in *National Westminster Bank plc v Inland Revenue Commissioners [1995]*.

3.4 Paid-up capital

Paid-up capital refers to the nominal amounts that have been paid up on the company's issued capital. For example, if a company has 500 shares of 50p each in issue, then the issued capital is £250. If they are fully paid, the paid-up share capital will be £250. However, if, for example, the shares are issued only partly paid, with 25p paid up on each share, with the balance due at some point in the future, the paid-up capital will be £125.

3.5 Called-up capital

Called-up capital means the amount equal to the aggregate amount of calls made on the shares (whether paid or not) together with any amounts paid up without being called and any share capital to be paid on a specific future date under the Articles, the terms of allotment or other arrangements for payment (CA2006 s. 547).

3.6 Equity capital

Equity capital means the issued capital of the company excluding any shares that have the right to participate in a dividend or return of capital only up to a specified amount (CA2006 s. 548).

3.7 Changes to capital

Chapter 8 of Part 17 of the Act sets out the provisions relating to the alteration of share capital. CA2006 s. 617 provides that a limited company with a share capital may not alter its share capital except as provided in Parts 17 and 18 of the Act.

Under Parts 17 and 18 of the Act, a company may:

◆ increase its share capital by allotting new shares;
◆ subdivide or consolidate all or any of its share capital;
◆ reconvert stock into shares;
◆ redeem shares;
◆ purchase its own shares;
◆ redenominate its share capital;
◆ cancel its shares (duty to cancel shares held by or for a public company); and
◆ reduce its share capital (CA2006 s. 617).

No other alterations are permitted.

3.8 Debt capital

Companies can also list debt capital including debt made up of loan notes, bonds or redeemable shares, which are treated as debt.

The directors have implied power to borrow money on behalf of the company under their general powers to manage the business of the company, subject to the provisions of the Act and the Articles of the company (Model Articles Plc & Ltd regs. 3 and 4).

3.9 Types of debenture

A debenture is defined in CA2006 s. 738 as debenture stock, bonds and any other securities of the company, whether or not constituting a charge on the assets of the company. In effect, a debenture is a document that creates a debt or acknowledges a debt.

The more common method is to issue a series of debentures in registered form. The conditions relating to interest, redemption or security will be printed on the reverse of each debenture issued. Registered debentures may be transferable on stock transfer forms under the Stock Transfer Act 1963 (STA1963) and such transfers are exempt from stamp duty (with a few exceptions). When a debenture or one of a series of debentures is transferred, the name and address of the new holder are endorsed on the debenture itself by the company.

Public companies normally issue their debentures in the form of debenture stock secured on the company's assets and constituted by a trust deed between the company and a corporate trustee, e.g. an insurance company or a trust company.

3.10 Loan stock

Unsecured loan stock carries a higher risk for investors. To compensate for this, it is usual for such stocks to bear a higher rate of interest than if it were a secured debenture stock. Sometimes it is also necessary to offer options in the form of a right to convert the stock into equity shares of the company at certain dates in the future (i.e. convertible loan stock; see below). The ratio is determined at the time of issue of the stock; alternatively, a right to subscribe for equity shares at a future date in a ratio and price determined at the time of issue is agreed. Like a debenture unsecured loan stock is constituted under a trust deed. The holder of the stock is entitled to be supplied with a copy of the trust deed at their request on payment of a fee (CA2006 s. 749).

3.11 Convertible loan stock

Convertible loan stock is a form of loan stock, usually unsecured, which includes provision for the stock to be converted into equity shares at ratios determined at the time of issue of the stock. There is a requirement for the company to give the stockholders notice of their right to exercise the conversion rights in every year in which the right exists. The company secretary or the company's registrar will be concerned with the proper procedure for dealing with applications from holders to exercise their conversion rights.

Test yourself 16.2

1.   **What is the difference between allotted and issued share capital?**

2.   **What is a company's equity share capital?**

4. Share capital

When issuing new shares, it is important to ensure that there is sufficient current authority in terms of CA2006 ss. 550 or 551 for the directors to approve the issue and that any rights of pre-emption, whether as set out in the Act or in the company's Articles, are observed or waived.

Once a company has issued shares, there are only limited circumstances under which they can be returned to the company as follows:

- purchase by the company;
- redemption;
- reduction of capital; and
- forfeiture.

4.1 Authority for allotment

In general, directors must not exercise the company's power to allot shares or grant rights to subscribe for shares unless authorised by CA2006 ss. 550 or 551 (CA2006 s. 549). This requirement does not apply to the:

- allotment of shares or grant of rights to subscribe for shares allotted under an employee share scheme; or
- allotment of shares arising on the conversion of a security into shares (CA2006 s. 549(2) and (3)).

The directors of a private company with only one class of shares can exercise the company's power to allot shares or grant rights to subscribe for shares without any additional member consent, subject to any restrictions in the company's Articles (CA2006 s. 550).

The authority to issue additional shares:

- may be given in general terms or made subject to conditions;
- must state the maximum amount of the relevant securities that may be issued; and
- must specify the date on which the authority will expire, which must be not more than five years after the authority was granted (CA2006 s. 551(3)).

Private companies with only a few members will often adopt the full five-year period.

The authority to allot relevant securities may be revoked, varied or renewed by ordinary resolution, even if the authority was given by a special resolution or contained in the Articles. A resolution renewing an earlier authority must state the aggregate number of shares that may be allotted and an expiry date, within five years. Securities may be allotted after the expiry of the authority, provided that the allotment relates to an offer or agreement authorised by the directors prior to the expiry of their authority. A copy of a resolution giving authority to directors to allot relevant securities must be filed with the Registrar within 15 days after it is passed (CA2006 ss. 30 and 551(9)).

4.2 Pre-emption rights

The Act provides that, unless disapplied in whole or in part by the Articles, whenever new shares are to be allotted, they must first be offered to existing shareholders in proportion to their existing holdings (CA2006 s. 561).

Pre-emption rights for existing members are provided in CA2006 ss. 561–573 and for many companies these provisions are excluded by the Articles or waived by special resolution of the members either annually where an AGM is held or on an ad hoc basis. Listed companies will routinely seek a waiver of the pre-emption provisions from members at each AGM for small issues of new shares, as noted above.

The allotment and issue of securities that can be converted into relevant shares are also included, but the following allotment and issues are excluded:

◆ shares taken by subscribers to the memorandum;

◆ shares that as regards dividends and capital carry rights to participate only up to a specified amount in a distribution;

◆ shares held by a person acquired through an employees' share scheme or which are to be allotted in pursuance of such a scheme;

◆ shares allotted under a capitalisation (bonus) issue; and

◆ shares allotted wholly or partly paid otherwise than in cash.

(CA2006 ss. 560, 564–566).

Any pre-emption rights contained in a company's Articles take precedence over the statutory pre-emption rights. The requirement of the Act is that no equity securities may be allotted unless they have first been offered to the holders of all the relevant shares in the company in proportion to their existing shareholdings. The detailed provisions with regard to the communication of the offer to the existing members, who must be given a period of not less than 14 days in which to accept the offer, are laid down in CA2006 s. 562. A record date to determine the members' entitlement under the offer must be not more than 28 days before the date of the offer (CA2006 s. 574).

4.3 Disapplication of pre-emption rights

Private companies may exclude the statutory provisions by provisions contained in their Articles even if inconsistent with the statutory provisions. It is also possible for both public and private companies to exclude the operation of the statutory pre-emption rights in CA2006 s. 561 if the directors obtain authority by a special resolution of the members, either in respect of a general waiver in conjunction with a general authority to issue shares or for a specific share issue (CA2006 ss. 570, 571). If the company's Articles do not already contain a suitable provision, an alteration to the Articles would be necessary and would require the approval of members by special resolution in a general meeting or by written resolution.

The authority to disapply rather than exclude pre-emption rights is contained in CA2006 ss. 569–573. It is also quite common for the special resolution required by CA2006 s. 570, giving the directors power to disapply the Act's requirements with regard to pre-emption rights on the allotment of new shares by a listed company to be proposed annually at each AGM. In most cases, listed companies will seek an annual waiver of pre-emption rights of up to an additional 5% of the issued share capital.

The grant of the power to directors to disapply the pre-emption rights makes it possible for the company to make a rights issue of its shares and exclude or make such other arrangements for certain (usually overseas) groups of members. Without the waiver it might be impossible to allot equity securities to all members of the company in proportion to their existing shareholding.

The disapplication of the pre-emption rights will cease when the general authority of the directors to issue equity securities under CA2006 s. 551 lapses. However, an offer made before the expiry of the authority to disapply the pre-emption rights would remain valid, notwithstanding the fact that the actual allotment did not take place until after that date.

4.4   Pre-emption group guidance

The Pre-Emption Group was established in 2005 to produce a statement of principles on acceptable practice for listed companies seeking waivers of pre-emption rights. The statement of principles was most recently updated in March 2015 and recommends that an annual disapplication of pre-emption rights under CA2006 s. 570 is acceptable provided:

◆   general authority is restricted to an additional 5% of the issued capital;

◆   authority for a further 5% may be sought provided it is only used in connection with an acquisition or specified capital investment; and

◆   the authority lapses at the earlier of the next AGM or 15 months after the date of the resolution.

In addition, the statement of principles notes that in any rolling three-year period use of pre-emption waivers should be restricted to 7.5% of the issued capital excluding any specific waivers or use of the additional 5% waiver for an acquisition or capital investment.

4.5   Allotment procedure

As discussed above, before any allotment of shares, the directors should ensure that they have sufficient authority to allot shares and that any pre-emption rights on the allotment of shares are not infringed or, to the extent that they are, that the necessary waivers have been received, either in writing or by a members' resolution (CA2006 ss. 550, 551, 561).

If the company's Articles restrict the aggregate number of issued shares, it will be necessary to obtain the members' approval to a resolution to increase the directors' authority to allot shares as necessary.

Checklist for the allotment of shares

1.   **An application form should be made available for those persons wishing to subscribe for shares. The application form serves to demonstrate their agreement to become a member as required by CA2006 s. 112 but is also used to collect the necessary information to allow entry in the register of members. Private companies must take care when drafting an application letter to make sure that it is not regarded as an invitation to the public to subscribe for shares.**

Only public companies can issue shares to the public (CA2006 ss. 755, 756).

2.   Those persons wishing to subscribe for the shares will complete the application form and return this to the company together with a cheque, or proof of bank transfer, in full or part payment for the shares, as appropriate.

3.   The application forms should be checked for completeness and the remittances banked.

4.   Convene a directors' meeting to approve the applications, issue of shares, issue of share certificates and updating of the register of members.

5.   As soon as possible, share certificates should be issued to the applicants and in any event not more than two months from the date of allotment (CA2006 s. 554).

6.   Public companies whose shares are publicly traded, members can hold their shares in uncertificated form in CREST.

7.   Within one month of the date of allotment, a return of allotments (Form SH01) should be filed with the Registrar (CA2006 s. 555).

8.   Shares that are fully paid, are not required to have distinguishing numbers.

4.6 Issue price

There are no provisions regarding the price at which shares should be issued other than a general rule that shares cannot be issued below their nominal value (CA2006 s. 580). In apparent contravention of this rule is the issue of bonus shares where no payment is required from the members with shares being issued 'for free'. However, these shares are issued as fully paid with the amount due being paid out of the company's **distributable reserves** rather than by the injection of new funds by members.

distributable reserves
Profit retained by a company which may be distributed to its members.

Directors have a duty to act in the interests of the members and so the price at which any new shares are to be issued must take that duty into account particularly in circumstances where it is expected that not all, if any, existing members will participate in the new share issue. Where members do not participate in a share offer the value of their holding is diluted by the new shares being issued.

4.7 Part payment

Although partly paid shares are generally rare, they are most often found in the case of a non-traded public company where the minimum amount payable on the shares is paid up, e.g. £12,500 rather than the full £50,000.

4.8 Payment for shares

There are two ways in which shares may be paid for:

◆ in money or money's worth, including goodwill and know-how (CA2006 s. 582(1)); and

◆ by way of capitalisation of the company's existing reserves (CA2006 s. 582(2)).

Payment in money (cash) is defined in CA2006 s. 583 and means:

◆ cash received by the company;

◆ a cheque received by the company in good faith that the directors have no reason for suspecting will not be paid;

◆ a release of a liability of the company for a liquidated sum;

◆ an undertaking to pay cash to the company at a future date; or

◆ payment by any other means giving rise to a present or future entitlement (of the company or a person acting on the company's behalf) to a payment, or credit equivalent to payment, in cash.

The allotment of shares at a discount, or in exchange for an undertaking to perform work or services is prohibited (CA2006 ss. 580, 552, 553 and 585).

Subsequent holders of shares may incur liability if any of the provisions relating to the payment for shares are contravened (CA2006 s. 588).

Model Articles Ltd reg. 21 do not permit the company to issue nil or partly paid shares.

4.9 Shares allotted for non-cash consideration

A public company is prohibited from allotting shares fully or partly paid for a non-cash consideration unless the consideration has been independently valued within the preceding six months and a copy of the valuer's report has been sent to the proposed allottee (CA2006 ss. 593, 596 and 597).

There are, however, three exemptions as follows:

◆ allotments of shares made in a takeover by way of share exchange if the offer is open to all shareholders in the target (CA2006 s. 594);

◆ allotments of shares made in a merger issued in exchange for all the assets and liabilities of another company (CA2006 s. 595); and

◆ shares allotted under a capitalisation issue by the capitalisation of reserves or the profit and loss account (CA2006 s. 593(2)).

The valuation report must be prepared by an independent person who is qualified to be an auditor of the company, unless they consider that it would be appropriate for another person with the required knowledge and experience to make the valuation or any part of the report on their behalf. The person must be independent and must not be an officer or servant of the company (CA2006 ss. 1150–1153).

The valuer's report must state:

1. the nominal value of the shares being allotted for the non-cash consideration;
2. the amount of any premium payable on the shares;
3. the consideration which has been valued and the method used to value it; and
4. the amount of the nominal value of the shares and any premium treated as paid up by the non-cash consideration.

A copy of the report must be filed with the Registrar when Form SH01 is filed (CA2006 s. 597). The valuer is entitled to call for any information from officers of the company they require, and it is an offence to give misleading or false information (CA2006 s. 1153).

Usually, a formal contract is entered into for the transfer of the non-cash consideration to the company and for the allotment by it of shares in consideration for the assets transferred. The agreement must be stamped and sent to the Registrar with Form SH01.

If there is no written contract, particulars of the agreed terms must be set out on Form SH01.

4.10 Financial assistance

A public company must not provide financial assistance for the purchase of its own shares or the shares of its holding company, public or private, whether at the same time as the acquisition of the shares or before. There are no such restrictions for the purchase of its own shares by a private company except that a private company may not provide financial assistance for the acquisition of shares in its holding company if that company is a public company (CA2006 s. 678).

Financial assistance is very widely defined in CA2006 s. 677 as:

1. financial assistance by way of gift;
2. financial assistance given by way of guarantee, security or indemnity, other than an indemnity in respect of the indemnifier's own neglect or default, or by way of waiver or release;
3. financial assistance by way of loan or other agreement under which any of the obligations of the person giving the assistance are to be fulfilled at a time when in accordance with the agreement any obligation of another party remains unfulfilled or by way of novation of or assignment of rights arising under such loan or agreement; or
4. any other financial assistance given by a company, the net assets of which are thereby reduced by a material extent or which has no net assets.

The following transactions are excluded from the general prohibition (CA2006 s. 681):

1. distribution of assets by way of dividend;
2. distribution on a winding up;
3. allotment of bonus shares; or
4. redemption or repurchase by a company of its shares.

Financial assistance by or for a public company is permitted by CA2006 s. 682 if the following conditions are met:

1. if the assistance is being provided by a public company that the company's net assets are not reduced or to the extent that they are the assistance is provided out of distributable profit;
2. the lending of money is part of the company's ordinary business and the loan is made in the ordinary course of business;
3. the loan is given in good faith in the interests of the company or its holding company for the purposes of an employee share scheme; or
4. where the loan is made to an employee, but not a director, in good faith for the purpose of acquiring shares in the company or its holding company.

The relaxation provided by CA2006 s. 682 is only available to a public company to the extent that its net assets are not reduced or, if they are reduced, that the payment is made out of distributable profit.

4.11 Share premium

The **share premium** is the amount of the issue price of a share in excess of its nominal value, e.g. in the case of a share that has a nominal value of £1.00 and is issued for £1.75, the share premium is 75 pence. The amount of any share premium must be credited to a special capital reserve – the share premium account (CA2006 s. 610).

share premium
The excess of the price at which shares are issued above their nominal value.

The use of the share premium account is restricted to:

◆ writing off the expenses of the issue of those shares;
◆ writing off any commission paid on the issue of those shares; or
◆ paying up new shares to be allotted to members as fully paid bonus shares.

4.12 Calls on shares

A call on shares is the name given to the process by which directors call on members to pay any amounts due on nil or partly paid shares. Although the Act provides that shares may be issued as nil or partly paid it makes no provision for the directors to call those amounts and the procedure must be set out in the company's Articles.

The procedure suggested below is based upon the provisions in Model Articles Plc regs. 54–62.

Where shares are held by joint holders, each holder is jointly and severally liable for the amount of any call. In the case of deceased shareholders, the estate continues to be liable for outstanding calls unless the shares have been transferred into the personal names of the personal representatives, in which case they are personally liable.

Procedure to call amounts due on shares

1. **Convene and hold a directors' meeting to approve the making of a call.**

2. **The company secretary should arrange the preparation and issue of call notices to members. Each call notice should be addressed to the registered holder or joint holders and should contain details of the registered member(s), the amounts currently outstanding and the amount now being called, together with details of where and when the payment is due, which must be at least 14 days after the date of the call notice (Model Articles Plc reg. 54(3)).**

3. **Each call notice should carry a distinguishing number and this number should be noted on the register of members, together with a note of the amount being called. The company secretary should compile lists of the payments as they are received and cleared by the bank. Once the date on which the call is due has passed, the list of payments should be reconciled with the register of members and a list of unpaid calls should be prepared.**

4. **A reminder letter should be sent to all members that have not paid the call, requesting immediate payment and warning of the potential penalties for non-payment, including forfeiture of shares.**

5. **Members should return their share certificates together with a copy of the call notice so that the company can endorse the share certificates, giving details of the paid call. The endorsed share certificate should be returned to the member. Alternatively, the share certificates can be cancelled and new, fully paid share certificates issued.**

6. **The register of members should be amended to include details of the additional amounts now paid on the shares.**

7. **If a call remains unpaid, interest is due at a rate to be set by the directors but not to exceed 5% above the base lending rate in force from time to time. Directors may waive the obligation to pay interest either in part or in full (Model Articles Plc reg. 57(3)).**

4.13 Forfeiture

If payments due on the shares are not paid, and if the Articles permit, it may become necessary to forfeit shares. As with the procedure with making a call the provisions are contained in the company's Articles and not in the Act.

It is important to ensure strict compliance with the requirements of the company's Articles since, if these are not followed, the forfeiture could be declared invalid. The power is rarely exercised in practice, and it is recommended that legal advice should be taken before setting up forfeiture arrangements. When the shares have been forfeited, the person concerned ceases to be a member of the company and the forfeiture should be entered in the register of members.

If the member cannot or will not pay the call, they may wish to surrender the shares. Shares can only be surrendered if they are already liable to be forfeited.

4.14 Purchase of own shares

Companies are permitted, under certain circumstances and subject to any restrictions in the Articles, to purchase or acquire their own fully paid shares. In general, companies may only purchase shares out of distributable profit or the proceeds of a fresh issue of shares.

Under certain circumstances private companies may purchase shares out of capital.

The following table sets out the various purchase options available to public and private companies.

Procedure	Ltd	Plc
Reduction of capital supported by solvency statement CA2006 ss. 642–4	✓	
Reduction approved by the court CA2006 ss. 645–51	✓	✓
Reduction of capital – simplified process CA2006 s. 692(1ZA)	✓	
Purchase of shares out of profit CA2006 ss. 690–708	✓	✓
Purchase of shares out of capital CA2006 ss. 709–23	✓	
Purchase of shares out of proceeds of fresh issue CA2006 s. 692(2)(a)(ii)	✓	✓
Redemption of shares CA2006 ss. 684–9	✓	✓
Treasury shares CA2006 ss. 724–32	✓	✓

Table 16.2 Purchase of own shares: plc versus ltd

There are some important differences between the various processes including:

- Shares can only be redeemed if they were issued as redeemable.
- Payments for purchases of shares, redemptions and acquisitions into treasury are subject to stamp duty, where the consideration payable exceeds £1,000, whereas payments under a reduction of capital are not.
- Solvency statements are required for reduction of capital supported by a solvency statement and purchases of shares out of capital. These also require the auditor's confirmation that the statement by the directors is reasonable and accordingly if the company does not have an auditor one will need to be appointed.
- Shares may only be held in treasury if the consideration paid to acquire the shares was made out of distributable reserves (CA2006 s. 724(1)(b)).

Under a scheme involving a payment out of capital, the company must use all of its distributable profit first.

The various procedures under which a company may acquire its own shares have many procedural processes in common as set out below. Whichever process is chosen it is necessary to ensure that the Articles contain the necessary authority and secondly it is recommended that tax advice and clearance is sought, to ensure that the taxation consequences for the company and the members whose shares are to be acquired are understood.

Procedure	Reduction with solvency statement	Reduction under simplified process	Reduction with court order	Purchase out of profit	Purchase out of capital	Redemption	Transfer to Treasury
Check articles to ensure no restriction on reduction of capital.	✓	✓	✓	✓	✓	✓	✓
If the company is a plc, will the reduction result in the issued capital falling below the minimum share capital requirement?			✓	✓		✓	✓
Convene and hold a directors' meeting, recommending the reduction of capital/purchase of shares to members and either to convene a general meeting or to circulate a written resolution to obtain members' approval.	✓	✓	✓	✓	✓	✓	✓
Meeting to approve giving of a solvency statement.	✓	✓	✓		✓		
Ensure valid quorum is present.							

Procedure	Reduction with solvency statement	Reduction under simplified process	Reduction with court order	Purchase out of profit	Purchase out of capital	Redemption	Transfer to Treasury
Where only part of the redeemable shares are to be redeemed the Articles will set out the process to determine which shares are to be redeemed which may be decided by ballot or as a percentage of each members' holding of redeemable shares.						✓	
Issue notice, signed by director or company secretary, on 14 clear days' notice or circulate written resolution for members to consider special resolution(s).	✓		✓	✓	✓	✓	✓
Included with the notice or written resolution must be a copy of the solvency statement.	✓		✓		✓		
The special resolution must be approved within 15 days of the date of the directors' solvency statement made under s. 642.	✓		✓		✓		
Audit report to be enclosed (CA2006 s. 714(6)).					✓		
Issue notice, signed by director or company secretary, on 14 clear days' notice or circulate written resolution for members to consider ordinary resolution(s).		✓					
Enclose with the notice a form of proxy if desired.	✓	✓	✓	✓	✓	✓	✓
A copy of the agreement, or a written schedule of its terms if the contract is not in writing, must be made available for inspection by the members of the company at the company's registered office for not less than 15 days prior to the meeting and at the meeting itself (CA2006 s. 696(2)(b)).		✓			✓	✓	✓
Directors to make a statutory declaration specifying the permissible capital payment within one week before the date of the meeting (CA2006 s. 714(2)).					✓		

Procedure	Reduction with solvency statement	Reduction under simplified process	Reduction with court order	Purchase out of profit	Purchase out of capital	Redemption	Transfer to Treasury
Hold general meeting or circulate written resolution. Ensure valid quorum is present. Resolution put to vote either by show of hands or by poll and to be passed by appropriate majority (special resolution by 75% majority).	✓		✓	✓	✓	✓	✓
Hold general meeting or circulate written resolution. Ensure valid quorum is present. Resolution put to vote either by show of hands or by poll and to be passed by appropriate majority (ordinary resolution by simple majority).		✓					
Within 15 days of the passing of the resolution:							
File a copy of the special resolution with the Registrar.	✓	✓	✓	✓	✓	✓	✓
Solvency statement, statement confirming the solvency statement made within 15 days prior to the resolution and circulated to members .	✓		✓		✓		
Form SH19 and filing fee of £10 must be filed with the Registrar.	✓	✓	✓				
Form SH03 filed with the Registrar.				✓	✓	✓	✓
Copy of the Form SH03 must also be submitted to HMRC for stamping at ½% of the consideration paid (not the nominal value) in excess of £1,000.				✓	✓	✓	✓
Application must be made to the court to approve the special resolution.			✓				
Provided the court is satisfied that the proposed reduction meets all the jurisdictional and procedural requirements, it will make an order confirming the reduction.							
A copy of the court order, a statement of capital on Form SH19 and the filing fee (£10) must be filed with the Registrar.			✓				

Procedure	Reduction with solvency statement	Reduction under simplified process	Reduction with court order	Purchase out of profit	Purchase out of capital	Redemption	Transfer to Treasury
Within one week of the passing of the special resolution, the company must publish a notice in the London Gazette giving details of the proposed payment and either notify creditors individually or by newspaper advertisement published within one week of the passing of the resolution.					✓		
The reduction becomes effective upon registration of the documents by the Registrar.	✓		✓				
Registrar must certify registration of the court order.			✓				
If no objections are received, the payment may be made at the end of the five-week period and must be made within seven weeks of the date of approval of the special resolution.					✓		
Copy of the Form SH03 must also be submitted to HMRC for stamping at ½% of the consideration paid (not the nominal value) in excess of £1,000.					✓		
Issue consideration cheques if appropriate and cancel share certificates relating to shares acquired. Update register of members. Issue balancing share certificates if appropriate.	✓		✓	✓	✓	✓	✓

Figure 16.3 Procedure for companies to acquire their own shares

Test yourself 16.3

1. **Can shares be issued at a discount?**

2. **If a call on shares is not paid what is the ultimate sanction available to the directors?**

3. **If directors have full authority to issue additional shares what protection do existing members have from having their holding diluted?**

5. Company share registrar function

As discussed in chapter 9, all companies are required to keep various statutory registers including the register of members. For the vast majority of companies maintaining their register of members does not present any practical difficulties as there are few if any changes year on year. Occasionally however there will be a request from, on behalf of or relating to a member that is unusual and might require the advice of a company secretary, accountant or solicitor. Such an event might be the death or bankruptcy or appointment of a Lasting Power of Attorney for a member.

Maintenance of the register of members is usually outsourced by companies whose shares are traded on a public market. These markets require that trading take place using the electronic settlement system CREST (see below), and the necessary system development makes designing a stand alone system by an individual company uneconomic. Additionally, the register size for these quoted companies, even for the smaller ones tend to be numbered in the thousands and for larger share registers in the millions of members. The logistics of issuing notices of general meetings or collating proxy votes are beyond the capacity of most company secretariats.

Whether a company has only a handful of members and maintains the register in-house or has hundreds of thousands of members and outsources the maintenance of the register, the actual processes and procedures to maintain the register of members are the same.

5.1 Role of the share registrar

The share registrar, sometimes referred to as a transfer agent, usually provides the following services:

1. **Issuance and transfer:** issuing new certificates or crediting electronic holdings following the issue of new shares and processing share transfers, cancelling old share certificates and issuing new certificates.
2. **Record keeping:** keeping and recording ownership of shares.
3. **Registration**: registering changes of ownership and other documentation received in connection with the shareholding/membership.
4. **Paying agent:** distributing interest, cash, dividends, or other payments to members. In addition, a share registrar may act as a tender agent (tendering shares in a tender offer) or exchange agent (exchanging a company's shares, options and warrants in a merger).
5. **Shareholder liaison:** facilitating communications between companies and their members. Acting as a proxy agent (sending out proxy materials) and a mailing agent (mailing the company's annual, interim and other reports).
6. **Meeting management:** organising and running general meetings, registering and verification of attendees, vote scrutineers, managing poll votes and increasingly supervising the technology application for virtual and hybrid meetings.

5.2 Dematerialisation

Companies whose shares are traded on a public market must enable their shares for electronic settlement. As the various markets offer trading on a T+1 basis (settlement the day after booking the trade) this means that the shares must be held digitally rather than in physical form as there is insufficient time to physically move share certificates from the selling broker to the share registrar for verification and cancellation and the new certificate to be printed and issued to the buying broker.

6. Register of members

This is considered in chapter 9.

7. Share transfers

7.1 Overview

Whether shares are admitted to trading on a public exchange or not, most shares are transferable although there is no automatic right to transfer ownership of shares in the Act and the authority will be set out in the company's Articles.

Many private companies' Articles contain pre-emption rights on transfer designed to ensure that the pool of issued shares is retained within a relatively small number of owners who are usually related to the company founders. The Model Articles do not contain pre-emption rights on transfer of shares.

The admission requirements of the public markets will require that there are no restrictions on the transfer of shares in order to facilitate the smooth operation of the markets.

7.2 Stock transfer form

Non-market transfers will be undertaken using a stock transfer form in the format set out in the STA1963 Sch. 1. The process to follow to transfer shares is set out below. The transferee does not have to sign the stock transfer form, provided the shares are fully paid.

Following registration, the company will issue a new share certificate to the transferee in respect of the shares transferred as well as any balancing share certificate to the transferor, if required.

7.3 Stamp duty

Stock transfer forms should be stamped by HM Revenue & Customs, if liable to duty or adjudication, prior to being lodged with the company for registration. Stamp duty is currently payable on transfers with a value of £1,000 or more at the rate of 0.5% of the consideration paid for the shares, rounded up to the nearest £5. Stamp duty is payable within 30 days of the date of the transaction.

If transfers, or other documents, are submitted for stamping late, interest and/or penalties may be payable.

Where liable to stamp duty, an unstamped stock transfer form does not provide a valid transfer. It is the responsibility of the person registering the transfer in the register of members to ensure that it is properly stamped or correctly certified as exempt (CA2006 s. 770).

Transfers of most shares traded on a growth market such as AIM are exempt from stamp duty provided the shares are not also listed on an RIE.

There are some exemptions from the requirement to pay stamp duty such as where shares are being transferred under a group reorganisation. An appropriate application should be submitted to the HMRC stamp duty adjudication section, claiming exemption from stamp duty. The most common exemptions from duty are given for transactions complying with the conditions of s. 42 of the Finance Act 1930 or s. 77 of the Finance Act 1986.

Transfer checklist to transfer shares

1. The transferor should complete a stock transfer form, giving details of the shares to be transferred, their own name and address as transferor, and the name and address of the transferee. The form should be signed by the transferor and, where the shares are partly paid, by the transferee.

2. Prior to registration by the company, it will be necessary for the stock transfer form to be stamped by HM Revenue & Customs unless the transfer is exempt from duty and has been signed and certified on the reverse. Stamp duty is payable by the purchaser of the shares. Duty is due on transfers with a consideration of more than £1,000. The current rate for stamp duty is 0.5%, rounded up to the nearest £5, of the consideration paid or payable (whether or not the consideration is cash).

3. The stamped stock transfer form, together with the original share certificate, should be forwarded to the company or its registrar (as appropriate) for registration.

4. Upon receipt of a stock transfer form, the company should check that the details of the transferor are correct and that the share certificate is valid. If the original share certificate has been mislaid, it will be necessary for the transferor to complete an indemnity in respect of this lost certificate.

5. Many private companies have detailed pre-emption provisions on the transfer of shares and care must be taken to ensure that these are followed. Alternatively, the pre-emption rights may be waived by the remaining members.

6. The transfer of shares requires approval from the board of directors, who should also authorise the issue of a share certificate to the

**transferee and of any balancing certificate to the transferor.
Companies with publicly traded shares will give their registrar
authority to register transfers as it is simply not practical to
authorise individual transfers.**

7. **Details of the transfer must be entered in the register of members.
Transfers must be processed or rejected within two months of
receipt. Where rejected, the company must provide the details for
the refusal that the transferee may reasonably request (CA2006
s. 771).**

7.4 CREST

Companies whose shares have been admitted to CREST will be authorised
to accept electronic instructions to affect the transfer of shares and these
details will be entered by a CREST participant such as a stockbroker. All market
transfers are undertaken via CREST.

Where shares are transferred via CREST the duty in the form of stamp duty
reserve tax (SDRT) is automatically collected and accounted to directly with
HMRC by CREST.

Test yourself 16.4

When payable, what is the rate of stamp duty?

8. Transmission of shares

'Transmission' of shares is a disposition of shares by operation of law, compared
with 'transfers' of shares, which are dispositions of shares by voluntary act.
Transmissions are most commonly used upon death or upon bankruptcy or upon
a member becoming of unsound mind and the subject of an order of the Court
of Protection.

Where a transmission of shares is required there will also need to be filed, with
or before the transfer forms are received, the documents providing the person
signing the forms with the necessary authority. For an executor, this is the grant
of probate.

9. Registration of documents affecting title

Companies and their share registrar will often receive documents for registration
that either grant authority over the shares to another party or restrict the right
of the registered member to transfer the shares or receive dividends.

A company registered in England and Wales is prohibited from recognising any trust holding of its shares and accordingly cannot note in the register any nominee or trustee capacity in which registered shareholders hold their shares (CA2006 s. 126). However, this does not preclude the use of designations or the use of words such as 'nominee' or 'trustee' in a corporate nominee shareholder's name.

It may be necessary to make endorsements or alterations to existing share certificates. These should be signed and marked with an official stamp, so as to prevent unauthorised alterations or endorsements being made.

9.1 Differences between English and Scottish law

There are substantial differences between the law of England and the law of Scotland on both matters of property law and common law as well as some differences in the application of the Act.

The Administration of Estates Act 1971 permits a company registered in England and Wales or in Northern Ireland to register a confirmation issued in Scotland. Some documents issued by the English courts are acceptable in Scotland, sometimes once validated by a Scottish court. In all other cases, however, documents issued by English courts are unacceptable in Scotland.

A similar position exists in England where, apart from confirmations, some documents issued by Scottish courts are acceptable in England, some require validation by an English court and others are unacceptable.

9.2 Documents issued by other jurisdictions

Orders or documents issued by courts outside England and Wales and Scotland are not acceptable for registration either by English or Scottish companies, and consequently should not be accorded any recognition.

9.3 Documents received for registration

In addition to notification of share transfers and changes of address companies and their registrars will often receive documents from or most often on behalf of members to be noted and registered in the register of members. The most important factor when registering these documents is to ensure they are correctly authenticated, are original or certified copies and that they correctly identify the member to which they relate.

Common registration documents include:

- death certificate;
- probate;
- letters of request;
- letters of administration;
- confirmation;
- small estates;
- lasting power of attorney;

◆ court protection order;

◆ bankruptcy order;

◆ order for rectification of register; and

◆ appointment of administrator, liquidator or receiver.

10. Share certificates

Proof that a person is or is not a member of the company is obtained by examination of the register of members. A sealed or executed share certificate is, however, *prima facie* evidence of title to those shares (CA2006 s. 768). The company is prohibited from denying the title of the person named in the certificate to the shares specified in it or that shares are fully paid if the share certificate states that they are.

Share certificates should contain at least the following basic information:

◆ a unique certificate serial number;

◆ the name and registered number of the company;

◆ the name of the registered holder(s);

◆ the number and description of the shares to which the certificate relates, including a statement as to the extent to which the shares are paid up; and

◆ the date of the certificate.

Listed companies must also comply with the detailed requirements of the Listing Rules (LR 9.5.16). For security reasons, it is recommended that the number of shares should be shown twice on the certificates of listed companies ideally once in figures and once in words.

It is not necessary to show addresses of shareholders on share certificates and this may be preferable, since this information is rarely kept up to date.

Companies whose shares are traded on a public market will also have their shares admitted to CREST to enable the holding of shares electronically without the need for a physical share certificate. For electronic holdings, the references below to the issue of share certificates will mean the crediting of the relevant CREST account.

10.1 Issue on allotment or transfer

Companies are required to issue share certificates to shareholders within two months after an issue of shares or the date when the documents necessary to effect a transfer have been received by the company (CA2006 s. 769).

10.2 Lost share certificates

Due to the enduring nature of share certificates and the prohibition on the company from denying the holders title to the shares represented by the certificate, indemnities are usually sought for the issue of a duplicate certificate to protect against the original share certificate being subsequently found and being used fraudulently to support a transfer of shares. This indemnity should be joined in by a bank, insurance or trust company.

On receipt of the duly completed indemnity, a duplicate certificate, clearly marked as a duplicate, is prepared and issued on payment of any fee required under the Articles. The register is amended to note that the original certificate has been lost and a duplicate issued in its place.

10.3 Certification

When members are transferring only part of their holding, they may be unwilling to forward their share certificate to the purchaser. Even when provided with a share certificate the purchaser may want verification that the certificate is valid before paying over the purchase monies which delays the transfer process.

To resolve this issue the transferor should forward the certificate and stock transfer form to the company for certifying. The company will then stamp the transfer form noting that the certificate representing the shares on the transfer form has been lodged with the company (CA2006 s. 775). This process can be undertaken in advance before the identity of the transferee is known, and accordingly avoid any delays once a purchaser has been found.

Test yourself 16.5

1. What comfort does certification of a stock transfer form give to the purchaser of the shares?

2. How long do companies have in which to issue share certificates following a share issue or share transfer?

3. Must shareholder addresses be shown on share certificates?

11. Distributions

Distributions are defined in CA2006 s. 829 as 'every description of distribution of a company's assets to its members, whether in cash or otherwise'. The following are specifically excluded from the definition of distributions:

1. an issue of shares as fully or partly paid bonus shares;
2. reduction of share capital involving the extinguishing or reducing the liability of nil or partly paid shares or by repaying paid-up share capital;
3. the redemption or purchase of any of the company's own shares out of capital; and
4. a distribution of assets to members of the company on its winding up.

CA2006 s. 830 states that a company may only make a distribution out of profits available for that purpose, more commonly referred to as distributable profits. These are the company's accumulated realised profits less its accumulated realised losses.

The amount of any distribution must be determined by reference to the items set out below as disclosed in the relevant accounts, which in most cases will be the most recent annual accounts circulated to the members:

◆ profits, losses, assets and liabilities;

◆ provisions of any of the kinds specified in SCG(ADR)R2008 Sch. 7 or the 2008 Regulations Sch.9; and

◆ share capital and reserves (including undistributable reserves).

If the last annual accounts do not show that there is sufficient distributable profit the directors can prepare interim accounts to justify the amount of the distribution.

If the annual accounts have a qualified auditor's report, the auditor must issue a statement confirming whether the qualification is material for determining if a distribution can be made (CA2006 s. 836).

If a public company needs to prepare interim or initial accounts, those accounts must be properly prepared in accordance with CA2006 ss. 395, 396 and 397. Where interim accounts are prepared, these must be signed and a copy filed with the Registrar. In the case of initial accounts these must be audited.

11.1 By public companies

CA2006 s. 831 places additional restrictions on the ability of a public company to make a distribution in circumstances where the following criteria are met:

1. if the amount of its net assets is not less than the aggregate of its called-up share capital and undistributable reserves; and

2. if, and to the extent that, the distribution does not reduce the amount of those assets to less than that aggregate.

11.2 By investment companies

Public companies that are also investment companies (CA2006 s. 833) face additional restrictions the principal one being the company's assets must represent at least 150% of the value of its assets after the distribution.

11.3 Cash dividend

The most common form of distribution is the payment of dividends to the members.

The declaration and payment of a dividend is, subject to the availability of profit and any restrictions in the Articles, at the directors' discretion (Model Articles Plc reg. 70, Ltd reg. 30). Interim dividends require no additional authority, but final dividends require the approval of the members by ordinary resolution.

Although tax credits relating to dividend payments were withdrawn in the 2015 autumn budget companies are still required to confirm the amount of tax deducted (currently nil) on dividend payments. This notification is called the dividend confirmation.

11.4 Mandates

The dividend mandate is the authority from the member to the company to pay dividends becoming due to an account at a specified branch of a specified bank.

Dividend mandates must be signed by the member. If there are joint holders, the dividend mandate should be signed by all the joint holders. In the case of a corporate body, the mandate may be signed by an official who should state their office. In the case of administrators, attorneys, executors, receivers, trustees in bankruptcy, etc., or any other person acting on behalf of the shareholder, the authority under which they sign the dividend mandate must be registered with the company.

11.5 Unclaimed dividends

When dividends are paid direct to members, warrants may occasionally be lost in the post or they may be mislaid by the member. Unpaid dividend warrants are a nuisance to the company and it is usual for them to indicate on the warrants that unless they are paid within six months (or sometimes 12), they will have to be returned to the company for re-dating or verification.

For obvious security reasons, it is desirable to stop sending dividend cheques to an address if mail is being returned marked undeliverable/gone away. In the case of listed companies, the UKLA requires that dividend warrants should not be withheld unless two consecutive dividend payments have been returned as undeliverable or left uncashed.

11.6 Scrip dividends

Some companies allow members to elect whether to receive dividends by the issue of fully paid shares to members in lieu of cash dividends, but authority to do this must be contained in the company's Articles.

Enhanced scrip dividends, under which the value of the shares being offered exceeds the value of the cash payment, are becoming increasingly popular. They are used by companies to encourage shareholders to take up the scrip dividend alternative.

11.7 Dividend reinvestment schemes (DRIP)

Dividend reinvestment schemes should not be confused with scrip dividend schemes, described above. Under these schemes, a shareholder signs a mandate to the effect that all dividends on their shares in future be paid to the company or its registrar to be used in the purchase of shares in the company on the market and added to their existing holding. The shares are purchased as a single transaction on the day the dividend is paid at the current market price, taking advantage of the lower dealing costs involved in a bulk purchase. The member will have to pay stamp duty on the transaction.

Stop and think 16.3

Failure to file interim accounts justifying the declaration of a dividend may seem to be just a technical breach of the Act. It does however mean that the dividend payment was not lawful and can make the directors liable to repay the amount of the dividend. In 2017 Next plc had to convene an EGM to rectify this procedural oversight.

Not only can this lead to reputational damage but there is a clear financial cost involved in convening and holding a general meeting.

Test yourself 16.6

1.   Cash dividend payments must be funded from what reserve?

2.   Scrip dividends and dividend re-investment schemes exchange the cash dividend for what?

12. Rights and warrants, debentures and bonds

12.1 Warrants

A warrant is a document rather like a share certificate which entitles the holder to subscribe for equity capital in the company at some future date or dates at a price which is determined at the time of issue of the warrant. Warrants do not form part of the company's capital and holders are not entitled to receive dividends or interest.

The company's Articles must authorise the issue of warrants. Warrants are often issued in connection with takeover offers in order to make the terms more attractive without immediate cost to the bidding company.

The terms of issue of warrants must include the procedures regarding transfer, inspection of the register, requests for copies of the register and the dispatch of annual reports and accounts to warrant holders, although there are no statutory provisions covering these matters.

12.2 Subscription rights

Sometimes the issue of a loan stock includes an associated right to subscribe for shares in the company concerned. This is not the same as the conversion rights under a convertible loan stock, where the loan stock is surrendered in exchange for shares. With subscription rights, the loan stock remains in issue and holders must subscribe additional money in order to exercise their subscription rights.

12.3 Debentures, loan stocks and corporate bonds

Debentures, loan stocks and corporate bonds are essentially the same and represent borrowing by a company which may be secured, convertible or listed. The legislation governing the registration of charges is contained in CA2006 ss. 859A–Q.

13. Capital events and role of share registrar

During the planning and implementation of capital events or corporate actions the company's share registrar plays a crucial role in ensuring that the administrative tasks are completed accurately and on time. For the purposes of this section both will be referred to as the share registrar.

The following are the more common types of capital events.

13.1 Share offer

A general share offer is perhaps the simplest of capital events from the perspective of the share registrar and the following steps should be followed:

- As application forms are received, they should be checked to ensure they contain the details of the applicant for adding to the register of members at the conclusion of the offer and that the necessary payment or evidence of a bank transfer is attached. Care must be taken to ensure that the application is in the name of a registrable person and that a trust or unincorporated company has not applied for shares.
- Schedules of valid applications with a running total of number of shares and subscription monies should be kept.
- Applications from existing members should be identified so that any new shares being issued are added to their existing account rather than a duplicate account opened.
- At the closing date of the share offer, the share registrar should forward to the company secretary, company directors and relevant professional advisers details of the applications received.
- If the total number of shares applied for exceeds the total number of shares on offer the applications will need to be scaled back. Although the offer document may set out details of how any scale back will take place, this is often left to the directors' discretion. There many different ways to scale back applications with the more common methods being:
  - all applications scaled back by the same percentage;
  - all applications up to say 5,000 shares being accepted in full and any larger applications being scaled back; and
  - applications being accepted in full on a 'first come, first served' basis.
- Once the schedule of applications is settled the directors should hold a meeting to formally approve the issue of shares, the register of members

should be updated and share certificates issued to the successful applicants and refund cheques issued in respect of unsuccessful applicants or partial acceptances.

13.2 Rights issue

Under a rights issue, the share offer is only made to existing members and in proportion to their existing holdings. They might also be offered the opportunity to acquire additional shares in excess of their entitlement, representing entitlements not taken by other members or for larger companies the rights issue might be underwritten in which case excess applications are generally not accepted.

The steps are broadly the same as for a share issue but with the following additional steps:

- Each members' entitlement under the rights issue will be calculated by reference to their holding of shares at the record date and entitlement forms printed showing the details of the member, a unique reference of the entitlement and details of the entitlement of each member usually expressed as both a number of shares and monetary amount. The form will include space for the member to indicate how much of their entitlement they wish to take up, including any additional shares if permitted.

- Forms will often be returned with the value of the payment received being different from the amount stated on the form as being applied for. In these circumstances, it is usual for the terms of the offer to state that where different the application will be accepted in respect of the value of the consideration received.

- At the conclusion of the rights issue, the schedule of valid acceptance will differentiate between shares accepted up to each members' entitlement and any excess applications. In the event that scaling back is required, this would only be applied to the excess applications.

- If the rights issue is underwritten, the underwriter will acquire the shares representing the shortfall between the number of shares applied for and the aggregate shares being offered for subscription.

13.3 Consolidation/subdivision

Under either a consolidation or subdivision there is no action required of the members other than voting at the general meeting at which authority of the consolidation/subdivision is sought. Following approval of the necessary resolution, the following steps will be required:

- Members' entitlements under the new share class are calculated as at the record date and a schedule of entitlements forwarded to the company secretary, company directors and any professional advisers. In practice, this is usually undertaken in advance of the general meeting to facilitate the consolidation/subdivision taking place at the close of business on the day of the general meeting, subject to the necessary resolutions being approved.

◆ The directors should hold a meeting to formally approve the issue of shares, the register of members should be updated, new share certificates issued and existing share certificates in the original class cancelled. There is no need for these to be returned by members but some may do so.

13.4 Takeover

The share registration work to issue the takeover offer documentation and receive acceptance is often undertaken by the share registrar acting for the offeror company rather than that of the target company. In these situations, it is important that the share registrar for the target keeps the offeror's share registrar up to date with any changes to the share register of the target during the course of the takeover offer.

The following steps are required:

◆ At the commencement of the offer, the share registrar to calculate the consideration to be offered to each member of the target. The consideration might be payable in cash, in shares of the offeror or a combination of the two.

◆ The acceptance form will contain the details of the member, a unique reference number and details of the consideration being offered. Where shares are transferred during the offer period the form of acceptance should be renounced in favour of the purchaser.

◆ As acceptance forms are received, these should be checked to ensure they are signed and have attached to them the share certificates for cancellation. Any incomplete acceptances should be returned for completion.

◆ Schedules of valid acceptances with a running total of number of shares and consideration monies/shares should be kept.

◆ Most takeovers are conditional on reaching a minimum level of acceptance, and once this level has been reached, the offeror will issue a statement that the offer is unconditional.

◆ At the closing date of the share offer the share registrar should forward to the company details of the acceptances received. This will also include details of applications received that are not valid in all respects. Depending on the reason for the acceptance not being valid the offeror may decide to treat them as valid anyway.

◆ Once the schedule of acceptances is settled the directors of the offeror should hold a meeting to formally approve the acquisition of the shares and the payment of any consideration monies or issue of consideration shares.

◆ A bulk stock transfer form will be included which details the aggregate number of shares being transferred supported by a schedule detailing the individual amounts. This form must be stamped by HMRC and then details of the transfers provided to the share registrar of the target in order that the target's register of members can be updated and the offeror's details added as a member.

13.5 Scheme of arrangement

For the share registrar implementing a scheme of arrangement is relatively straightforward and does not require the existing members to do anything other than vote in respect of the scheme proposals at the general meeting.

Following approval of the scheme of arrangement, the following steps will be required:

◆ Members' entitlements are calculated as at the record date and a schedule of entitlements forwarded to the company. In practice, this is usually undertaken in advance of the general meeting to facilitate the scheme of arrangement taking place at the close of business on the day of the general meeting, subject to the necessary resolutions being approved.

◆ The directors should hold a meeting to formally approve the issue of shares, the register of members should be updated, new share certificates issued and existing share certificates reflecting the original holdings cancelled.

Test yourself 16.7

1. **Who are offered shares under a rights issue?**

2. **If a member transfers their shares during the course of a takeover, what should happen to the form of acceptance issued for those shares?**

14. Key features and establishment of employee share schemes and their ongoing administration

Employee share schemes provide a way for employees to acquire a financial stake in their employer. This encourages loyalty and motivates employees in a way that normal remuneration does not.

For an employer, there are several perceived and actual advantages, including:

◆ aligns employee and shareholder interests;
◆ aids employee retention and recruitment;
◆ remunerates employees in a tax-efficient way; and
◆ raises working capital.

There are also disadvantages that should be considered before launching such a scheme, including:

◆ adverse effect on morale if the share price falls;
◆ administration costs – initial set-up costs and long-term costs of administering the scheme;

- dilution of share ownership;
- risks of unrealistic financial expectations among employees; and
- difficulty in selling shares post-exercise for employees in an unlisted company and potential need and costs to establish employee benefit trust.

The most common schemes are:

- Enterprise Management Incentive;
- Company Share Option Plan;
- Save As You Earn;
- Share Incentive Plan; and
- Unapproved share options.

14.1 Enterprise Management Incentive (EMI)

An EMI scheme is a discretionary scheme allowing an award of share options with more favourable tax treatment than unapproved schemes. EMI schemes are the most popular due to their tax advantages and flexibility.

The employer must have assets of not more than £30 million, not more than 250 employees and must be carrying out a qualifying trade, at the date of issue, to qualify to issue EMI options.

EMI options can be granted up to the value of £250,000 per employee in a three-year period and an employer limited to an aggregate of £3 million. The option period is capped at 10 years with no minimum initial holding period.

The chief tax benefit of an EMI scheme is that no income tax or NI contributions are charged on the grant of EMI options, and, provided that (i) the exercise price is at least equal to the market value at the date of grant; and (ii) the options continue to qualify until the date of exercise, then there will also be no income tax or NI charge at the point of exercise.

14.2 Company Share Option Plan (CSOP)

A CSOP scheme is also a discretionary scheme also offering tax incentives.

CSOPs may be offered by any company regardless of size. The maximum option-value is £30,000 per employee based on the market value at the date of the grant. The option period must be between three and 10 years.

Income tax and NI are not due when the option is granted or exercised, making this scheme very tax efficient. Any options issued must be in the ultimate parent company of a group, and must be of the same class as those held by the group controllers.

14.3 Save As You Earn (SAYE)

An SAYE scheme must be made available to all employees although this can be subject to an initial period of employment of up to five years.

Under an SAYE scheme, employees are granted options to buy ordinary, fully paid and unrestricted shares after three or five years' of service with the company at a discount of up to 20% of the market value at the date of grant.

The employees can contribute between £5 and £500 per month for either three or five years in order to purchase the shares at the end of the option period.

Provided that the minimum option period of three years is observed, there is no income tax charge on the grant or exercise of the option. Additionally companies will receive corporation tax relief on the cost of establishing and administering the SAYE scheme.

14.4   Share Incentive Plan (SIP)

There are four types of SIP shares that a company can offer to its employees either alone or in combination. These are:

1.   free shares;
2.   partnership shares;
3.   matching shares; and
4.   dividend shares.

SIP schemes issue shares and not options over shares.

The company is entitled to provide each employee with free shares up to a value of £3,600 per year with no income tax or NI consequences. Free shares can be awarded by reference to an employee's pay grade, performance, length of service or hours worked.

Employees may also instead be offered the opportunity to purchase the lower of £1,800 or 10% of their salary in partnership shares per year out of their pre-tax and pre-NI salaries.

The company may then match these partnership shares at a ratio of up to two matching shares for each partnership share purchased by the employee, effectively allowing a further £3,600 worth of 'free shares' to be given by the company each year.

The company may also allow participants to reinvest any dividends paid on the shares by purchasing dividend shares. There is no income tax charged on the dividends that are paid out.

SIP shares must be held for a minimum of five years with the shares being held by an employee trust during the holding period. Corporation tax relief can be obtained by the company for the cost of setting up and administering the scheme.

14.5   Unapproved share options

Options under an unapproved share option scheme do not benefit from any tax incentives and are not subject to any external restrictions on their grant, exercise or value. The employee will be subject to income tax via Pay-as-you-earn tax and potentially National Insurance contributions on exercise of the option. The company may also need to make an NI contribution.

Test yourself 16.8

1. Under which type of option scheme might an employee receive partnership shares?

2. What main benefit do unapproved share options not enjoy compared to approved option schemes?

3. What is the maximum monthly payment that an employee can make under an SAYE scheme?

Chapter summary

◆   Role of the tri-partite oversight of the securities industry

◆   Discussion of the terminology used to describe different attributes of shares

◆   Overview of the role of the share registrar for traded companies

◆   Review the process required to transfer shares

◆   Consideration of the various documents that might be lodged by members or others in respect of members and their shareholding

◆   Review of distributions and the authority required

◆   Rights and warrants, debentures and bonds

◆   Capital events and role of share registrar

◆   Overview of employee share schemes

Test yourself answers

Chapter 1

Test Yourself 1.1

1. Which of these cannot be appointed as company secretary of a public company: company secretarial manager of the company's auditor, a chartered secretary or an unqualified compliance officer?
Company secretarial manager of the company's auditor and an unqualified compliance officer

2. Which of these cannot be appointed as company secretary of a private company: company secretarial manager of the company's auditor, a chartered secretary or an unqualified compliance officer?
Company secretarial manager of the company's auditor

3. What is the basis of a company secretary's executive authority?
Employment contract

Test Yourself 1.2

1. Why are there two appointment forms for a company secretary, Forms AP03 and AP04?
Form AP03 is for the appointment of a natural person, Form AP04 is for the appointment of a corporate company secretary

2. Are there any benefits for a sole director appointing a third party as company secretary rather than themselves?
The same person cannot sign documents in both capacities and so where two signatories are required such as on deeds they would need to either appoint an authorised signatory or have an independent party witness their signature

3. Does the removal of a company secretary also terminate their employment contract?
Only if their contract stipulates that they are specifically employed as company secretary

Test Yourself 1.3

1. The Governance Code recommends that the company secretary report to two people. Who are they and for which aspects of the company secretary's role would each have oversight?
The chairman of the board in respect of governance issues, CEO in respect of executive matters

Test Yourself 1.4

1. Who is authorised to convene meetings of the directors?
Any director may convene a meeting or request the company secretary to do so

2. How might minutes of directors' meetings differ between a regulated and unregulated company?
Minutes of a regulated company will often be more detailed and contain details of challenges, reviews and reports in the decision-making process

3. Is it good practice to permit directors to amend meeting minutes to reflect what they meant to say?
No

Test Yourself 1.5

1. Can companies print documents in very small 'fine print'?
Documents must be legible with the naked eye

2. Can companies unilaterally decide to issue their report and accounts by email only to their members?
No. Consent is required and members can elect to receive a hard copy

3. A company has developed its own secure encrypted web technology which requires anyone using the service to pay an annual subscription. Can the company use this platform to make its annual report and accounts available to its members?
No. Copies of the report and accounts must be available free of charge when made available on a website

Chapter 2

Test Yourself 2.1

1. What are the key differences between an executive director and an NED?
Executive directors are employees usually full-time and responsible for implementing company strategy, NEDs are not employees, usually part-time and responsible for setting corporate goals and strategy

2. Must directors have the word 'director' in their job title?
Not a requirement

3. What criteria prevent an individual from being independent?
Long association with the company
Being an employee
Share options
Recent material business interest
Cross directorships
Represents a significant shareholder

Test Yourself 2.2

1. What form should be used to notify the Registrar of the appointment of an individual as a director?
Form AP01

2. Which statutory registers should be updated on the appointment of a director?
Register of directors
Register of directors' residential addresses

3. What information should be obtained from the new director?
Full name
Date of birth
Service and residential address (if different)
Nationality
Occupation

4. Who cannot be appointed as a director?
Person under the age of 16
A disqualified person
A bankrupt
An auditor or employee of the audit firm
A director of an insolvent company cannot be appointed as a director of a company with a prohibited name without consent of the court
Anyone not meeting any specific criteria in the Articles

Test Yourself 2.3

1. What are the seven codified duties of directors?
To act within their powers
To promote the success of the company
To exercise independent judgement
To exercise reasonable care, skill and diligence
To avoid conflicts of interest
Not to accept benefits from third parties
To declare interests in any proposed transaction or arrangement

2. Do directors have unfettered authority to exercise the company's powers?
No. Their authority is subject to any provisions in the Articles, their service contract and any authority limits adopted by the board

3. Can directors delegate any of their powers and duties?
Yes to committees of the board

4. How many directors may be appointed?
Any number subject to any maximum set out in the Articles

Test Yourself 2.4

1. Under what circumstances can a director be disqualified?
For unfitness
On conviction
For breach of statutory obligations
For fraudulent or wrongful trading
In the public interest
By voluntary undertaking
On competition grounds

2. Do the remaining directors need to approve the resignation of a director?
No

3. How soon must notification of the vacation of office by a director be notified to Companies House?
14 days

4. How many directors should retire at the first AGM of a public company?
All

Test Yourself 2.5

1. Why is succession planning important?
To ensure an orderly succession and to maintain the necessary balance of skills, experience, diversity, independence and balance

2. If a listed board has two executive directors, a chairman and a non-independent NED, how many independent NEDs must be appointed?
Three

3. Is positive discrimination permitted to address board diversity imbalance?
No

Test Yourself 2.6

1. Can any company take out directors' indemnity insurance?
Yes

2. Can a director be indemnified against personal liability to pay fines and damages?
No

3. Can the details of any indemnity insurance be kept secret?
No, must be available for inspection by members

Test Yourself 2.7

Can a person be co-opted to a board without their consent?
No

Chapter 3

Test Yourself 3.1

1. Which companies are required to undertake board evaluation?
All listed companies

2. Which companies must carry out external facilitated board evaluation and how often?
FTSE350 companies – at least once every three years

3. Who should evaluate the performance of the company chair?
The NEDs led by the senior independent director

Test Yourself 3.2

1. When should directors receive induction training?
Shortly after appointment

2. Is it necessary for experienced directors to receive induction training?
Yes as all companies have different processes

3. Is it better for directors to receive training all in one session or spread out during the year?
It is better to drip feed the updates rather than overload with say one annual update session

Test Yourself 3.3

1. Why should board committees have written terms of reference?
To ensure there are clear objectives, authority and parameters for the matter delegated to them

2. Who is responsible for notifying the FCA where a PDMR deals in the company's shares?
The PDMR but often delegated to the company secretary

3. Can an employer legally sack a whistle-blower for blowing the whistle?
No

Chapter 4

Test Yourself 4.1

1. What two criteria must be met in order to be a member of a company?
Consent to be a member, be entered in the company's register of members

2. Other than as a shareholder what other forms can company membership take?
Guarantor or for an unlimited company without a share capital some other method of dividing ownership

3. Is there a minimum or maximum number of members that a company must have?
Minimum of 1, no maximum

Test Yourself 4.2

1. What are the main disadvantages of registering shares for a long-term investment in children's names?
As minors children can void any obligation to pay funds to the company and a minor cannot deal with any transaction themselves which would require a court order to ensure it was in their interests

2. Can anyone become a member of a company?
Subject to the Articles any natural person or entity with legal capacity may be a member. However subsidiaries are generally prohibited from owning shares in the parent entities

3. A professional partnership wishes to acquire some shares. How should they be registered?
In the name of one or more partners unless it is a Scottish partnership which can register the shares in the partnership name

Test Yourself 4.3

1. In order to establish the rights of a shareholder which documents should be referred to?
The Articles or any separate terms stipulated at the time of the issue of the shares

2. Are members always shareholders?
No – some members are guarantors

Test Yourself 4.4

1. How can a guarantor transfer their membership to someone else?
They can't

2. Does the guarantee cease immediately on the guarantor resigning?
No it remains for one year

3. Which type of organisation is best suited to use a guarantee company structure?
Not for profit

Test Yourself 4.5

1. Why is aligning the interests of directors and shareholders difficult to achieve in practice?
Shareholders have many different reasons for becoming and remaining as shareholders so their interests are not aligned with each other

2. What are the main differences between activist and pressure group shareholders?
Activist shareholders use their holding and influence to bring about change. Pressure group shareholders try to bring about change through publicity achieved through campaigns and meeting disruption

Test Yourself 4.6

1. Rights attaching to shares can be divided into three broad categories, what are they?
Rights to vote, rights to distribution of profits and rights to capital

2. What protection is given to members holding non-voting class shares if the members holding voting shares resolve to amend the Articles in general meeting to increase their dividend rights?
Rights attaching to shares of a class cannot be amended without their consent, even if they are non-voting shares

3. Can a company with two classes of shares, ordinary shares and redeemable shares, purchase back all of the ordinary shares?
No

Test Yourself 4.7

What two tests must be satisfied in order to bring a claim for unfair prejudice?
The conduct complained of must be unfair and the conduct must have caused or is causing prejudice or harm to the interests of the members or a group of members

Test Yourself 4.8

Can anyone bring a derivative action claim against a company?
Must be brought by a member

Test Yourself 4.9

What is the difference between beneficial and legal ownership of shares?
Legal ownership is where the person is the registered member, the beneficial owner retains the economic benefit of ownership but is not the legal owner as the shares are registered in a nominee name

Chapter 5

Test Yourself 5.1

1. Certain words and expressions require consent before they may be used as part of a company name. Which of the following require consent?

◆	Britain	Yes
◆	French	No
◆	Accountant	No
◆	Insurance	Yes
◆	Royal	Yes

2. What are the different types of company that can be incorporated under the Companies Act 2006?
Public company limited by shares
Private company limited by shares
Private company limited by guarantee
Private unlimited company, with or without a share capital

3. Why must a public company apply for a certificate under CA2006 s. 761 before it starts trading?
To ensure that the amount paid up on the aggregate nominal value of its issued share capital is not less that the authorised minimum

Test Yourself 5.2

1. Hard copy, paper filing is available for all statutory forms and documents. What other methods of filing these documents are there?
Online filing
WebFiling
Software filing

2. Does it matter to which Companies House office documents are delivered?
No, as any documents filed at one registry that relate to a company registered at another will be forwarded

Test Yourself 5.3

Is it sufficient to post documents to Companies House prior to the expiry of the appropriate filing period?
No – the requirement is that they must be received, and be acceptable for filing, prior to the deadline

Test Yourself 5.4

1. What is the comply or explain principle?
Listed companies should apply the principles of the UK Corporate Governance Code and explain any non-compliances with the provisions of the Code

2. What are the five categories covered by the Governance Code?
Board Leadership and Company Purpose
Division of Responsibilities
Composition, Succession and Evaluation
Audit, Risk and Internal Control
Remuneration

Test Yourself 5.5

What is the benefit of acquiring at least 90% acceptances on a takeover?
Achieving the 90% threshold permits an acquiring company to compulsorily acquire all remaining shares on the same terms if it wishes

Test Yourself 5.6

1. The City Code applies to what type of company?
All public companies or companies that have been public in the previous 10 years

2. *What is the significance of a share offer being conditional on reaching acceptance of 50%, 75% or 90% of the issued shares?*
These thresholds provide different degrees of control:
50% allows the holder to pass all ordinary resolutions and is treated as the holding company for accounting provisions
75% permits the passing of special resolutions as well as ordinary resolutions and gives control to the holder
90% is the level at which dissenters in a takeover can be acquired

Test Yourself 5.7

1. *How long after ceasing to trade can an application for dissolution be made?*
Three months

2. *What action might occur if the Registrar believes a company is defunct?*
The Registrar may take action to strike the company off the register and dissolve it

Test Yourself 5.8

Which of these activities disqualifies a company from being able to file dormant company accounts?

1. *A late filing penalty being imposed on ABC Ltd, an authorised insurance company.*
No

2. *Payment for the amounts due on the subscriber share relating to XYZ Ltd.*
No

3. *A dividend being paid by a non-trading entity?*
Yes

Chapter 6

Test Yourself 6.1

1. *What are the differences between listed and quoted companies?*
A listed company is one listed in the Official List maintain by the UKLA. A quoted company is a company whose equity share capital has been listed in the UK, officially listed in an EEA State or admitted to dealing on the New York Stock Exchange or Nasdaq

2. *A listed company has additional disclosure requirements, where can these be found?*
Listing Rules and Disclosure and Transparency Rules

Test Yourself 6.2

1. Do micro and small companies need to file their profit and loss account with the Registrar?
No

2. Which legislation governs the content of corporate governance statements for listed companies?
Companies Act 2006, Listing Rules, Disclosure and Transparency Rules, UK Corporate Governance Code

Chapter 7 Test

Yourself 7.1

1. Which documents and records are auditors entitled to have access to?
All

2. What are the three categories of companies that can claim exemption from audit?
Small companies
Dormant companies
Subsidiaries

3. Is an audit intended to provide reassurance as to the future prospects of the company?
No

Test Yourself 7.2

1. What type of individual or firm cannot be appointed as a company's auditor?
An officer or employee of the company or an officer or employee of a connected undertaking, any person or firm that has a business relationship with the company

2. There are a number of non-audit services that auditors are prohibited from providing to a PIE, name five of them.
Tax services
Any part in management or decisions-making
Bookkeeping and preparation of accounting records
Payroll services
Design or implementation of internal control of risk management processes
Valuation services
Legal services
Internal audit
Services linked to financial, capital structures, investment strategies
Promoting, dealing or underwriting in shares of the audit entity
HR services

3. *What is the ratio of permitted audit:non-audit services fees for public interest entities?*
70%

Test Yourself 7.3

1. *Can anyone be appointed as a company auditor?*
No must be a registered auditor, or audit firm and not be prohibited from being appointed

2. *Can the liability of the auditor be limited?*
Yes but requires consent of the members

3. *How many consecutive years can an auditor be appointed to a PIE?*
Ten years plus an additional ten years if a tender has been carried out

Test Yourself 7.4

1. *What does audit partner rotation guard against?*
Threat to auditor objectivity and independence

2. *Do all companies need to change their audit firm regularly?*
No only Public Interest Entities (PIE)

Test Yourself 7.5

1. *When does an auditor of a PIE need to make a statement if they cease to hold office as auditor?*
Always

2. *Who are the relevant audit authorities?*
The auditor's recognised supervisory body and in the case of a PIE the FRC

Test Yourself 7.6

1. *Who is the audit report prepared for?*
The members

2. *Is the audit process expected to uncover all errors or fraud?*
No – only material errors and omissions

Chapter 8

Test Yourself 8.1

1. *What are the two market functions provided by the LSE?*
Primary market to raise capital and secondary market for investors to buy and sell shares

2. *Why are applications to both the UKLA and LSE required to list on the Main Market?*

Application for listing is made to the UKLA, admission to trading on the Main Market is made to the LSE. The Main Market although the largest is not the only market where listed shares can be admitted and traded

Test Yourself 8.2

Which of the following transactions will trigger a notification obligation under DTR:

1. *Sale of shares taking a holding from 5.9% to 5.1%.*
No

2. *Purchase of shares taking holding from 3.9% to 4.1%.*
Yes

3. *Company purchasing and cancelling shares held by shareholder A resulting in shareholder B's holding increasing from 2.9% to 3.0%.*
Yes

4. *Sale of shares taking a holding from 5.1% to 4.9%.*
Yes

Test Yourself 8.3

What is the purpose of comply or explain?
It is recognised that although the Code represents best practice in the field of corporate governance one size does not fit all and companies should be able to depart from the code provisions but should explain why that approach is appropriate

Chapter 9

Test Yourself 9.1

What is the difference between a CREST stock deposit and stock withdrawal?
A stock deposit is the movement of shares from the certificated part of the share register to the uncertificated, dematerialised part of the register

A stock withdrawal is the opposite of a stock deposit

Test Yourself 9.2

1. *Must the statutory records be kept at any specific location?*
Yes at one of the registered office, the SAIL address or in the case of a private company on the central register

2. Must the statutory books be books or are other formats permitted?
The statutory records may be held in hard copy or electronically and there is no specific format provided the required information is kept

3. Why must directors provide both a service address and residential address?
The residential address is required in case letters addressed to the service address are returned undelivered then the registrar will send mail to the residential address

Test Yourself 9.3

1. What is the fee to obtain a copy of the register of members for a company with 500 shareholders?
£65

2. Can a request for a copy of a register specify that the information is to be provided in the form of an Excel spreadsheet?
No – the request can require delivery in hard or soft copy but not the format of the soft copy

Test Yourself 9.4

1. Should minutes of all meetings involving directors be minuted?
Yes

2. Can directors' and members' minutes be kept together?
Yes but not recommended as members' minutes must be available for inspection while the directors' minutes need not

3. How long must a company keep its original minutes of meetings?
Ten years

Test Yourself 9.5

1. Directors have no statutory right to access board papers, why is this?
They have the right of access to all records and so do not require a specific right to board papers

2. Is there any statutory requirement to retain notices of either directors' or members' meetings?
No

Test Yourself 9.6

1. Companies must keep accounting records with sufficient detail to enable the directors to assess what?
To show and explain transactions, disclose with reasonable accuracy the company's financial position and enable the directors to prepare accounts and financial statements as required by the Companies Act

2. For how long must companies keep minutes of meetings of their directors and members?
Ten years

3. Do a company's members have to pay a fee to inspect the registers or documents that must be available for their inspection?
No

Chapter 10

Test Yourself 10.1

1. Which gateway is used to software file at Companies House?
Companies House XML Gateway

2. In addition to an appropriate software package what else is required to software file?
An account with Companies House for the collection of any fees payable

3. What is GIGO?
Garbage In Garbage Out

Chapter 11

Test Yourself 11.1

1. Is it acceptable for minutes of members and directors to simply record decisions?
No – the reasoning behind decisions must be recorded also, to provide context for those not at the meeting.

2. Is it necessary to record attendees at directors' meetings?
Whilst not a legislative requirement, keeping a record of attendees is considered best practice.

Test Yourself 11.2

1. Why should a record of votes for and against resolutions be maintained?
Recording the votes cast in respect of a resolution in the minutes is conclusive evidence of the vote unless a different result can be proved

2. What is the purpose of keeping directors' minutes?
To keep a permanent record of the decisions of the directors and ideally a sense of the discussions and reasons for any decisions reached

Test Yourself 11.3

1. What are the differing minute retention periods for meetings held before or after 1 October 2007?
Permanently and 10 years respectively

2. What are the dangers of not keeping minute books secure?
Loss of confidentiality, total loss or tampering and alteration

3. How long must a company keep its original, authenticated minutes?
Ten years

Chapter 12

Test Yourself 12.1

1. How often should listed companies undertake a board evaluation?
i)   Internally   Every year
ii) Externally facilitated At least every three years – FTSE 350 companies

2. Must every director be evaluated every year?
No

3. Should evaluations follow the same format and cover the same topics each year?
No

Test Yourself 12.2

1. What are the two main options available to members under the Act to take action against directors?
Actions for unfair prejudice or derivative action claim

2. Of whose interests should directors be most mindful?
The members

Test Yourself 12.3

1. In general how is the power of entry and search granted and who to?
By the courts/magistrates to a police constable

2. Can an HMRC inspector with the power of arrest make an arrest for any criminal offence?
No their power is limited to HMRC offences

Chapter 13

Test Yourself 13.1

1. What are the seven GDPR principles?
Lawfulness, fairness and transparency
Purpose limitation
Data minimisation
Accuracy
Storage limitation
Integrity and confidentiality (security)
Accountability

2. GDPR is supplemented in the UK by which additional legislation?
Data Protection Act 2018, Privacy and Electronic Communications Regulations

Chapter 14

Test Yourself 14.1

1. Can any member request that a resolution be circulated?
No. The member or members must hold between them not less than 10% of the voting rights at a general meeting

2. Who has the right to exercise the voting rights on that written resolution?
The registered member

3. On what basis can members of a public company approve a resolution other than at a general meeting?
By proxy or by unanimous written resolution under the duomatic principle

Test Yourself 14.2

1. Under what circumstances must a private company hold an AGM?
If it is a quoted company or required by its Articles

2. What additional resolutions would a quoted company routinely add to its AGM notice?
Receipt of directors' remuneration report, approval of directors' remuneration policy (triennial), authority to issue shares, waive pre-emption rights on allotment and approval of political donations, authority to convene general meetings on 14 days' notice

Test Yourself 14.3

1. Which documents should be available for inspection by members at an AGM?
Register of members
Directors' service contracts
Notice

2. Are amendments to resolutions allowed?
For ordinary resolutions only to correct obvious typographical mistakes, no amendments may be made to a special resolution

3. Can members ask questions about anything?
At a general meeting any question relating to the business of the meeting, at the AGM of a quoted company questions may be raised on any topic however directors only need to ensure that questions relating to the business of the meeting are answered

Test Yourself 14.4

1. What does clear days mean?
Clear days excludes the date the notice of a meeting is given, or deemed given, and the date of the meeting

2. What must a traded company have done to allow members' meetings to be held on 14 days' notice?
Obtained consent at the previous AGM or a general meeting held since the previous AGM

3. Do notices of general meetings need to distinguish between ordinary and special resolutions?
Yes

Test Yourself 14.5

1. If one of two members refuses to attend general meetings can a meeting be held?
Under the Model Articles no but check the Articles

Test Yourself 14.6

1. What is the key difference between an ordinary and a special resolution of the members?
Ordinary resolution is approved by a simple majority and a special resolution requires a 75% majority

2. What advantage does passing a resolution at a meeting have compared to the same resolution circulated as a written resolution?
At a meeting the majority is of those voting and on a written resolution it is of the entire voting share capital

Test Yourself 14.7

1. Can proxies speak at meetings?
Yes

2. Who has authority to adjourn a general meeting?
The chair

Test Yourself 14.8

1. What options does a corporate member have in order to cast their vote at a general meeting?
Appointment of corporate representative or appointment of a proxy

2. What is the maximum period before a general meeting for the cut-off for the receipt of forms of proxy by the company?
48 hours (excluding non-working days)

3. How many proxies can an individual member appoint?
As many as they like but proxies must represent different shares

Test Yourself 14.9

1. Can a member appoint more than one proxy?
Yes

2. Can proxies vote both for and against the same resolution?
Only if they represent different members or different shares of the same member

3. If a member's proxy does not attend the meeting are their votes still counted as recorded on the proxy appointment form?
No

Test Yourself 14.10

1. What, if any, are the practical differences between voting on a show of hands and on a poll?
On a show of hands each member has one vote on a poll each member has the number of votes attached to their shares – usually one vote per share

2. Must a chair always call for a poll?
If a poll is validly demanded by members yes in other circumstances the chair has discretion but does have a duty to ensure that the sense of the meeting is correctly recorded

3. If an abstention is a not a vote, why do some members insist on ensuring their abstention is recorded?
To demonstrate dissatisfaction

Test Yourself 14.11

1. In order to constitute a valid meeting what must all attendees be able to do?
Participate in the meeting, to hear the speakers and to be able to ask questions

2. How has digital voting promoted the use of poll voting as a matter of course?
Digital technology has enabled almost instantaneous vote count whereas a manual count can take hours

Chapter 15

Test Yourself 15.1

1. Who can elect the chairman of the board?
The directors

2. Where are the rules and procedures governing the holding of directors' meetings?
The company's Articles

Test Yourself 15.2

1. What is the main risk associated with having professional advisers present at all directors' meetings?
Might be deemed to be a shadow director

2. What do committees of the board, and especially non-executive members contribute to the board?
More in-depth analysis and review of topics. Committee members tend to have greater experience/interest in the committee's brief than the full board

Chapter 16

Test Yourself 16.1

1. Which organisations have oversight of the UK financial services industry?
FCA
PRA
The Treasury
Bank of England
Financial Policy Committee

2. *What is the name of the process through which the FCA supervises the employment of financial services professionals?*
Controlled functions

Test Yourself 16.2

1. *What is the difference between allotted and issued share capital?*
Allotted shares are those where the investor has acquired an irrevocable right to be registered as the holder of the shares. Issued shares are those entered in the register of members and for which a share certificate or CREST credit has been issued

2. *What is a company's equity share capital?*
These are the ordinary voting share capital

Test Yourself 16.3

1. *Can shares be issued at a discount?*
Yes up to 10%

2. *If a call on shares is not paid what is the ultimate sanction available to the directors?*
Forfeiture

3. *If directors have full authority to issue additional shares what protection do existing members have from having their holding diluted?*
Pre-emption rights on the allotment of new shares

Test Yourself 16.4

When payable, what is the rate of stamp duty?
0.5% of the value of the consideration

Test Yourself 16.5

1. *What comfort does certification of a stock transfer form give to the purchaser of the shares?*
Confirms that the holder does hold sufficient shares to complete the transfer and that the company, or share registrar, is holding the share certificate

2. *How long do companies have in which to issue share certificates following a share issue or share transfer?*
Two months

3. *Must shareholder addresses be shown on share certificates?*
No

Test Yourself 16.6

1. Cash dividend payments must be funded from what reserve?
Distributable reserves

2. Scrip dividends and dividend re-investment schemes exchange the cash dividend for what?
Fully paid shares

Test Yourself 16.7

1. Who are offered shares under a rights issue?
Existing members

2. If a member transfers their shares during the course of a takeover, what should happen to the form of acceptance issued for those shares?
It should be forwarded to the transferor or their broker

Test Yourself 16.8

1. Under which type of option scheme might an employee receive partnership shares?
Share incentive plan (SIP)

2. What main benefit do unapproved share options not enjoy compared to approved option schemes?
Tax relief either on issue of the options, on sale of the shares or both

3. What is the maximum monthly payment that an employee can make under an SAYE scheme?
£500

Directory of Resources

Organisations

Advisory, Conciliation and Arbitration Service
www.acas.org.uk

Bar Council
www.barcouncil.org.uk

British and Irish Legal Information Institute
www.bailii.org

Chartered Institute of Management Accountants
www.cimaglobal.com

Chartered Institute of Legal Executives
www.cilex.org.uk

Companies House
www.gov.uk/government/organisations/companies-house

Company information
https://beta.companieshouse.gov.uk

Company name checker
https://beta.companieshouse.gov.uk/company-name-availability

Competition & Markets Authority
www.gov.uk/government/organisations/competition-and-markets-authority

Confederation of British Industry
www.cbi.org.uk

Court of Justice of the European Union
https://curia.europa.eu

Courts and Tribunals Judiciary
www.judiciary.gov.uk

Department for Business, Energy & Industrial Strategy
www.gov.uk/government/organisations/department-for-business-energy-and-industrial-strategy

Domain name registrars
ICANN
www.icann.org

Nominet UK
www.nominet.uk

Internic
www.internic.net

European Business Register
www.ebr.org

European Court of Human Rights
http://echr.coe.int

European Patent Office
www.epo.org/index.html

European Union
https://europa.eu

Financial Conduct Authority

FCA Handbook
www.handbook.fca.org.uk/handbook

Listing rules
www.handbook.fca.org.uk/handbook/LR

Financial Services Register
https://register.fca.org.uk

Mutuals Public Register
www.fca.org.uk/firms/mutuals-public-register

Financial Reporting Council
www.frc.org.uk

Audit resources
www.frc.org.uk/auditors

Corporate governance
www.frc.org.uk/directors/corporate-governance-and-stewardship
www.frc.org.uk

HM Courts & Tribunals Service
www.gov.uk/government/organisations/hm-courts-and-tribunals-service

HM Land Registry
www.gov.uk/government/organisations/land-registry

HM Revenue & Customs
www.gov.uk/government/organisations/hm-revenue-customs

Stamp duty
www.gov.uk/topic/business-tax/stamp-taxes

Information Commissioner's Office
www.ico.org.uk

Institute of Chartered Accountants in England and Wales
www.icaew.com

Institute of Chartered Accountants in Ireland
www.charteredaccountants.ie

Institute of Chartered Accountants in Scotland
www.icas.com

Institute of Chartered Secretaries and Administrators
www.icsa.org.uk

Guidance material
www.icsa.org.uk/knowledge

Publications
www.icsa.org.uk/shop

Institute of Directors
www.iod.com

International Corporate Governance Network
www.icgn.org

Judicial Committee of the Privy Council
www.jcpc.uk

Law society
www.lawsociety.org.uk

London Stock Exchange
www.londonstockexchange.com/home/homepage.htm

Admission and disclosure standards
www.londonstockexchange.com/companies-and-advisors/main-marketdocuments/admission-and-disclosure-standards.pdf

AIM rules
www.londonstockexchange.com/companies-and-advisors/aim/advisers/rules/aim-rules-for-companies-updated-october-2018.pdf

Dividend timetable
www.londonstockexchange.com/traders-and-brokers/rules-regulations/dividend-procedure-timetable-2019.pdf

Panel on Takeovers and Mergers
www.thetakeoverpanel.org.uk

Patent/Trademark Office
www.gov.uk/government/organisations/intellectual-property-office

Prudential Regulation Authority
www.bankofengland.co.uk/prudential-regulation

Supreme Court of the United Kingdom
www.supremecourt.uk

Trade Union Congress
www.tuc.org.uk

UK Legislation
www.legislation.gov.uk

UK Listing Authority
www.fca.org.uk/markets/ukla

UK Parliament
www.parliament.uk

Publications

Armour, D: *The ICSA Company Secretary's Checklists*, 10th ed. (ICSA Publishing Ltd, 2017).

Armour, D: *The ICSA Company Secretary's Handbook*, 11th ed. (ICSA Publishing Ltd, 2016).

Bruce, M: *Rights and Duties of Directors 2018/19*, 17th ed. (Bloomsbury Publishing Plc, 2019).

Coyle, B and Hill, T: *Corporate Governance,* 6th ed., (ICSA Publishing Ltd, 2017).

Coyle, B., Atrill, P. and Sayers, J. *ICAEW Professional Stage Accounting Study Manual*, volumes 1 and 2. 5th ed. (ICSA Publishing Ltd, 2005).

Frederick, D: *Accounting*, 2nd ed. (ICSA Publishing Ltd, 2018).

Herbert Smith Freehills LLP: *A Practical Guide to the UK Listing Regime*, 4th ed. (ICSA Publishing Ltd, 2017).

Impey, D and Griffiths, M and Loose, P: *The Company Director: Powers, Duties and Liabilities*, 12th ed. (Jordan Publishing, 2015).

Impey, D and Montague, N: *Running a Limited Company*, 8th ed. (Jordan Publishing, 2013).

Lai, J: *Tolley's Company Secretary's Handbook*, 2th ed. (Tolley, 2018).

Robson, R and Davis, P: *Effective Minute Taking*, 2nd ed. (ICSA Publishing Ltd, 2018).

The Institute of Chartered Accountants in England and Wales (2006). *ICAEW: Professional Stage Business Finance Study Manual*. 6th ed. (The Institute of Chartered Accountants in England and Wales, 2006).

The Institute of Chartered Accountants in England and Wales *ICAEW: Professional Stage Financial Reporting Study Manual*. 6th ed. (The Institute of Chartered Accountants in England and Wales, 2006).

The Institute of Chartered Accountants in England and Wales *ICAEW: Professional Stage Business Management Study Manual*. 6th ed. (The Institute of Chartered Accountants in England and Wales, 2006).

Walmsley, K: *Butterworths Company Law Handbook*, 32nd ed. (LexisNexis Butterworths, 2018).

Weisgard, GM: *Company Voluntary Arrangements and Administrations*, 3rd ed. (Jordan Publishing, 2013).

Online resources

Companies House
Forms
www.gov.uk/topic/company-registration-filing/forms

Guidance
www.gov.uk/government/collections/companies-house-guidance-forlimitedcompanies-partnerships-and-other-company-types

Institute of Chartered Secretaries and Administrators
CSP Online
www.companysecretarialpracticeonline.co.uk

Research
www.icsa.org.uk/knowledge/research

Practical law
https://uk.practicallaw.thomsonreuters.com

Magazines and newsletters

Company Secretary's Review (LexisNexis). The long-established monthly journal.

Director (Institute of Directors). IoD magazine, available in print and online at www.director.co.uk/editions.

Governance & Compliance. ICSA magazine, available in print and online at www.icsa.org.uk/products-and-services/governance-and-compliance.

PLC Magazine. Monthly magazine for subscribers to the Practical law corporate and law department services. (https://uk.practicallaw.thomsonreuters.com.

The Register (Companies House). A free quarterly magazine on Companies House and other company law developments.

Glossary

Abridged accounts – A condensed version of the annual accounts which small and medium-sized companies (according to the specified size criteria) are allowed to file with the Registrar of Companies. They may not be used as a substitute for the full annual accounts for the circulation to members.

Administrator – A person appointed by the court to manage a company in financial difficulties in order to protect creditors and, if possible, avoid liquidation. The administrator has the power to remove and appoint directors. Also a person who administers the estate of a deceased person in the absence of any executors.

Agent – Someone who is authorised to carry out business transactions on behalf of another (the principal), who is thereby bound by such actions.

Allotment – Shares are taken as allotted when a person acquires the unconditional right to be included in the company's register of members which is generally accepted to be once the contract of allotment is completed and acceptance of the application notified to the applicant.

Allottee – A person or company to whom shares have been allotted.

Alternate director – A person appointed by a director to represent them, usually at board meetings, and who assumes the responsibilities and duties of their appointor when acting in their place.

Annual accounts, annual report and accounts – The accounts which are prepared to fulfil the directors' duty to present audited accounts to members in respect of each financial year. Annual accounts of limited companies must be filed with the Registrar of Companies.

Annual general meeting (AGM) – A general meeting of the company's members, which must be held in each calendar year within 15 months of the previous AGM. Under Companies Act 2006, private companies are (generally) no longer required to hold AGMs, although the requirement remains for public companies.

Articles of association – The constitutional document setting out the internal regulations of the company. Unless modified or excluded, the specimen Articles in the relevant version of Table A/Model Articles in force on the date of incorporation have effect.

Audit – The independent examination of, and expression of opinion on, the company's accounts. All persons or firms offering audit services must be registered auditors and belong to one of the recognised accountancy bodies.

Bonus issue – Issue of additional shares to existing shareholders, in proportion to their current holding, already paid up in full out of the distributable reserves of the company.

Call – A formal notice issued by a company requiring shareholders to pay all or part of the amounts unpaid on partly paid issued shares.

Capital – The money or money's worth used by a company to finance its business.

Certificate of incorporation – A certificate issued by the Registrar of Companies on receipt of specified constitutional and other documents of the company. The company assumes its identity as a legal person on the date of incorporation shown on the certificate.

Charge – A means by which a company offers its assets as security for a debt. A charge is a general term that includes, but is not limited to, a mortgage. A fixed charge relates to a specific asset or assets. A floating charge relates to whatever assets of a specified class are in the company's possession at the time the charge crystallises (if it does so).

Class rights – Where a company has more than one class of shares, the rights attached to those different classes of shares.

Common law – The body of law based on custom and usage and decisions reached in previous cases. The principles and rules of common law derive from judgments and judicial opinions and not legislation introduced by parliament.

Company – An association of persons which, on incorporation, becomes a legal entity entirely separate from the individuals comprising its membership. In the Companies Act 2006, 'company' is restricted to companies registered under that Act or previous Companies Acts.

Company secretary – An officer of the company with a number of statutory duties, such as to sign the confirmation statement and accompanying documents, and usually charged with a range of duties relating to the company's statutory books and records, filing requirements, etc. Under the Companies Act 2006, private companies are no longer required to appoint a company secretary.

Compulsory liquidation – Winding up of a company by order of the winding up court.

Confirmation statement – A form filed each year with the Registrar of Companies, confirming that specified information about the company's directors, secretary, registered office, shareholders, share capital, notified to Companies House is correct or that any changes to the information are being notified at the same time as the confirmation statement. Replaced the annual return from 1 July 2016.

Contract – An agreement between two or more legal persons creating a legally enforceable obligation between them.

Corporate director – A corporate entity that is appointed as a director of another company. Quite common within groups of companies.

Creditor – A person or company owed money.

Creditors' voluntary winding up – Insolvent winding up of a company by resolution of its members.

CREST – Operated by Euroclear UK & Ireland Limited, CREST is the major UK securities settlement system for UK equities, government bonds and a range of other securities, providing simultaneous and irrevocable transfer of cash and securities for all sterling and euro payments and real-time settlement.

Debenture – A written acknowledgement of a debt owed by a company, often – but not necessarily – secured. It is common practice for a debenture to be created by a trust deed by which company property is mortgaged to trustees for the debenture holders, as security for the payment of interest and capital.

Debt – An amount of money owed by one person, the debtor, to another, being the creditor.

Department for Business, Energy and Industrial Strategy (BEIS) – The government department responsible for the administration of company law. The Companies Act confers certain powers on the Secretary of State. Formerly called the Department for Business, Innovation and Skills (BIS).

Director – An officer of the company responsible for determining policy, supervising the management of the company's business and exercising the powers of the company. Directors must generally carry out these functions collectively as a board.

Directors' report – A statement attached to the annual accounts containing certain information laid down in the Act.

Distributable reserves – Profit retained by a company which may be distributed to its members.

Distribution – The transfer of some or all of a company's assets (usually cash) to its members, generally by way of dividend or on a winding up.

Dividends – The distribution of a portion of the company's assets (usually cash) to its members.

Dormant company – A company which has not traded or has ceased trading and has no accounting transactions that need to be entered in its financial records.

Duomatic principle – The 'Duomatic principle' (called after the case of the same name, *Re Duomatic Ltd [1969]*) provides that where it can be shown that all shareholders having the right to attend and vote at a general meeting of the company assent to some matter which a general meeting of the company could carry into effect, that assent is as binding as a resolution in general meeting would be. This can in some cases obviate the requirement to hold a general meeting to pass a resolution – so long as all the shareholders agree to that resolution.

Fiduciary – Having a position of trust, such that the power and authority conferred by the position must be exercised solely in the interest of the person with whom the fiduciary relationship exists. Trustees are in a fiduciary position, as are solicitors in relation to their clients. Directors have a fiduciary duty to the company, obliging them to act always in good faith and not to derive a personal profit from their position.

Financial statements – The term adopted by the joint accountancy bodies to signify 'balance sheet, profit and loss accounts, statements of source and application of funds, notes and other statements' which collectively are intended to give a true and fair view of financial position and profit or loss.

Financial year – The period in respect of which the company's profit and loss account is drawn up; it need not coincide with the fiscal or calendar year and need not be a period of twelve months.

Floating charge – Security, usually for a loan, over a class of assets the individual components of which vary over time, such as stock or book debts. (*See also* charge.)

Formation – *See* registration.

Gazette – Official publication for formal announcements. Published daily by TSO on behalf of the National Archive.

General meeting – Any general meeting of the company's members that is not an annual general meeting.

Guarantee – A formal agreement under which a guarantor undertakes to meet the contractual obligations of one person to another in the event of default. A company limited by guarantee is one in which the liability of the members is limited to a specified amount in a winding up.

Holding company – A company which has subsidiaries.

Incorporation – *See* registration.

Initial Public Offering (IPO) – An initial public offering is the first sale of shares issued by a company to the public and is usually associated with its stock market launch. Prior to an IPO a company will typically have a relatively small number of shareholders made up of the founders, early stage investors such as venture capitalists or angel investors, family and friends of the founders and employees. The IPO usually involves the raising of additional funds by the issue of shares to the public which will include both institutional and retail investors. An IPO might only add a few shareholders if the shares are all taken by institutions or many hundreds of thousands of retail investors if the IPO is more widely available such as the Royal Mail Group IPO in 2013.

Inside information – Is information that is precise, has not been made public, relates directly or indirectly to the company and if made public is likely to have a significant effect on the price of the company's shares or securities (that is information that a reasonable investor would be likely to use as part of the basis of their investment decisions).

Insider dealing – Buying or selling shares on the basis of an unfair advantage derived from access to price-sensitive information not generally available. Insider dealing is a criminal offence.

Issued capital – *See* share capital.

Judgment creditor – A creditor who has obtained a court order in their favour.

Limited company – The commonest form of company, in which the liability of members for the debts of the company is limited – either to the amount of share capital for which they have applied (a company limited by shares) or to a specific amount guaranteed in the event of a winding up (a company limited by guarantee).

Limited liability partnership (LLP) – A corporate body where the partners have limited liability but undertake the management themselves rather than appointing directors to manage the company on their behalf.

Liquidation – The process under which a company ceases to trade and realises its assets for distribution to creditors and then shareholders. The term 'winding up' is synonymous.

Listed company – A company whose shares are listed by the Financial Services Authority on the Official List of the UK and admitted for trading on the London Stock Exchange or PLUS Listed markets.

Member – A subscriber to the memorandum of association and any other person who agrees to be a member and whose name is entered in the register of members.

Members' voluntary winding up – Solvent winding up of a company by resolution of its members.

Memorandum of association – A constitutional document setting out details of the subscribers on incorporation.

Model articles of association – The specimen articles of association for a company limited by shares incorporated under the Companies Act 2006. Unless specifically modified or excluded, the version of the Model Articles in force at the time of a company's incorporation automatically applies to the company.

Natural directors – Companies are required to have at least one natural director by which is meant a human being rather than a corporate entity.

Officer – Includes a director, manager or (where appointed) the secretary of a company. Not everyone with the title of manager is sufficiently senior to be regarded as an officer, who must have a level of supervisory control which reflects the general policy of the company. Also includes the company's auditor.

Ordinary resolution – A resolution at a general meeting carried by a simple majority of votes cast.

Ordinary shares – The most common form of share in a company, giving holders the right to share in the company's profits in proportion to their holdings and the right to vote at general meetings (although non-voting ordinary shares are occasionally encountered).

Paid-up capital – Refers to the amounts paid up on any issued shares.

Panel on Takeovers and Mergers – An independent body (the Panel), established in 1968, whose main functions are to issue and administer the City Code on Takeovers and Mergers (the City Code) and to supervise and regulate takeovers and other matters to which the City Code applies. Its central objective is to ensure fair treatment for all shareholders in takeover bids.

Partnership – A business run by two or more persons where the owners share ownership (partners) and have unlimited liability for the business's debts.

Person with significant control (PSC) – An individual owning or exercising control over 25% or more of a company's equity shares or voting rights.

Pre-emption rights – Preferential right of existing members to purchase new shares to be issued or existing shares being offered for sale by way of transfer by an existing member.

Preference shares – Shares carrying the right to payment of a fixed dividend out of profits before the payment of an ordinary dividend or the preferential return of capital or both.

Prima facie – On the face of it, at first sight.

Private company – A company that is not a public company.

Prospectus – Any prospectus, notice, circular, advertisement or other invitation to the public to subscribe for purchase of a company's shares or debentures.

Proxy – A person authorised by a member to vote on his behalf at a general meeting. A proxy need not also be a member of the company.

Public company (plc) – A company that meets specified requirements as to its minimum share capital and which is registered as a public company. Only public companies can offer shares and debentures to the public.

Quasi-loan – A loan where a company reimburses the director's creditor.

Redeemable shares – Shares which are issued as redeemable may be bought back by the company at a future date at the option of the company or members depending on the terms of issue.

Registrar of Companies – The official responsible for maintaining the company records filed under the requirements of the Companies Act.

Registration – Process by which companies are created by filing (or registering) several specified documents at Companies House.

Regulatory information service (RIS) – An information provider approved by the FSA to disseminate information to the market.

Resolution – A decision at a meeting reached by a majority of members voting.

Retirement by rotation – The annual standing down of directors (usually one third) for re-election by members at an annual general meeting.

Return of capital – An amount paid back to members being a repayment of the principal originally invested. A return of capital will occur if shares are redeemed or otherwise purchased by the issuing company.

Service contract – A director's contract of employment.

Shadow director – A person, not appointed as a director, managing or directing the affairs of a company or who directs the actions of the directors.

Share – A unit of ownership of the company, representing a fraction of the share capital and usually conferring rights to participate in distributions. There may be several kinds of shares each carrying different rights. Shares are issued at a fixed nominal value, although the company may actually receive a larger amount, the excess representing share premium. Members may not be required to subscribe the full amount immediately, in which case the shares are partly paid. The members then await calls, which require them to pay further amounts until the shares are fully paid.

Share capital – The capital of a company contributed or to be contributed by members. Nominal capital represents the nominal value of the shares issued and excludes any premium paid.

Share premium – The excess of the price at which shares are issued above their nominal value.

Shareholder – A member holding shares of a company with a share capital. The most common form of company member.

Special resolution – A resolution required either by the Companies Act or a company's Articles which must be carried by at least 75% of the members voting at a general meeting. Such resolutions tend to be required where the proposal would change the nature of the relationship between a company and its members, such as an amendment to the Articles.

Statute law – The body of law represented by legislation, and thus occurring in authoritative written form. Statute law contrasts with common law, over which it takes precedence.

Stock transfer form – Document used to transfer ownership of shares from one person (transferor) to another (transferee).

Subscriber – A person who subscribes to the memorandum of association and agrees to take up shares in the company on incorporation.

Subsidiary – A company controlled by another, which usually holds a majority of the issued shares.

Table A – The specimen articles of association for a company limited by shares incorporated under former Companies Acts. Unless specifically modified or excluded, the version of Table A in force at the time of a company's incorporation automatically applies to the company.

Takeover – The process under which one company acquires control of another usually by acquiring all the shares.

Three-way proxy – A proxy form, which must be used by a listed company, which allows a member to instruct his proxy to vote for, against or abstain on each resolution.

Transfer – Process where ownership of shares passes from one person to another usually by way of a sale.

Transferee – A person acquiring shares by way of transfer.

Transferor – A person disposing of shares by way of transfer.

UK Corporate Governance Code – The code on corporate governance that applies to UK listed companies. It is a voluntary code rather than a legal requirement.

Index

A

abridged accounts 130, 450
access to records and registers
  inspection
    fees 232
    in person 231
    right to request copies
      231–232
    location 231
accounting reference date
  listed company 202
activism
  investor 79
  member 78
  pressure group 80
administrator 43, 450
agent 5, 450
allotment
  meaning 71, 450
  right of pre-emption 83
allottee 70, 450
alternate director 26, 450
annual accounts
  listed company 202
  meaning 14, 450
annual general meeting (AGM)
  335
  business 335–336
  company secretary, role of
    338–342
    after 342
    before 338–340
    during 341–342
  meaning 40, 450
  members' right to propose
    directors 336
  notice 343
annual report
  additional disclosure 140–145

company secretary, role of
  129–130
full accounts 135–137
  content of accounts 135
  requirements 136–137
legislative developments
  161–163
listed companies 139, 202
meaning 14, 450
medium sized company
  133–135
  content of accounts 135
  eligibility 133–134
  exclusions 134
  thresholds 134
micro companies 130–131
  content of accounts 131
  eligibility 129
  exclusions 131
  thresholds 130
quoted company
  annual report and accounts
    140
  definition 139–140
  filing obligation 140
small companies 132–133
  content of accounts 133
  eligibility 132
  exclusions 132
  thresholds 132
summary information 140,
  297–298
arrangements 115–116
articles of association
  classes of shares 81–82
  meaning 17, 450
  members' rights 80
  rights attaching to class of
    shares 82

audit 28, 451
  external see external audit
audit committee report 158–159
auditor's report 157–158
  listed company 202

B

best practice 59–67
  authority limited 61
  code of conduct 61
  committee terms of reference
    63
  directors' remuneration report
    154
  expense policy 62
  independent standards for
    NEDs 62–63
  matters reserved to board 60,
    375–380
  risk management policy 66–67
  share dealing policy 64
  tenure policy for NEDs 61–62
  whistle-blowing policy 64–65
board evaluation 49–54
  benefits 278
  external 54
  governance 51
  internal 53
  internal v external 277
  monitoring 51
  principles 276
  processes and interactions
    52–53
  reasons for 276
  structure 50–51, 275
board meetings 362, 363–364
  chair 366
  committees 374–375
  company secretary

after 368–369
   at meeting 368
   preparation 367–368
conflicts of interest 383
   duty to avoid 383–384
convening directors' meetings
      364–365
corporate governance
      proposals 373
delegation of authority and
      responsibility 369–371
executive discretion 381
interests in contracts 384
loans to directors 386–387
management 363
management and advisers,
      reliance on 372–373
matters reserved for board
      375–380
   board membership 378–
      379
   communication 378
   contracts 378
   corporate governance
      379–380
   delegation of authority
      379
   financial reporting and
      control 377
   internal controls 377
   other 380
   policies 380
   remuneration 379
   strategy and management
      376
   structure and capital
      377
minutes of directors meetings
      365–366
motions 382
quorum 365
resolutions 382
substantial property
      transactions 385–386
types 363
bonus issues 193, 451

C
call 74, 451
capital   68, 451
capital events 422

consolidation/subdivision
      423–424
   rights issue 423
   scheme of arrangement 425
   share offer 422–423
   takeover 424
certificate of incorporation 101,
      451
charge 104, 451
class meetings 336–337
class rights 84, 451
committee report 159–160
common law 39, 451
companies limited by guarantee
      69
company 4, 451
company insolvency 123
   creditors' voluntary winding up
      123–124
   liquidator 124
   members' voluntary winding
      up 123
   phoenix companies 125
   report on conduct of directors
      124
   restoration 125–126
   Scotland 125
   strike off and dissolution 125
   winding up by court 124
company secretary
   adviser, as 14
   annual report, and 129–130
   appointment 11–12
   background 6–8
   chair, and 13–14
   communication with
      shareholders 19–20
   directors, and 13–14
   document delivery
      by company 21–22
      to company 20–21
   duties 8–9
      board 8
      company 8
      shareholders 9
   external audit 165
   information dissemination
      15–18
      after board meeting 17–18
      before board meeting
         15–16

during board meeting
      16–17
   meaning 4, 451
   prohibited appointees 9
   qualifications 9
   removal 12–13
   resignation 12–13
Competition and Markets
      Authority 119
   investigatory powers
      291–292
compulsory acquisition 119–120
compulsory liquidation 304, 451
confirmation statement 43,
      451–452
contract 5, 452
corporate bonds 422
corporate director 19, 451
corporate governance
   background 109
   culture 121
   development 110
   policies
      diversity and discrimination
         121
      employment handbook 122
      remuneration 122
      whistleblowing 122
   setting tone from top 121
corporate records 241
   accounting records 241–242
   contracts for purchase of own
      shares 242
   director service contracts 241
   directors' indemnities 241
   documents for purchases out
      of capital 242
   minutes 241
   report to members of
      investigation by public
      company into interests in
      shares 243
creditor 28, 452
creditors' voluntary winding up
      123, 452
CREST 118, 223, 452
cumulative preference shares 82

D
data protection 318
   Data Protection Act 319–321

fee tiers 320
freedom of information 326
GDPR 321–324
  grounds for lawful basis
    323–324
  general data processing
    319
  intelligence service processing
    320
  law enforcement processing
    319
  public access to corporate
    information 324–
    326
  registration regime 320

  regulation and enforcement
    320
  right to request details of data
    held by an employer or
    company 325–326
debenture 17, 82, 422, 452
debt 77, 452
dematerialisation 217
  current proposals 217–218
Department of Business, Energy
    and Industrial Strategy
    163, 452
  investigatory powers 283–
    286
derivative action claims 87
  alternative remedy 89–90
  application for permission to
    continue 88
  application to continue action
    brought by another 88–89
  grounds 88
  permission to continue 89
director
  addresses 32, 221
  alternate 26
  appointment procedure
    29–31
  collective responsibility
    34–35
  contracts of employment
    33
  co-option 47
  CPD 59
  de facto 26
  defective appointment 33

disputed appointments 33
disqualification 43
  competition disqualification
    order 44
  competition undertaking
    44
  conviction 43
  fraudulent or wrongful
    trading 43
  public interest 43
  undertaking 44
  unfitness 43
duties 35–39
  act for benefit of its
    members 35
  act within powers 35
  authority to exercise
    company's power
    38–39
  avoid conflicts of interests
    36–37
  common law 38
  contractual 38
  declare interests in any
    proposed transaction or
    arrangement 37
  exercise independent
    judgment 36
  exercise reasonable care, skill
    and diligence 36
  liability for actions or
    inaction 39
  not to accept benefits from
    third parties 37
  promote success of company
    35–36
  regulatory 38
  statutory duties, other
    37–38
education 55
executive 24, 34
indemnification and liability
    insurance 46–47
induction 31–32, 55
  checklist 56–59
  meaning 5, 452
  non-executive 24-25, 34
  number 32
  qualification 27–28
  recruitment 28
  regulatory approval 28

removal of directors 42
retirement by rotation 41
rotation and re-appointment
    32
shadow 25–26
support 59
types 23–26
vacation of office 40–41
directors report 150–152,
    452
  listed company 203
directors' remuneration report
    152
  best practice 154
  Companies Act requirements
    152–153
  implementation report
    disclosures 155
  listed company 202–203
  Listing Rule and Governance
    Code requirements
    153–157
  remuneration policy disclosures
    156
disclosure
  accountability, and 295,
    312–315
  business model reporting 317
  clear and concise annual
    reporting 315–318
  dividends 316–317
  inside information 206–209
  interests in voting rights
    209–213
  listed companies 296–311
    auditor's report 297
    availability of annual
      accounts and reports
      298
    Companies Act obligations
      296–298
    directors' remuneration
      policy 298
    directors' remuneration
      report 297
    directors' report 297
    disclosure and transparency
      rules 299, 305–312
    FCA enforcement actions
      312
    filing obligation of quoted

companies 298
general obligations 301–305
inside information
  305–306 *see also* inside
  information
listing principles 300
listing rules 299–305
listing suspensions,
  cancellation and
  restoration 301
Market Abuse Regulation
  305
notice of general meeting
  298–299
sponsors 301
strategic report 296–297
summary information
  297–298
types of information 296
performance metrics 317–318
risk and viability reporting 317
trust, and 312–315
disclosure of financial statements
availability of annual accounts
  and reports 160
FCA 161
filing requirements 160–161
registrar 160–161
disclosures of interests in
  shares
contents 213
disclosure obligations
  212
exemptions 212
filing 213
form 212
notification thresholds
  211–212
obligation to notify an interest
  209
relevant interest 211
relevant issuer 210–211
distributable reserves 402, 452
distributions 77, 418–419, 452
cash dividend 419
dividend reinvestment schemes
  (DRIP) 420
investment companies, by 419
mandates 420
public companies, by 419
scrip dividends 420

unclaimed dividends 420
dividends 68, 452
disclosure 316–317
listed company 203
divisions 115
document retention periods
  243–246
dormant companies 127, 452
duomatic principle 333, 453

E
employee share schemes
  425–428
Company Share Option Plan
  (CSOP) 426
Enterprise Management
  Incentive (EMI) 426
Save As You Earn (SAYE)
  426–427
Share Incentive Plan (SIP) 427
unapproved share options
  427–428
external audit
access to documents
  165–166
annual accounts 164–165
appointment 170
appointment by PIE 172–173
appointment of partnership as
  auditor 174
audit firm 177
audit partner 176
audit tender 173–174
auditor's right to information
  183
company secretary's role 165
company's obligation on
  cessation of appointment
  179–180, 181
duties of auditor 182–
  183
exempt companies 174
independence 166–167
liability 175
maximum engagement period
  173–174
non-audit fees 169
non-audit services 167–168
notification to authorities 180
notification to Companies
  House 180

private company that is not PIE
  170–171
public company that is not a
  PIE 171
Public Interest Entities 171–172
remuneration 175
report to members 183–185
report to PIE committees
  185–186
resignation of auditors
  177–179
rights of auditors who
  are removed or not
  reappointed 179
role 182
rotation of auditors 176
signing report 186
termination of appointment
  177
UK's competent authority
  176

F
fiduciary 85, 453
filing company returns 104
late submission 107–108
online 104–105
software 105
web 105
Financial Conduct Authority and
  Prudential Regulation
  Authority
investigatory powers 289–291
financial records 239
inspection 240
required information 239–240
retention periods 240
where kept 240
financial statements 97, 453
listed company 203
financial year 82, 453
floating charge 104, 453
formation 97
meaning 43
process 99–103
types of company 99

G
gazette 114, 453
general meetings 335–337
adjournment 350

agenda 346
annual *see* annual general
    meetings
attendance
    corporate member, by
        355–356
    disruption 356
    member that is a natural
        person, by 356
communication with members
    and other stakeholders
    361
independent proxy report 360
materials 346
meaning 29, 453
notice 342–346
    agreement to short notice
        344
    clear days 343–344
    content of 345
    entitlement to 344–345
    periods 343
    special notice 345–346
polls 353
    demand 353–354
    publication of results 355
    when demanded 354–355
procedural motions 348
proxies 350
    appointment 352
    at meeting 351
    evaluation 352
    form and dispatch of forms
        351–352
    three-way 351
quorum 346
regulations governing 337–338
resolutions 347–348
role of chair 348–349
rules of order 349–350
share registrar 359–360
speaking 349–350
standing orders 349–350
technology 358
    audio-visual conferencing
        358–359
    electronic or hybrid meeting
        359
    electronic voting 358
    online proxy submission
        358

voting 357
    abstaining 357
    guarantee 68, 453
    guarantors transferring
        membership 77
    specific provisions 77

H
HM Revenue and Customs
    investigatory powers
        286–289
holding company 41, 453
incorporation
    matters to be considered
        98–99
    types of company 99

I
Initial Public Offering (IPO)
        453–454
inside information 201, 454
    closed periods 209, 310
    control 307–308
    disclosure 206
    disclosure committee 208
    disclosure of PDMR share
        transactions 209, 309–
        310
    financial information
        310–311
    information requirements 311
    MAR and DTR 206–207
    payments to governments
        311
    PCA 309
    PDMR/PCA dealing
        208029
    PDMRs 309
    prevention of 308–309
    selective 306–307
insider dealing
    Criminal Justice Act 215–216
    meaning 207, 454
    Proceeds of Crime Act 2002
        216–217
integrated reporting 161
    implementation 162
    purpose 161–162

J
judgment creditor 124, 454

L
legal persons 73
liability
    offences 106–107
limited company 68, 454
limited liability partnership (LLP)
    8, 454
liquidation 43, 454
listed company 6, 187, 454
    additional requirements 202
    constitutional changes 206
    financial 202–203
    issues of securities 204–205
    listed companies 214–215
    UK Corporate Governance
        Code 213–214
listing requirements listing and
        FCA 188–189
    admission and disclosure
        standards 200
    communication 200
    eligibility criteria 200
    settlement 200
    authorised persons 190
    Disclosure and Transparency
        Rules 201
    eligibility 190–191
    LSE as secondary market 199
    premium and standard 190
    principles 188–189
    process 192–193
    regulated activity 190
    regulatory regime 189
    role of advisers 194
        corporate broker 194–195
        Financial Public Relations
            consultants 195
        lawyers 195
        other advisers 196
        reporting accountant
            195–196
        share registrars 196
        sponsor 194
        types of issue 193–194
loan stocks 82, 422

M
meeting materials 237
    access rights 239
    board papers 237–238
    directors 237

member meetings 346
members communications 238
member meetings 333 *see also*
    general meetings
members 6, 69
  activism 78–80
  agreement to become 70
  beneficial ownership 90
  entry in register 70–71
  guarantors 77
  legal person 73
  liability 69
  meaning 69–70, 454
  minors 74–75
  number 71
  registered members 90
  restrictions in Articles 73–74
  restrictions on 72–73
  shareholders 76
  types, other 78
memorandum of association 68,
    454
mergers 114
minute books 233
  access rights 236
  directors 235
  members 235–236
  security 234–235
  where kept 234
minutes
  due diligence demonstration
    263–264
  evidence, as 264–265
  need for 257
  proof of existence 262–263
  record of decisions and actions
    263
  required information
    257–260
    static data 259
    variable data 259–260
  retention 266–267
  risk management 268–270
  security 266–267
  six C's
    clarity 260
    coherence 261
    completeness 261–262
    conciseness 261
    consistency 261
    correctness 262

Model Articles of Association 8,
    454

N
narrative reporting 145
natural director 27, 454

O
officer 5, 455
ordinary non-voting shares 81
ordinary resolution 33, 455
ordinary shares 81, 455
  right to dividends 83

P
paid-up capital 71, 455
Panel on Takeovers and Mergers
    117, 455
  investigatory powers 292–293
partnership 7, 455
persons with significant control
    (PSC) 224, 454
pre-emption rights 83, 454
preference shares 81, 454
prima facie 88, 454
private company
  company secretary 4
  meaning 5, 454
prospectus
  approval 199
  contents 197–198
  exemptions 197
  meaning 455
  offer to public 196
  rules 96
public company
  company secretary 4
  meaning 6, 455

Q
quasi-loan 386, 455

R
reconstructions 115–116
redeemable shares 82, 455
Registrar of Companies 11, 456
registration 99–100
  community interest company
    101–102
  companies' registered
    members 102

documents affecting title
    415–417
  English and Scottish law,
    differences between 416
  issued by other jurisdictions
    416
  received for registrations
    416–417
  meaning 68, 456
  process 100–101
  public company 101
  re-registration 103
  right to manage company 102
  same-day 102
regulatory information service
    (RIS) 17, 456
regulatory oversight 271
  assessing performance
    274–279
  board performance 275–279
  Competition and Markets
    Authority
    power of entry 291–292
    production of documents
      291
  Department of Business,
    Energy and Industrial
    Strategy 163
    overseas regulatory
      authorities 286
    power of entry 283–284
    power to investigate affairs
      of company 284–285
    power to investigate
      ownership 285–286
    production of documents
      295
  Financial Conduct Authority
    and Prudential Regulation
    Authority
    power of entry 290–291
    production of documents
      289–290
  HM Revenue and Customs
    direct tax investigations
      287–288
    indirect tax investigations
      288–289
  investigations 286–287
    investigatory powers
      283–293

OECD: Principles on Corporate
    Governance 273–274
Panel on Takeover and Mergers
    production of documents
        292–293
    right of entry 293
    procedures 272–274
    securities industry 392–395
    stakeholder protection
        279–282
    Wates principles 280–281
resolutions 347, 456
    ordinary 347
    special 347–348
    written 333–334
retirement by rotation 41, 456
return of capital 81, 456
rights attached to shares
    capital 83
    conversion 83–84
    pre-emption 83
    redemption 83
    right to receive dividend
        83
    right to vote 82
    variation 84

S
secretarial software
    benefits 254–255
    categories 247
    factors to consider 250–251
    group record keeping 248
    implementation 252–253
    need for 248–251
    ongoing maintenance 255
    process 249
    security 253–254
    uses 254–255
securities industry
    authorised firms 393–394
    controlled functions 394–395
    regulated investment activity
        393
    regulation of 392–393
service contract   33, 241
    creation 11
    meaning 24, 456
    resignation 12
shadow director 25, 456
share capital 68, 391, 398, 456

allotment procedure
    401–402
authority for allotment 399
calls on shares 405–406
disapplication of pre-emption
    rights 400–401
financial assistance 404–405
forfeiture 406–407
issue price 402
part payment 402
payment for shares 403
pre-emption group guidance
    401
pre-emption rights 399–400
purchase of own shares
    407–411
share premium 405
shares allotted for non-cash
    consideration 403–404
share certificates 417
    certification 418
    issue on allotment or transfer
        417
    lost 417–418
shareholders
    members 76
    specific provisions 76
    meaning 7
share premium 405, 456
share registrar 412
    dematerialisation 413
    role 412
share transfers 413
    checklist 414–415
    CREST 415
    stamp duty 413–414
    stock transfer form 413
shares 456
    allotted capital 396
    authorised capital 396
    called-up capital 396–397
    changes to capital 397
    convertible loan stock 398
    debentures 397–398
    debt capital 397
    equity capital 397
    issued capital 396
    loan stock 398
    paid-up capital 396
    transmission of 415
    types 395

special resolution 84, 456
stamp duty exemptions 120
statute law 40, 456
statutory registers 219
    access 231–233
    central register 229–231
    charges 223–224
    CREST 223
    debentures 224
    directors 220–221
    directors residential addresses
        221
    format 226
    interests in voting shares of a
        public company 226
    location 227, 231
    members 221–223
    people with significant control
        224–226
    registered office 228
    required records 220–226
    SAIL address 228–229
    secretaries 221
stock transfer form 71, 456
strategic report 145–150
subscriber 68, 457
subscription rights 421
subsidiary 13, 457
succession planning 45
    balance 46
    diversity 45
    independence 46

T
Table A 8, 457
takeover
    action following first closing
        date of public offer 118
    agreement with individual
        members 117
    City Code 118–119
    CREST 118
    meaning 116, 457
    public offers 117–118
    purchases in market 117
    Takeover Panel 118–119
    transfers to offeror company
        118
    types 116
three-way proxy 351, 457
transfer 70, 457

transferee 74, 457
transferor 114, 457

UK
UK Corporate Governance Code
   109–113
  listed companies 213–214

meaning 6, 457
UK Stewardship Code 113
  listed companies 214–215
unfair prejudice
  meaning 85
  members rights 86
  protection from 85

remedies 87
unfair conduct 86

W
warrants 421